I Was a Teenage Norwegian

by Peter Dublin

Illustrations by Marit Bockelie

For information address
    Press-Tige Books
    291 Main Street
    Catskill, NY 12414

First Press-Tige Edition 1997

Printed in the United States of America

ISBN 1-57532-109-2

To:
Mor og Far Thyholdt
Mor og Far Norbye
Mom and Dad Dublin

I have taken a number of literary liberties with this book. It is based upon real experiences, and in that sense it is true. Not all of it is factual, but where I have fabricated people and situations I have kept them true to the time, place, and story.

Along with my story, I teach the reader a little Norwegian. I define Norwegian words when I introduce them, and then I don't use the English word ever again. There is a Teenage Norwegian-English Glossary at the end of the book. Norwegian has three letters in its alphabet in addition to the twenty-six English letters—æ, ø, and å—and they come *after* the other twenty-six.

Many people have helped me with my story. Special thanks go to Marit Bockelie for her willingness to let me use her illustrations in this work. I am indebted to Franck Pettersen for his description of the Northern Lights, his well-kept student journal, and his tape recording of my first theatrical event.

I began work on this book at the Cambridge Adult Education Center. I thank Jeff Kelley for getting me started, to Sally Brady for helping me continue, and to Mopsy Strange Kennedy for enabling me to finish. And I thank all of the students in those classes for their supportive and critical suggestions.

I had two editors—Barbara Ravage and Russ Atkins—and they both allowed me to write my book and helped me make it a better book.

Finally, I thank Jana for her patience and her willingness to allow me my linguistically-rich fantasy life.

-1-
Tromsø At Last

I couldn't have been more anxious. For two months I had waited for this moment. For twenty-four hours I had been on the coastal ship staring at the fields, with their little houses and animals, that covered the coastline of both the mainland and the islands. The water, the gorgeously deep blue water, was everywhere, but it was the mountains that were over-powering. Many were snow-covered; almost none of them sported trees very far above the farms at their base. The drama was enhanced because of how close we were.

I washed my face, gathered my suitcases together, and wandered up to the railing on the upper-most deck of the *hurtigruten*, the Norwegian coastal ship euphemistically referred to as an "express." We had been ploughing through the water past the mountains and the villages when I heard the engines slowing down slightly. Then I saw it: Tromsø Island. I could make out the southern tip of the island first, with a small cluster of houses and what looked like a beach: I would believe that when I saw it up close. As we steamed along, there were more and more houses and, finally, the town itself.

I Was a Teenage Norwegian

Tromsø was the biggest town in North Norway and bigger than any town I had seen on the entire *hurtigruten* trip. There were boats in the harbor, not just fishing boats, but freighters and even a tourist ship. There were brick and stone buildings as well as the wooden houses; some were even four or five stories high. Everything was colorful, and it didn't look all that strange. There were houses, offices, stores, cars, people, horse-drawn carts...all the comforts of home. And it was going to be my home, my new home.

There I was, standing on the deck, hanging over the railing, looking at my new home, wondering what I was doing there, wondering if perhaps I shouldn't just stay on the *hurtigruten* and head back to America. I spent seven weeks, four days, and twenty-three hours getting to Tromsø and Tromsø was where I would stay. I was scared as hell and as anxious and nervous as I had ever been in my life; I didn't deny it. But I was there, a lot of people had confidence in me that I could be the ambassador I was sent there to be, and I was about to get off the *hurtigruten* and meet my new family and begin my new life as the person Tromsø would enable me to become. I was at the end of a two-month journey that had taken me to the threshold of a twelve-month adventure that would change me forever.

But who was this seventeen-year-old kid standing on the deck of the world's slowest "express" ship looking out at an island 200 miles north of the Arctic Circle? How did I get there and what did I think I was doing?

Although at the time I combined an over-bearing degree of self-importance with an almost complete lack of self-esteem, I probably was a more ordinary teenager than I would ever have admitted. I was smart. My native intelligence earned me a spot in all of the advanced classes at Staples High School and my C average wasn't quite bad enough to warrant losing that spot. I was surrounded by the smartest kids at school. We had our three or four kids a year who got five 800s on the SAT tests (including achievements). Although I wasn't the smartest, I made up for that by being one of the most intellectually arrogant and judgmental.

I had lots of friends growing up, and by the end of elementary school I was having parties at my house with the closest thing elementary schools had to the "popular crowd." Everything changed for me when I went to junior high school; I was no longer popular. I joined the football team because I thought it would bring me into the popular crowd; it didn't. I wasn't asked to join the fraternities, the symbol of popularity for boys at Staples; I was devastated. I strove to be part of a crowd that had no interest in me.

I had never "fit in" at Staples. Being different was not just my fate; it was the way in which I defined myself. On the one hand, I hated the social isolation: having few friends, having little social life, not being "popular." On the other hand, I basked in the aura of my difference. I wanted to be "popular," but I didn't have any desire whatsoever to be "normal." That ambivalence dominated my high school years.

More than anything, I was moody. My most common response to the tensions and frustrations I experienced was to go into my room and sulk. I would shut the door, listen to the radio, play my imaginary guitar in front of my mirror as I pretended to be a rock star, and do everything I could to forget about my troubles. Neither I nor anyone else could get me out of my moods; they took their own time to pass.

So what was an intelligent, serious, unpopular, socially-inept, somewhat overweight, cynical (to cover his low self esteem) 17-year-old doing taking his first steps on Northern Norwegian soil? I grew up in an internationally-minded family. Throughout the 1950s, my family was a strong supporter of the United Nations, when such support was considered not just liberal but left-wing. Every year, Westport invited delegates from the UN to spend a weekend with Westport host families; we were always a host family. One year there were two delegates from Ouagadougou, Upper Volta (now Burkino Faso). We laughed all weekend; we taught them American card games. Every year I got to meet people from different parts of the world.

It was this background which prompted me to apply for an AFS scholarship, even though I hadn't much confidence in being selected. AFS was exceptionally competitive at Staples; there were usually forty or fifty kids who applied each year. I thought my interview with the AFS Selection Committee had gone well, but I was still surprised when I was selected in October as one of the finalists. I was even more surprised when I received a letter on May 17,1961 that I was going to Tromsø and I had three weeks to prepare.

As I sat in my room that fateful night, getting ready for bed, thoughts came at me from all directions. I wanted to get out of that town; I felt that strongly. In fact, I couldn't wait to get out. But what would it mean? Was it really going to be any better in Norway than in Westport? Why were they sending me there, anyway? Norway, of all places. Nobody had even heard of Norway. What would it mean about college? I would miss my senior year and all my advanced placement courses. How would I take my SAT exams?

The next day I went right to see Miss Barrie, my champion. Every outcast needs a champion and Miss Barrie was mine. She was my guidance counselor and she understood me.

"Come on in, Pete," Miss Barrie opened her door. "I just heard the great news. Come in. What's on your mind?"

"I'm wondering." I started talking even before my butt had reached the seat, "what kind of effect this might have on my getting into college? Isn't it going to make it harder to get in? I won't have my senior year; I won't have all my advance placement courses; I won't get to visit all my colleges; I won't have any interviews; I won't ..."

"Wait a minute," Miss Barrie interrupted. "I can see you don't understand the meaning of an AFS scholarship. Anyone wanting to got to college would trade all of what you're going to miss for the one thing you're going to be: an exchange student. If you're worried," she said reaching for the telephone on her desk, "I can call Earlham right now and confirm your acceptance. That's your safe school; I can get you into Earlham today."

"Really?"

"Of course." Miss Barrie was important to me because she had much more confidence in me than I had in myself. "I understand your fears, but they are groundless. Schools look at an AFS exchange student as a great benefit to their campus. Only a couple of thousand high school seniors are chosen a year; you're in an elite group. The last thing you have to worry about is whether this hurts your chance to get into the college you choose. The last thing."

I hardly noticed the next three weeks; they passed quickly, if not effortlessly. I got my inoculations. I got my passport. I got most of my clothes. I took pictures of my family and house and school and church. By the end of two of those three weeks, I'd taken care of most of the details and I got back to worrying.

Shortly after I had heard from AFS, I had written a letter to my Norwegian family: The Románs. I introduced myself, told them how excited I was to be coming, and asked them what they must have felt were a thousand questions: How old is my brother? How cold is it in the summer? How cold is it in the winter? What kind of clothes do I bring? What is Tromsø like? I had gotten a letter back, but it didn't tell me much.

FORSIKRINGSSELSKAPET TOR A/S

May 31, 1961

Dear Pete,

We have received your letter of the 29 inst. and I'll just write you a few words to tell you will be welcome to us.

It seems as if your father and I have almost the same profession as I am working in insurance business too, fire, motorcar and accidents.

Today I am going to Harstad by car—a distance from Tromsø of about 350 kilometers.

As now I am in a hurry and I'll therefore write you in a few days— and so will Karl Arvid too.

I don't know what information you need about Tromsø—who is situation in the north of Norway. Perhaps you have to notice that the winter is long up here, and warm clothes will therefore be useful most of the year.

Sincerely,
Karl Román

Three weeks exactly from the day I got the letter from AFS, I climbed into my family's pink 1956 Plymouth station wagon for the one-hour drive into NYC. After dinner with my family around the corner from AFS headquarters, I boarded the bus for Montreal, along with forty other teenage Americans.

The bus was full of kids. Most were going to Europe for the summer; a few, like myself, were leaving for the entire year. I talked with some of the others. A few of the kids started singing *Cumbaya*. I felt myself falling into my grumpy, unpleasant, and cynical self. Sulking was my second home; I spent a lot of time there. It was so easy for me to slip into self pity; it was a comfortable and familiar place. I knew I was supposed to be happy and excited, full of myself, honored with my selection. But, mostly, I was scared. One year was a hell of a long time, and I just didn't know if I could do it. Had AFS made the right choice?

At about five o'clock the next morning, we arrived at the Queens Hotel in downtown Montreal. I spent the better part of two hours saying hello to those AFSers who were now beginning to arrive at the hotel. Our trip was brief compared to that of the kids coming from other parts of the country.

"Hello, I'm Chuck. I'm going to Switzerland for the summer."

"Hello, I'm Pete. I'm going to Norway for the year."

"Hi, I'm Jinny. I'm going to France for the summer."

"Hi, I'm Pete. I'm going to Norway for the year."

"Hello, I'm Jim. I'm going to be in Spain for a semester."

"Hi. Pete. Norway for a year."

"Hello, there. I'm Nan. I'm going to Italy for the summer."

"Pete. Norway. Year."

After breakfast, eight of us groggily wandered around the neighborhood in which the hotel was situated, finally deciding a tourist bus trip around the city was better suited to our lack of slumber the night before. When we got back to the bus terminal the eight of us climbed into two cabs and headed for the docks, arriving at about two o'clock. I boarded the boat, taking my last step on the fertile concrete of the North American continent. I almost got sentimental, but I walked on board with a funny buddy from the bus trip and all I could do was to superimpose my frown on my already upcurved lips.

I walked around, met people, found my cabin, met people, and in general, met people. I felt like I did that all day but, then again, there were eight hundred of us going by boat to Europe; there were a few new people to meet. I showered and went to dinner.

"Hello, I'm Charles. I'm going to Austria for the summer."

"Hello, I'm Pete. I'm going to Norway for the year."

"Hi, I'm Jane. I'm going to Belgium for the summer."

"Hi, I'm Pete. I'm going to Norway for the year."

"Hello, I'm John. I'm going to be in Portugal for a semester."

"Hi. Pete. Norway for a year."

"Hello, there. I'm Nell. I'm going to Greece for the summer."

"Pete. Norway. Year."

The 10-day trip aboard the MS SEVEN SEAS was the perfect next leg of my journey. There we were, 800 American teenagers selected by AFS. There I was, with a social life on board. At the dances, everyone I asked to dance with me consented, and a number of girls asked me to dance with them...unheard of in my personal experience. And yet, by the middle of the dances, I would usually slip back into my "I do not get pleasure out of anything I do" mode. My ambivalence overwhelmed me. I was happy to be there, but my happiness could not deflect my mood swings: up one minute and down the next.

Most evenings progressed sluggishly. I periodically expressed some of my sentiments but no one understood me.

"Don't you wonder sometimes," I asked, "what we're doing here?"

"This is great."

"Shouldn't we be studying Norwegian?" I asked.

"The nights are for dancing."

"Aren't you afraid?" I asked.

"I've been on boats before."

"What do I do if my family hates me?" I asked.

"What did you say?"

We were on board the SEVEN SEAS for ten days but the time felt condensed. And, there were occasions when I began to feel slight changes coming over me. I was elected to the Ship Council by my group of eighty-three AFSers on their way to Norway. People looked up to me for leadership. I organized soap slides in the corridors; talk about leadership. And the days were always full of people. Throughout each day, I continued to meet new people.

"Hello, I'm Chiz. I'm going to England for the summer."

"Hello, I'm Pete. I'm going to Norway for the year."

"Hi, I'm Jessie. I'm going to Luxemburg for the summer."

"Hi, I'm Pete. I'm going to Norway for the year."

"Hello, I'm John. I'm going to be in Turkey for a semester."

"Hi. Pete. Norway for a year."

"Hello, there. I'm Natalie. I'm going to Finland for the summer."

"Pete. Norway. Year."

After breakfast each morning all 800 of us broke into our country groups for language classes. The logistics were staggering; the AFSers were headed for more than fifteen different countries. I never did find out what happened after breakfast to those kids going to England.

"*God morn,*" Bente Dahl said cheerfully each morning. Bente always wore a traditional Norwegian outfit: colorful skirt with a matching top, white blouse, silver pendant around her neck, and a colorful hat. She was clearly intent on getting us in the mood.

"Goo more-en," we responded cautiously. I had always been a good student in French class and I did have a good ear for languages. But, I still worried about how quickly I could pick Norwegian up and I worried about how that might limit my ability to speak when I got to Tromsø. I did have a *year*, so I worried about how little I would know on my first *day* in Tromsø. I worried about the language camp we would attend for three weeks in Oslo before even getting to Tromsø. I worried about not worrying enough.

Day by day, the phrases were getting more difficult, but they were still relatively easy.

God dag: Good day.

God morn: Good day.

God aften: Good evening.

Hvordan står det til: How are you?

Det gleder meg å treffe deg: Pleased to meet you.

I found learning Norwegian to be pretty easy for me. The grammar remained a snap and the phrases were not too complicated. We even learned how to count from one to a hundred.

en	*ti*
to	*tyve*
tre	*tredve*
fire	*førti*
fem	*femti*
seks	*seksti*
syv	*søtti*
åtte	*åtti*
ni	*nitti*
ti	*hundre*

What fun!

Meeting new kids and learning new Norwegian phrases every day was exciting, but even more exciting were some of the differences I began to feel in myself. I was a little happier and a little more at ease (and at peace) with myself. Recognizing the select group in which I found myself made it possible for me to think a little more highly of myself. I was both a social wall flower and a campus/ship personality: elected to the Ship Council, working on the ship newspaper, organizing soap slides. The beginnings of the struggle between the old and the new Petes, the different parts of my personality, began to emerge and define both the tension and the growth that would characterize the entire year.

After our last breakfast on the SEVEN SEAS, we put into effect the debarkation procedures the staff had gone over with us the day before. Since the staff had their passports checked first and left the boat before us, I was put in charge of the Norway contingent.

"Listen up, you guys," I shouted over the roar of 800 high school students itching to get their journeys started for real. "It's important that everything go smoothly and quickly. Keep in mind, we have an 11:00 o'clock train to catch. Personally, I hope all of us make it, but I'll guarantee you that I will. So, if you cooperate and follow me, there's a good chance you will, too."

"Where do we go?" Rosie asked.

"Find Bente and just wait near her."

"How do we get to the train?" Leslie asked.

"Take a plane?"

"What about our luggage," Ben asked.

"Carry it?"

It always felt good to be put in charge—even if I did have trouble answering stupid questions—but that didn't really take my mind off what I had to do: leave the boat and most of the kids on it. I felt unhappiness settling in; perhaps I liked some of those kids more than I had realized.

"Okay, Norwegians," I addressed my multitude. "Step lively. This is a gangplank we're walking."

One-by-one we stepped off the ship onto our first bit of European soil. Believe it or not, it really didn't feel any different from that of America!

We got on the train and I had my first taste of the European train compartment. I was used to American trains, where the seats were side-by-side through the entire length of the car, with a narrow aisle down the middle. European trains were divided into compartments. There was a long, narrow aisle down one side of the car, along the windows. Off that hall were eight or ten compartments, or little rooms, each with its own door. Each compartment had two benches, facing each other.

"Did everybody make it?" I asked, sticking my head in one compartment after the other. Was I really expecting someone to say no?

"I didn't," Tom Holbrook said, making me feel I had asked a worthwhile question.

"If you guys don't stop moving around, "I threatened, "I'll have to assign seats."

"I don't want to sit next to Rosie," Leslie complained, "for the whole trip. She snores even when she's awake."

"We'll change partners in Copenhagen," I suggested.

As we slowly pulled out of Rotterdam, I had never seen such beautiful land in my whole life. I took the train a lot from Westport to New York; those trains made a habit of going through the ugliest section of each town along the way. Germany looked a lot like Holland, but more industrialized, bigger, and less quaint. The houses were packed a little tighter, even though we were still traveling through the countryside. There were a few more factories, and they were a little bigger. All of the buildings appeared a little more austere and functional...not quite as pretty as their counterparts in Holland. I found it remarkable that an invisible line, like a border, could bring about such a noticeable change.

By 6:30 the next evening we were about an hour southeast of Oslo. I was completely awe-struck by the beauty of the land we were passing through. The land itself was flat, not the mountainous Norway we saw in a movie on board the SEVEN SEAS, but it was moist and lush, especially in the morning as the sun came up. It was farm land, and there were fields and animals and barns everywhere. I could almost feel the land's softness, with the hay drying sometimes in stacks and sometimes hung over wires, like clothes drying on a clothesline. I had not picked up a book or attempted to write a letter the whole train ride from Rotterdam for fear of missing something special in the landscape.

On my last night in Westport, I wrote a letter to myself.

June 6, 1961

Dear Self,

Tomorrow I'm off to New York for the bus to Montreal and the boat to Europe. So, what have I learned about Tromsø, my home for the next year? Tromsø is a little village so far north in Norway that it is one of the few places in Europe that is never included on a European map. At the Arctic Circle, most forms of animal life—at least normal animal life—cease to exist; even trees are too scared to grow. But when I was told that I am to live 200 miles above this "line of no return," I was more than a little taken aback; perhaps when I am actually there I will wish to be taken aback to my home in Connecticut.

I think I now realize why no picture of either my new family nor my new house was ever sent to me: they don't have any cameras! Originally, I assumed that the Gulf Stream would warm up this ice-box a little, and my research indicates that warm it up a little it does. But the five or ten degrees added to the year-round sub-zero temperatures of Tromsø obviously don't make it like the French Riviera, in spite of its nickname, "Paris of the North."

I hear there is at least the beauty of the midnight sun in the north of Norway. Beauty my foot! Maybe some people think that to have day-light for two solid months, followed by complete and utter darkness twenty-four hours a day for the next ten months is beautiful, but for me, it's too dark to see anything.

I have also heard that the skiing will be wonderful, too. Are people serious? We're talking about skiing on the beautiful, sloping, ninety-degree mountains of Norway. Get real. I'm not certain where everyone gets their ideas of Norway, but I am afraid they don't come from the northern part of Norway.

But I have a lot to look forward to; I really do. Who wouldn't look forward to living for one whole year in the luxurious interior of an igloo? And what fun it will be walking ten miles to a quaint, old, unheated, one-room school house? It will be Thoreau's paradise, living all by oneself, completely isolated from civilization...and four miles from the nearest bathroom. But we'll always have cold running water, every spring when the two-foot snowdrifts begin to melt.

I Was a Teenage Norwegian

I am really looking forward to the rugged Norwegians, the beautiful countryside, and my long underwear. I wonder why AFS doesn't send more of us to Norway?

This story is about how becoming a teenage Norwegian enabled hidden parts of me to be expressed. Neither I nor anyone else could, for example, rid me of my teenage American moods; that took traveling 5,000 miles to a town I couldn't even find on a map. Tromsø changed me, although elements of my past, even my moods, hung on. The tension between the emerging Norwegian Peter Dublin and the old American one is what this story is about.

-2-
Norway At Last

My first day in Oslo was the beginning of my journey, although within ten days I came closer to leaving Norway than at any time during the remainder of the year. My year-long adventure as a teenage Norwegian came perilously close to ending before it began.

Trollvasshytta was the name of the language camp. "*Hytta*" means cabin or cottage and everyone knows what a troll is. I thought of that place as the Cottage of the Trolls, although it was more of a small compound than a single *hytta*. The approach to Trollvasshytta was through woods, which gave the place a lot of character. The compound was like an island in the middle of the woods. In one direction was the *trikk*, the trolley line to the center of Oslo; in the other direction, we could walk for hours through a forest.

There was a main house, where we ate, had classes, and where most of the kids slept. It looked more like one of the central buildings in an American summer camp: one story, slightly pitched roof, painted clapboards, a few windows, a porch in front. Then there were two smaller *hytter* where the rest of us slept. All the buildings were painted barn red and it appeared more like a farm in the mountains than a language camp in Norway's largest city.

The roof of my *hytta* was a lawn, but the roof-lawn was only a small part of what made that place so remarkable. I began to get a sense of how remarkable on the bus from the railroad station the day before. Everything was cool and normal as we started to wind our way from the station through the city for ten or fifteen minutes. We were in a city and it looked like a city: lots of cars, buses and trucks, *trikks* to watch out for, flat stretches of city blocks, traffic lights, everything I expected. All of a sudden, we started climbing. We didn't climbed a little hill and stop climbing. We climbed a mountain, not a hill. It may have been a small mountain as mountains go, but it was still a mountain and we climbed, and climbed, and climbed, seemingly forever.

It was a steep, narrow, and exceedingly curvy road. About ten minutes into our climb, it was evident that we could not make it around a particular corner under a bridge that carried the *trikk* up the mountain. The driver drove the bus on a side street and backed up under the bridge into another side street and finally straightened the bus out in order to be able to continue our climb up the Oslo mountainside. That whole little routine took close to ten minutes itself and the entire bus applauded his efforts, including the chaperones.

Still, we were only half-way to Trollvasshytta. As I looked out the windows, I got a sense of how far we had already come and how high up we already were. I could see the center of the city growing smaller in the background; we must have been five or six miles away from it by then. From another angle I could see farms and farm-land.

"Where are we?" I asked Bente.

"Oslo," Bente answered.

"Where are those farms?" I asked Øystein, our new chaperone, hoping for a better answer.

"Oslo," he smiled.

Bente and Øystein assured me that we were still within the city limits and that the farms, mountains, and forests we could see all around us were also all within the Oslo city limits. Trollvasshytta itself was within the city limits too, even though it was almost at the top of the mountain in the middle of the woods. People could go out for a walk in Oslo, not come back for a couple of weeks, and never have left the city limits!

Øystein was the newest addition to my emerging AFS family. He was typically Norwegian: blond hair, blue eyes, tall, and slender. He was a great guy—good sense of humor, understanding, and supportive—and a fine athlete; none of us could keep up with him in the woods. He had been an AFS student in the United States a few years earlier. Bente was the ski champion of all of Norway and one of the best downhill racers in all of Europe. AFS really did pick exceptional people. Me included? I wasn't completely convinced, but I was getting there.

Our first full day in Norway provided us with our first opportunity to sample Norwegian food and adjust our eating schedule to the pattern of Norwegian meals. I saw two major differences almost immediately. First, Norwegians ate four meals a day instead of the three we were used to in the States. We had breakfast, lunch, and dinner—that I was used to—except we ate dinner at 4:00 in the afternoon. We had dinner relatively early because the Norwegian eating schedule included an evening meal, *aftens*; we ate *aftens* around 10:00 PM. At least in the summertime, it wasn't as strange as it sounded, since it was still light out at that hour and we rarely went to bed before midnight. In fact, as our weeks at Trollvasshytta wore on and we became used to this new schedule, I found myself growing fond of *aftens*. It was almost as much of a social time as it was a culinary one: all of us sat around, chatted about the day's events, marveled at the sunset, wondered about our new lives.

The second major difference I noticed was that all the meals except dinner were comprised of a single food: sandwiches. Breakfast (difficult to believe): sandwiches. Lunch (of course): sandwiches. *Aftens* (no precedent there): sandwiches. Sandwiches with that frequency took a lot of getting used to and the three weeks at Trollvasshytta were an insufficient transition time. It might have been slightly easier if the sandwiches were familiar: two pieces of bread stuffed with ungodly amounts of a great variety of possibilities. In Norway, however, sandwiches were open-faced; there was only one piece of bread with only one topping on it.

"Pete," Bente looked aghast, "what are you doing?"

"I'm making a sandwich."

"But what are you making it with?" she asked again.

"Salami and cheese, I think."

"That's not allowed," Øystein said, with a serious face.

"What do you mean?" it was my turn to look surprised.

"You can't have two toppings on a sandwich," he explained distinctly.

"You can't be serious," I couldn't tell if Øystein was being serious; I didn't know him well enough.

"Oh, yes," he said, his face still serious. "Norwegian sandwiches are open-faced with one topping."

"This is a law?" I asked.

"This is Norwegian," he answered.

Hey, I thought, when in Oslo.... Luckily for me I wasn't especially hungry anyway and I didn't care to eat that much. But what would happen if I were hungry?

June 22, 1961

Dear Mom and Dad,

Just a quick letter to let you know we arrived in Oslo and we're all settled in our new home: Trollvasshytta. I am sending with this letter the first installment of my journal, which will give you a more detailed sense of what has happened these past two weeks. Has it really only been two weeks?

I think things are starting to fall into a more definite routine, and everything will not seem as wonderful, new, and exciting as it has every day since I left home. We will certainly have new and different experiences, but I sense they will be more infrequent now. But when I do look at everything and try to evaluate it for what it is really worth—not in comparison to what has already happened—it does take on more significance and a more valuable meaning is quite apparent.

I have wanted to leave Westport for as long as I could remember. I'm still glad I'm here but it is harder on me than I could have ever imagined. But I've got a job to do and I'm going to do it!!

Love,
Pete

I Was a Teenage Norwegian

Those of us at Trollvasshytta obviously had a great deal in common, sharing the same adventure, fears, and hopes. I found it easy, at least sometimes, to talk with them about things that I gathered mattered to them but had never mattered to me, such as clothes and music. And there were also discussions about things that I cared about, such as politics. I still hung back sometimes and I didn't participate in every activity (often preferring to be by myself), but I felt an increasing level of comfort with these kids, with myself, and with my situation.

We had our first Norwegian class from nine until twelve with our new teacher, Liz. Liz worked on both grammar and vocabulary, with an emphasis on those words which would come in most handy during our first few months in our new homes and towns. And Liz worked a lot on our pronunciation, especially the vowels.

"In English," she said, "there are five vowels—a, e, i, o, and u—and sort of a sixth: sometimes y. In Norwegian, we have those six vowels, and three others that don't exist in English at all: *æ, ø*, and *å*."

Liz provided us with a difficult, but fun, exercise. She wrote the nine vowels on the board, so we could remember what they were. She had one of us go up to the board and she gave that person a pointer. Then she would start pronouncing the vowels and the person at the board would have to point to the vowel she was saying. We did that exercise every day for a week; it was much harder than it sounded, because so many of the vowels had completely different sounds than their English equivalents and sounds that were difficult for us to distinguish from each other. But it was fun—almost like a game—and completely non-competitive. As the week wore on, and all of us got better and better at it, we actually fought among ourselves for a chance to go up to the board and see how accurate our hearing had become.

"I realize that most of you," Liz announced toward the end of dinner that evening, "are anxiously awaiting evening study hall. And I understand that having to postpone this most exciting part of your day may be a great blow to you. But, I fear, you will have to wait one more day for the pleasure of that study hall, because we are expecting a group of Norwegians to visit us any minute."

And within minutes, about twenty students from Oslo came up to Trollvasshytta to visit us, students who would be AFSers in the US.

"Hello, I'm Knut. I'm going to Detroit for the year."

"Hello, I'm Pete. I'm going to Tromsø for the year."

"Hi, I'm Karen. I'm going to Arizona for a year."

"Hi, I'm Pete. I'm going to Tromsø for a year."

"Hello, I'm Gunnar. I'm going to be in Los Angeles for a year."

"Hi. Pete. Tromsø for a year."

"Hello, there. I'm Berit. I'm going to a small town outside of Atlanta."

"Pete. Tromsø. Year."

14

I had a lot to think about as I got into bed that evening. On the one hand, I had a good feeling that with people such as those I had met and a land such as I had begun to experience, I could be happy in Norway. On the other hand: what was I doing here? I wasn't as fun-loving or as talented as any of the Norwegian AFSers-to-be with whom I had spent the evening. Did I really know what I was doing? Could I really manage?

There was one major item that Trollvasshytta lacked: a shower. Had there been a shower at my disposal for half an hour each morning, I might not have minded getting up as much as I did. I could have combed my hair, washed my hair and face, shaved my stubble, and done all those other things that one was supposed to do in the morning. Without a shower I was very much of a slob. Not only in my dress habits, but in other habits as well. There were, in fact, many days I overslept, missed breakfast, and was even late for class. On the weekends, I sometimes missed whole activities.

One afternoon, we all went for a three-mile hike to a lake somewhere hidden in the woods. I just loved the way we could walk out of our *hytta*, through the back yard of Trollvasshytta, and right into the woods.

On the way, I struck up a conversation with Leslie.

"Isn't the water great?" I asked.

"It's a lot like our lakes in Minnesota," Leslie answered.

"How's everything going for you," I wondered out loud.

"You know," Leslie continued, "I'm really feeling pretty good about everything. I'm not too homesick and I'm learning some Norwegian. How about you?"

"Sometimes I wonder why I was ever chosen," I responded, "but more and more I feel pretty good, too. I feel I'm going through this change, you know what I mean?"

"I know; I kind of feel like I'm changing, too. What kind of change do you think you're going through?"

"Well, it's mostly that I feel I'm coming out of my pessimistic shell. I feel I'm slowly making my way into the stage of normal optimism."

"But I sense," Leslie ventured, "that you still keep a lot of things in, a lot of stuff to yourself."

"Yeah, you're probably right. There's a part of me that thinks it's not good to talk of change; I should just let it happen."

"But don't you find," Leslie persisted, "that it helps if you talk about what's happening to you?"

"Yeah, I guess. In a way, when I talk it's like getting another optimistic shot in the arm."

Little did I know that the tensions I was feeling, the tensions I expressed in that brief conversation, were about to come to a head, an almost disastrous head.

Now, thirty five years later, I can see it coming...as clear as the midnight sun. But it doesn't surprise me at all that I couldn't see a thing at the time. I know now what I didn't know then: there was a struggle bubbling within me—not raging, not even boiling over, but churning around inside me. I had spent the previous four years wallowing in self-pity and an effort to be someone I wasn't; the results were moodiness, pessimism, cynicism, and sarcasm. I can now see that it was those parts of myself, not Westport, that I so desperately wanted to leave behind. I can now see that leaving Westport was probably the quickest way to jumpstart the process of allowing other parts of me to emerge, crowding out those parts which had so dominated those teenage years.

One afternoon, I felt a little sick, so I lay down and slept right through dinner. I felt sick off and on ever since I arrived at Trollvasshytta. Nothing serious, just a stomach ache, a headache, other aches, slightly nauseous. I missed some of the meals because of it, but it wasn't much of a loss; I hadn't been eating much since I left Montreal. I woke up four hours later and couldn't get to sleep for another three. That was par for the course, both in Norway and in Westport. I couldn't relax; I couldn't turn my mind off. I didn't do it continually, just at night when I couldn't get to sleep or when I went for walks in the woods by myself. I knew I shouldn't feel blue about my present situation, but I did some good thinking about it and, anyway, I couldn't turn my mind off even if I wanted to.

When I got up the next morning I was still not feeling too well. I decided to stay in bed for a while. I wasn't hungry anyway and I didn't mind missing another breakfast. I lay in bed and begin thinking, as I did the previous evening, about the States. I thought of my family and my mind drifted off into the fantasy of my return in 1962. I thought about home and the train ride back to Westport; I imagined in my mind the trip from the station to my house in every detail. I had been at Trollvasshytta for almost two weeks and waking up, feeling sick, and staying in bed had become something of a pattern. I didn't know exactly what it was, but even I was wondering if the physical pain had its basis somewhere in my emotions. I finally got up at 10:00 AM and made my way lethargically into Norwegian language class.

"*God morn*, Pete," Liz addressed me. "*Her er dine vitaminer.*"

I had hardly made it through the door and Liz immediately presented me with one box of vitamins and instructions for taking same.

"You cannot afford," she said to me, but loud enough for everyone to hear, "to be a sick AFSer in Norway!"

The next morning I was up bright and early; I surprised everyone by making it to breakfast. I wasn't even feeling poorly. I could just about begin to see Tromsø in my mind. By dinner, however, I was not feeling well. I had a big dinner of half a glass of water and two aspirin tablets. I somehow managed my way through the two-hour study session that evening before I headed off to bed early.

I hadn't been in bed more than fifteen or twenty minutes when Øystein came into the *hytta* and began a talk I would remember for the rest of my life. I hadn't seen it coming, but it had been inevitable.

"Pete," Øystein began, "Are you physically sick?"

"I don't know," I answered. "I'm never hungry and I get headaches."

"Well," he persisted, "can you tell me exactly what is the matter?"

"I don't know. Sometimes I have headaches."

"Can you point out specifically what ails you?"

"I'm not sure. One day I'll feel fine, and the next day I feel ill. Last night was great, and today was terrible. Some days I feel good about myself and being here, and the next day I don't know why I'm here. The feelings and the pain come and go. I've always had headaches, but I get them more frequently here and more unpredictably. I've always felt nauseous sometimes, but now it's more often. And then it just disappears...for a while."

"I'm going to give it to you straight, Pete," Øystein continued. "If you cannot point to something specific that is the matter with you, you should get out of bed and begin to do what everyone else does. No more missing breakfast and part of class and study hall or not going on walks."

"But sometimes I need to study for my finals," I objected. I felt guilty about my Staples finals, and my promise to the principal that I would take them in Norway.

"Forget about studying for the finals," Øystein's voice was more forceful than I had ever heard it. " You will be better off flunking the tests if the only time you can find to study is when everyone else goes on a hike."

I was the kind of kid who struggled with this kind of conversation, a conversation in which someone else told me how stupidly I was behaving. I had conversations like this with my father for years; he would constantly get on my case for thinking too much and doing too little, for trying too hard and enjoying myself too infrequently. I even had this kind of conversation on board the SEVEN SEAS when Joan told me she had never seen someone so full of so much self pity.

"See, Pete," Øystein pushed on, "you are here on a mission. That's really what AFS is. You have to get hold of yourself and begin to take all of the experience a little more seriously. I have seen many Russian students come to Norway and let me tell you, they take their experience a hell of a lot more seriously than you do, Pete. This isn't a summer vacation; you're here for a year...maybe

"Just because you are selected to come here doesn't guarantee you success. There are always a number of AFS failures; you cannot afford to be one of them. You have to work hard to succeed.

"Pete, you have a choice. You can get up out of that bed and begin to take part in this experience. You can eat with us, study with us, walk with us. Or you can go home...tomorrow. That's your choice. I hope I see you tomorrow at breakfast. Good night."

If a good swift kick in the butt was what I needed, that certainly was exactly what I got. Øystein threatened me with expulsion. Ever since I had heard on May 17th that I was going to Norway, I had doubts about whether or not I could handle the experience. I found out on the

I Was a Teenage Norwegian

SEVEN SEAS that I wasn't alone with either my doubts or my dreams. Even at Trollvasshytta everyone was willing to share his and her concerns for the year. But no one had let the fears and self-doubts become demoralizing and debilitating, except me. If only I could take hold of myself and overcome these doubts and fears. If only I could fulfill Øystein's image of an AFSer. If only I could live up to his aspirations for me. If only I could, I knew that my AFS year in Norway would be a success and I would feel contented. If I couldn't, God help me.

As the sun streamed in the *hytta* the next morning, I felt that the new day began the life of another, a new Pete Dublin. If Øystein had hoped to scare the hell out of me, he had most certainly succeeded. There was no way I was heading back home, mission incomplete. I may not have fully understood why I wanted to leave Westport, but I sure as hell knew I wanted to leave, and I sure as hell wasn't going back after four weeks. I wasn't mad at Øystein; I wasn't even mad at myself. More than anything else, I was determined. I wanted this experience and I wasn't going to screw it up. Period.

Even today I can still see that cabin, I can still see Øystein, I can still hear that conversation after all these years. Even with hindsight, I don't blame anyone for the situation. I don't blame AFS for not having adequately prepared me; I don't blame my family and Westport's former AFSers for not having talked to me. There really wasn't anything anyone could have said which would have prevented this situation. It was a situation waiting to happen, the result of an interaction between the situation and my own biography, my own personality. And its resolution, as clear to me today as the crisis itself, depended on other aspects of that same personality and the support structure that AFS had provided.

"*God morn*," Øystein greeted me as I entered the big room with the tables set for breakfast.

"*Værsågod*," Liz welcomed me to the table. I still didn't quite get the use of the word, but I welcomed the invitation: I was starving.

We usually started with either an egg or a bowl of corn flakes; this was the American portion of our breakfast. The rest of the meal was open-faced sandwiches: *smørbrød*. These *smørbrød* were made out of one piece of bread or something comparable to Rye Crisp, called *knekkebrød*. Since we were only allowed one topping per *smørbrød* and all the toppings—cheese, jams, and salami—were fabulous, most of us had made up for it by having six or eight *smørbrød* per meal. Up until that morning, "most of us" had not included me. The old Pete had lost, thus far, seven pounds, and I was down to 181 pounds in my stocking feet! The new Pete was about ready to make up for lost time; he began his new life with six *smørbrød*. The first benefit of the new Pete.

After lunch, we all hiked to the chapel near the famous Holmenkollen ski jump. Out the *hytta*, through the back yard, into the woods we went; I loved it. It felt good to be with the group and to be

18

active. I loved walking in the woods and now I could experience the woods with the others, not just by myself. When we got back home, we ate dinner, studied Norwegian, and threw ourselves into our beds. Our stay at Trollvasshytta got everyone tired. I was tired, but I was far from exhausted; I was exhilarated. I had made it from New York to Montreal. I had made it on the SEVEN SEAS. I had now made it at Trollvasshytta. Two more days; I could hardly believe it. Two more days and I would be heading off to Tromsø. And I would make it in Tromsø, too.

It didn't bother me at all getting up early on my last full day at Trollvasshytta. Although I had gotten a lot out of my stay in Trollvasshytta, I wanted to get up to Tromsø.

"Let's get out of here," my heart egged me on.

"We're not quite ready," my head objected.

At breakfast I was selected by the others to give the two house-keepers a handkerchief, and the celebration was pretty funny given my scanty Norwegian.

On that last day at Trollvasshytta, I headed out on a walk into the woods by myself. I had walked through these woods almost every day, and I had walked them often by myself under less pleasant circumstances, but this was the first time I walked there by myself full of hope and joy. I was getting a little nervous on my last day at Trollvasshytta.

It was clear to me that I needed the three weeks at Trollvasshytta, if for no other reason, as a buffer, a quieting down from my original fears and super-emotions of the pre-ship time and my feelings on the SEVEN SEAS. It was equally clear as I wandered those woods for the last time that I had gained a few insights into other people and a few into myself, too. I felt the stay at Trollvasshytta would help me in the future to tolerate others more and be able in the future to live more compatibly with other people. So what if there was too much food and if I hadn't lost as much weight as I would have liked.

Right after dinner, some of the kids began to leave. Tom was the first one to go and rightly so, because for the past two and one-half weeks he lived about two hundred yards from his new house. He couldn't believe it. His Norwegian family lived right in the woods surrounding Trollvasshytta and we literally walked past it almost every day. Imagine how difficult it was for Liz and Øystein not to tell him.

The remaining twelve of us went to bed early, or at least what was early for us: at about 9:00 PM. I could barely manage a brief letter before I headed off to never-never land myself.

July 7, 1961

Dear Mom and Dad,

I can't believe this is the last letter I will write you from Oslo. Tomorrow morning I begin the last leg of my trip.

I have all those many thoughts that Øystein brought forth: I would be on a mission, I would be an ambassador for my country, I would have to work hard to succeed. I have advice that I was given before I left Westport: be yourself, listen hard, let your new family become a family for you. I have these thoughts, ideas, and I feel that if I keep them at the front of my mind there is a chance that I can abide by some of them. I am grateful to all the people who have said such thoughts to me, for I can sense that these thoughts will take on some real meaning for me during this stay.

And I am deeply indebted to you, my two parents, who have given me the basis for almost 100% of my thinking. And to my best friends, I will always be thankful for their criticism, advice, and warm friendship. With a background of friends, family, and acquaintances such as these, and with the ideas and thoughts that they have—though not really preached to me—I cannot see but that I can make this whole thing a success if I will only work, try, exercise self-control when necessary, and enjoy myself.

With this I sleep.

Much love,
Pete

"Hey, Pete," Liz shouted through the *hytta* window. "How long do you expect to stay here at Trollvasshytta? I thought you wanted to get up to Tromsø. Was I wrong? Should I just let you sleep?"

It was six o'clock in the morning. It was the day I had waited for, and all I wanted to do was bury my head under the covers and get a few minutes' more sleep. But no, this was the day to get up and get out, and that's what I did.

"You guys," Liz was already in her chair eating as I entered the dining room, "had better eat a hearty breakfast. Most of you have many hours of travel ahead of you."

Never had a truer word been spoken; I had a two and one-half day trip ahead of me.

Pete Dublin

Leave Oslo East-Station Saturday morning at 9.10.

Arrive in Trondheim Saturday night. Met by AFSer and later followed on the train to Fauske.

At Fauske in the morning Sunday. Ask for directions to get on the bus to Bodö. Met in Bodö by AFSer. Given dinner and taken on the boat to Tromsø. Arrive Manday afternoon. Met by your family.

God reise, and don't get lost!

Bente

There were only twelve of us left; the other six lived close enough to Oslo that they were picked up by their families the previous evening. The rest of us had longer trips to make, and I had the longest. After all, I was going to the land of the midsummer winter. I was going to Tromsø.

Three of us headed off for the train station in downtown Oslo. I grabbed my two, unbelievably heavy suitcases (I may have lost seven pounds since I left but my two suitcases—starting the trip weighing in at ninety pounds—hadn't lost an ounce between them) and began the short walk from Trollvasshytta to the *trikk* station. I took one last look at the Cottage of the Trolls which had been my first home-away-from home: the large central building where we ate and studied, the smaller *hytta* for sleeping, my *hytta* with its growing-grass roof, the opening from the back yard into the woods. I took this one, last mental snapshot, turned away, and headed for the *trikk*. Damn if I wasn't a little sad to be leaving the place.

"Liz," I said, with increasing panic spreading over my face, as we entered the railroad station, "I think I left my passport and tickets at Trollvasshytta."

"Where have you looked?" Her face showed no panic whatsoever.

"Every place except where they are," I smiled as I found both necessities underneath my camera in my smaller suitcase. Nothing quite like getting off to a shaky start. A little drama just in case the trip proved to be boring.

Once I got over my initial jitters as the train pulled out of the station, I found the ride itself dull, but the trip interesting, because of what I saw. As we traveled farther and farther north of Oslo, we saw more and more beautiful mountains. The mountains were big and bold; they rose gradually from the valley floor and then immediately towered over it. One of the mountains was tree-covered from the valley floor half-way up and snow-covered from there to the top. For those who love running rivers and streams, for those who love to see quiet, peaceful eighty-mile-long lakes, for those who love to watch logs drift serenely down a slowly moving river, for those I suggest the 9:10 out of Oslo for Trondheim.

The 9:10 from Oslo pulled into Trondheim at about 9:30 in the evening. The first leg of the final leg of my northward trip ended, but I hardly had time to think about it. I felt as if I were back in Copenhagen with only fifteen minutes to change trains. It was probably better that way. I certainly didn't have any time to be worried or sad; I barely had enough time to catch my train. I was finally on my own but I was almost too hurried to notice.

Physically, Norway looks like a thermometer, with a little tail going off eastward at the top. Most Norwegians, and all three Norwegian cities, were located in the big, circular area at the bottom of the thermometer, where most of the mercury was stored. Oslo was at the southern end of this bubble, Bergen at the western end, and Trondheim at the northern top. Once past Trondheim, the country narrows dramatically. Fauske was my next destination—the last stop on the railroad line—and it lies almost smack on the Arctic Circle, at about sixty five degrees North Latitude. Tromsø was farther north, almost at the top of the thermometer; it lay at almost seventy degrees North Latitude. Where was I going? How far away from everything familiar to me could I get? What

was I doing in that icicle of a country? Why was I going to a place I would never have chosen myself? Was I crazy?

The train pulled into Fauske at about 10:15 in the morning, and I immediately boarded a bus to Bodø. The bus ride to Bodø was short; Bodø was only an hour due west of Fauske and that was where I was to board the *hurtigruten*. I was supposed to be met in Bodø by an AFSer. I arrived in Bodø at 12:00 noon and there was no AFSer to meet me. I was met instead by a friend of the AFSer; the AFSer was in the army at that moment.

"I don't know how it is in America," Lars explained, as he helped me with my luggage, "but here in Norway every boy has to spend one year in the army. Here in Norway," Lars continued as we checked my luggage at the bus station, "it's only for one year, but everyone has to serve; there are no exceptions." I was already glad Lars had met me; I would never have known *to* check my luggage at the bus station, let alone *how* to check it.

Lars was twenty-one and had already served his one year in the army. He was tall, with fluffy blond hair, a pleasant smile, and friendly. He had been born and raised in Bodø and worked in his father's company, selling wholesale auto parts throughout Northern Norway.

"Bodø and Tromsø are very much alike," Lars continued as we settled into our chairs at a restaurant for lunch. "They're both big coastal towns in the north of Norway; they are larger than the villages, people have more to do there, and they have high schools."

"What do most people do?" I asked, taking a bite of my *smørbrød*.

"Well, there's a lot of fishing, since they are both on the coast. But most of the fishing takes place out in the coastal villages, not big towns like Bodø. Bodø and Tromsø are commercial centers for their areas: a lot of stores, warehouses and distribution centers, wholesalers, and the like."

"Like your father?" I asked.

"*Jada,*" Lars responded. Definitely had something to do with *ja*, the Norwegian word for yes.

"How big is Bodø?" I asked, looking around. Lars kept talking about Bodø and Tromsø as big towns.

"About 8,000-10,000 people," Lars smiled proudly. I had to get familiar with a different scale than the one I was used to.

At 3:00 in the afternoon, Lars escorted me to the boat, after we picked up my ninety pounds of baggage at the left luggage counter in the bus station. At least I had someone to help me carry all my stuff.

"*Takk,*" I said as I headed up the gangplank, having learned the Norwegian word for thanks almost as quickly as I had learned *ja*.

"*Ha det,*" Lars waved good-bye.

Have it. What a strange way to say good-bye. It was short for, "*Ha det godt,*" which literally meant "have it good." But it got shortened to "have it."

Most Norwegians lived along the coast in small towns or coastal villages. The only easy way to get from one place to the next—in some cases the only way—was by boat. For all towns along the coast, a boat was the best way of getting goods transported, everything from radios and food to refrigerators and automobiles. So, the Coastal Express—or *hurtigruten*—was not exactly a passenger ship, although it carried passengers, and not exactly a freighter, although it carried freight.

As we pulled out of Bodø harbor, I wandered around the *hurtigruten*. There were two decks for cabins; I walked through the corridors, but I never got an opportunity to confirm my suspicions that they weren't as fancy as those on the SEVEN SEAS. As with my lack of a sleeping bunk on the train from Trondheim to Fauske, I didn't rate a cabin on this leg of my trip; I had to sleep on the deck. It was about 70°F at 3:00 PM; I hoped it wouldn't get much colder at night. I forgot. I was in Northern Norway: what night?

We steamed briefly up a *fjord* and I got a first-hand glance at the mountains and waterfalls. That was the part of Norway everyone heard about, but hearing about *fjords* had little meaning until I had actually seen them. The dictionary defined a *fjord* as a narrow inlet of the sea between cliffs or steep slopes. That was what they were, but the words just didn't do them justice. The mountains went straight down into the water. Sounded simple; looked spectacular. There were no fields, because the angles were too sharp. The *hurtigruten* went so close to the mountains that I felt as if I could have touched them. Trees covered the mountains literally down to the water's edge. It was a little *fjord*—hardly half a mile in length—but by the time we got to the back of it, it felt eerie. It was as if we had passed into the twilight zone; we were in a different time and space.

The basic pattern on the *hurtigruten* was to ride for three or four hours, stop in a small town for an hour to drop off passengers and freight, and then steam along for another few hours before the next stop. If our arrival at a town was a break in routine for us, it appeared to be a situation of sheer excitement for those in the town. Everyone in each town came out to see the arrival of the *hurtigruten*; it was clearly the event of the day. Little kids, mothers, school-age kids, workers of all sorts, even kids in their teens and early twenties. They waved at us, talked to the crew members as if they were family, smiled, joked...I had never seen anything like it. It was easy to see how the *hurtigruten* tied coastal Norwegians together. I kept telling myself that I would have to get off the *hurtigruten* at one of the stops; it looked easy to do and lots of people did it.

At about 12:30, I got my first glimpse of Northern Norway's famous Midnight Sun. What I had never appreciated when I heard about the Midnight Sun was that it was exactly that: the sun shining bright in the sky at midnight, and all through the night. Shining bright meant close to broad daylight all night long. Shining bright meant wearing sunglasses while I looked directly into the sun at 12:30 AM. Shining bright meant glare as the midnight sun reflected off the water. As I watched the sun for a couple of hours, off and on during my conversation, it dipped a little and then started its ascent higher into the sky. But it never disappeared from view; it never dipped below the horizon; its shine always bounced off the water. My favorite part was seeing its reflection off the water: broken up when the water was choppy, undulating when the water was wavy, and almost glass-like when the water was still.

All good things must come to an end, even a nightless night. I found one of the benches on deck, spread my sleeping bag out on it, and crawled in. That was the easy part; getting to sleep was another story. First of all, it was daytime at 3:00 AM. Second of all, the boat plunged to and fro in the water. Finally, there was a convention taking place on the deck: boat-hands cleaning the floors, tourists taking pictures of the Midnight Sun, people out for a stroll. There was another problem: excitement. I was almost in Tromsø.

-3-
Home At Last

There I was, standing on the deck, hanging over the railing, looking at my new home, wondering what I was doing there, wondering if perhaps I shouldn't have just stayed on the *hurtigruten* and headed back to America. I had just spent the previous seven weeks four days and twenty-three hours getting to Tromsø and Tromsø was where I would stay. I was scared as hell and as anxious and nervous as I had ever been in my life; I didn't deny it. But I was there, a lot of people had confidence in me that I could be the ambassador I was sent there to be, and I was about to get off the *hurtigruten* and meet my new family and begin my new life as the person Tromsø would enable me to become. I was at the end of a two-month journey that had taken me to the threshold of a twelve-month adventure that would change me forever.

Getting off the boat was easier said than done. I had my ninety pounds of luggage to carry. I managed to find the gangplank and stumbled hesitantly down it onto the Tromsø soil that would become so familiar to me over the next year.

My new father and brother were at the dock to meet me and they waved at me. They both wore slacks, white shirts, socks, and sandals; they appeared pleasant and friendly enough, but they didn't look "Norwegian." During the previous few weeks I had decided that slender, tall and blond were the Norwegian national characteristics. Román and his son were both short.

"You must be Pete," Mr. Román greeted me in English. "I'm Karl Román and this is my son, Karl Arvid."

"Hello," Karl Arvid said quietly, but with a slight smile. He, too, spoke English, with a Norwegian accent even slighter than that of his father. Almost everyone I had met who spoke English, spoke it well and with only a slight accent.

Mr. Román looked younger than my father; I thought it was his fair, smooth skin that gave him that appearance, because his eldest daughter was older than me. He was short, slender, and had a full-head of slightly graying hair. Karl Arvid resembled his father. Like his father he was short and slender, although his full head of hair was light-brown and was parted on the right side. When he smiled, I thought I noticed something clever and a little rebellious behind the smile. Since that was the way I thought about myself, I was pleased to see similar characteristics in my new brother.

I hoped Karl Arvid and I would get along. I had thought about him a lot, especially during the trip from Oslo to Tromsø. I had an American brother, but I didn't have a brother exactly my own age and having one in Norway was one of the many things to which I looked forward.

"You must have had a long journey," Mr. Román continued. I carried my two suitcases as we walked toward the parked cars.

"Yes," I answered. "I've been traveling for more than two days. I left Oslo Thursday morning."

"How did you come?" Karl Arvid asked. That was a strange question; I assumed there was only one way.

"I took a train from Oslo to Trondheim, a train from Trondheim to Fauske, a bus from Fauske to Bodø, and the *hurtigruten* from Bodø to Tromsø."

"Well," said Mr. Román as he put one of my suitcases in the trunk of a small, blue Volvo, "let's get you to the house."

That wasn't exactly the conversation I had fantasized when I imagined my first words with my new family. It was mundane. But we were still on the dock and my new mother wasn't there. Perhaps their English wasn't as fluent as it sounded. I hoped it was that; I wanted this new Norwegian family to care about me.

The house on Karl Pettersensgate was only a short drive from the dock. We crossed what I assumed was the main street of town. I glanced quickly at the stores in either direction and on both sides of the street, but we didn't slow down and neither Mr. Román nor Karl Arvid said anything as we drove. All I could tell as we drove up a steep hill was that Tromsø was bigger than any of the other coastal towns I had seen, including Bodø. We parked the car next to a fairly plain, reddish house. It was made of painted wooden clapboards, like all the other houses I had seen in Tromsø and throughout Norway. There were fewer windows than I was used to on American houses, none on the northern exposure, and no shutters at all. All the windows were casement windows, not the double hung I was used to in New England. It was smaller and even plainer than my Westport house, and it had no yard. I had figured that Tromsø, being in the middle of nowhere, would be rural; almost none of the houses had yards. There was also no garage; we parked the car in a space next to the house.

The front door was like our "front" door in Westport: a back door into the kitchen. Along with the kitchen, the first floor included a living room and a dining area. There was a small eating table in the kitchen, but it wasn't big enough for the entire family. Although there were fewer windows than in a comparable American house, there were windows in the dining area that looked out toward the water separating Tromsøy from the mainland. There was a mountain on the mainland facing the island and we could see it clearly. What a spectacular sight; that we did not have in Westport.

My youngest sister and Mrs. Román were the only other family members home to greet me; I felt disappointed that my other two sisters weren't there. My other two sisters weren't even at home. In all, there were four Román children. Karin was the oldest; she was already at the University in Bergen and the University was on summer vacation. Karl Arvid was the only boy. Maria was ten and Bergljot was seven. Bergljot was cute as she hid behind her mother's apron. She was small, with straight blond hair down to her shoulders. She was eight or nine years old and small for her age. She wore a blue dress with white socks and no shoes. Mrs. Román, like her husband and son, was short; she was a little on the plumpish side. She shared Karl Arvid's impish blue eyes and her face was more wrinkled than her husband's. Her apron covered a plain, grey dress.

"Welcome here," Mrs. Román broke into a broad smile as she spoke. "We make ourselves happy to have you with us."

"Takk," I answered with one of my few, experienced Norwegian responses. I could ride the *trikk* and say thank you.

Bergljot giggled at my Norwegian. It felt good to get some of attention.

"Take Pete upstairs to his room," Mr. Roman suggested to Karl Arvid.

"Sure," Karl Arvid said. Karl Arvid appeared to be a man of few words.

As Karl Arvid and I made it to the second floor, Karl Arvid pointed to the small bedroom at the top of the stairs. "This is your room. It is right next to my room."

I was disappointed. From the point of view of the Románs, it was probably special for me to get my own room. But that was not what I wanted. I had my own room in Westport and valued that almost more than anything, but Tromsø was supposed to be different from Westport. I didn't want a younger brother; I wanted a brother the same age. I didn't want my own room; I had looked forward to sharing a room with my new bother, with Karl Arvid. Talking late at night, laughing together like real brothers, getting help with my Norwegian...that was what I had longed for.

I didn't say anything. In part, I kept my disappointment to myself because I had been there only twenty minutes and I hardly knew the Románs. In part, I kept it to myself because I was certain they felt they were treating me in a special way. But I felt crushed as Karl Avid and I went back downstairs.

"Well," Mr. Román suggested, "why don't we take Pete on a drive around the island?"

"Sure," Karl Arvid said.

The drive gave me my first real glimpse of Tromsø and Tromsøy. Except for the main street in downtown Tromsø, none of the roads were paved. As we drove around the island, everywhere there was the overwhelming smell of herring—which I saw drying on huge racks. And with the sun still high in the sky, its reflection off the water was dazzling. But it was the island mountains in the background that made the view. They were mostly snow-covered, and they extended in every direction.

"This road runs around all of Tromsøy," Mr. Román explained. "There are still a few farms, as you can see, but only a few."

"Where does the ferry go?" I asked. A bridge connected Tromsøy to the mainland on the other side of the island; on the western side of the island, there was a ferry.

"The ferry goes to Kvaløya, Whale Island," Mr. Román answered. "There still are very few people on this side of the island."

There were few houses and virtually no stores. There were a few small factories or warehouses and a large number of fishing boats, but the western side of Tromsøy looked almost as desolate as most of the islands I saw from the *hurtigruten*. Once we turned around the northern tip of the island, I noticed more and more houses and more and more buildings as we approached the center of town. I estimated that Tromsøy was 4 or 5 miles wide and 10-12 miles long.

We drove through the center of town again, one long main street with only a few side streets. There were shops on both sides of the street, but more on the side farthest away from the water. There were sidewalks, but the one on the upper side was clearly a little wider. There were one or two concrete or stone buildings, but almost all the buildings were made of wood and were brightly painted.

"Are most of the stores old?" I asked. They looked old to me.

"Most of them are," Mr. Román answered. "The Germans bombed a lot of the towns in Northern Norway during and at the end of the war, but Tromsø wasn't bombed. This is one of the few Norwegian towns that still has most of its old buildings."

Although by Norwegian standards, Tromsø was a big town, there were almost no cars on the main street. Instead, lots of were people walking up and down the sidewalk, even though almost all of the stores were closed. And everyone walked on one sidewalk: the one on the upper side of the street.

"Why are so many people walking when all the stores appear to be closed?" I asked.

"That's what people do in Tromsø," Mr. Román answered. "Go to town and walk along Storgate, our Main Street."

"But why does everyone walk on just this side?" I pointed to what I thought of as the upper side.

"That's where we walk," he answered again. "Only the boonies walk on the other side."

We were talking in English. I didn't know whether this was a Norwegian word that he couldn't translate or an attempt to say something in English.

"Boonies?"

"Farmers," Mr. Román answered. "People not from Tromsø; people who have grown up in the country on farms who come to study or live in Tromsø. You will walk on this side, too," Mr. Román said, pointing to the upper side.

For me, Tromsø itself was the country. I was not prepared to think of Tromsø as a "town" surrounded by rural areas with country bumpkins who didn't know which side of the street to walk on. But I didn't think it was a question of confusion: people not knowing which side of the street to walk on. I sensed a little snobbery, the first hint of it since coming to Norway. I was particularly sensitive to snobbery; there was more than enough of it in Westport.

After we traversed Storgate, we drove over the bridge to the mainland and north to a whale "factory."

"As far as I know," Mr. Román explained as we got closer, "this is the only whale factory not on a boat."

I got a whiff of the worst smell I had ever experienced in my life, worse than rotten eggs, worse than diesel fumes, worse than the Saugatauk marshes at low tide. Although I could barely see the building Mr. Román pointed to in the distance, the stench was already pervasive.

"Now you know you have really been to Tromsø," Mr. Román smiled.

As it turned out, the smell—as pungent and awful as it was—was not the most difficult part: seeing the whale disturbed me even more. The "factory" was a large concrete parking lot with a huge whale on it. Boats had dragged the captured whale to the factory. It was my first whale; it was the biggest animal I had ever seen...by far. The thing was the size of a basketball court! Men were crawling all over that huge, dead carcass slicing the blubber off the dead whale. There was blood everywhere.

I Was a Teenage Norwegian

"Have you ever had whale steak?" Mr. Román asked.

Where do you think I live? I wondered silently to myself. I've never even seen one of these animals before. I can hardly hold back the vomit and you ask me if I've eaten whale before. This is my first day here; give me a break.

"*Nei*," I answered aloud, more politely than I thought to myself, having added the Norwegian word for no to my emerging vocabulary.

"We'll have to serve it to you. It tastes just like beef steak, only moister and more flavorful."

With the sights and smells of whale guts still vivid, it was fine with me if he didn't deliver immediately on that promise.

"I think they are expecting us at home for *aftens*," Mr. Román said.

We got back to the house at about 8:00 o'clock and Mrs. Román had the *smørbrød* waiting for us.

"*Værsågod*," she invited us to the table.

"I'll be right down," I said heading up the stairs. "There's something I want to get."

As I sat down to *aftens* I realized how accustomed I was already becoming to the Norwegian eating patterns. By eight or nine o'clock at night I was expecting my fourth meal of the day, especially in Tromsø where it was still so light. And I expected—no, almost looked forward to—the *smørbrød*. I never would have thought six weeks before that I could eat *smørbrød* three times a day and like them.

"I brought something for you from America," I said to the Románs as we finished *aftens*. "It's a puzzle, a plastic puzzle called 'Hexed.' I hope you enjoy it."

It turned out that the Románs were great puzzle players but they had never seen a puzzle game; they were only used to regular puzzles. I could see countless hours of frustrated enjoyment.

We finally all headed up to bed at around two o'clock in the morning and it was still bright daylight outside; sleeping in daylight was going to take some getting used to. For the moment, however, my thoughts were mostly on my reactions to Tromsø and the Románs. The land was beautiful, even the view from my window. My new parents were in many ways like mine at home in America. Mr. Román was eager to tell me of his work at his life insurance company and he labored constantly on the puzzle, as I knew Dad would have. *Fru* Román was a good cook, very sweet, had a pleasant disposition, and appeared to be a good housewife and mother. My littlest sister was a little afraid of me at first sight, but she was only seven and would get over that. Maybe my brother would talk more as we became friends.

Thinking about the Románs got me thinking about the day I heard about coming to Norway and how that day typified my feelings for my family.

"There's a surprise awaiting your eyes," my twelve-year-old sister smiled as I came home. But of course the little dear wouldn't think of showing the surprise to me until Mom came home. I had a one and one-half hour wait to rack my feeble brain and do some amazingly inaccurate guesswork. With still six weeks of school left, it couldn't be grades. I had no plans yet for the summer, so it couldn't be that. There were a couple of things I was counting on my parents not finding out, but I felt safe there. What I forgot, however, was that it was May 17th the day in 1814 that the constitution of Norway was signed; every-now-and-then even such overwhelmingly important facts such as that slipped my mind.

When my mother finally arrived, I clawed open the following letter from AFS.

May 15, 1961

Mr. Peter H. Dublin
12 Red Coat Rd.
Westport, Conn.

Dear Mr. Dublin,

We are delighted to accept you as a participant in the American Field Service School Program for 1961. You have been selected to live with a family and attend school for one year in Tromsø, Norway.

Please confirm your acceptance to us by return mail.

Your experience will be a most challenging one. In addition to fitting into a family and into a new way of life, you will also attend a school quite different from what you have known. The demands made upon you will be great, but we have faith in your eagerness, willingness and ability, and we know you can contribute much and gain a great deal.

Above all, you must learn the language of your host country, and we urge you to begin your study today. Unless you are fully able to handle the language, your experience cannot be the successful one you hope for.

Our primary concern, as it is with all AFS students, is that your stay abroad be a rewarding and happy one. So we urge you to ask our help, and later, that of the AFS committee caring for you abroad, with any questions or problems you may have.

You will hear from us soon again with information and material, but once again, we are happy to welcome you into the AFS family.

Sincerely,

Stephen Galatti
Director General

"Norway?" I asked my Mom.

"Norway," she smiled.

"Where's Norway?" Peg asked both of us.

"Norway?" I asked no one in particular. "Okay, Okay. Let me think. Maybe it's all right because people say that Norway is quite pleasant and spectacular with its mountains and fjords."

I Was a Teenage Norwegian

"Where's Norway?" Peg was only twelve but she was stubborn. She didn't like getting nothing for an answer.

"And blonds," I continued, sort of muttering to myself, thinking out loud. "There are vikings, and skiing. I haven't studied about Norway since 4th grade. How can I be expected to know anything about Norway?"

"Oh," my mother interrupted my sputtering. "I also got a 'letter' from the town where you'll be staying." My mother had many sides. She had her bitchy side; she had her depressed side. She had her supportive side; she had her playful side. She walked onto the kitchen porch, reached into the chest freezer, and pulled out a block of ice surrounding a note reading "Greetings from Tromsø." Those were the days when the mail still arrived in the morning and she had all day to prepare my special surprise in her own special way. She thought her "note" was really amusing. Peg thought her "note" was really amusing. I started to shiver.

"So, Pete, what do you think? How do you feel," Mom asked.

"I don't know. I had forgotten, you know. It's been so long since anyone's heard from AFS. I just figured no one else was going anywhere."

"I know, but you're going somewhere now...and soon."

"Where is Norway?" Peg asked again.

"But why Norway?" I pleaded.

"I'm sure AFS knows what it's doing," Mom continued. "They've been doing this for years. They want to match you with the right family, regardless of the country."

"Yeah, yeah. I know what they say. I'm just surprised, that's all. I wasn't expecting AFS at all and I sure wasn't expecting Norway."

"So, is there a convention or something in the kitchen?" my father asked as he entered the kitchen. Dad worked at Metropolitan Life in New York City and five days a week he left the house at 7:15 AM and returned home at 6:45 PM, weather and train permitting.

"Guess what? Guess what?" Peg blurted out. I could have killed her.

"Shut up." I cut her off. "I'll tell him, OK? I got this letter. Show him the letter in the freezer, Mom." I could see she was proud of her joke as she showed the frost edged letter to my father.

"What's this all about?" Dad asked.

"I just got a letter from AFS," I answered proudly. "Guess what? I'm going to Norway for a year, That's Mom's way of breaking the ice."

"That's great," Dad said as he gave me one of his patented congratulatory hugs. He was tough on me at times, but I always felt he supported me. "That's wonderful. I'm so happy for you."

All through dinner we could talk of nothing else. Mom and Dad were clearly proud, and a little anxious about my leaving home. Peg was excited, but it began to dawn on her what it all meant and she clearly didn't want me to go. She and I were close and I knew that it would be difficult for her having me gone at all, let alone for so long.

"Are you coming home for Christmas?" Peg asked.

"Of course he's not," my brother Tom chided her. "Norway's too far away. Don't you know where Norway is?"

I had a close relationship with my parents, specifically, and my family generally. It wasn't that I didn't struggle and argue with my parents throughout my teenage years; I did. We did a lot together and I felt loved and supported. My father, in particular, spent hours talking to me and giving me advice, even though I always argued with him and never seemed to listen. He understood it took me a while (sometimes years) to comprehend his wisdom.

Back in my new bedroom, I realized I was getting used to some of my new life. For example, I was already getting used to eating three or four *smørbrød* for breakfast; I wasn't sure I would want to eat that kind of breakfast when I got home but I was getting used to it. I could even begin to appreciate how tied to their own ways of doing things people got. I was sure, for example, that Karl Arvid would have had problems eating eggs, cereal, or pancakes for breakfast; he would have felt that such food was as strange as I initially felt eating *smørbrød* three times a day was. I could just hear him saying, "What a strange country; people only eat sandwiches once a day. And what strange sandwiches: two slices of bread. You can't taste anything but the bread. And most every sandwich has two or three toppings on it. I wonder if I'll ever get used to this way of eating?"

Dad had always told me that everything worthwhile in life required hard work. Øystein made it clear that this year would require hard work on my part. I had worked hard to stifle my moody parts. I worked hard to ask questions, to be upbeat with my new family, but I was still unsure as to the outcome. What did I have to do and who did I have to become to succeed?

Before leaving for Norway, I had decided to write what I thought of as a "Dear Friend" form letter to my friends and extended family. I used the end of my first full day in Tromsø to compose my first "Dear Friend" letter and to sort out my thoughts and feelings about reaching my new home at last.

July, 1961

Dear Friend,

I am here at last and I am very happy and contented with my new Norwegian home. A great deal has happened in the past few weeks and I hope I can relate it to you in an interesting manner. The land is so beautiful that I am afraid I cannot do it justice with my words...but nevertheless, I will try.

Tromsø is a small town of about twelve or thirteen thousand people, situated on a small island off the coast of Norway, at about 70° North Latitude. Fishing is one of its major industries, and the luscious fragrance of herring drying pierces the air more than once or twice a day. Connecting

I Was a Teenage Norwegian

Tromsø to the mainland is Europe's largest all-concrete bridge, covering a distance of one kilometer. Situated in Tromsø is the world's only land whale factory (where they kill, not produce the whales) and the world's only teakwood quay (made from the wood of a German ship sunk off the island during World War II). It also has a post office, a movie theater, three banks, a football stadium (not exactly made to cater to the needs of the major leagues), and a ski lift. So, Tromsø is equipped with all the necessities of modern life.

During my first day here, it did not get dark at all. From what my family tells me, one gets to bed sometime between twelve and three in the morning; consequently, one sleeps through the entire morning. In the summer, we have meals at noon, 3:00, 8:00, and 10:00; in winter, we will have meals at about 7:00 AM, noon, 3:00, 8:00, and 10:00. They do not change the times of the meals, they just add another.

From what my brother has told me, there is very little to do in Tromsø. Every evening, most of the town's teenage population makes a trip to town and walks back and forth, up and down the main street. One does not make a date with a girl, but if she wants to see him...why, she will be there, too. Five or six times a month, one goes to the kino, *or movie theater. It is not as expensive as it sounds, for the admission fee is only KR2 (or a little over a quarter)*

I am still healthy and as happy as can be with everything that has happened, with everything that is happening, and with all that will surely happen in the future. And already I am beginning to learn more about others and more about myself. My only hopes are that you are as well and happy as I and that I have been able to express myself in an enjoyable and informative manner. Until my next letter, I remain

THINKING OF ALL OF YOU,
Pete Dublin

-4-
A Rough Start

I had been away from home for six weeks, I had been in Norway for four weeks, I had been in Tromsø for one week. I was worried before I left home; I was worried in Oslo; I was even more worried in Tromsø. Mr. Román gave me the impression that he didn't feel I appreciated all that he did for me and this was not good. Karl Arvid and I would walk together to town in silence; we couldn't talk at night because we had separate bedrooms. I hadn't even met two of my sisters. Tromsø was where I was and the Románs were who I was with. I had to make it work; they were my new family.

"Karl Arvid," I asked at breakfast, "what will we do today?"

"I don't know," he answered. It was his most common answer. It was still summer vacation for us, Karl Arvid and I normally slept until noon.

"Let's walk to town, *til byen*," I suggested. Walking to town was our usual afternoon activity.

"Sure. Maybe we need to buy some milk anyway. But we have to be back by 2:00 o'clock."

"Why so soon?"

"Your uncle's funeral."

My uncle's funeral? That's it? That was the first I had heard that I had a Norwegian uncle, let alone that he was dead. Wasn't it a big deal to die? How could Karl Arvid be so matter-of-fact about his uncle's death? I was having trouble figuring out the people in my Norwegian family. Part of my difficulty was that I couldn't tell whether individual people reflected themselves as individuals or Norwegians in general. It was particularly difficult with Karl Arvid, who was so quiet. Was a funeral a more commonplace experience in Norway, did Norwegians take their funerals casually, or was this just the way Karl Arvid was? I assumed I would eventually be able to make such distinctions; all I could do at that time was walk *til byen* with Karl Arvid.

Karl Arvid had a job at one of the local newspaper from the time school ended until the day I had arrived. We first stopped at the newspaper office so that he could get his last paycheck. I went to the bank and cashed my first allowance check from AFS in Oslo: KR100. $14.

We both felt flush with money as we walked along Storgate. On the proper side, of course.

"*Hei*, Karl Arvid," one of his friends greeted us.

"Geir," Karl Arvid answered.

"I just saw Knut and Lars at the Samfunn Kafé. Why don't we join them."

"Sure."

The three of us joined Knut and Lars at the *kafé*. Kids didn't seem to plan anything or even call friends on the phone. They just walked up and down Storgate and saw whoever they met; then they got together with whoever was there.

"Have you been out to your *hytta* yet," Knut asked Geir.

"Not yet. I think we're going at the end of July. Have you asked your father," Geir asked Karl Arvid, "whether or not you can come?"

"No. But I think your father has talked to him."

"I think we're going to our *hytta* sometime in August," Knut said.

The conversation went on like that for half an hour. The entire conversation was in English, for my benefit. I understood why they did it; I understood that it represented a certain degree of consideration for me. They spoke much better English than I spoke Norwegian. But I hadn't come to Norway to help them practice their English; I had come to learn Norwegian.

Yet, none of Karl Arvid's friends asked me anything and I didn't say anything at all during the entire conversation at the *kafé*. It was not easy for me to take the initiative and these kids didn't make it any easier. I had assumed that I would be instantly popular with my new brother's friends, that being friends with me would be a treat and an honor for them. I saw AFS as my big escape from my own unpopularity at Staples; I wanted to be popular so badly I assumed it would happen instantly. That conversation brought my damn doubts creeping back. Could I do it? Could I make friends in Tromsø?

Karl Arvid and I walked home; we had to dress for the funeral. I thought back to a trip my mother and I made to the Factory Store in Norwalk just before I left for Norway.

"What can I do for you?" the salesman asked.

"We need a sports jacket and a pair of slacks and a suit," Mom announced proudly.

"Any particular color," he asked as we moved down the aisle toward the suits. Blue, brown, gray; I didn't know what to think. Anything would probably be fine, as long as it wasn't black. I may have been serious, but I was not *that* serious.

"I think charcoal gray is the most practical," Mom answered immediately. How did she know so quickly? Had she been thinking about the suit all week? I hadn't given it a moment's thought until we began walking through the aisle here.

Throughout my teenage years, clothes were an issue of some tension between my mother and myself; interestingly enough, my father stayed out of that issue completely. Like most other boys my age, I had some definite ideas about clothes: I wanted to wear whatever everyone else was wearing. I was a non-conformist who wanted to be popular; in terms of clothes, the latter desire outweighed the former trait. My mother, however, had her own ideas of what was proper for a boy my age to wear: whatever boys my age had worn in Germany when she was my age. I wanted chinos; she bought me grey flannel slacks. I wanted sneakers; she bought me shoes. I knew the suit would involve a test of wills, a test I assumed I would probably lose.

"I have to measure to be sure, but I would guess a size forty," the salesman stopped in front of the small white circle (with the 40s spread out to its right) which hugged the bar and divided the different sized suits from each other.

"That's black," I mentioned without the least bit of enthusiasm.

"Charcoal gray," Mom corrected.

"This is for a funeral."

"You never know," she defended her choice. "It's the most practical color; you can wear it for any occasion."

Any occasion as long as it's a funeral, I thought to myself sullenly. That may have been how you did things in Germany when you were growing up, but it is 1961 in America. A black suit? She could call it whatever she wanted; it was still a black suit.

"Let me take a quick measurement," the salesman interrupted my thoughts. They weren't getting me anywhere anyway. "Your chest's about forty; just what I thought. Waist is thirty-six; that figures. Why don't you take this one into the dressing room and come back out when you've got it on. Don't forget to put your shoes back on so we can measure for the length of the trousers."

He handed me the suit and I promptly dropped the pants. It was going to be difficult enough to win the battle over color; being nervous didn't do much to improve my chances.

I found the dressing room, closed the door, and started putting on the suit. I couldn't believe I was getting into a black suit. What kid wore a black suit? I didn't know what kids in Norway wore, but I was sure none of them would get caught dead wearing a black suit. Charcoal gray my ass.

"Why don't you come over here and stand in front of the mirror," the salesman motioned. He started tugging at the arms, smoothening out the front of the jacket. He seemed pleased with his selection, as did my mother. Hell, they didn't have to wear it.

"The jacket looks fine. We may want to take a little off the sleeves, but that's all. You're a forty all right. Why don't you take off the jacket and let's look at the trousers."

"Trousers?" Why couldn't people call pants pants? People called pants "trousers" and they charged twice as much money for them.

"How do they feel," Mom inquired as I took off the jacket.

"The trousers feel a little loose," I told her. I said the word in as snotty a fashion as I could muster on short notice, but neither Mom nor the salesman seemed to notice. "I think they might be ready to fall off, in fact."

"They do seem big," he said, his head tilted (like an artist inspecting a model) and his face screwed up, registering his surprise. "I measured your waist at thirty-six inches and these trousers are for a thirty-six inch waist."

"I know," I said knowingly; I had been through this conversation many times before. "I always wear pants that are two inches less than my waist measurement."

"That doesn't make any sense. Why don't you turn around."

I wasn't quite sure what effect turning around would have on my waist size or its relationship to the size of my pants but I accommodated to his whim and slowly did a 360° turn.

The salesman looked even more surprised and he screwed up his face even more than before. "You don't have any ass," he said incredulously. "No wonder the trousers are so loose."

"What do you mean," my mother interrupted indignantly. "What do you mean, no ass? My son has a fine ass. Look at that," she pointed pointedly.

My words had come back to haunt me. How had I known that the first time I would wear my new suit would be to a funeral?

We walked together to the cemetery farther up toward the top of the island, Mr. Román, Karl Arvid, and I in our charcoal grey suits. The cemetery was about a 10-minute walk from the Román's house. My Tromsø funeral was my first funeral. The only death in my American experience was my grandmother, just the year before I came to Norway. There was a memorial service but no funeral. I had no point of reference.

When everyone was assembled, we sang a few hymns together. There were between twenty five and thirty people all together, a mixture of adults and children. There were hymn-books, so I could read some of the words and sing along with the others. I didn't recognize any of the hymns; I doubted the Lutherans and Unitarians shared much music. Our voices were the only sound. The priest said a few prayers; I could only understand the "amen" at the end of each one. The kids were rest-

less, but not overly so, and the parents were tolerant of their movements. The priest was somber, but the mood of the gathering was more respectful than sad. I couldn't understand the words, but I felt I could understand the sentiment. In spite of the language difficulty, I found that I was genuinely moved. I wasn't religious, but there was a spiritual part to me and the ceremony, the gathering, touched that part.

Although death had played almost no part in my life until that moment, I had often thought about it in the abstract. Although I had often wondered about the feeling of death by the dead, I had decided that it wasn't important how death feels to the person who has died; the the person was dead, right? What mattered were the thoughts that went through the minds of those who still lived. I had thought a great deal about death in the past, but it nevertheless surprised me to see what thoughts went through my mind when I was confronted face-to-face with death, even in an indirect manner. I was certain the ceremony itself, and the willingness of the Románs to include me in it, stirred many of those thoughts and feelings.

After the ceremony the six of us walked back home, and that was that. No reception, no food, no nothing else. Once again, confusion reigned. Was that a Román thing or a Norwegian thing? In spite of the seriousness of the occasion, there was a casual informality at the cemetery. Was that a Román thing or a Norwegian thing? I needed to make some friends quickly, or I might never find out.

* * * * * * * * * * * * * *

I Was a Teenage Norwegian

My days with the Románs were uneventful. Karl Arvid and I usually woke up at noon. We usually walked *til byen* in the afternoon. We ate supper and sat around the house in the evening playing canasta or putting puzzles together, before going to bed at 1:30 or 2:00 AM. Having nothing to do so much of the time was one of the problems I had with that family. The other was that I couldn't do anything about it. I asked them questions and started conversations, but I felt uncomfortable and I stopped. I would sit in the living room, often in silence, completely unable to move or take any initiative. I planned everything out in my mind to say to them, and then I couldn't do it.

One day after I had been there two or three weeks, we finally had something to do. At 5:30 in the afternoon, Karl Arvid and I walked down to the pier to meet his (our) 13-year-old sister, Elin, who was coming on the *hurtigruten*; she had been in Oslo attending a Girl Scout camp, although no one had explained the situation to me until that morning. She wasn't on the boat. Ordinarily, this would have been great cause for concern, but in the summertime there were two *hurtigruter* a day and Elin was on the one that arrived at 11:30 at "night."

"Elin is only going into the seventh year of elementary school," Karl told me while we were waiting. "She is so small that my parents kept her out of school an extra year in the beginning."

Elin and I did not get along right away. She hardly said hello to me at the pier and she didn't say a word to me as we walked home together. She chatted away with Karl Arvid, so I knew she could talk, but it was all in Norwegian and not a word to me. Elin glanced at me once or twice, so I knew she could see me, but all I got was a shrug and a cold eye. Was it her room I had taken over? I was certain it was Karin's—the pictures on the wall made that clear—and she was at the University. By the time I went to bed at 1:30 she still hadn't talked to me or asked me a question or anything.

Throughout my first few weeks in Tromsø, about the only people I saw were my Norwegian family, Karl Arvid's friends, and the other American AFSers. Although I was the only AFSer in Tromsø for the entire year, there were six other AFSers in Tromsø for the summer. Lorni Grenfell was the one I knew best. I had seen her on the boat to Rotterdam and the train to Oslo and I had seen her a couple of times since coming to Tromsø. She was the only person I could talk to about the Románs. I would see her occasionally on one of my evening trips *til byen*.

"I wonder sometimes," I said to Lorni as we seated ourselves at a table in one of the *kafés*," if the Románs even wanted an exchange student. I wouldn't say they have greeted me with open arms, let alone open hearts."

"But my Norwegian sister says they already had an AFSer. They must have known what it was like."

"She must have been Karin's AFS sister," I said. "Karin's the only one in the family I haven't met yet. Maybe she's different. Maybe she's an older version of Bergljot."

"How old's Bergljot?" Lorni asked.

"Eight, I think. And she's great. We play all the time; she's the only one who talks to me in Norwegian; I feel she genuinely cares that I'm there."

"So that's good. That's a start, at least. You know, Pete, you're going to be with them for an entire year. Start with Bergljot and work your way up through the rest of the family."

I remembered a conversation I had had on board the SEVEN SEAS with Jack Simons, a kid from somewhere in the South whose cabin was just across the corridor from mine and Chuck-going-to-Switzerland's.

"The reason I'm stubborn," Jack argued, "is that I'm usually right."

"For me," I proceeded along a somewhat different line, "being argumentative and stubborn is just my way to figure things out. I take a position and then argue it forever. I expect other people to argue back, and the more stubborn I am, the better their arguments have to be. I'm that way with my father all the time."

"So what happens?" Jack inquired. He listened in a way that said to me he was genuinely curious about my experiences. "What's the end result?"

"For me, I take all the arguments and I reflect on them. Very often, I will eventually change my mind. For the person I'm talking to, I would guess the end result is mostly frustration. Even if I eventually see the logic of that position, the other person may never know I've come around. I know for a fact my father can't stand my stubbornness."

"I feel a little less dogmatic on this boat," Jack offered, "than I usually do at home. When I listen to other people's ideas here, I seem to be more open to them."

"Maybe," I offered, "it's because we're all in the same boat."

I didn't know if my stubbornness was preventing me from hearing what Lorni was saying to me or if my stubbornness was insuring that I would stick it out with the Románs no matter what.

There was one area where I could honestly say my stubbornness was paying dividends: eating *geitost*. *Geitost* is a brown cheese made from goat's milk. It comes in large rectangles and you cut thin slices from the block with a strange cheese cutter. You were supposed to put two or three slices on a piece of buttered bread and feel you were in heaven when you ate it. *Geitost* was served at every sandwich meal, literally morning, noon, and night; only at dinner were we spared. That is, *I* was spared, because clearly every Norwegian loved the stuff .

Geitost has a unique taste. It is a hard, almost sweet, cheese that melts in the mouth, almost like caramel. It was like no other taste I had experienced, and I didn't like it at all.

I Was a Teenage Norwegian

That was the problem. *Geitost* was the Norwegian national cheese. I remembered what Liz said at Trollvasshytta.

"Pete, have some *geitost*."

"I don't really like it."

"Pete, have some *geitost*."

"But I don't like it. Can't I eat *jarlsbergost* instead?"

"Pete, you are going to live here for an entire year. You had better get used to *geitost*. You wouldn't want an exchange student coming to America who didn't eat hot dogs and hamburgers, would you?"

I thought of only one way to solve my problem: eating the stuff. For the first three weeks with the Románs, I ate *geitost* at every sandwich meal: literally, morning, noon, and night. I still couldn't stand the stuff—the almost sweetness, the caramel-like texture, the melt-in-my-mouth sensation—but I decided to keep eating it until I liked it! In fact, it took only three weeks of that daily regimen to break the *geitost* barrier. One day I suddenly loved the stuff. From that day on, I ate *geitost* two or three times a day for the rest of the year and I couldn't get enough of it. Thirty five years later, it is still my favorite cheese.

There was a message there. I didn't know what it was, but I got it anyway. I had successfully struggled with adversity and had conquered through a combination of determination, commitment, and will-power. I knew I couldn't succeed at everything. I still couldn't take the same initiative with the Románs as I had with the *geitost*; the cheese didn't talk back or give me a cold eye. But slowly, bit by bit, I utilized the same strategy to resolve many of the struggles I encountered that year.

Two days after Elin arrived, we all piled into the family Volvo and headed for the beach. The beach in Tromsø was on the southern tip of the island. To be accurate, the use of the word "beach" was generous. When I thought of a beach, I thought of sand and swimming. The Tromsø beach had neither; it consisted mainly of small rocks, big rocks, and grass. There was water; Tromsø was an island and, therefore, surrounded by water. Swimming, however, was another story. That water was cold; that water was freezing.

"How's the water?" I asked Elin, who raced in as soon as we arrived.

"Fine." Elin still didn't smile at me, but we were at least on speaking terms.

"Do you have any idea how cold it is?"

"Actually," answered Mr. Román, "the water is pretty warm so far this year; it's about 50°F."

"Come on in, Pete," Bergljot screamed up to me from the water in Norwegian.

I just waved back. In my experience, 70°F was about my bottom limit. Of course I didn't tell anyone that and they probably just thought I didn't like to do anything they did. I just sat in the sun and got a first-hand look at some of the pretty girls and their even prettier bikinis.

What was most striking, however, was to see how the Norwegians—men and women alike—changed clothes on the beach.

It was a neat trick, especially for the girls and women. They changed into their bathing suits underneath their street clothes. They slipped off their underpants and pulled up their bathing suits under their skirts—wriggling constantly—and then took off the skirts. Half done, they stood with their bathing suit bottoms and their shirts or sweaters on; this was Tromsø summer. Then they took off their bras—from underneath their shirt or sweater—and pulled up their bathing suits—still underneath their shirts or sweaters—and finally took them off, too. It was a neat trick but it also reflected a different set of standards than I was used to regarding bodies and the public display of bodies. Most of the very young children, for example, went completely naked and some of the women changed from the waist up in the open; obviously nobody had any qualms about doing so. Mr. Román didn't have a bathing suit; he went swimming in his underpants. I didn't feel embarrassed; I had a bathing suit but underpants would have been all right, too. I had led a pretty sheltered life; seeing bras and breasts had some appeal to me.

"*Hvor ofte kommer du til ...*" I began. "What's the word for 'beach'?"

"*Badestrand,*" Karl Arvid offered.

"How often do we come to the *badestrand*?" Mr. Román repeated in English. "In the summer we like to come when it is warm like today. Perhaps every weekend, yes."

"I wish we could speak," I said in English, "more Norwegian to each other. I think that would help me learn more quickly and be better prepared for school when it starts in August."

We began to speak a little more Norwegian at the *badestrand*, perhaps because we were all a little more relaxed. But neither I nor the Románs were pressing the issue of Norwegian a great deal. And when I asked them to speak more Norwegian to me, even if they responded, eventually they just started speaking English again. That was not going to help me prepare for the coming year; that was not going to help me become a real family member.

Sunday evening, I walked *til byen* by myself. I walked up and down Storgate, making sure I walked on the correct side; I wouldn't want to be considered a boonie. I passed by strangers, some of whom might very well become my friends during the year. I heard them all talking that strange language, a language which I hoped would be second nature to me before long.

"*Hei,* Lorni," I said smiling at the sight of someone I knew.

"Hi," she responded. "This is my sister, Ragna Kjellman."

"Hi, Pete," Ragna said. "Lorni has already told me a lot about you."

"Why don't we go have some coffee or a soda?" Ragna asked.

We headed off to a *kafé*. The routine was to walk *til byen*, walk up and down the one approved sidewalk, meet some friends, and go off to a *kafé* for something to eat or drink.

"*Hei*, Marit," Ragna called out. "*Får vi være med?*"

"*Jada*," Marit answered.

"I've asked Marit," Ragna explained, "if we can join her and Bjørg. They're both in your class at school. They speak very good English."

It took all my courage to ask the Románs if they would speak more Norwegian, and my asking didn't make a difference anyway. I didn't have the guts to ask Ragna and her friends to speak Norwegian to me. And if they did, I probably wouldn't have understood anything anyway.

"Hi, Pete," Marit began. "I think we shall be in the same class."

"Marit and I," Bjørg continued, "are in the fifth year English line. That's usually where they put the AFS students."

We talked for maybe a half an hour and the more we talked the more it was obvious to me how well Lorni and Ragna were matched.

"It's a little difficult for me," I said to Lorni, "to see how well you two get along because I don't feel Karl Arvid and I are well matched at all."

"You may be right," Lorni responded, "but it really isn't as important for you that you get along well with Karl Arvid. You have a whole year to meet new friends; you won't be with your brother all that often."

"When school starts," Marit suggested, "you'll make many new friends. Our class is small and everyone is friendly."

"Last year," Bjørg continued, "there was an AFSer at school who was not too friendly with her own sister, but she had many friends and she was very happy."

"I met Jo Ann just before she left for home," Lorni said. "She told me that she was unhappiest at the beginning, because she wasn't close to her sister. But she had a fantastic year, one she will never forget."

I understood what they were saying, but this was not what I had hoped for. Obviously, I could have fun even if I didn't get along that well with Karl Arvid, but it would make a big difference if I felt more like a member of the Román family. As Lorni and Ragna walked me home, I began to wonder how I might feel if Karl Arvid and I got closer, got to be more like Lorni and Ragna. Maybe I could work a little harder at that. Maybe there was something I could do to bring us closer together. I would love it if we could be more like brothers.

My slowly emerging optimism was in for a rude shock the next day. The day started just like all the other days: a late breakfast, a walk *til byen* in the afternoon, a snack with Karl Arvid. But then came the surprise.

"Pete," Mrs. Román announced at dinner, "I feel you are not too happy to live with us. Maybe it would be best to write to AFS and see about getting your family changed."

Mrs. Román's unexpected candor hit me like a bombshell and that created a cloud of tension everyone felt. The air was so thick I could have cut it with a knife if I hadn't been hanging on her every word.

-5-
Calm After the Storm

I felt like such a failure. I thought I had worked at becoming a part of my new Norwegian family, even if I hadn't felt especially welcome in it. I didn't feel they worked as hard at making things work as I did, but I felt the failure was mine. I was the AFS student and it was my job to fit into their family. What a way to start my year.

Two days of simmering gave me the distance I needed. There was clearly something amiss in my family relationship. Mr. Román told me he didn't feel I appreciated all that he did for me; I felt that I was appreciative, that I thanked him for what he did, that I did the best I could to enjoy the few things we did together, but he didn't *feel* that I did. Bergljot was the only sibling I got along well with, and she was only seven and didn't even speak any English. On the other hand, Karl Arvid and I were almost completely non-verbal; we were almost completely non-everything else, as well.

But, damnit, Tromsø was where I was and the Románs were the only family I had, and I had been there less than three weeks and I had no intention of giving up.

"Pete," I remembered Mrs. Ottinger's words to me a couple of days before I left Westport, "do you have any room left for a little advice?" For a family friend, she could be a little motherly at times.

"Oh," I answered, "there's a little space left in my suitcase. I figured someone would fill it up; might as well be you."

"A lot is going to happen to you, particularly at the beginning. And you're going to have a lot of feelings—positive and negative, both— right away. And you do tend to be a little judgmental at times. This I have noticed."

"So...."

"So," she forged ahead, oblivious to my sarcasm, "I want to advise you to take the 'two-month test.'"

"The two-month test?"

"No matter what problem you have early on in your year, give it two months. Don't make any judgments until you've given yourself and the problem two months. It may sound like waiting a long time, but I think any serious problem deserves the two-month test."

"Pete," Karl Arvid woke me out of my reverie, "are you ready? Dr. Jenssen is waiting."

"I'll be right down," I said, packing the rest of my clothes. Karl Arvid and I were off to Dr. Jenssen's *hytta* with his son, Karl Olav, and another friend, Geir. Maybe my family was ready to give me another shot, just as I had decided to accept Mrs. Ottinger's advice. No one had mentioned Mrs. Román's comments during the previous two days. And now Karl Arvid and I were about to do something together, and to spend time with some of his friends.

We drove over Tromsøbrua, along the sound that separated Tromsøy from the mainland and into the adjacent *fjord*. It was the first time I had driven that far into the mainland, away from the coast. I had already become quite familiar with the coast and its mountains that dropped right to the water, with barely enough land for a string of small farms. In many ways, what was most astonishing about driving farther inland was how much the landscape resembled that of the coast. We had driven inland for forty-five minutes and we were still just wandering along the edge of a *fjord*.

"Is this considered a big *fjord*?" I asked.

"No," Dr. Jenssen answered looking most amused. "Lyngenfjord is not even particularly big by Northern Norwegian standards, but it's nothing compared to some of the longer *fjords* in western Norway. You can drive for hours and hours before you get to the end of some of them."

Forty-five minutes was long enough for me, thanks. Even after the water disappeared from view, the mountains never ceased. The biggest ones we could see off in the distance, bordering on Sweden. But we always drove up and down some more modest height, or rode along the top of another. One thing was immediately obvious: there were a lot fewer people inland than there were along the coast, and fewer towns as well. There may have been fewer people and fewer towns, but there were just as many farms.

The farms were all small; some of them couldn't have been more than a few acres, especially those on the coast. I saw tractors everywhere, but not much else in the way of heavy equipment. Every farm had some animals: mostly a few cows, usually sheep, a few goats. And they all dried their hay in a completely unfamiliar way. The Norwegian farms were dotted with long wire fences, and the hay was hung over the fences to dry.

"Here we are," Dr. Jenssen announced as we arrived after our three-hour drive. "Our *hytta*."

There is a special relationship between Norwegians and their *hytta*. Almost everyone I knew had a *hytta*: Dr. Jenssen, Geir's father, the Románs. Dr. Jenssen was pretty well off by Norwegian standards, but none of the others were. The differences among so-called rich and poor people in Norway appeared to be quite a bit less than they were between rich and poor people in America. Many Norwegians could afford to own a *hytta* and most of them had one.

Americans had a special relationship with their car, and they liked their car fancy. Norwegians had a special relationship with their *hytta*, and they liked their *hytta* simple. Dr. Jenssen's *hytta* was quite isolated: off a quiet gravel road, on a small lake, surrounded by mountains, in the middle of the interior of Northern Norway, 200 miles above the Arctic Circle. The *hytta* had the same grass roof I had encountered at Trollvasshytta. The *hytta* was made of logs. The whole scene resembled a color illustration of a Scandinavian folk-tale.

"*Ingen strøm,*" Dr. Jenssen explained that there was no electricity. The lack of electricity was common. What was not common was that Dr. Jenssen spoke Norwegian to me.

I had assumed our *hytta* trip, our *hyttatur*, would last a few days, but after a week I began to understand that I was going to be there a while longer. No one had told me how long we were going to be gone for, and I found it difficult to ask. I don't really know why I didn't ask; sometimes I think I was being polite. I was with them, they knew what they were doing, and I just tagged along, taking what was given. The *hyttatur* was more than long enough for me to establish a new relationship with an old activity: fishing.

Living on the Connecticut coast almost all my life, and vacationing one summer at Lake George, New York I was familiar with fishing, and it was not one of my favorite pastimes. In part, this was undoubtedly due to my complete and total lack of success in the endeavor. I did it a few times with my father during a rain-filled week on Lake George in New York when I was twelve. But neither of us ever caught anything, and I couldn't say that I much enjoyed the experience.

Remembering Mrs. Ottinger's words of advice, I did the best I could to look forward to our fishing expedition, as fishing most definitely was a deeply embedded tradition of Norwegian *hytta* life.

"See that river?" Dr. Jenssen asked, as we pulled over to the side of the road for a minute. We were back in English for the time being. I sensed a complicated explanation, hence the shift in language.

"With all the people fishing?" I asked in return. The river must have been close to 100 feet wide and it flowed powerfully through a densely wooded area near the road. There were people standing on both shores,and others wading in the river, but I didn't see any people fishing from boats.

"Yes. In fact, you can only see some of the people fishing on this river; there are probably hundreds of others out of sight in both directions. This place is well-known for its fishing."

"Are we fishing there?" I ask.

"No. We don't have reservations."

Was it a river or a hotel? I often had thoughts I tended to express only to myself. Given my continued sarcasm, it was probably a good thing I kept them to myself.

"This is one of Norway's most famous, and expensive, rivers," Dr. Jenssen continued. "It's also one of Norway's few *private* rivers. In fact, people own parts of this river and rent their parts out to others who want to fish. You have to pay, and you have to have a reservation. We, on the other hand, are going to another river nearby. Not as many fish," as he started the car again and switched to Norwegian, "but we don't need a reservation."

It took only a few minutes to get to where we were going: an equally picturesque river down the road a few miles. This river was nowhere as wide as its more famous cousin but it flowed just as strongly. It was less straight and shallower, but it wandered through equally appealing woods and it felt more subdued and peaceful.

"Karl Olav," Dr. Jenssen turned to his son. "Can you get the boots out of the trunk?"

"Sure."

"We brought a pair for you, too, Pete," Dr. Jenssen continued in slow, easy-to-understand Norwegian. "Have you ever worn fishing boots before?"

"No."

"When you fish in a river," Dr. Jenssen switched to English, "you want to be able to fish in the river, not just from the shore. That's the reason for the boots."

I put on the elongated rubber boots which fit over my shoes and extended all the way up to my thighs, almost to my waist. I took the fishing rod Karl Olav handed me and tentatively made my way into the river. I felt the river rush around my legs. It was completely different feeling from fishing in a boat. I was in the river; I could feel its power. I could go anywhere in the river I wanted. I felt closer to the fish; we were both in the river.

Karl Olav had prepared the fishing rod with whatever bait or hook or fly the situation demanded. I was more than willing to let others do things for me. I cast out as far as I could, and slowly reeled the line in. Even with nothing hooked, the power of the river surprised me; reeling in on Lake George had never been this forceful.

"I think I have something," I shouted.

"Pull it in carefully," Geir advised. He was closest to me at that momentous moment.

"It's pulling like crazy," I continued with great excitement. I had never caught a fish, never really. The dogfish I caught once in Long Island Sound didn't really count. It was small and unbelievably ugly.

"Well," Geir remarked more skeptically, "the river is running pretty fast here. It's difficult to know."

"It feels big to me," I continued with the same degree of enthusiasm. I anxiously pulled and reeled in the line, a continuous movement in anticipation of a great result.

To my embarrassment what was dangling from my line was a 3-4" fish.

"The river is running fast here," Dr. Jenssen did his best to reduce my embarrassment. "It is difficult to know how big the fish is on the end of the line until you actually have it in your hand. Of course, more experience will help, too."

I didn't care; it was fun: the fast river, the whole scene. I discovered I enjoyed the fishing more than I cared about catching the fish. We stayed there for three hours, just standing in, and walking through, that beautiful, fast-flowing river. I loved wandering through the river, feeling the water move against my legs, while they remained dry. I understood the appeal; I could have stayed there for days.

And that was just river fishing. A few days later, Dr. Jenssen let me go out by myself in his canoe on the lake near his *hytta*. It was not dangerous. I appreciated the opportunity.

"Why don't you take one of the fishing rods," he suggested in Norwegian. I still wished Karl Arvid and the others were more sensitive to my need to hear and speak Norwegian, especially the easy, slow variety Dr. Jenssen used with me. "Maybe you'll have more luck than you did in the river."

Fishing on a fast-moving river was a special experience, the mixture of excitement and solitude. Fishing on a lake was completely different. The lake was peaceful and quiet, not even close to exciting. But it allowed for a kind of relaxation, that contrasted with the need for attention required by the river. I was still alone on the lake, but I felt more connected to my surroundings without the constant struggle of the river. I was on that crystal clear, mirror-smooth lake in a world of my own. The sun had just set: at 11:30 PM. I didn't know if it was the latitude or the time of night, but the colors were magnificent and the patterns of color spectacular. I was sitting alone, out in the middle of the lake, not a ripple on the water, surrounded by a sky full of gorgeous red colors bouncing off the few, scattered clouds. It was like the Fourth of July without the noise.

And for the first time in weeks I thought about my parents and how little time I would be with them for the rest of my life. I began to realize how much I was on my own, on my own for the rest of my life. No matter what help I got in Tromsø, no one could take care of things for me, no one could solve my problems.

I thought about how I had always needed to feel different as a teenager; I needed to feel like an outsider. I needed to be rejected by the popular kids, so that I could define myself in opposition to them. Even when the parking lot at Staples was full, nobody had trouble spotting our 1956 pink Plymouth station wagon. I loved that car. It was an automatic; it had no gear shift stick, not on the steering wheel column nor on the floor. Just to the left of the steering wheel there was a set of push-buttons for shifting gears. Most of all I loved the color. There was no mistaking our car for any other car. That car made me different. It wasn't a cool car, like the Hot Rodders had. It wasn't a fancy car, like the rich kids had. And it wasn't a non-descript car, like everyone else had. It was a different car, like me, and I loved being different.

The *hyttatur* was an important event for me because I realized I didn't want to be different; at least I wanted to be treated like everyone else. Dr. Jenssen had come the closest of anyone in Tromsø of treating me like everyone else. I felt a part of the *hyttatur* as I had not yet felt a part of the Román family. I was eating *geitost* like everyone else. I was fishing like everyone else. I was one of the guys.

By the time we got back to Tromsø, we had been away for three weeks! I had left Tromsø thinking I would be away for three days. Clearly, there was still a rather large communication problem. But Mrs. Ottinger's two months were not yet up, and I continued to work toward resolving as many family problems as I could. *Fru* Román hadn't mentioned my finding another family before I left for the *hyttatur,* and I was working hard to make sure she never would again. I asked her questions whenever I could, and I even offered to wash the dishes, something no other male in the household ever did.

I was feeling a little more comfortable about going *til byen* myself. I was slowly experimenting more with my Norwegian, and I could understand a lot of what people said to me, if they spoke slowly and distinctly. Karl Arvid helped me pick out a pocket dictionary, and I literally stuck it in my back pocket where it remained until my parents picked me up in Hoboken almost a year later. I was even getting used to Storgate and the rituals surrounding walking up and down the street. I never thought of walking on the other side of the street; maybe I was becoming a bit of a *Tromsøværing*—what people from Tromsø called themselves—myself.

"Pete," said Karl Arvid one evening shortly after we had come back from the *hytta*, "do you want to go to the *kino* to see a movie?"

"Sure," I answered enthusiastically. "That sounds great." And it really did. Karl Arvid asking me to do something with him. I might even meet more of his friends. That's what brothers were for.

We walked *til byen* and then up and down Storgate. I was now used to the routine. I knew which side of Storgate to walk on and I knew the end boundaries: the Grand Hotel to the south and the *Kino* to the north. Even going to the *kino* meant arriving early enough to walk up and down Storgate a couple of times, just to see who was there.

"Geir, Karl Olav," Karl Arvid greeted them in Norwegian. "Do you want to go to the movies with us?" I still couldn't speak much Norwegian, but I was beginning to understand more and more.

"What's playing?"

"The third show," Karl Arvid answered, "is an American movie: *The Beat Generation.*"

"Karl Arvid," I inquired, "I don't understand 'third show.' What does that mean?"

"We only have one *kino* in Tromsø, but the *kino* has three showings each day, and each show is usually a different movie."

Verdensteatret

TROMSØ

Nr. 9 6 3 7 9

3. Forestill.

Voksne kr. 2,50

"Helge," Karl Arvid shouted to a boy across the street.

"Karl Arvid," Helge answered equally loudly, "I haven't seen you all summer. Where have you been?"

"We've all been to Karl Olav's *hytta* for the past three weeks."

"Who's with you?" Helge asked, turning toward me. "Is that Pete?" The conversation automatically changed from Norwegian to English as soon as I heard my name.

"*Ja.*"

"Hi, there. I'm Helge. Glad to meet you."

"*Hei*, guys," Karl Olav interrupted. "Let's go to a *kafé*; I'm starved."

As we headed off, I noticed Karl Olav's most distinguishing characteristic: a toothbrush sticking out of his back pocket. He literally brushed his teeth after every meal. When I first met him, I figured this was one of those quaint Norwegian customs I could write home about; probably had its roots in Viking times. It turned out that wasn't it at all; it was just the price he paid for having a dentist for a father.

"So," Helge began as we finally sat down with our food, "did you meet any girls?"

"We never do. You've been there; there's no one there."

"You guys should have been here," Helge continued. "Tromsø has been full of girls all summer. I've been picking them up every night on Storgate."

"Pete," Karl Olav was the one who finally had something to say to me, "I'm having a party a week from this Saturday night. It's the last Saturday before school starts."

"You are expected to invite a girl," Geir added.

"Don't worry, Pete," Karl Olav continued. "It won't be as difficult as you imagine. We've already picked out the girl."

"Who is it?" Helge asked with an almost professional curiosity.

"Anna Karen Smestad," Karl Arvid answered.

"Aren't you the lucky one," Helge whistled softly. "Now, that's one pretty girl."

"Does she know about this?" I asked apprehensively. I had only met her once before, briefly, as we walked up and down Storgate.

I Was a Teenage Norwegian

"We've already talked to her," Karl Olav answered, "and she says it's fine. It's not an arranged marriage; it's just a party."

"I hope you know how to kiss, Pete," Helge smiled, "because Norwegian girls are used to kissing."

"I think you can count on this as a kissing party, too," Karl Olav smiled.

"And one thing you have to know about Norwegians," Helge offers. "We kiss with our tongues. I don't know if you are used to that in America."

As Karl Arvid and I walked home, I realized that this was a part of my year I hadn't given much thought to. I had Sue; Sue Osborne was my girlfriend. I was neither popular nor happy at Staples, but I did have an alternative social group: LRY, Liberal Religious Youth, the youth group of the Unitarian Church. I didn't really have any girlfriends at Staples, but I dated a couple of girls from my local LRY group. And then there was Sue Osborne. Sue was from New Jersey and I met her at one of our regional conferences; we had been going steady for about five months when I heard from AFS.

I thought of our relationship in those terms, but it was difficult for two people to "go steady" when they didn't even live in the same community; it was difficult to do everything together when you couldn't do anything together. We got to see each other at LRY conferences and she had visited my house a couple of times. It was important to me that I thought I had a girlfriend—it made me feel more acceptable to myself as a teenage boy—and that was probably why I thought of myself as going steady, in spite of the distance. I took a picture of Sue with me to Norway. I needed to have a girlfriend, or perhaps I needed *to feel* I had a girlfriend.

"Sue? It's Pete," I had said when I called her the evening I heard about going to Norway.

"Hi, Pete," Sue answered in her perky voice.

"You're never gonna guess what's just happened; I won't even give you a chance to try. I don't think I ever told you I had applied to be an AFS exchange student; it happened before we met, and I had long since forgotten about it because I had never heard and I came home from playing tennis today, and my sister said there was this letter but she wouldn't show it to me until my mother came home, and when she did I opened it and it was from AFS and I'm going to Norway."

"Wow, that's great."

"Yeah, I guess so. I mean, it is great; it's just that I never expected Norway. You know how much I've studied French and how good I am at it. I guess I just assumed that I'd go to France. I guess I was hoping I would go to France. Actually, I haven't thought about it at all since last fall when two of the finalists in our school were selected. I figured that was the end of it and no one else would be selected. And then I heard: Norway! The only problem is that it's for an entire year."

"Oh."

"Listen, Sue, it'll be OK; you'll see. We'll work it out somehow; I'm sure we can. This is real important to me, but so are you. I want to go, but I don't want to lose you."

"A year's a long time."

"I know; it's going to be difficult for me, too. But we have something special and special it will stay. Listen, I've got all this stuff on my mind, and all this stuff I've got to do and I have only three weeks. Somehow we can make this all work out; I know it. I'll call you again when I have more time. Take care. Bye."

I had, finally, received a letter from her. The letter was a good one, with an enclosed composition. The letter made me realize how little, over the previous two months, I had thought of her. I was not sure whether this was good or bad, but I was surprised. She was my girlfriend, wasn't she? I had so much wanted a girlfriend and I was so pleased that I had one. I felt good that I had Sue as an anchor as I headed for the uncharted waters of Norway and Tromsø; Sue would be one of the constants in my otherwise ever-changing life.

But I was in Tromsø for a year, and she was in New Jersey. I hadn't thought much about her or what I was going to do about girls. I still didn't know what to do but the time was fast approaching when I could put this issue off no longer.

August 18, 1961

My Darling Susie,

My every thought of you is summed up in the first three words. You certainly are a darling (or would it be better to reuse the words, and say you are my darling) but you are not a Sue any more; you have now moved into the Susie class (I guess it sounds as if you are a boxer or a sports car...both of which I hope you are not). In your letter, you are still your old self: extremely intelligent, still using "Gad," thinking as you do. But there is life and humor in your last letter that completely overwhelmed me.

There are many, many attractive girls here in Tromsø and a great many of them have quite the figure to back up the face (this does not mean that a good figure or a pretty face is important, merely that it is pleasant to look at). The most popular bathing suit for them is, naturally, the bikini. I honestly believe, even without seeing the "new" you, that you are more than a match for any one of them (not that it is important...but it will be pleasant to look at).

I, too, have come to enjoy camping. I am not too sure how kosher it is, but possibly we could take a camping trip when I get back. I can think of no better way to "get acquainted" again (and I hope you know me and trust me well enough to realize that I do not mean sexually).

You are more than 100% right about adjusting to others' faults. My minister said to me just before I left, "It is easy to like another person for his good points; what is difficult is to like and appreciate that person for his faults." It is more than difficult; it is necessary. It is easy to like a person for his good points, but only if that person has good points. How is it possible for a person to have good points? Why only if he does not have many faults. And how is it possible for a person not to have many faults? Why only if he is made aware that he has faults? And how can a person be made aware of his faults? Why merely by criticizing him and his faults. In other words, Susie dear, try to live with and adjust to my faults, yes, but also try to help me rid myself of these faults.

I love you,
Pete

Every day, for the five days since Karl Arvid told of my date, the party was uppermost on my mind and foremost in my conversations. On the one hand, I was definitely excited: my first Norwegian party, my first Norwegian date, a chance to meet new friends, a chance to see if I had changed. On the other hand, I was scared: I didn't like parties, no one would dance with me, what if Anna Karen wanted to make out? The party had formed a focal point for my final few days of summer vacation.

I was feeling much more comfortable about going *til byen* myself. One evening I was walking Storgate by myself, practicing my role as *Tromsøværing* when I was greeted in Norwegian by a girl. It was Anna Karen.

"*Hei*, Pete," Anna Karen greeted me in Norwegian. I had met her briefly once before, walking up and down Storgate. She had typically Norwegian blue eyes, a smooth-as-silk complexion, and a captivating smile.
"*Hei*."

"This is my friend," Anna continued in Norwegian, "Ingrid. She's at the *gymnas*, the high school, too."

"*Det gleder meg,*" I continued in Norwegian as well. It may have been a formal way of saying I was pleased to meet her ("It pleases me") but at least it was Norwegian. It was time for me to speak as much Norwegian as I could with anyone who was willing to suffer through my broken speech and poor grammar.

"Do you want to go to a *kafé* and get something to eat," Anna Karen asked.

"*Ja.* Samfunn?" I said like a native. There were many *kafés* in town, and I had visited a number of them, but Samfunn was the only one whose name I could remember and pronounce. But Anna and Ingrid didn't know that, and I sensed they were terribly impressed. I certainly was.

So here we were together, just the three of us, sitting together in a *kafé*, and what the hell was I going to say? I certainly never had to worry about this situation in America; nobody would go out with me. But Tromsø was different; I could walk up and down Storgate any evening and meet people and go to a *kafé* with them. Easy. But now I had to talk to these girls, something that I would have found discouragingly difficult in English. But I had started the conversation in Norwegian; I couldn't back out now. I may have been away at the *hytta* for only three weeks, but even those few weeks made a difference.

"I'm looking forward to the party," I blurted out. I hadn't talked about anything else with the boys for so long I didn't know what else to talk about.

"Oh, didn't Karl Olav tell you?" Anna Karen asked. "I have to take care of my younger brother. I'm not going to be able to go to the party."

"Oh, that's too bad," I said. It was difficult enough getting used to getting set up with a date, but I had spent the past three or four days getting used to it and by the time Anna Karen pulled out I was more than excited. This was to be my first Norwegian party and my first Norwegian date and my first Norwegian girl.

Aside from the fact Anna Karen was pretty and she talked to me in Norwegian, this meant that the gang of four was going to have to start all over again picking someone for me. It was difficult enough getting used to my first arranged date; it was not going to get any easier the second time. Maybe I would just sit that party out and wait until school started, the teenage American whispered. No such luck, the teenage Norwegian knew better.

-6-
The First Fest

I had a call from Adele Berg. Adele was the AFS head in Tromsø. She had been away for the summer, which was why we had never met before. One of the major aspects of her job as AFS head in Tromsø was to make sure everything was all right and help me out. *Fru* Román had told me that Adele had said she wanted to talk to me about school...by that time only days away.

I walked to her house, which was only ten or fifteen minutes away. I walked everywhere and got around Tromsø pretty well by myself. Getting to Adele's house was child's play for someone as experienced on the streets of Tromsø as I was.

"*Velkommen*, Pete," Adele greeted me at the door. "You can leave your shoes in the hall."

"I got a call from Rektor Riksheim this week," Adele began in Norwegian when we were seated. "He wants to see you tomorrow so that he can talk with you before school starts on Monday."

"That's fine," I answered, also in Norwegian.

"He'll go over your schedule and answer any questions you might have. I doubt he will be very helpful, but he does want to talk with you."

"That's fine," I answered. I understood most of what Adele said, but I still didn't feel I had enough vocabulary or confidence to say much in Norwegian myself.

"But that's not why I asked you over here, today," Adele abruptly switched to English. Here it was. I had done my best to push it to the back of my mind but I really knew, when I was summoned to Adele's house, what the real subject of our conversation would be. Talking about school and the principal wanting to see me was just to soften me up. Switching from Norwegian to English...I knew it was serious.

"I got a call from your mother this week, too, and we had a long talk. She told me that she senses that you are not happy living with them and that you will be happier living somewhere else."

"I don't even know how I feel, but I am not sure they want me to stay with them. I want it to work out so badly, but I'm not sure what to do. I sense that the Románs don't want me living with them."

"Is there anything in particular?" She had a matter-of-fact way of talking, but I felt she was sensitive.

"I don't know. My father tells me I don't appreciate all he does for me. I thank him, I do whatever he suggests, but nothing I do gets through to him. Karl Arvid is still pretty quiet with me. I see him with his friends, now, and he's not quiet with them at all. I can't tell whether he doesn't like me or if he is uncomfortable speaking English, which is all he speaks with me, which is strange if he's uncomfortable with English. No one in the family talks with me much in Norwegian, and that makes it difficult for me to learn. I went away on a *hyttatur* for what I thought was a three-day camping trip with some of Karl Arvid's friends, and we didn't come back for three weeks. We went fishing and I had a good time, but I thought maybe the Románs just wanted to get rid of me." That was the longest speech I had made since leaving Trollvasshytta and coming to Tromsø. It surprised even me; I hadn't realized how many pent-up feelings I had. I knew the Románs had gotten to me, but I hadn't realized how much.

"Do you want to change families?"

"No," I said more quickly than I would have imagined possible. "This is my family; I want it to work out. It hasn't even been two months yet."

"What's special about two months?" Adele asked.

"There's this friend of my parents, Mrs. Ottinger," I explained. "The advice she gave me before I left home was that no matter what problem I have early on in my year, I had to give it two months. She said any serious problem deserved the two-month test."

"Pete, I'm here to help you in any way I can, as long as I'm in Tromsø," Adele continued. "You'll have to decide for yourself what you want to do about the Románs. If you want to see how it goes, that's fine with me and I'll support you in that decision. I just want to give you a chance to talk, to get any issues off your chest and out on the table."

"I really appreciate that," I said. "Right now, that's what I need most: to have someone to talk to and to know someone is there for me."

"And we'll talk again, right?" Adele got it; she had switched back into Norwegian as the intensity of the conversation lessened. Adele was especially sensitive to my need to talk, on the one hand, and my need to talk Norwegian, on the other. "After school has started."

"*Ja,*" I said.

"Don't forget," she told me as I got my shoes back on and headed out the door, "to meet me in the school-yard at 10:30 tomorrow morning; we still have to meet the principal. You're going to have to get used to getting up early anyway."

Later that evening, Karl Arvid and I walked *til byen*, wandered up and down Storgate a few times, found Geir, Karl Olav, and Helge, and headed for the *kafé*. I had definitely gotten into the Norwegian teenager evening routine. I was even beginning to feel that I belonged.

I Was a Teenage Norwegian

"This is serious business about Pete," Helge said almost before we had all sat down with our food. The conversation among that little group of ours had remained in English ever since the first time I had met the other three. The big change, however, was that I was included in the conversation. Perhaps because they were talking about me. But I didn't care what the reason was; I was happy just to be included.

"We've got to find someone else now that Anna Karen cannot come," Geir stated the obvious. The others nodded their assent. There we were, the five of us, sitting around a table at the Samfunn Kafé, eating our *smør-brød* and drinking our sodas. I was certain that to any outsider we looked so serious, discussing affairs of state, or was it the state of my affairs?

"Maybe it would be better," I began tentatively, "if I don't go to the *fest*. I'm still a little scared about going to a *fest* with all these kids I don't know, and especially with a girl I don't know."

"*Hei*, Pete," Karl Olav chimed in, "there's nothing to be scared of. It's just a *fest*; it'll be fun. There will be lots of kids from school. We'll find you someone nice."

"But I'm afraid anyone you choose will be bored with me because of everything I can't do."

"What do you mean?" Helge asked.

"I still can't talk much in Norwegian. And I don't think I can make out."

"You can't make out?" Helge asked, his face screwed up in disbelief.

"It's more that I'm not sure I want to."

"You don't want to make out?" Helge asked, his face now complete-ly distorted with disbelief. Helge couldn't imagine any teenager from

58

anywhere in the world who didn't want to make out. Until I saw his response, I hadn't realized at all how strange my words must have sounded. A seventeen-year-old who didn't like to make out? That sounded strange even to me. And it wasn't exactly that I didn't like making out; I did, and to that extent I was normal. But sex was tied into a whole range of other feelings and insecurities.

"What do you guys think?" I finally asked.

"Look," Geir said. "Else Maria is at the table in the corner. She's nice and pretty and isn't going with anyone now. Here's what I suggest. We ask her over here and introduce her to Pete. If she wants to go, that's fine. Leave the decision up to her. How about that?"

The other three nodded in agreement, and then looked at me.

"OK," I relented. "That's fine. If she wants to go with me, I'll go with her."

It was Geir's suggestion and he got the honor to start the show. I watched him as he walked over to a table in the corner and started talking with one of the girls sitting at it. I couldn't tell if she was nice, but she was pretty: dark blond hair, cut short to curl around her ears, a slightly sloping nose, slender with a more-than-adequate chest. She looked younger than us, another one of Karl Arvid's *småpiker* friends. Many of his friends, especially many of the girls, were two or three years younger than he was. *Småpiker*, young girls. Anna Karen was a *småpike*; it looked as if Else Maria was, too. She looked even better when she stood up: her chest was much more than adequate and her legs were smashing. I couldn't believe I was thinking all this when I didn't even know if I wanted to make out.

"Pete, this is Else Maria," Geir said to me as the two of them walked back to the boys table. "Else Maria, this is Pete, Karl Arvid's American brother."

"*Det gleder meg,*" Else Maria said to me, a small but distinct smile on her face.

"*Jeg også,*" I said in my finest Norwegian. Me, too. I was in love already; she spoke Norwegian to me.

The other three guys at the table all looked at me, nudging me with their eyes. Panic had already set in. I doubted I could have handled the situation in English and Else Maria was talking to me in Norwegian. There was nowhere to turn for help. I could see her girlfriends at the table in the corner paying strict attention to the drama unfolding at our table. I concentrated on the Norwegian. How did I say "would you like?" in Norwegian. I knew the word for party: *fest*. How about if I just looked at her sincerely and said "*fest,*" raising my voice at the end of the word in the hopes that she would sense a question mark, in the hope that she might catch my drift.

"I would love to go to the party with you," Else Maria continued in Norwegian, saving me from any further embarrassment. Clearly Geir had made the proposition to Else Maria and she had made up her mind already. I didn't even have to ask her; she made it pretty simple for me. I had a date again.

* *

Adele was waiting for me in the school-yard at 10:30. She whisked me in the door so quickly I hardly had a chance to look around and see what the place looked like.

"Rektor Riksheim is very precise," she said quickly, almost dragging me up the stairs to the second floor. "You do not want to keep him waiting, especially not on your first interview.

"*God dag,*" Rektor Riksheim said formally as Adele and I entered his office. Rektor Riksheim was about my height, with a full head of curly grey hair and a military posture. His smile was as formal as his voice. It was clear that he would conduct this interview standing up and that he would demand the same of me.

"*God dag*, Rektor Riksheim," Adele began. "This is Pete Dublin."

"You will be in the fifth year English line," Rektor Riksheim announced. No hello; no how are you? Didn't ask about the *hurtigruten* trip or what I had done on my summer vacation. This was definitely someone I was going to like...a lot.

Adele spoke Norwegian and Rektor Riksheim also spoke Norwegian, but they didn't speak the same Norwegian. I had read about those two Norwegians, but this was the first time I heard *nynorsk,* or New Norwegian. *nynorsk* was, of course, the older of the two Norwegian languages; I should have known that from the name. They were both official languages, but many more people spoke *bokmål,* the Norwegian I was learning. Mostly, people from the rural areas—farmers, some fishermen—spoke *nynorsk.* And, Rektor Riksheim; anything to make my life difficult.

"You will study English, French, Biology, History, Norwegian, Religion, Physical Education, and *bokmål.* You will not have to study *nynorsk,*" he said, with an audible drop in his voice indicating his disappointment that I would not have to study his language. I, on the other hand, was relieved. That sounded like the world's easiest schedule: only eight courses. But it definitely would have been a killer with *nynorsk.* What a lucky guy I was to avoid that dreaded subject.

"There are many differences between Norwegian and American schools. We expect you to understand and observe our rules. We have ten-minute breaks between classes and all our students go outside during the breaks. Fresh air is healthy for you so you must go outside.

"Keep in mind," Rektor Riksheim continued, "that it is an honor and a privilege to go to this *gymnas.* This is not like an American high school, where everyone is expected and obliged to go. Norwegian students take an entrance examination for *gymnas* and only the best are admitted. You will have a heavy schedule. This will be a difficult year for you and you will have to work hard. You can expect to do nothing but work this year if you intend to succeed.

"Personally, I was rather hoping for another girl. We have had two exchange students in the *gymnas* and they were both girls. They were very good students. In fact, Joanne from last year got a better result on her Norwegian exam than some of our Norwegian students. I hope you will take your year here as seriously as Joanne did."

Give me a break, was all I could say to myself. School hasn't started and you're comparing me to some brain who was here last year. I don't want to hear it. I'm still on summer vacation. I've got a *fest* to go to tomorrow night; I've got to get my priorities straight. And I still can't speak more than a single sentence in Norwegian. And you have the gall to tell me to take this all seriously, in *nynorsk*?

As we walked down the stairs, Adele winked at me. "Aren't you glad we weren't late?"

"I could hardly understand the man," I said almost out of breath from having concentrated so hard trying to understand Rektor Riksheim's *nynorsk*. "I knew this wasn't going to be a vacation, but school can't be all that bad, can it?"

"Don't worry," Adele smiled. "You will probably find some corners to cut. And, seniors don't have to go outside during breaks."

Luckily for me, I still had a couple of days before I had to worry about school. That was fine with me because it let me concentrate my worrying on the *fest* the following night. As Karl Arvid and I walked *til byen* that evening, I realized that there was more to worry about than I had originally imagined.

"Karl Arvid," Geir shouted as he saw us walking Storgate. "Did you hear? Else Marie is sick; she can't go to the *fest*, either." A coincidence? A coordinated effort? A conspiracy?

"That's okay," Helge chimed in. This was a man prepared for all eventualities. There was no way he was letting me off the hook. I didn't even bother to hold out any hope for a reprieve. "I have another idea: Marit."

"Marit who?" Karl Olav asks. "No...Marit?"

"Sure," Helge acknowledged what Karl Olav had just figured out. "Marit. My sister."

"No," I said firmly. "I'm not going with any sister." It was Helge's sister in particular that worried me. Partly, the idea of going with the sister of one of Karl Arvid's friends was quite scary. Partly, I was afraid that Marit might have been like Helge.

"It's too late," Helge smirked. "I already asked her when I found out that Else Maria was sick." I gave up; he was incorrigible. To be honest, I appreciated the attention I was getting, regardless of how uncomfortable the substance of that attention made me feel. I wanted to be with other kids my own age, I wanted to go to a *fest*, and the price I had to pay—overcoming my fear—was an acceptable cost.

Finally, the day arrived: my first *fest*. I spent it nervously, aimlessly. What was the worst that could happen? Marit could be bored? At least I was an American; at least she wouldn't have to be bored by something familiar, like a Norwegian. And for me? What was the worst that could happen? I could be bored? When I thought of it that way, nothing even remotely bad could happen.

"Are you ready, Pete?" Karl Arvid asked at the top of the stairs.

"I guess I am. What about Marit?"

"She'll be there," he answered, not a trace of doubt in his voice. "It is her house, after all."

"Enjoy yourselves," Mrs. Román wished us well as we put on our shoes and headed out the door.

As we walked, I began to understand some of my fears. Perhaps more than the Norwegianess of the *fest*, what worried me most was the festness of the *fest*. I was never particularly popular in Westport and I hardly ever went to any parties there. In fact, one of the few parties I attended was my last, where I came to understand my intellectual friends had a social life of their own.

"Are you off to the party, now?" Mom had asked on my final Saturday evening in Westport.

"Yeah, I guess. I think I've gotten as much done today as I can."

"Have fun," she said. She didn't get many opportunities to wish me well on my way to a social gathering. "Remember we're going to church tomorrow, so don't stay out too late."

"Right," I mumbled as I walked out the door. Westport parties were an unknown for me; I couldn't imagine what kind of celebration party Jim Wunsch had in mind. There were three groups of kids at Staples. There were the working class Italians: the hoods. There was the Jewish intellectual crowd; those were all the kids in my classes. Finally there was the popular crowd; they were the WASPs. Jim was in the intellectual crowd and he had just been elected school president. He wasn't exactly the party type; on the other hand, neither was I. He and Judy Schine and the others were pretty cerebral; I couldn't imagine them at any kind of party.

"Hi, Pete, glad you could come," Judy answered the door. "I think you know most of the people here."

"Hey, Dubs," Larry Duberstein called out. Larry and I were in the same class, sitting next to each other ever since first grade.

"Duber," I answered, "what are you doing here? You weren't even running for anything, and I didn't notice you campaigning, either."

"That's true, but where there's a party, I follow."

That I understood. Although Larry and I had grown up together and were best of friends for most of our lives, we drifted apart at high school, even though we were still in the same classes. He became popular, and I didn't. His coming to a party I could understand; I just couldn't understand his coming to *that* party. These kids weren't his party friends; they were just the kids who were with him in class.

And that was when I discovered how big a mistake I had made. I had always seen the three social groups at Staples as discrete. The popular kids partied; the smart kids studied. A few smart kids partied, but always with the popular kids. As I looked around, a light-bulb of awareness and understanding turned on: the Jewish intellectual crowd partied!

As I wandered through the rooms, talking to all the kids I shared class with everyday, I realized that they had a social life. For the past two years, I had invested all my energy trying to be accepted by the popular crowd. I didn't know any better, but the kids in this crowd did. I had no reason to be in that crowd, and they knew it. What I completely overlooked was that all of the kids with whom I spent all my time in school had created their own social group. They knew they didn't belong in the popular group. They had none of my warped aspirations. They simply went about the business of taking care of themselves. Here I was in the middle of the social group I had always longed for and never even knew existed.

"*Hei*, Pete," Helge welcomed me to his house. His party, his house, his sister. "Just leave your shoes near the door and come in."

"*Takk*." To hell with his English; I would dazzle him with my Norwegian.

"Most everyone is here," he continued, "and the getting is good."

That was Helge, I reminded myself. A one-track mind, always on girls, always thinking about who was getting what from whom.

"Pete," Helge moved me toward an attractive blond, perhaps a year or two younger than we were. "This is Marit, my sister. Marit, this is Pete...from the United States of America. You know, good old Uncle Sam."

"*Det gleder meg*," Marit said in Norwegian. Already, I felt better. Maybe it was just boys my age who spoke English; all the *småpiker* spoke Norwegian with me.

"*Takk*," I responded in kind. Over and above her willingness to speak Norwegian to me, I noticed two additional things immediately about Marit. First, she wore no lipstick. Second, her skirt was short. Since I was always in a position of never knowing whether what I encountered was peculiar to a particular person, or peculiar to Norwegian culture as a whole, I took a quick look around the room, and confirmed my suspicions: no lipstick and many short skirts.

"Do you want to dance?" Marit asked. Her voice was comforting; I heard in it a concern for me, a desire to insure that I was not overwhelmed. Although Marit resembled Helge physically—about the same height, the same light brown curly hair—I didn't feel in her the same assertiveness or aggressiveness. Even her face appeared more calm and more relaxed than Helge's.

"*Ja*," I answered, actually meaning it.

"How long have you been in Norway?"

"I arrived about two months ago?"

"And how long have you been in Tromsø?"

"Four or five weeks."

"Is it difficult for you to talk Norwegian?"

"Yes," I admitted. "But I want to do it if I can. I need to be able to speak and most people still speak English to me."

"I know," Marit responded sympathetically. "Kids here love to speak English. You will have to stop them from doing so, you know."

"I know. I already have an idea."

It was a slow dance and I did all right. There weren't really any steps; I just shuffled my feet around in time with the music and Marit followed me. She had a firm hold on me, which made me feel even more comfortable with her; I couldn't stand girls who sort of wilted in my arms when we danced. As the dance ended, we walked over to one of the sofas, our arms around each other's waists quite naturally. That, too, was new and different. In America, only people going steady held hands or put their arms around each other's waists. I fantasized about doing it, but it never happened. But there it felt okay, even on our first date. In fact, it felt rather nice.

"I often wonder," Marit continued, "what it must be like to be an exchange student. To leave home and all your friends. Go to a strange place and live with a new family."

"I always wanted to be an AFS student," I told her. "Now that I'm here, it's harder than I thought." I couldn't believe it; I was actually having a real conversation in Norwegian. I actually spoke in more-or-less complete sentences. And Marit was laughing at me. Maybe I was doing all right.

"I can apply to be an AFS student in two years," Marit said, "and that's what I plan to do. But it's difficult to get accepted, I think."

We kept talking and dancing through most of the evening. At one point, I kissed Marit on the neck. I didn't plan it; I didn't even think about it for minutes on end before I did it, turning the thought over in my mind and imagining it endlessly as a way of building up the necessary courage for action. It just happened, sort of grew out of the moment. And Marit didn't pull away. If I wasn't mistaken, I think she even liked it.

"Getting any?" shouted Helge. This guy was talking about his own sister! Helge may have been one of the boys, but I didn't like him. He had no tact, manners, or thought for other people. He was a big talker, but I was beginning to wonder if that was all there was to him. Besides me, the only one not getting any was Helge; ironic, wasn't it? Everyone else was making out; even I had gotten one kiss.

"Do you have a girl friend in America," Marit asked, seemingly oblivious to her brother.

The moment of truth had arrived. I had known for months that at some point early on in the year someone would ask that question. I was not one hundred percent positive I had a girl, but I thought I did; I felt as if I did. I wondered why Marit was asking. Did she want to make out, like everyone else?

"If I do," I said, holding her tight but not looking at her, "I don't know about it."

There it was; the lie was out. It was the tiniest of lies—just barely escaping the truth—but it was not a true statement.

I had written to my parents sharing with them all that had happened recently: the situation with the Románs, my trepidation and fears about the start of school, my interview/interrogation with Riksheim. I felt close to them, and wanted them to know everything that was happening to me. And, I needed an opportunity to share my thoughts and feelings.

I felt close to both my parents, but I had a special relationship with my father. We always had long talks, just the two of us. He listened, gave advice, and I argued with him. It must have frustrated him, but it worked for me. And, I wanted to maintain a semblance of that special relationship with him during that year. Occasionally I wrote to him alone, although I knew he would share my letters with Mom.

August 26, 1961

Dear Dad,

I have just returned from my first Norwegian party, so full of thoughts I have to share some of them with you. Everyone at the party was making out, except me and my date. She was real nice; it wasn't that. It's just that I'm off and I want to stay off. Perhaps I'd better explain "off."

I have now been "off" for about six months...off sex, or in other words, not making out, etc. Sue placed this idea in my head with her virgin viewpoint that it is vulgar to make out unless one is in love. I eventually modified "vulgar," but I have adhered to that policy for over half a year. I want to make the kiss a more sacred action. In other words, I will not make out merely to make out, but because I am making out with a certain girl that I am very fond of. It must be that I like the girl more than I like to make out.

I was also dishonest. My date asked me if I have a girlfriend in America. I kind of beat around the bush and then said that if I had one, I didn't know about it. Stretching the truth is always a lie.

I remember Reverend Westwood's statement about not displaying a sign you are a good person, but to let others realize this for themselves. I guess that he was well aware that I often try to prove myself to others. I am going to slowly work toward being honest so that people will see that I am honest because I am honest. I won't have to tell them.

I am going to constantly think of everything I do or immediately have done, and continue to benefit from my mistakes (and even less painfully, from the mistakes of others). I realize now that only by making myself a better person will I be able to convince other people that I am a better person.

I Was a Teenage Norwegian

If I can only work now for the goals I have set, and work in earnest to correct my faults and make myself a truly better person, this letter may be looked upon as the cornerstone of all my efforts. And God help me if I fail. But if I fail, it will be because of myself, and God only helps those who help themselves.

Love

Pete

It was four o'clock in the morning as I finished my letter, my first father/son letter of the journey. It had been some day, and some two and one-half months. I felt as if I had been through a fantastic voyage, but my voyage had hardly begun. In two days, school would begin. I could hardly wait. I could hardly wait to see what would happen. I could hardly wait to see what I would become.

-7-
Norwegian At Last

"*Hei*, Pete," Bergljot screamed at my door, when she heard me getting up. "Come down and play with me."

"*Jeg kommer. Jeg kommer.*" I answered back in Norwegian. I'm coming. I'm coming. Bergljot was my favorite Román, right from the start. Even on that first day as she hid behind *fru* Románs apron, we had clicked. She had remained a bright light when everything else had appeared dark.

"*Snakk langsomt,*" I pleaded. Speak slowly. She cocked her head in semi-wonderment. It simply didn't make sense to her that she had to talk slowly to an adult; it didn't make sense to her that she could know more than an adult about something.

As soon as I was finished with my *geitost* breakfast, she was on me in a flash. Bergljot may have been as cute as kids came, but she loved rough-housing and all other such playful pastimes that were natural for children her age. Sometimes she snuck up on me and I hardly knew what hit me. That morning, it was a set of keys. Right to the head.

"*Nok,*" I complained. Enough. The rough-housing I could take, but when she started throwing things at me, I had to say *nok*. My sense was that Norwegian parents put fewer limits on their kids than what I was used to in America. Bergljot could do almost anything she wanted: run around the house screaming, play with ashtrays too heavy for her to handle, physically maul her parents (and her American brother). I was about the only person I ever heard say *nok* to her. So what did she do then? Raced toward me, leapt into my lap, and cuddled. How could I get angry at such a kid?

My relationship with Bergljot had always been great; my relationship with the Románs was getting a little better. One reason was, I hadn't spent all that much time with them. Various members of the family—Elin and Karen, for example—were away for part of the summer, Karl Arvid and I went to the *hytta* without the rest of the family, and the family (minus Karl Arvid and *fru* Román) were away for the last week of summer. This lack of interaction cut down on the frustration and conflict, but it didn't help me become a real member of the family.

I Was a Teenage Norwegian

In Westport I would have relished that amount of independence: being on my own, allowed to stay up all hours of the night, getting money to eat out at a restaurant. In Tromsø, though, what I longed for was more of a *connection*, not more independence.

The other reason things felt better had to do with *fru* Román herself. During my first month, everything I did seemed to annoy her. I guess I was making mistakes—not maliciously, but out of ignorance of Norwegian customs—but since she never said what about me was bothering her there was no way I could correct it. She must have had a talk with Adele Berg, whose straightforwardness had impressed me when we met. Soon afterwards, *fru* Román started telling, directly and without annoyance, when I had done something wrong.

"You have to take your shoes off when you come into the house," she now explained to me. "You'll always see shoes just inside the front door in a Norwegian home." In time I also learned that I was expected to pass food to Román first at mealtimes, and offer to buy the daily milk or bread.

That alone was probably enough to break the tension between us, but I was also beginning to speak enough Norwegian so that we could conduct a conversation in her language; that appeared to be the icing the cake needed. I hadn't called her *mor* yet, but I could at least imagine doing so. I was definitely not a Norwegian yet, but I was no longer simply a tourist. I was not a member of the Román family yet, but I no longer felt like an unwelcome guest.

* * * * * * * * * * * * * * * * * * *

Twas the night before school started and all through the house everyone was stirring...and then some. That evening I had a visit from a girl who would be in my class: Jorunn Pettersen. She was quite attractive, and dressed in a skirt and a blue Norwegian sweater with reindeer pattern across the top. She cocked her head to one side when she smiled, which she did often.

"I've just come back from Michigan," Jorunn said in Norwegian. "I was an AFSer myself, and I thought you might like a chance to talk a little before school starts tomorrow. Have you talked with any other kids in our class?"

"I met a couple of girls at a *kafé* early in the summer," I responded in Norwegian, too, "but I don't remember their names. Those are the only ones from our class. All the others I have met are younger. Lots of *småpiker*." I figured I would dazzle Jorunn with my deep sense of cultural understanding. "I did visit the *rektor* with Adele Berg."

"Oh, you have talked with Adele? That's great."

"She really was helpful. I could talk about the difficulties I've had, and she helped me think about ways to improve."

"What did you think of the *rektor*?"

"I don't know," I answered tentatively, not wanting to tread on any sensitive ground. Maybe he was her uncle or something. "He struck me as pretty serious. He kept talking about how much work there would be and how great Joanne was last year and how disappointed he was that I was a boy."

"Rektor is a little *gammeldags*, you know, old fashioned. I wouldn't worry much about what he says because you really won't have much to do with him now that he's talked to you."

"You've been to school in America and school here. Is there as much work as he says? That was a little scary."

"To tell the truth, ordinarily school is much harder in Norway than in America," Jorunn answered. "But I don't think this year will be that difficult for you. You see, you'll be in the 5th year English Line. Most students have five years of *gymnas*, so you'll be a senior. The English Line had many of its final exams—German, French, Mathematics— after the 4th year, so really, this is not the hardest year. In that sense, you're lucky."

Wait a minute! Wait just one minute!. What was going on here? I had just been talking with Jorunn for almost half an hour...entirely in Norwegian! My God, it had finally happened, and I almost didn't notice it. A real conversation, not just a few sentences back and forth. I had been waiting for that moment all summer.

"Jorunn," I said excitedly, "this is really my first conversation in Norwegian."

"I think you're doing quite well," she replied.

I couldn't help but think of the first time I had managed those few sentences back and forth. It occurred on the *hurtigruten* trip from Bodø to Tromsø. By 7:00 o'clock in the morning we approached another town. I plucked up my courage and decided I was ready to get off the *hurtigruten* and go for my first Norwegian coastal town excursion on my own. I didn't know where we were or what the town was called; the docks were not like railroad stations with signs on them. The town was small, and looked like all the other towns we had stopped at since Bodø: hugging the coastline, surrounded by a backdrop of snow-covered mountains and colorful wooden houses. The boat slowly pulled up alongside the dock, and the crew made it secure with the help of their counterparts on shore.

Immediately, people moved the freight off the boat; this was the priority. The first people walking down the gangplank were those who were actually bound for this particular town; then it was the tourists' turn. I felt the eyes of the entire small town on me as I walked down the steep gangplank and onto shore. Those people knew everyone in town; they knew I was a stranger and that I must be a tourist. I wanted to feel like someone other than a tourist, but that was all I was, and I assumed it showed.

I Was a Teenage Norwegian

Although it was only 7:30 in the morning, the town looked as if it had been wide awake for hours. Of course, it had been light for hours already; in fact, it had been light for almost two months! The people who were not down at the dock were about town, doing their business. Most of the few shops were already open. They were all on either a single, long main street or one of the few side streets. None of the streets were paved, even the main street. There were few cars; most of the people were walking.

I decided to go into a store to buy something. I didn't really care what it was; I just wanted to be able to manage on my own. So, where to go? What to buy? I didn't want to spend much money; I just wanted to make a transaction in Norwegian. How about a postcard?

"*Værsågod*," the woman behind the counter said in a friendly voice.

There was that word again: "*Værsågod*." It got used for almost everything. People used it for "you're welcome," after someone said thank you, "here you are," when they gave me something, and, in my current situation, "can I help you."

"*Værsågod*," the woman said again with her smile intact.

"*Jeg vil kjøpe et kart*," I said, mustering all my internal fortitude. Damn! I just said that I wanted to buy a map.

"*Unnskyld*. Excuse me *Jeg vil kjøpe et kort*." I want to buy a card; that was a little better.

"*Et kort?*"

"*Et postkort.*"

"*Javel, et postkort. Hvilket postkort?*"

Now I was already in trouble. I needed some time to figure this all out in my head. I talked to myself. What is her question? What's this "*hvilket*" word mean? I don't remember it. Wait a minute. "*Hvilken*" means which. Right. Nouns have gender and we usually learn adjectives in their masculine form. *Hvilken* means which when it's used with masculine nouns. Postcard is a neuter noun in Norwegian, so *hvilket* must be the neuter form of "which." So, she's asking me which card I want. I hope it doesn't take me this long to figure out everything someone says to me in Norwegian.

"*Denne postkort*," I pointed to one of the town, obviously taken from the neighboring mountain. I was hopeful the woman was still there and that she hadn't gone on her coffee break while I was figuring out what she said. Damn! Another mistake. It took me fifteen minutes to figure out what *hvilket* meant because *postkort* was a neuter noun, and then I used the wrong form of "this one."

"*Unnskyld. Dette postkort. Hvor mye koster det?*" How much does it cost? I was pretty certain I got those four words right.

"*Det koster 50 ører.*"

"*Værsågod*," I gave her a 50 *øre* coin.

"*Takk*," she answered, still smiling. She probably got enough tourists in her store that she could speak better English than I could speak

Norwegian, but maybe not. I didn't know and I didn't care. What was important, was that she didn't speak English with me and she was patient. That made it possible for me to succeed.

Mission accomplished. I made mistakes but I corrected them; that was important. Most important, I was on my own and I still managed. I felt great!

"But I must warn you," Jorunn snapped me out of my short trip down memory lane, "most of the kids at school will want to speak English to you."

"I figured that would be the case," I said. "But I have an idea for stopping them."

"What will you do?" Jorunn asked.

"That's my little surprise." I had an idea for the past couple of weeks, but I didn't want to tell anyone. I liked surprises. "You must know the teachers?" I asked.

"I do," she answered, "but perhaps that will be a surprise for you. You can tell me tomorrow after school what you think of them and which ones you like. You must understand that teachers in Norwegian schools are a little different than what you are probably used to in America?"

"How so?"

"Well, they are usually a little bit more formal and serious. You would never have a teacher who is a pal like you do with some teachers in America. Even the younger ones—even the ones we have grown up with here in Tromsø—are usually more distant from the students than many American teachers."

"I think this is the first time I've wanted summer to end and school to start."

"How have things been for you so far? How are things with the Románs?"

"They're definitely getting a little better. Things have been a little difficult for me, especially with Karl Arvid."

"I don't know if anyone has told you this," Jorunn confided, "but Karl Arvid used to be a pretty wild kid a few years ago."

"Boy, you would never know it now," I said, my mouth open in disbelief.

Jorunn and I went on like this for almost an hour and a half. An hour and a half! I was talking Norwegian with a Norwegian about Norwegian schools and my Norwegian family. Now I felt as if I were ready for anything, including school.

The next morning I wasn't so sure. What was I doing 200 miles north of the Arctic Circle going to a *gymnas* when I could hardly speak the language?

"Pete," Mrs. Román explained as I ate breakfast, "don't forget you have to bring a *matpakke*."

I Was a Teenage Norwegian

How could I forget; the infamous food pack. Schools in Norway didn't have cafeterias. All Norwegian children brought their own lunch to school: their *matpakke*. And what was in a typical *matpakke*? Surprise, surprise: *geitost smørbrød*. Finally it was time to reap the rewards of having worked so hard to get to like *geitost*.

As I worked my way through my two *geitost smørbrød* for breakfast, I had to make my two *geitost smørbrød* for lunch.

"You can have bread or *knekkebrød*," *fru* Román explained.

For a moment, I had feared that I would have no variety, no options, no choices. But just as my greatest fears were about to become true, Mrs. Román indicated a level of variety I had not experienced up until that moment. I could have my *geitost*—there was little choice there—on regular bread or Norwegian crisp-bread, *knekkebrød*.

"Thanks," I responded. "I think I'll just have it on bread." No sense in breaking with tradition on my first day of school.

"Come on, Pete," Karl Arvid said, "we have to go."

"*Ha det.* Good luck," Mrs. Román called out.

The *gymnas* was a short walk from our house. The gravel roads were full of kids, walking to school, talking to their friends. There was only one *gymnas* in Tromsø. It was a big building, with red-painted plaster walls. It was three stories high and almost a city block long. It sat up on a hill overlooking the center of town. The school was bordered on the back by a road, and on the front by the schoolyard, which in turn was surrounded by a fence. The schoolyard was itself pretty big, maybe 100' x 200', and the students were milling around in the schoolyard before school started. There must have been two or three hundred of them.

Karl Arvid went off to stand with his friends from the 4th Year English Line class, leaving me to stand alone just outside the entrance to the schoolyard. I saw a blond-haired boy moving toward me and I knew that my big moment had arrived. I reached into my jacket, pulled out a folded cardboard sign, straightened out the string attached to it, and put the string around my neck. I was ready.

"Hi there," the boy smiled. "You must be Pete. I'm Arnulf." He was speaking English; how could I have guessed?

There we were: face to face. He was speaking English to me and I was saying nothing. I had decided never to speak English again.

"Pete?" Arnulf said again, his face reflecting his confusion. Here he was, being as friendly as he could, and I stood there silently. Could I be deaf? Could I be mute? Could I be lost?

Then he noticed the folded sign. It was obviously not typically Norwegian to wear a piece of folded cardboard around one's neck, and I was certain he had seen enough American movies to know that it was not typically American either. By that time, our interaction had attracted a small crowd surrounding us. Slowly, dramatically, I unfolded the cardboard sign.

EXCUSE ME BUT I CANNOT UNDERSTAND ENGLISH

I had decided to wear that sign until it was no longer needed. Whenever anyone at the *gymnas* spoke to me in English, I would refuse to respond in any way except to open the sign. All I could do was hope that it would work.

"Of course," Arnulf replied in Norwegian. "*Unnskyld.* My name is still Arnulf, and now I know you must be Pete."

"*Det gleder meg,*" I replied in Norwegian. I couldn't believe it; it had worked! I got him to talk to me in Norwegian. "Are you in my class?"

"Yes, I am. And that's the bell for us to go in. Why don't you come with me and we'll figure out which seats to take."

We walked through the schoolyard as all of the kids crowded through the only two doors leading into the building. Arnulf looked something between impish and intellectual. He had taken my joke well; in fact, his response was tinged with no small degree of respect. Definitely between impish and intellectual.

Our classroom was on the second floor. It was small—only twenty desks—but Arnulf assured me that we only had eighteen students in the class.

"Personally," Arnulf confided, "I don't like to sit right up in the front row. I know it's a small room anyway, but I like to be back a seat or two."

"I can understand that," I nodded my head in agreement. It struck me as an appropriate strategy.

"I'm going to sit in the third row," he pointed to a desk. There were only four rows. "I'm going to sit next to Randi, my girlfriend."

"I'll sit behind you," I indicated. "That puts me in the last row, as far away from the teachers as I can get."

"Pete," Jorunn said as I took my seat. "Can I sit next to you?"

"*Jada.*"

"I see you've taken a place as far away from the teachers as possible," Jorunn smiled. "But perhaps you'll need some company, and someone has to protect you from Arnulf's influence."

I Was a Teenage Norwegian

"*God morn*," a teacher said as he walked into the room. He had a bit of a spring to his walk; he was relaxed, at ease with himself and the class. Actually, he looked something like Ozzie Nelson.

"*God morn.*" The class stood up and spoke in unison. Was that what Jorunn meant the previous night when she talked of formality?

"Don't worry," Jorunn whispered to me, as if she had just read my thoughts. "We have to stand up when the teachers walk in the room, but we don't have to stand up when they leave."

"As you know," Engelsen began, "I will be your *klasseforstanden*, your main teacher, this year. I will have you for English and French. Here is the list of books you must buy for both these classes. I would like to take a minute to write your schedule on the board.

Monday	Tuesday	Wednesday	Thursday	Friday	Saturday
Free	English	Gym	Norwegian	French	History
Norwegian	English	Norwegian	History	Religion	English
English	English	English	Biology	English	Gym
French	French	French	Biology	Norwegian	Free
Biology	History	Norwegian	French	English	Norwegian
French	Biology	History	History	French	History

"I hope you won't find this too tough of a schedule. I realize you are all looking forward to the typical 5th year English Line schedule as your easiest year here and I will do everything I can to disappoint you."

"Engelsen, how is *fru* Engelsen," Arnulf asked playfully.

"She is well, thank you. I believe she is having much the same conversation with the 4th Year English line, for whom she is *klasseforstanden*."

"Are we on a regular schedule, today?" Randi asked.

"No, we will have short hours, today. But before I leave, I would like to offer a welcome from the faculty at Tromsø *gymnas* to Pete Dublin. I assume you are Pete?" Engelsen asked, turning in my direction.

"*Ja*," I answered with one of my better-known Norwegian phrases. With that one I didn't even have trouble with the pronunciation, and there was not much grammar to get wrong, either.

"*Velkommen*, Pete. I am glad to hear you speak Norwegian. I have already heard about your sign."

The class laughed as everyone looked in my direction. The sign was still hung around my neck, although it was folded. It was also the first period of the day, I had only opened the sign once, and that only ten minutes before. I found it difficult to believe the faculty would have heard about my sign already. I had left Westport hoping for popularity in Tromsø; I hadn't bargained for having my every move known almost before I made it.

"I do hope, however," Engelsen continued, "that you will not forget all of your English. As you can see, your schedule calls for eight hours of English instruction per week, and I do not allow Norwegian to be spoken in my English classes. Perhaps I will have to wear my own sign, in English, of course: Excuse me, but I do not understand Norwegian."

The class laughed as Engelsen left and a much more severe-looking man strode in. It was Andreassen, our Norwegian teacher, and he was as different from Engelsen as the midnight sun was from the darkness. If Engelsen reminded me of Ozzie Nelson, Andreassen reminded me of Ichabod Crane. He was tall, brusque, completely serious, and somewhat stooped. And I couldn't understand a word he said. He had a way of talking into his chest without looking at me or anyone else in the class. At one point he must have been listing the books we were supposed to buy, because I could make out the word "*bøker*." But that was about it. When he was done, he walked out as quickly as he walked in.

"What did he say?" I asked Jorunn.

"He is difficult to understand," Jorunn said, her face reflecting the understatement in her voice. "Even we Norwegians have some difficulty understanding Andreassen. He is a brilliant man, a scholar, but his teaching style leaves much to be desired and his speaking style makes his teaching style seem pretty good."

The school day continued that way, one teacher after the next with ten-minute breaks in between, until we left right after lunch. We all walked down the hill into town. As I left school, I took off my sign. I had a feeling I wouldn't need it again. The damn thing had worked. I had worn it all day, and opened it up maybe twenty or thirty times. By the end of the day, word had gotten around: Pete wouldn't speak English.

That evening, I sat down to write another letter. My letters often provided me with a way of reflecting on what was happening to me. As I shared my thoughts with family and friends, I often found I gained new insights into my experience.

In July I had begun a form letter to those family and friends I didn't write to personally.

August, 1961

Kjære Venn,

I think those first two words help to explain one of the bigger changes that has come over me in the past few days (they mean, by the way, "Dear Friend"). Starting with today, the first day of school, I speak only Norwegian. I stutter and stumble sometimes and I cannot always find the exact word I need, but I can usually say what I want, be understood, and understand what my friends say to me.

I Was a Teenage Norwegian

There are many different features in the school day here as compared to America. The gymnas is open from 7:30 in the morning (the first class begins at 8:30), but there is nothing resembling homeroom. Probably the main reason for this is that each class stays in the same room during the entire day and the teachers are the ones to walk. This means that we are with the same group of kids for every class during the entire year. Each class has one teacher more than any other teacher—the klasseforstanden—*and this teacher is the closest thing we have here to a homeroom teacher.*

Another interesting facet of gymnas *life in Norway (and one that all students in America would be anxious to have) is what is called "friminut-ter:" recess. After each forty-five minute class, all the students must go outside into the schoolyard for ten minutes. The theory is: fresh air is good for you; you must have fresh air. At least that was what Rektor Riksheim, the principal, explained to me.*

Almost all the classrooms are identical. The teacher sits at a desk which is on a slightly elevated platform in the front of the room. The students always rise when the teacher enters the room, and sometimes rise when the teacher leaves again. Other than that, their respect for their teachers seems to be on a personal basis (making it possible for students to play cards with one another in one of the classes). The relationships among the kids in the class are much closer and friendlier than in the American classes (perhaps because the same group of people has been together for two or three years) and all of my classmates are both friendly and helpful. I could not be luckier or happier than I am now.

Hilsen *(Greetings),*
Pete

Jorunn. Arnulf. Engelsen. Andreassen. The cast of characters in my life began to fill out. What a surprise I had for that school! What was in store for tomorrow? And the days after? I was actually beginning to feel a little optimistic. I was beginning to talk as if I really enjoyed myself in Tromsø. I had a great day; I felt proud of that. I switched to Norwegian and I made my mark on the school. I would probably be okay, as long as the rest of my teachers were more like Engelsen than they were like Andreassen.

-8-
Settling In

"*Hei*, Pete," Arnulf greeted me as I entered the *skolegård*. "*Kor det går?*"

"*Jeg forstår ikke*, I don't understand," I said, something I was already quite used to saying.

"It means...." Arnulf began to translate into English.

"*Nei, nei*," I interrupted quickly, remaining in Norwegian. "Tell me what it means in Norwegian. Explain in Norwegian; don't translate into English." That was another one of my strategies for insuring that no one ever slipped into English with me, and that I never slipped back into English myself.

Wearing that sign around my neck the first day of school was more of a sign of things to come than I had initially realized. It was a sign that I was to play a different role at the *gymnas* than I had played at Staples, that I would be viewed differently by my Norwegian classmates than I was viewed by my American classmates. But it was also a sign that I was different, not just that others viewed me differently. My inaction over the summer with the Románs may have reflected a part of me, but it had angered another part of me. That anger had built up, albeit silently, over the summer and had erupted that first day of school in a flurry of decisiveness. I would no longer be a victim of my linguistic passivity; I would decide my fate and my fate was to speak Norwegian.

"It means," Arnulf continued in Norwegian, too, "How are you doing? How is it going? How are you?" He used three different Norwegian phrases, all of which I understood, but none of which had the word "*kor*" in them.

"I don't understand '*kor*'."

"It's *Tromsøværing*," Johnny Ingebrigtsen, another kid in my class answered. There was by now a small group of us from *femte Engelsk*— the fifth year English Line—standing in the *skolegård*. I hadn't realized that my Norwegian class started before first period.

"I thought *Tromsøværing* referred to someone who lived in Tromsø," I said.

"It's both," Johnny continued. Johnny was also in my class: third seat from the front, in the row next to me. He was over six feet tall and had the longest hair of any of the boys in class. He combed the sides straight back, where they met in the back like a duck-tail; he wouldn't have looked at home in the intellectual group at Staples. "It means someone who is *from* Tromsø, but it also refers to the Tromsø dialect."

"I thought there were just two Norwegians," I said, undoubtedly showing my frustration at the prospect of there being a third.

"In a way you are right," Arnulf responded, looking professorial.

"For *you*, however," Johnny continued, "there's a third : *Tromsøværing*."

"It's really more of a dialect," Arnulf explained. "We use a lot of different words than *bokmål*; actually it sounds almost like *nynorsk*."

"If you're really going to be one of us," Johnny said, with something between conviction and humor in his voice, "you have to learn to speak *Tromsøværing*."

"You guys had better get going," Jorunn admonished us as she joined the group. "This Norwegian lesson is running over into our first real class of the day."

As we walked up the stairs into our classroom, my head swam. I couldn't understand any of my teachers as it was; was I now going to have trouble understanding my friends?

"*God morn*," Sætter, our history teacher greeted us as he wandered through the door with little sense of where he was.

"*God morn*," we responded in unison, standing up and sitting down in one motion. I already sensed a degree of ambivalence in that show of respect. There was an almost perfunctory aspect to the rising when the teacher entered the room. Was that a senior thing?

"We will study European history this year," Sætter began, "starting at approximately the 14th century. I realize you haven't had a chance to read anything yet, so I will begin by discussing some of the critical events of that period."

Within moments, Sætter had leaned back in his chair and was talking about the current election for the Norwegian Parliament. I feared that if he leaned back any further (or opened his eyes and saw what he was doing) he would fall right out of the chair and crack his head on the blackboard.

"What's he talking about?" I asked Arnulf.

"He's analyzing the positions of the conservative parties," Arnulf said slowly and distinctly, knowing that this was not the easiest of topics for me to understand in Norwegian.

"Is this European history?"

"This is Sætter," Randi answered with a broad grin. Arnulf had said he wanted to sit next to his girlfriend, Randi. She was taller than Arnulf by an inch or two, wore large-rimmed glasses, and looked somewhere between nervous and serious.

Toward the end of the morning, we had French, also with Engelsen.

"Is Engelsen the one you thought I would like?" I whispered to Jorunn as we sat down.

"*Ja,*" she answered. "He's firm, but friendly. He's smart, but he's also more sensitive than most Norwegian teachers. He's the closest teacher here to what I had, and what you probably had, in America."

"You were right. I like him. I'm sure glad he's the one we have the most."

"Pete," Engelsen addressed me in French. "Perhaps you can answer a question for me."

"*Jeg kan prøve,*" I answered. I can try.

"En francais, s'il vous plait," Engelsen requested me to speak in French.

"Je peux *prøve,*" I stumbled, to the howls of the other kids in the class.

I had studied French at Staples, and I was close to fluent, thanks to my mother. But here, I had to translate everything from French to Norwegian, not to English. It was clear from my stumbling over a simple answer that my mind was on my Norwegian, and it was not at all clear there was enough room in that mind for two foreign languages simultaneously.

"That's it for this morning," Johnny told me as Engelsen left the room. "We can eat lunch now. What did you bring?"

"*Geitost,*" I said proudly as I took my two *smørbrød* out of my *matpakke.*

"Ugh," Johnny scowled in disgust. "Do you really like that stuff? I can't stand it. Personally, I prefer peanut butter."

That couldn't be happening. *Nei,* that wasn't real. I had just spent three weeks of my life getting used to stuff I couldn't stand: two *smørbrød* a meal, three meals a day. People told me *geitost* was the Norwegian national food, and that everyone loved it and I had better love it too. And, during the first week of school I discovered that some kids didn't like it and didn't eat it.

"Arnulf," Bjørg Wilhelmsen said during our lunch-time conversation, "did you hear what the Labor Party says about the Common Market?"

"That it's not for the common man?" Arnulf laughed.

"Very funny. Very funny." Bjørg was our political intellectual. She had short, dark hair, glasses, and a serious look to her.

"Have you been able to follow the election at all, Pete," Randi asked me. Randi struck me as being a little ditsy, but then she surprised me with serious questions.

"I see the posters," I answered, "but I can't read the newspapers yet, and I can't really understand much of the news on the radio, either."

"Do our Norwegian elections strike you as different from your American elections?" Lillian Ingebrigtsen asked me. I sat in the last row between Lillian and Jorunn. She looked at me in the oddest way—as if she were laughing at me—but this was the first time she had spoken to me.

"They sure appear a lot different, even though I can't understand all the issues. If nothing else, they are a lot noisier."

"Elections are a big deal in Norway, especially in small towns like Tromsø," Pål Ytreberg explained. Pål was tall, dark, and handsome...as well as quiet. I hadn't heard him utter a word until then. He sat next to the window, staring out of it most of the time. Romantic? Poetic? Political? Politics touched all of those kids.

"We don't have anything else," Arnulf smiled, "way up here in the Arctic Circle. This is our only form of entertainment."

"Keep in mind," Pål explained, "that a big reason for that involvement is that there are six main political parties in Norway: Left, Right, Center, Communist, Socialist, and Labor. People get very excited about their party."

"Instead of having just the Democrats arguing against the Republicans," Arnulf began...

"Boring," Johnny interrupted, taking time off from his peanut butter *smørbrød*.

"...you have Labor against the Left, the Right against the Center, the Left against the Socialists, the Right against the Left, the Center against Labor, Left against center, Socialists against the Right, the Center against the Socialists...

"The Communists against all of the other parties," Johnny interrupted again.

"I wish," I said, "I knew a little more Norwegian; it sounds like great fun."

"Speaking of fun," Jorunn interjected, "fun is over. Andreassen is here."

After school, Jorunn asked if she could walk home with me. "It's not that far out of my way anyway."

"I'd like that," I said.

"How are things going with the Románs," Jorunn asked, never one to beat around the bush.

"I really never know. That's part of the problem. Sometimes everything feels fine; sometimes I'm not so sure.

"What about Karl Arvid?"

"I remember what you said about his being wild, but I still can't believe it. He's so quiet. I'm hoping that we may get closer when I can speak better Norwegian. There's no hostility between us...there's not much of anything between us."

"And Román and *fru* Román? Any change there?"

"I don't know that I'll ever be able to call Román *far*, but I do feel I get along a lot better with *fru* Román. We are not mother and son now, but we can talk to each other more and more. As my relationship with her becomes more stable, so does my relationship with the rest of the family."

"I'm glad things are better," Jorunn said as we reached the road where she walked up toward the top of the island. "I hope you'll feel free to talk to me about them. I want to help you get the most out of your year here."

"I know you do, Jorunn, and I really appreciate all the help. It makes things a lot easier for me having someone to talk to."

I was settling in with my Norwegian family. It had taken a while, and things weren't perfect, but I felt a degree of comfort I hadn't felt before. I could talk to everyone, I knew how to make my own *matpakke*, I took my shoes off when I entered the house, I knew where most everything was in the kitchen.

After dinner, I settled down to my evening homework; that was a problem. It wasn't because the work was so difficult or that I felt an overwhelming need to succeed; it was mostly because I didn't understand a word that I read. For example, my history textbook:

19

Det varte også nokså lenge før de fulgte eksemplet fra Storbritannia og begynte å nytte de nye maskinene; industrien var derfor lite utviklet.

Bare ved universitetene holdt minnene fra den store tid under frigjøringskrigen seg; her levde tankene om «Tysklands enhet og frihet» både hos professorer og studenter. Mange av dem hadde selv kjempet med i krigen, og i sine foreninger (B u r s c h e n s c h a f- t e n) sang de ennå krigs- og frihetssangene fra den tiden og drev fekte og turnøvinger for å stå ferdige når fedrelandet skulle trenge dem. Frigjøringskrigen hadde ikke ført til noen e n h e t. Men en stor forenkling hadde funnet sted: de 300 à 400 stater som landet hadde vært delt i før Napoleonskrigene, var nå redusert til 39, Østerrike medregnet. Videre var disse statene sammensluttet i et løst statsforbund, som fikk navnet D e t t y s k e f o r b u n d. Dets organ var f o r b u n d s d a g e n, som bestod av utsendinger fra de enkelte staters regjeringer. Den østerrikske utsending førte her forsetet. — Forbundets myndighet var sterkt begrenset, og behandlingsmåten på forbundsdagen langsom og innviklet. Forbundet fikk derfor liten betydning; de enkelte stater var suverene som før.

Med den politiske friheten stod det heller ikke rart til; for fyrstene hadde glemt sine løfter om fri forfatning. I nesten alle tyske stater var det enevelde, sensur og religionstvang.

PREUSSEN skulle synes best skikket til å ta førerskapet i Tyskland; det var ingen stat som etter 1815 hadde på langt nær så mange tyske undersåtter. Som grensestat både mot Russland og Frankrike kom Preussen i tyskernes øyne til å stå som deres vakt både mot øst og vest. Preussen hadde alminnelig verneplikt, og dets utpregede embetsstyre var iallfall samvittighetsfullt og velordnet. Enda mer fikk det å si at Preussen i årene etter 1815 gikk i spissen for en viktig reform av Tysklands tollforhold. I 1818 hadde det av praktiske grunner opphevet

81

I Was a Teenage Norwegian

On that one page, I had to underline forty words. Forty words on one page and my assignment was to read over twenty pages. That second night of school, I worked on my homework for over four hours. My record during the first week of school was one and one-half hours to read half a page from my Norwegian Literature text. That couldn't go on.

"*God morn,*" Johansen said to the class on my first-ever school on Saturday.

"*God morn,*" we answered. Gymnastics was the only class where we didn't have to stand up when the teacher entered the room. First of all, that was one of the few classes where we went to the teacher instead of the teacher coming to our room. Second, that was the only class where we remained standing almost all the time anyway.

"We are going to work on some tumbling, today," Johansen began. "We'll need these mats pulled over near the horse," Johansen said. Some of the boys did as he asked, and others just kept talking to themselves,or wandering around the gym as if Johansen wasn't even there.

The gym was tiny, more like an oversized classroom than a gym. There were no basketball nets, and no equipment except for some old gymnastics apparatus and a few mats.

"Let's form a line and vault over the horse, please," Johansen requested. Some of the boys were quite athletic, strong in the arms, and graceful. Arnulf was not one of them, and he crawled over the horse. Johnny didn't even run up to the horse; he walked up to it and then around it. I didn't know whether what I saw was typical Norwegian behavior in gym class, or if the behavior was reserved especially for Johansen. When it was my turn, I ran up to the horse, placed my hands on it, pushed hard, and knocked the horse over. It wasn't that I had joined my classmates in their antics; it was just that gymnastics had never been one of my better sports.

"Pete," Johnny said as we walked back to our own classroom from the gym, "We have inspection today."

"What's inspection?" I asked.

"You know how we have *friminutter* after every class?"

"Right. Fresh air is healthy for you so you must go outside.

"What you probably think of as lunch," Johnny continued, "we simply call our big *friminutter, storefriminutter.* Everyone except the seniors has to go outside then, too, and it's the seniors' responsibility to make sure that everyone else is out of the building during the *storefriminutter.*"

"And that's inspection?" I asked.

"That's inspection," Pål answered.

"And it's your turn today," Arnulf smiled.

"Okay. Sure. Do I eat lunch first or do inspection first?"

"Inspection first," all three said in unison.

I didn't see inspection as such a big deal. All the kids knew they had to be outside. I would just walk around to all the classrooms, and make sure the kids were out. If they weren't out, I knew how to say "Please go outside." That was a short sentence.

As I wandered through the building, my expectations were confirmed: most of the kids were already outside. The few I met went outside themselves as soon as I asked. No problems on the first floor. No problems on the second floor. A piece of cake; I could do anything. It was on the third floor that I encountered a classroom, immediately over our own, where there were eight or ten kids still inside...eating their lunches.

"Please go outside," I said.

"Why?" one of the boys asked.

This was going to be a little harder. I had practiced saying "Please go outside," but I hadn't thought through an answer to that question.

"It's the *storefriminutter* and everyone has to go outside."

"Why?" the same kid asked again. He was definitely annoying me.

"Fresh air is healthy for you so you must go outside," I answered, hoping this was some standard kind of response that everyone knew, understood, and acknowledged as the truth. If, however, that was an excuse they used only on ignorant Americans, I might be in trouble.

"Who are you, anyway?" one of the girls asked belligerently.

"I'm Pete." I had assumed everyone in the school knew who I was.

"And why aren't you outside," another girl asked, equally seriously, "if everyone has to go outside."

"I'm a senior," I answered proudly, boasting of my new-found status.

"So are we," they said, unable to control their laughter. "This is the Fifth Year Mathematics Line. Why don't you get your lunch, bring it up here, and we can introduce ourselves."

There was a part of me that was worried about joining them for lunch; I couldn't be sure what other tricks they might have up their Norwegian sleeves. But I figured if I were invited, it was only polite to accept.

"I see you, too, have *geitost* in your *matpakke*," one of the boys said to me smiling. I felt a little more relaxed, but I was still cautious. "My name is Gunnar. Gunnar Brox."

Gunnar struck me as a happy-go-lucky kind of guy. He talked quickly; he didn't slow down for me. He was one of the boys pulling my leg about inspection; the jury would stay out for a while on Gunnar.

"Don't mind Gunnar," one of the other boys said. "He only looks friendly. My name is Franck. Franck Pettersen."

If Franck had played American football, he would have made a perfect tight end. He had a dramatic air about him: he cut the air with his hands when he talked, he sat up straight when he ate, and he had a deep, resonating voice. He was all smiles as he talked to me, but he was right in there with Gunnar pulling my leg.

"Listen, Pete," one of the other boys said. "You have to be careful with tall Norwegians. They are not to be trusted. You don't have to be afraid of Odd and me; we're short. By the way, I'm Per. Per Sparboe,"

I Was a Teenage Norwegian

"Other than us," Gunnar asked, "How are things going for you?"

"*Bra*," I answered. Fine. "Inspection has been the most difficult time so far in school. Actually, *inspection* was fine; *you* were the problem."

"We had heard about you," Franck said, "and we had seen you in the *skolegård*. All we needed was a chance to meet you."

"Your Norwegian sounds pretty good," Odd remarked. "I heard about your sign."

"I haven't heard," Per offered, "that business about fresh air being healthy for you since elementary school. That was pretty amusing."

"That's what Rektor Riksheim told me," I answered. "It was all I could think of. I can't say much in Norwegian yet."

"You're doing okay," Franck said. "Did you know any Norwegian before you came here?"

"*Nei.*"

"Nothing?"

"Not a word," I answered.

"I think it's pretty impressive," Per added. "But we will have to work on your *Tromsøværing*."

I was settling in with my Norwegian school. It had taken a surprisingly few days, and I felt surprisingly comfortable already. I had my seat in my class, I recognized most of my classmates, I had encountered all of my teachers (even if I couldn't understand them all), and I had passed muster with one of the other senior classes (even if only barely).

One of the ways in which school there was noticeably different from what I was used to, was that I could leave the *gymnas* if I didn't have a class; and there were no study halls. Students at the *gymnas* were a little older than students at Staples. I walked down the hill *til byen*.

I had heard there was USIS—United States Information Service—office on the second floor of a small building adjacent to the Tor Insurance Company building where Román worked. Right next door was Pedersen's bakery, but I didn't want to spoil my lunch.

The office was small and looked like a library. There were American newspapers—all of which were weeks old—and the International Herald Tribune, which was only days old. And, there were shelves full of American books.

"You must be Pete," a tall, boyish-looking man addressed me in Norwegian.

"*Ja*," I answered in Norwegian. I didn't recognize the man at all.

"Don't be surprised that I know who you are," he continued. "Tromsø is a small town. We know within a day or two when someone new comes to town, especially an AFS exchange student. I have seen you eight or ten times already, but I thought I'd wait until you found us here to introduce myself. My name is Appelbaum and I'm the USIS officer here in Tromsø."

"*Det gleder meg*," I said as we shook hands. There were two ways in which shaking hands in Norway was different from shaking hands in America. First, if you were sitting down, you stood up to shake hands. Second, you were supposed to nod your head when you shook hands. It wasn't exactly a bow, just a little nod of the head. It made the whole process feel more formal; in fact, it made me feel a little Norwegian when I did it. I just hoped I was getting it right.

"Feel free to read the newspapers if you want," Appelbaum continued. "A lot of Americans are following Roger Maris."

"Roger Maris?" I asked.

"The baseball player."

"I know. But why?"

"*Han slår mange* home run," Appelbaum answered, using the American expression as there was no Norwegian equivalent. Soccer was THE sport in Norway; they didn't even know how to play baseball, let alone follow it. I didn't know what was going on with Roger Maris, but I was curious.

I couldn't believe what I was reading. Roger Maris and Mickey Mantle—both on the Yankees—were in a home run race. It looked as if they would both hit more than 50 home runs in one season, and Maris had a chance to beat Babe Ruth's season record of 60 home. Maris already had fifty three. I hadn't completely left America, although Roger Maris' quest to break Babe Ruth's home run record was my last tie to America.

* * * * * * * * * * * * * * * * * * * *

Within the first two weeks of school I was already thinking about a second girl. I had enjoyed myself immensely with Marit at the party and

I Was a Teenage Norwegian

I could still taste the kiss on her neck. It was an evening filled with conflicting emotions: pride (that I had managed at all), joy (from the pleasure of the party), desire (for Marit), and guilt (because I had lied about Sue). But the heat of that moment was replaced by a sense of promise. Girls smiled at me all the time in the *skolegård*. I could hardly walk fifteen or twenty feet up and down Storgate without some girl saying hello and smiling genuinely. And now there was Gunn Mathisen. I wasn't in love or anything. It was just that she, Gunn, was phenomenally cute and always happy and always smiling. And, when I met her we always got to joking around, doing funny things, saying funny things, and laughing and having a good time. We met occasionally in town.

"*Hei*, Pete."

"*Hei*, Gunn. *Hvordan går det?*" How's it going?

"*Det går bra*," Gunn answered. Fine. "Have you seen Elin Fosse?"

"*Nei*," I answered. "Where is she?"

"She's working after school at the bookstore. Can you believe it? Elin working at a bookstore."

"What do you think? Perhaps a visit?"

"Great idea. It's just down the street next to the *kino*."

"That's the store," Gunn pointed across the street.

"I remember," I said. "That's where I got my textbooks."

"When I think of Elin," Gunn smiled, thinking of Elin, "it's not exactly books I think of. Let's go."

We raced across the street, never bothering to look for cars. This was, after all, Tromsø: no cars, even in Storgate.

"Can you see her?" Gunn asked, slightly out of breath.

"She's over there, to the left. She's helping someone."

"Let's wait," Gunn suggested, "until she gets closer to us. Wait until she's behind the counter right in front of us."

"Then what?" I asked.

"Then we stick our noses up against the window and make funny faces. Let's see her keep a straight face with her customers, then."

Which was exactly what we did. Boy, did we get Elin. She was talking to a customer and by chance looked in our direction. She laughed so hard, I thought she was going to collapse on the floor. The customer didn't have the faintest idea what was going on.

I was still not completely used to the social routine in Tromsø, but certain features emerged, at least regarding social life at night during the week. Nothing was planned and people walked *til byen*. When I got *til byen*, I walked up and down Storgate. When I met other kids that I knew, we stopped to talk; we did not just say hello in passing as we did after school. Sometimes kids decided to go off to a *kafé* for drinks and food, but that hadn't happened to me often.

"*Hei*, Pete," Jorunn greeted me as we stopped to talk one evening toward the end of the second week of school.

"*Hei*, Jorunn," I responded.

"Do you want to walk together?" Jorunn asked me. "I hear you're buying your books from Elin Fosse, now." Word traveled fast in a small town.

Jorunn and I spent a lot of time together, both in and out of school. We often ate lunch together and we often walked *til byen* together after school.

"*Hei*, Pete," Arnulf greeted me. He was with Johnny and Pål from 5GE.

"*Hei, dokker.*" It was one of my first words in *Tromsøværing*. '*Dokker*' was used for the plural 'you,' and it meant something like 'you guys.'"

"We were thinking of going to the *kino*," Arnulf continued. "Do you want to come with us?"

"*Ja*," I agreed. "What's playing?"

"It's an American movie: *On the Beach*."

"Oh," I said, slightly disappointed. "I've seen it already."

"No problem," Arnulf answered. "See it again, and this time you can read the *norsk* sub-titles. It's a great way to learn *norsk*."

I didn't learn huge amounts of *norsk* that evening, but the movie certainly did provide me with the beginning of a letter home.

September 11, 1961

Dear Mom and Dad,

I saw the movie "On the Beach" tonight. It made me think about how I want to spend my life. I first wanted to be a lawyer (remember eighth grade?) because I liked to argue with people. Then I thought of the Unitarian ministry, partly because I thought that I could help people that way. But, after seeing this movie, I want to help people in a different way. I do not merely want to help people lead happier lives while I aid them in their search of the truth. I want to permit them to live.

I do believe that this world has the potential to do and be good. It has the potential to be bad, unfair, unjust, cruel, and on and on, but I feel that it has the same potential to work in a constructive way toward the bettering of this Earth. And, I want to be a part of the large force it will inevitably take to prevent the picture of a stark, naked San Francisco depicted in the movie.

Many kids say, as I just heard one of my Norwegian classmates say again this evening after the movie, "It is just a matter of time before that will happen to us here."

There is so much that has to be done to insure continued peace and tranquility for the rest of time, and all this person can do is shrug his shoulders and accept the philosophy that bad can only turn to worse. Why does he not say that the world is not faring too well these days, and what can I do to make it better?

It hurt me so much walking home tonight wanting to do what I can but not knowing what I can do and what must be done. What is of paramount importance now, is to continue to merely live and gain everything I can from life now so that I can put it to use later.

Oh, why the hell should I go on speaking? Speaking such as I have done now is not worth anything by itself; it must be followed by action. And I do

I Was a Teenage Norwegian

not even have any ideas as to what I can do. But my chin shall stay up, even if I must work toward an unmarked goal by unmarked means. "When there is so much to do and so few that are doing it, even I, a mere individual, a mere personification of the race, am important."

All my love,
Pete

The next day I walked to the USIS office. I read the International Herald Tribune and discovered that Maris had hit Number 54.

That evening, there was an AFS*møte*, an AFS meeting. Our task was to begin the process of selecting a student to be an AFS finalist for next year. There were five of us on the committee. Adele Berg was still the chair of the committee, although she would be leaving Tromsø within a few weeks to study in Germany. Liz Arnett—our *norsk* language teacher from Trollvasshytta—had finally arrived in Tromsø, where she was a student at the Teachers College; she would be taking over for Adele when she left. Jorunn was on the committee because she was an AFSer in the United States the previous year. Finally, there was Knut Følstad, another returning AFSer, although he was in the 4th Year.

There were thirteen applicant papers; I managed to read seven of them in the time it took the others to read all thirteen. Many of the essays read as if they were written by thirteen or fourteen year-olds. Perhaps it was just that some kids couldn't write well; maybe they didn't get as much training as I got in the States. Maybe I was being too critical.

Jorunn and I started to walk home together at 11:30. We shared about five minutes of the same road on our way to our separate homes.

"Do you notice how dark it is getting," Jorunn said, looking at the setting sun.

"In another few weeks," I said, "I bet we can see stars at 11:30."

"We're going to have our first *russefest* next weekend," Jorunn announced, as we walked slowly together. "You're a *russ* now, a real senior, and there is nothing *russ* like better than a *fest*."

"That's great," I said. I had heard about *russefest* ever since school started, and finally the first one was upon us.

"*God natt*," Jorunn bid me good night as we parted. Jorunn headed up the hill toward her house and I bore off to the right for the Románs. As she left I had an eerie and scary thought: Did Jorunn like me?

I was settling in with my Norwegian girls. It had taken less than two weeks, although I was not completely comfortable with either my success or my feelings. I had been to my first party, I had kissed my first Norwegian girl and I was playing and having fun with someone who was more than just a friend. I thought that Jorunn might like me in that way, also, and I was too happy to let thoughts of Sue get in my way.

-9-
The First Russefest

With thoughts of Marit, Gunn, Jorunn, and Sue sloshing around in my mind, I went to the USIS office again the following day; I felt a compelling need to see how Maris was doing. According to the International Herald Tribune, he was up to 55. He could actually do it; he might actually break Babe Ruth's record!

Sue remained one of the big question marks as I headed off into the unknown year ahead. I felt I loved her, but I had no sense of what would happen when I was away for a whole year. There was nothing much I could do about it; I was going away. We had talked about it a lot; we thought we could do it, stay together when we were apart. At least that was what we both said and that was what we planned to do. My father didn't think it was such a good idea—he thought I should keep my options open—but it was what Sue and I said we wanted.

Actually, I didn't have the faintest idea what I wanted. With hindsight, it is clear to me now that what I *wanted* was not the governing issue. What mattered was what I *needed*. I wanted to go to Norway; I wanted to leave Westport. That was why I went. But I was much more afraid, and I had many more doubts and self-doubts, than I ever sensed. Feeling that Sue was my girlfriend, feeling that I had a girlfriend, enabled me to leave for Norway while still leaving a little part of me behind in the States.

Whatever it was exactly that was churning around inside me, Sue was at its core.

September 18, 1961

Sue Dear,

There are two things I need to talk to you about. First of all that seemingly age-old problem of the "friendliness of the Tromsøværing.*" I'll try to list the pros and cons. First of all, it is fun to hold hands with a girl, but I am a little afraid. Second of all, everyone else does it and I should just accept holding hands or keeping your arm around the girl's waist at the end of a dance (and she keeps hers on my shoulder) as the custom it is and no more, but I am not sure I would feel right doing it, and I feel that things like that*

I Was a Teenage Norwegian

should be worth a little more. But you said you would accept holding hands as a symbol of friendship and that is all it means to them. This is the conversation I was having between the devil and angel within me...but the big problem is to decide who is the devil and who is the angel. I just cannot figure this out and I do not know what I can do to help the problem. I think I will speak to Jorunn Pettersen, for she is about the best person I could talk to.

The second thing is that I missed you and wanted to be with you more than I ever have. I was listening to some quiet music on the radio and thought of the time we were driving back from New York in the rain. I thought of that weekend because we listened to Johnny Mathis together, but my thoughts were with that drive. It was nothing special maybe, but I won't forget it for a while. As I look at it now, it was the greatest time we ever spent together for there was nothing that happened, but it was just you and me who were doing nothing. And God, I thought of that and missed you so much that I almost broke down. The feeling was so powerful inside of me that I could not take it and I had to turn off the radio. It was awful, but it was beautiful. Maybe it was love....

All my love,
Pete

I walked *til byen* after school the next day and visited first, as had become my pattern over the past week or so, the USIS office. For someone who was becoming a teenage Norwegian, I was surprised at my continued interest in Roger Maris and his quest to break Babe Ruth's single-season home run record. I was informed that Maris was up to 56 home runs; he needed only four more to tie, and five to break the record. There must have still been a little bit of the American left in me, even then.

I had a chance to talk with Jorunn sooner than I had imagined, as we met walking up and down Storgate and she agreed to walk home with me; it was more or less on her way.

"I've been thinking a lot," I began in English, "about the upcoming *russefest* and my first *fest.*" This was the first time in over two weeks that I had spoken English; the stuff was too important for me not to talk about and impossible to talk about in *norsk.*

"What is bothering me is the fact that all the kids here are very friendly with one another."

"Why is that bothering you?"

"I can't figure out whether or not I should join you in that friendliness. How friendly should I get with all of you?"

"But you can do whatever is comfortable for you. You can be like us, or you can be like you have always been. We will be your friend in either case. You don't have to be like us to be liked by us."

"I understand that. I know you guys have accepted me and the choice is entirely mine. I have so much trouble explaining this; I just can't do it."

"You know, Pete," Jorunn explained, "the kids here are friendly with each other—as you put it—because they are such good friends; that's all it is."

"The sense I get from watching," I said, "is that everything you do—except for the few couples that are going steady—is done in fun, with no seriousness intended."

"Of course. I haven't told you but I'm going with Tore who is in the Army. But I'll still hold hands with some of the *russ* boys because they are my good friends. It's just an indication of our affection for each other, nothing more. In fact, it's fun holding hands."

"I guess that's what I'm not sure about," I stumbled, up the hill and in the conversation. "I'm not sure I can do this because I may be a little too afraid."

"Afraid of having fun?" Jorunn asked.

"Well, actually," I reluctantly agreed, "there have been some times when I had fun and there have been some groups of kids I had fun with. I'm really glad I have you to talk to Jorunn; you make it possible for me to see all the problems and responsibilities and tensions that are within me."

"You have to see them to get rid of them," Jorunn said.

"I knew this girl last year; she showed me the need for physical expression as a means of relieving inner tensions. She used to jump, do gymnastics, and take judo lessons, but I imagine hitting a wall or yelling would do the trick."

"What about here, in Tromsø?"

"That's the problem, I guess. I cannot yell here in Norway. I have no physical outlet whatsoever. I can't yell at *fru* Román or Bergljot; I don't have a younger brother to beat up on. When I become unhappy, I just stay that way because it is difficult to relieve such tensions."

"You're home," Jorunn said as we reached the Román's house. "I guess it still doesn't feel like home, does it?"

"*Nei*, I guess not," I answered. "I can't really yell. But I do appreciate that you talk with me. That really helps a lot. *Takk. Tusen takk.* I don't know what's more than 1,000 in *norsk.*"

"You're having a tough time, Pete," Jorunn said, "but you're doing pretty well; you really are. You're going to make it; you're going to do just fine."

"We're ready for dinner, Pete," *fru* Román announced as I came through the door and took off my shoes.

"What's for *middag*, for dinner?" I asked.

"*Torsk og poteter*," she answered. Boiled cod and boiled potatoes, I muttered to myself. Again. Once or twice a week, that was our *middag*. Most of the other days it was just another kind of fish. I hadn't been fond of fish when I left America, but I didn't actually hate it. It was a lucky thing for me that I didn't hate fish, because we had fish four or five times a week. And it was always boiled and it was always served with potatoes. And the potatoes were always boiled. The only real choice was whether or not *fru* Román peeled the potatoes before or after she boiled them.

"How was school today?" Román asked.

"It was fine," I answered.

"And for you, Karl Arvid?"

"Fine."

"Will you play with me after *middag*?" Bergljot asked.

"*Ja*," I answered. Bergljot was still the fun part of this family for me. I assumed everyone else meant well, and I did get along with the family a little better now than over the summer, but I still didn't get the feeling that they really cared about me, even when they asked questions. I was used to more conversation, especially at meals; that was the way it was in Westport. Now that I was in school and I was making lots of new friends, it wasn't as much of a problem not having such a great family. I could manage.

After school the next day, I made my daily pilgrimage to the USIS office to check on the progress of slugger Roger Maris. Maris had 57, Mayor Wagner won re-election in New York City, and we were still yelling at, and warning, the Russians as they continued to eat up the Free World. I felt perfectly safe in Tromsø. Well, perhaps not perfectly safe; I still had a need to cling onto my last remnant of American culture. I had grown up as a Brooklyn Dodger fan; I was one of those who never forgave them for moving to Los Angeles. Otherwise, I would never have been caught dead following one Yankee struggling to beat another Yankee's record, no matter how historical the quest. And now it was this little piece of baseball history that provided me a last piece of connective tissue to my past.

"Are you all set for the *russefest* this evening?" Jorunn asked me in school the following Saturday morning. I was still having a little trouble adjusting to going to school on Saturday, even if it was only half-day and we got out at 1:00 PM

"I guess so," I answered somewhat tentatively. I was tentative, in part, because I always approached parties tentatively, even with my initial success with Marit. Would I have to dance? Would girls dance with me? In addition, I was tentative because of Sue. I wrote her every few weeks, but she never responded. That worried me: Did she still love me? Did she ever think of me? Was she still my girlfriend?

"Oh, don't worry," Arnulf assured me. "It will be lots of fun."

"This is what being a *russ* is all about," Johnny explained. "Your last year of *gymnas* is supposed to be a study year, but it's really a *fest* year."

"It's just that I never really go to parties in America."

"Well," Arnulf said, "this definitely isn't America, is it? This is Tromsø. And this is not just a *fest*, is it? This is a *russefest*! And this isn't just a *russefest*, is it? This is the first *russefest*!"

"The *fest* is out at Nyløkken Kafé," Johnny said. "It's one of the *kafés* out of town a bit, toward the southern tip of the island. Do you know where it is?"

"*Nei*," I answered. "I've only been to the *kafés* right in town."

"Look," Arnulf offered. "I'm walking out to it anyway and the Román's house is on my way. I can pick you up and we can walk together. OK?"

"That would be great," I answered with some relief.

After dinner that evening, the talk turned to the *russefest* again.

"I hear," Karl Arvid said, "that the first *russefest* is this evening. I assume you are going,"

"I guess so," I responded.

"What are you wearing?" he asked.

"I don't know. What am I supposed to wear? This is my first *russefest*."

"I think," *fru* Román suggested, "that you should wear one of your jackets and a tie. I don't think you will need your suit."

I Was a Teenage Norwegian

Well, wasn't that a shame, I thought to myself. Wouldn't Mom be upset that I didn't get another chance to wear my "charcoal grey" suit? Since the funeral, I hadn't been required to take that sucker out of the closet and it looked as if it would stay put in there, where it belonged, for a good while longer. Sorry, Mom.

"I think that sounds right," Karl Arvid agreed with his mother. "Even though it's the first *russefest*, you don't really have to get that dressed up for it."

"Where is the *russefest*?" Román asked.

"At the Nyløkken Kafé," I answered.

"That's a nice spot," she commented.

"There's plenty of room for dancing," Karl Arvid added. "Did they explain any of this to you, about the *kafé* I mean?"

"*Nei.*"

"What happens is that the seniors rent the *kafé* for the evening," Karl Arvid continued. The conversation was turning into the longest conversation Karl Arvid and I had ever had. He was actually explaining something to me. I was amazed. "That way they have it all to themselves. They don't have to pay money for rent, but they can't bring their own beer. The *kafé sells* the *russ* beer and they have the *kafé* all to themselves. And that's how there is enough room for dancing."

"What if you don't drink beer?" I asked.

"You can buy *brus*, soda," Román answered. "Solo or Coca Cola, you know."

The beer thing was one of the aspects of the *russefest* that worried me. I heard from everyone that there was always a lot of drinking at *russefester*. The legal drinking age was eighteen in Norway and all the *russ* (except me) were over eighteen. They would have let me drink; that wasn't the problem. The problem was that I had never much liked the taste of beer.

The end result was that I didn't drink and I didn't want to drink. But I was in a culture where, apparently, people drank a lot, particularly *russ* at their *russefester*. I hadn't talked about this with anyone and I was worried that my friends would think I was a prude, or that I was critical of them for their drinking habits. Along with the worry was inexperience: I didn't really know what it was like to be around drunken kids. I never got invited to any parties in Westport, where lots of kids drank, even though the legal drinking age was twenty-one. I would have to jump off that bridge when I came to it, and it looked as if I would come to it that very evening.

"Pete," *fru* Román yelled upstairs at a little after 7:00 PM. "Someone is here for you at the door."

"*Hei*, Arnulf," I said when I saw him.

"Are you ready," he smiled.

"I guess so," I answered, still somewhat tentatively.

"You'd better wear a coat over your jacket," Arnulf suggested. "It's not too cold out, but we have a bit of a walk. At least a half hour."

That part of life in Tromsø, at least, I was used to: walking. As far as I knew, none of the *russ* had a car; at least I hadn't seen any of them driving, although they were all over eighteen and probably had their licenses. It wasn't even that common to take the buses, although there were plenty of them, going all over the island and even back onto the mainland; I certainly hadn't taken one. All of my friends walked...everywhere. Walking was fine with me.

Although I had been to the southern end of the island when I went to the *badestrand* with the Románs, I hadn't ever walked there. Arnulf and I passed the *gymnas* and headed down to Storgate. We walked to the Grand Hotel, the point at which we turned back when we walked up and down Storgate. We continued south past the Grand Hotel, past the brewery, past all of the stores. Then the hospital was on our right, the water separating Tromsøy and the mainland was on our left, and the wind was whipping off the water. Arnulf was right about wearing a coat. We walked along the water's edge most of the way, mostly through single family houses, in which most people in Tromsø lived. It must have been two or three miles because the walk took us close to forty-five minutes.

"Here we are," Arnulf announced as we approached a small, wooden building just off the road and in the midst of a small woods. "Nyløkken."

The *kafé* had two rooms. There was a food counter in the near room, which was full of tables and chairs...just what one would expect in a *kafé*. The other, larger room, had all the tables and chairs pushed to the outside, leaving a large space for dancing...just as Karl Arvid had described.

"Well," Arnulf responded, "*russefester* are a big part of senior life and most of the *russ* usually come. Remember, there are three lines at the *gymnas*: English, Math, and Natural Sciences. I don't even think you've been in the Natural Science Line's room, have you?"

"*Nei*, just the Math Line, when I was on inspection."

"Oh, yeah," Arnulf laughed. "I heard about that. Gunnar got you good, didn't he? All together there are sixty *russ* at the *gymnas*."

"It looks like," I observed, "that there are probably forty to forty-five of them here tonight."

Right from the start, I merely sat and watched and thought. It usually took something, or someone, to get me off my ass and get going. The main reason was that I felt a little lost and I found it easier being alone.

One evening, at a party on the SEVEN SEAS, I found myself in a similar situation. "Joan," I asked one of my new-found friends. "Am I making a complete ass of myself."

"You sure are," Joan answered without a moment's hesitation. "I don't think I've ever seen someone so full of self pity. Here you are, one of 800 kids chosen to go abroad with AFS. And you go moping around the ship pitying yourself. What do you have to pity? You're pitiful the way you pity yourself.

"I've never seen someone with so much going for him who has so little self-confidence, either," Joan was on a roll and had no intention of stopping. "Your pessimism dominates you; you have a pessimistic lack of self-confidence. Are you making an ass of yourself? You sure are!

"Listen, Pete," Joan continued, never letting up, "just be yourself; people will like you for who you really are. All of you. I do."

"*Hei*, Pete," Per, one of the boys from the Mathematics Line, said as he put his arm around my shoulder. "What are you doing sitting over here by yourself? And you don't even have anything to drink. Odd, get this boy a beer." Per barely managed to stay on his feet; his arm was draped over my shoulder more for his support than as an act of friendship.

"Really," I said, quite quietly, "it's okay."

"*Nei*, Pete," Per slurred, "this is our first *russefest*. How can you be a real *russ* at your first *russefest* and not get drunk?"

"What are you," Odd chimed in, "some kind of damn Yankee? This is Tromsø and you are a *russ*, isn't that so?"

"I don't really like beer," I said, without much emphasis or conviction.

"*Hei*, you guys," Johnny from my class joined us. He was clearly a little drunk, too. "Pete's okay. A real *Tromsøværing*. He doesn't have to drink *Mackøl* to be a *russ*. Have you heard of *Mackøl* before," Johnny asked me.

"*Nei*, I don't think so."

"It's our local brew, beer from the Mack brewery. It's the best beer in Norway. Don't tell me you don't have *Mackøl* in the US?"

"I guess not," I responded.

"They'll leave you alone, now," Johnny said with a grin, as we walked over to the food counter to get me a Solo. "Odd and Per are fun, but they get a little rowdy when they're drunk...which they will be most of the time at our *russefester*. You'll get to like them more as you get to know them better, even when they're sober."

"Thanks for helping me out," I said. "I'm still not used to all this drinking."

"We are brought up drinking *øl* and even *brennevin*, our aquavit," Johnny explained as we sat down at a table. "A lot of Americans I have met feel that drinking is bad, but we are not brought up to think that at all.

"It's kind of interesting," Arnulf said as he joined us, *Mackøl* in hand. "In Norway, we tell the kids it's okay to drink a beer, and they do. In America, you tell the kids it's not okay to drink a beer, they rebel, and drink it anyway. Two different ways of bringing up kids, and they both have the same result: drunken teenagers."

"Does it make any difference, " I wondered out loud, "that it's legal for you to buy drinks?"

"I don't notice much difference," Arnulf observed. "Even our lack of guilt doesn't prevent us from having fun."

I hadn't been to many Americans parties, but I was surprised to see that virtually nothing was broken; there was little damage or destruction, outside of a couple of broken glasses. And the kids didn't *appear* drunk— with two notable sleeping exceptions—merely a little high. Even more surprising was the music. They played a lot of records, mostly American songs. It was difficult for me to become a *norsk russ* at a *russefest* when so much of the music was American rock 'n' roll. What was neat, however, was that there was a band: a two-piece band, comprised of a guitar and an accordion. I couldn't be sure whether that was something special to a *russefest*, special to that *russefest*, and exception to every rule, or something typically Norwegian. I felt as if I might spend half of my year in Tromsø discovering toothbrushes in the back pocket of dentists' sons.

Although there was a lot of dancing, there was no making out. I wouldn't say absolutely none, because I noticed that various couples at various times went outside to "watch the stars" for a couple of minutes. But mostly, the kids danced. There were few couples; there was more of a communal spirit. I got the feeling that those kids had grown up together. It was just real friendly; I guess that was the best word for it.

"Pete," Jorunn interrupted my reverie, "you look a little sad. Some of the other kids are worried that you are not enjoying yourself."

"Oh, I'm fine."

"We are worried because you are just sitting and not dancing. Would you like to go outside and talk a little?"

"*Ja*," I said, feeling happier at the prospect of talking with Jorunn than I probably sounded.

"Is the reason you are not dancing because of any AFS pressure you feel on your shoulders?" Jorunn asked bluntly. Jorunn had been through this herself.

"I guess," I began somewhat uncomfortably, "there are just some times when it is easier for me to be alone." It was always difficult for me to know how honest I could be with others, especially my Norwegian friends. Then there was the question of how honest I could be with myself.

"It's difficult for us to understand why someone wants to be alone in the middle of a *fest*. That's why so many of us are worried that you are not having a good time."

"Actually...." For one of the few times since school started, I switched to English. I felt it necessary to *say* something, not merely *talk*. "It's more complicated than that. Before I came to Norway, I had a girl-friend and for the past six or eight months I have been 'off.'"

"That's an expression I never heard before," Jorunn looked puzzled.

"It's one I made up," I responded. "It means I am off sex. I can't kiss a girl unless I have very strong feelings for her. It's a philosophy that my girlfriend has, and I have adopted it, too."

I Was a Teenage Norwegian

"That's difficult for me to understand," Jorunn said sympathetically. "As you know, I am going steady with a Tromsø boy who lives in Southern Norway now. I love Tore very much, but that doesn't mean I can't have fun with my classmates this year. Being friendly with the boys here doesn't in any way affect my love for Tore."

That was an eye-opener, a light bulb. It was one of those moments when a lot of confusing data suddenly made sense. I had watched Jorunn off-and-on during the evening. She danced with everyone and was real friendly with lots of the boys...about as friendly as she could get without making out. I put that together with how friendly she was with me, perhaps even more than friendly, and I realized my sense of reality conflicted dramatically with hers. The two cultures clashed, and the clash had clouded my observations and judgment.

"I just don't think," I said, stuck in my own parochial mindset, "that I can turn it on and off like that. I respect you for being able to do it, perhaps, because it is too difficult for me to do. It's not just that I like Sue and that I feel I should be true to her, and all that; I'm just not sure how good or right it is for me to get *too* friendly with girls."

"Well," Jorunn suggested, the wiser and more pragmatic of the two of us, "let's go back inside and see if we can at least dance together. How's that sound?"

"That sounds great," I said smiling a little.

"*Hei*, Jorunn," Bjørg from our class yelled out after Jorunn and I finished our first dance. "Don't I get a turn, too?"

"I hope there's enough of me for everyone," I joked sheepishly." So Bjørg and I danced for a while, and before I knew it, I had danced and joked for the next two hours. I certainly had more fun during those two hours than I did during the first two. What was particularly gratifying was how interested so many of those kids were in insuring that I had a good time. Some of their habits (drinking) I couldn't accept, and others (being as "friendly" as they were) I wasn't sure I could handle, but I was happy and I was lucky to be with such a caring group of kids.

"Rest assured," Jorunn said, "I and the others will work on your shyness and see to it, dance by dance, that you dance more and have more and more fun. We're going to make sure that someday soon you will be able to just throw your arms around a girl in the center of the dance floor, and kiss her just because you feel like it. Who knows, maybe someday I'll just throw my arms around you and kiss you just because I feel like it."

"Is that what I have to do," I asked with a smile, "to convince you I am happy and having a good time?"

"Don't you worry," Jorunn said with confidence. "We'll get you there, and soon."

Not on your own, Jorunn, I thought to myself. If that were the case, it would probably be futile. Therefore, there was going to be one other person to help the *russ* in their case: me. Sure, one of the reasons would be that I wanted to be happy and have fun. But more important was that I did not want those people—those wonderful people who wanted me to feel at home and to be happy—to see me sitting all alone and to think that something was wrong and that I was forlorn. It just wasn't fair to make people who were trying to help me feel happy feel that all their efforts were in vain.

These were my new friends. In just three weeks, Jorunn had already become quite special. She understood me and what was going through my mind better than anyone else, and she was always there for me, even when I didn't realize I needed support. She was a bit of a straight-arrow, but everyone liked her anyway. Johnny looked like what we in Westport called a "hood." He wore a leather jacket and combed his hair back on the sides. It wasn't greasy, but he looked greasy. And yet, he was as sensitive to me as any of the other kids: asking me questions about America, asking me questions about myself, helping explain Norwegian words I couldn't understand, helping to explain teachers I couldn't understand, telling me names of *småpiker* I saw in the *skolegård*. Arnulf was caustic and funny, and the closest thing to an intellectual that I'd found in Norway. But he was as much of a clown as he was an intellectual; I particularly liked that combination. He slept through many of the classes, but never missed a word, either of our conversation or the teacher's.

"So, Pete," Arnulf asked as we walked home, not realizing what a martyr he was talking to, "what do you think of your first *russefest?*"

"A lot of drinking, a lot of dancing, and a lot of fun," I said honestly.

-10-
Transitions

"Thank you all for coming this evening," Karl Arvid began. "This is our first *Bragemøte* of the year and I am glad so many people are able to be here."

Karl Arvid was the Brage President. Brage was the only after-school activity sponsored by the *gymnas*. Even Brage was hardly "sponsored;" the school merely let Brage use one of its rooms for meetings. There wasn't even a school advisor. That was a far cry from what I was used to at Staples, with its tons of after-school clubs—French Club, Spanish Club, UN Club, Ham Radio Club, Calculus Club, Science Club, AFS Club, Chess Club, on ad nauseum—each with its own faculty advisor and photograph in the yearbook.

"I want to talk a little about the *Bragerevy*, and then we'll hear our speaker for the evening," Karl Arvid continued.

The *Bragerevy* was the closest thing to a high school play, even though it was actually a revue, a *revy*. An adult from the town was the director of the *revy*, and all of the participants were kids from the *gymnas*. I suspected that I was expected to be involved.

"Now that we have gotten our business out of the way," Karl Arvid continued. having decided when the next *Bragemøte* would take place, "we can hear our speaker. I am happy to be able to introduce Pete to you all. Many of you have seen him around the school already, but I have seen him around my house every day. Here's my brother: Pete Dublin."

My brother? Where did that come from? That was certainly the first time Karl Arvid had ever talked about me in that way. Calling me a brother was a big step for him and a big change for me.

"Good evening," I began in my halting *norsk*. "My name is Pete Dublin and I am an AFS exchange student." Good God, I suddenly thought to myself. I was standing in front of forty or fifty people, almost none of whom I knew. It was the third week of school and I was supposed to talk to them...in *norsk*. I froze.

"All I want you to do," Karl Arvid had explained over the previous weekend, "is to give a five-minute talk on why you wanted to get an AFS scholarship and why you wanted to come here."

There was a rule for AFSers in America giving talks: they were not allowed to give a talk before January, until they had been in the United States for six months. On the other hand, I had been in Norway less than three months, I had not been able to speak a word of *norsk* before I came, and I had only been speaking *norsk* in complete sentences (let alone paragraphs) for less than three weeks. Where was Adele Berg to protect me when I needed her? Unfortunately for me, she was right there in the audience and she wasn't going to do a damn thing but listen.

I gave the speech in *norsk* and the *norsk* I used was rudimentary. What follows is the translation of the *norsk* into comparable English, mistakes and all.

Hello. I am Pete Dublin and I shall be going to the *gymnas* here in Tromsø in this year—this whole year. Perhaps you have seen my picture and you know a little about me. If you have seen it not I am 17 years from the state of Connecticut (about 70 kilometers from the town of New York) and I shall be in the senior English Line. But perhaps some of you here make an application for an AFS scholarship and perhaps you will gladly to hear a little about Pete Dublin and AFS. So now I shall try to explain why I wanted to get an AFS scholarship. I have lived in Westport in 13 years on the east party of America in my whole lives.

After I made my first mistake, there wasn't a sound in the room…until I laughed and made fun of myself first. Then everyone else in the room felt they could laugh, too. I was, after all, killing *their* language.

Therefore, almost all of all my ideas come from from just one party of America and of the world. I thanked that it was not so good to have so much of my brain formulating in that way and I thought that it would be a good idea to try to another *plass*.

I had the habit of putting in an English (shown as Norwegian here) word wherever I didn't know the correct Norwegian word. I knew they could understand me, but I assumed they preferred me to learn the real Norwegian words.

Went I was tolded that I would walk to Norway I was a little happily because I would be on now a country that is very different a Westport…very different. Also, it is very usual for teenagers to be a little unlucky where everyone is or everything that one has and many teenagers wish to leave your home and try to be happily with some other people on another school in

another town. I didn't think that I would try in another countries also. I also like people and like to be with people. And if I
have the chance to meet new people I tear it (if I not am too
afraid). An AFS scholarship would give me that chance. Win I
heard that I would walk to Norway (I heard May 17) and I
would be there on a whole year, I was happy, unlucky, and afraid.
I have hoped to get an AFS scholarship and I was happy when I
got it. Also, it is a very good honor to be chasing by AFS
because they are not so many that get an AFS scholarship. But I
was unlucky also because there were so many thinges that I
would must leave, so many thinges that I liked so very much.
But I knowing then that an AFS scholarship is very valuable,
more valuable than any other thing. I knowing that then and I
knowing that better now. And I was afraid also. I had not
watered to go to another country on a whole year because I
knowing not one word Norwegian and I am always a little
afraid. And I am very happily now in Tromsø and I am still a
little afraid. To thank you for listening.

Fifty people listening to me butcher their language. Fifty people listening to me stumble through what would have otherwise been a simple, little speech. But I made it through the speech. Somehow, both I
and the Norwegian language survived.

This first time on my own in *norsk* in front of lots of people reminded me of my first time in *norsk* in front of one person. We had been at
Trollvasshytta for a week when we finally got an opportunity to make
something of an excursion into Norway, not just the forest around us.
After lunch, Ken and I walked to the *trikk* and took it down to the center of Oslo.

"Well, Pete," Ken suggested as we walked together down the completely unfamiliar, and somewhat scary, streets of downtown Oslo.
"What do you think about getting a map?"

"I think," I answered, "your question raises two more: where do we
get it and do we get it in English or Norwegian?"

"The answer to your first question is: at that bookstore on the other
side of Karl Johan."

"I'm impressed that you already know the name of this street. Does
that mean that the answer to the second question is yes and that I have
to do it?"

"You got that right," Ken smiled as we crossed the street and headed for the bookstore.

"*Værsågod,*" the clerk greeted us.

"*Kan...jeg...få...et...kart...over...Oslo?*" I sputtered slowly and deliberately. It was my first complete sentence in Norwegian, the result of my
three weeks of Norwegian language classes.

"*Jada. Et kart over Oslo,*" the clerk answered promptly and naturally. "*To kroner femti ører.*"

"*Vær...så...god,*" I managed as I handed him the money.

"We did it," Ken smiled as we walked out of the store with our purchased-in-Norwegian possession.

"What do you mean *we* kemosabe?"

Apparently, people in Tromsø didn't have any problems with what I did to their language either. One of the Lutheran priests who taught religion classes at the *gymnas* was at the *Bragemøte* and afterwards he asked me to discuss religion in America and Norway in his classes. After three weeks, I was the expert? Still, it was satisfying to be asked—a boost to my ever-fragile self-confidence—and I knew I was supposed to do everything that people asked of me.

"How did it go?" *fru* Román asked in *norsk* as Karl Arvid and I got home.

"Fine," I answered.

"How long did you speak?" Román asked. It appeared that he and *fru* Román had waited up for us, just as my Mom and Dad would have.

"Five or ten minutes," I answered, "but it seemed like hours."

"Don't listen to him," Karl Arvid jumped into the conversation, as animated as he was at the meeting itself. "Pete was great. It was a great speech."

"I made so many mistakes...."

"But you laughed at your own mistakes," Karl Arvid interrupted, "and that made it easier for everyone listening."

Well, if that wasn't a real family conversation, I had never had one.

After school a few days later, I went to the USIS office. For someone who was becoming a teenage Norwegian, I still had difficulty fully breaking my connection to America. Psychologically, it was easier that the connection be baseball. I was informed that Maris was up to 58 home runs; he needed only two more to tie, and three to break, the record. I watched a film on New England which I imagined I would be able to use in one speech or another during the year. What with the *Bragemøte* already under my belt and the Religion classes just around the corner, I assumed I would be in demand all year. Could this be a way to supplement my AFS allowance?

We got a monthly allowance of KR100. Norwegian money was simple; there were 100 *ører* in a *krone*, and a *krone* equalled about 14 cents. It didn't sound like much to me, and I wasn't shy about expressing my opinion of the subject.

"You shouldn't have any trouble living on that," Bente had assured us at Trollvasshytta, "for everything costs less here in Norway than it does in the United States." Bente was right and our allowance was fine, but I kept my eyes open for ways to supplement my allowance nevertheless.

The next day after school I walked a few times up and down Storgate before walking home for dinner, just to see who was there. I didn't have much homework anyway.

I Was a Teenage Norwegian

"*Hei*, Pete," Johnny from my class greeted me. He was walking with Pål and Arnulf.

"Did you vote, yesterday?" Pål asked.

"*Hei, dokker*," Arnulf interrupted, "Pete's an American. You forget, sometimes, because he speaks such fluent *Tromsøværing*."

We all laughed. Arnulf was at the *Bragemøte*; he knew the kind of "fluent" *norsk* I spoke. I was glad he was sensitive to the state of my *norsk*, but I was equally glad he could laugh at it and at me, and help me laugh at myself. We decided to go to Sagatun for something to drink and to continue our conversation on the elections. The *kafés* were spread throughout the center of town. Samfunn was all the way at the northern end of Storgate, next to the *kino*. Kaffistova was on the second floor of a building on Storgate across from the Tromsø Cathedral. Sagatun was on one of the side streets leading from Storgate, past the cathedral, toward to docks. It was in a small building with a statue of Roald Amudsen, the famous Norwegian polar explorer, out front.

"What's different here for me," I explained. "is that everyone votes for the party, not the candidate."

"That's true," Johnny nodded his head. "I'll be damned if I even know who the local Labor Party candidates are, but you can be sure I'll vote for them."

"Here in Norway it's the party that matters," I continued. "The party decides its position, and everyone votes that way"

"I had never looked at it that way," Pål nodded in agreement. "Perhaps I've always been too close to our own elections. Perhaps I needed the perspective of a naturalized *Tromsøværing*!"

"*Han e' ikkje så dum som han se' ut,*" Arnulf said with a smile. He turned to me and explained. "That's a particularly Tromsø expression. It means that you're not as dumb, not as stupid, as you look. We use it a lot—even for ourselves—and we use it only for those we really like— even ourselves."

"What was most exciting for me to watch," I continued, "was how involved kids were in the elections."

"That's true," Pål agreed. "It is a passion for us, perhaps because there are so many political parties and the parties here have quite different views on issues."

That night, I realized that a routine was setting in. Every day I woke up, went to school, went *til byen* after school, came home for dinner, went *til byen* in the evening. Some days broke the routine, but I actually liked having a routine and the stability it provided me. I was generally feeling pretty good about my life in Tromsø, even though everything wasn't perfect: my family, my *norsk*, my studying. But there were days when I felt that everything had collapsed for me. Sue was a major reason for this, and a reminder came every day that I didn't get a letter from her. My final exams—which I never took— at the end of my junior year at Staples was about the last such American issue, and the reminder for that came in one of my Mom's letters, recounting a conversation she had with Mr. Lorentzen, the principal.

September 14, 1961

Dear Mom and Dad,

Every-now-and-then I get a little discouraged, but I always pull out of the mood in a minute or two (or even less). Today, the mood has lasted longer. I just got to feeling blue when I realized how much I have to do and how little I am doing.

There is all the school-work I have to do; it is not difficult but there is a great deal of it. I started right in on it at the beginning of school (working harder than I ever did at Staples) but I have eased off a little and that is not too good. And there is always the language difficulty. I can speak better now, but I am not learning as quickly as I used to (or maybe I am just imaging things).

There are just so many things to get me down, and if they all hit me at the same time, it takes a little time to recover. Then I read a letter like the one I got from Mom today, when I came home from school and was feeling particularly low. It ended by saying that all you wanted to hear about were my Staples tests and that I had finally taken them. I haven't. They continue to be a problem and I cannot afford to have them bothering me now. So, I wrapped up my books, addressed them to Staples, and went to the post office to mail them. I have no time to study; that is why I sent the books back. It is obvious I will fail all of them for I cannot study and it has been almost three months since I last saw one of those school textbooks. But maybe failing my Staples finals is merely one of the sacrifices I have to make to come here.

I Was a Teenage Norwegian

I'll be all right, but sometimes I am not so sure.

> *All my love,*
> *Pete*

"*Hei*, Pete," Bjørg greeted me as she walked through the classroom door the next day. "You're early today, too, like the rest of us."

School didn't begin until 8:30, but it was open from 7:30 and lots of kids came early...mostly to talk.

"Good morning," Engelsen said in English as he entered the class for the first of three English periods in a row.

"*God morn*," we said in unison, standing up and sitting down again quickly.

Engelsen was our *klasseforstanden*, the teacher with whom we had the most classes. We had Engelsen for both English and French, which amounted to almost fifteen hours of class a week. Of all the teachers I had, Engelsen was by far the most understanding and sympathetic. He was also the closest thing to the kind of teacher I was used to in America. Generally, the teachers in Tromsø were quite formal and distant. They sat or stood at the front of the room, on their little raised platform—to keep them "over" the students—and they generally lectured at us. Some lectures were forceful, while others bordered on the lazy and anecdotal.

For the most part, when the teachers didn't talk at us, we recited...we were heard. The teacher picked one of us to be heard, and asked us to speak on a particular topic. It wasn't at all like questions and answers, and there was no give-and-take between student and teacher. In fact, the students just fed back whatever in the textbook they had memorized. It was rote learning at its worst: uninspired and boring. The kids knew that once they were heard, they wouldn't get another turn again for a while, so they didn't even have to bother memorizing the material in the textbook for the next week or two.

Engelsen was the only teacher I had who tolerated interaction approximating a class discussion. He often entered into conversations with the students, instead of asking them to recite what they had memorized. At other times, he actually asked the class to discuss a topic. He did this mostly in English classes, and the class had to discuss the topic in English.

I had been in school for almost four weeks, and my *norsk* was improving noticeably. Unfortunately, I still had huge problems understanding most of the teachers. So, I came up with a technique I called "total concentration." Once a day, I picked a class and decided to concentrate totally on the lecture for that period. History and Religion were my usual choices, because those teachers were the easiest for me to understand. I concentrated all my attention and energy on understanding what the teacher said. I could generally understand only one or two words a minute. By the end of the forty-five minute period, I was exhausted...completely drained, which was why I could use the technique only once a day. But there was a clear improvement; when I first started the technique after the second week of school, I could only understand 5-10 words in the entire forty-five minute period. By the fourth week of school, I was well into the 30-40 word range.

"Do you want to go up to the 5th Science?" Johnny asked at lunch time. "You look a little tired. You've had a hard day, sitting in class and all."

"I've been concentrating," I said.

"That's more than I can say for you, Johnny," Arnulf chided his classmate.

"They're not as much fun as we in 5GE, Pete," Johnny continued. "but you might as well meet all sorts while you are here. So, do you want to go upstairs?"

"Sure." We each took our *matpakke* and headed upstairs. 5th Science was also on the third floor—along with 5th Math—facing the *skolegård*, but in the southern corner of the building.

"Have you all met Pete?" Johnny asked as we entered the classroom. "He thought it might be nice to pay a visit."

"*Hei,*" I said, somewhat meekly. It was still a lot easier for me to let Johnny take the lead.

"*Hei,* Pete," a number of them said in unison. Their *matpakker* were open, spread out on their desks, and they were already eating their lunch.

"My name is Knut," one of the boys introduced himself. I remembered him from the *russefest.* "*Kor det går?* How is everything going? I hope it hasn't been too difficult for you having to be in 5th English."

"As long as they let me out for lunch," I responded, "I think I'll be okay."

"Your *norsk* is getting much better," one of the girls commented. "I was at the *Bragemøte* and it was pretty good then; it's a lot better already."

"That sign," one of the boys said, "was the neatest idea I had ever seen. I've never seen so many Norwegians stop speaking English so quickly."

"And now," Johnny bragged, "Pete's started concentrating."

After school, I made my daily pilgrimage to the USIS office to check on the progress of slugger Roger Maris. I found out that he had hit number 59. One more to go for the tie; two more to go to break the record. Poor Mickey Mantle. He was having a fabulous year himself, but who noticed, given that he trailed Roger Maris?

"We're just about ready for *middag*, Pete," *fru* Román said to me as I left my shoes in the hall and walked through the kitchen into the living room/dining area. It was common in the few Norwegian houses I had visited to have a small hall, or mud room, where people took off their shoes when they entered a house. The Román house had a small entrance room, which lead right into the kitchen.

"How are things at school?" Román asked.

I Was a Teenage Norwegian

"I had lunch with the 5th Science today," I answered. "That was the first time I had visited them." Even if the dinner talk was brief, at least all our conversations were in *norsk*. It was amazing how quickly that particular transition had occurred. I had my lengthy conversation with Jorunn the night before school started, went to school the next day with my sign, and returned home to *middag* in *norsk*. I had assumed the Románs had changed; maybe it was me.

I took a little nap after *middag*, which was one of the more pleasant Norwegian customs. After the nap, I got a rare phone call. Talking *norsk* was getting easier; talking on the phone was not.

"Pete," *fru* Román called up to me. "It's Adele Berg."

"*Hei*, Adele," I said when I got on the phone.

"Pete," Adele began, "do you think you could come over here this evening for a chat?"

"I guess so. I don't have any plans."

"Good," Adele said. "Perhaps around seven, for coffee?"

"I'll see you then. *Ha det*."

"What did Adele want," *fru* Román asked.

"She wants me to come over for a chat," I answered.

"She's leaving, you know," Román says. "Going to Germany to study."

"She did mention that before," I said. "I just didn't remember when she was leaving."

"I think it's soon," *fru* Román said. "I think at the end of this week."

As I walked over to Adele's, I realized how much I would miss her. She was supportive and helpful.

"Thanks for coming over," Adele said as I entered the house and took off my shoes. "You don't have to take off your shoes." I noticed that the only custom more common than taking of your shoes when you entered a house was the custom of telling guests they didn't have to take off their shoes when they entered your house. But I took them off anyway.

"Coffee?" Adele asked, cup in hand.

"*Takk*," I answered. I never drank coffee in America, and I could never imagine drinking coffee at breakfast. But I was already used to drinking coffee at the sort-of meal between *middag* and *aftens*, called *kaffe*.

"I also hear you like cake with your coffee," Adele said as she handed me an already-cut piece.

"It's a small town," I smiled.

"I want to talk about your family," she began abruptly, switching to English. Clearly Adele didn't want to simply chat a bit before leaving for Germany next week. "I want to talk about changing families."

Boom. It had come at last. It wasn't exactly a surprise, but to hear the actual words—"changing families"—was a bombshell. Especially since things were getting better, and I had come to the conclusion that they were good enough, especially since I was making so many fiends at school.

"I don't know," I said.

"This is going to be difficult for you," Adele continued, "and my leaving at the end of the week will not make it any easier. But you're still at the beginning of your stay here, and I think now is the time to do it, if you're going to do it at all."

"I guess I feel that perhaps I need to give it a little more time," I said without a great deal of conviction.

"You have been with them for two months, now," Adele persisted. "I have talked with Jorunn. She tells me that you have told her that your family relationship was cool."

"That's about right. I figure maybe that's good enough for now."

"I'm not sure it is," Adele continued. "Even I have noticed that you and Karl Arvid aren't good friends. You don't show much affection for each other."

"That's true."

"That kind of relationship really hurts both sides," Adele said. "Karl Arvid has a lot to do at school. Having to adjust to you at home could be distracting for him."

"The problem is that even if it makes sense to leave, even if it is the wisest thing to do, I feel defeated. I feel I have failed."

"You haven't been here long enough to fail," Adele said. "But if you don't resolve this problem, and resolve it now, you could. You have enough to worry about without having troubles with your family."

"I know you're right," I said. "I guess I'm still a little scared."

"There's nothing I can do to make it feel less scary, Pete," Adele said, "but I can get you into another family."

"You can?"

"Of course. It may take a while to find another permanent family, but I think I can get you into an intermediate family more quickly. Someplace where you'll feel more comfortable while Liz looks for a more permanent family. I'm sure Jorunn and Knut will be able to help her."

"Thanks, Adele," was all I could say, although I felt much more. As I walked home, I realized how defeated and excited I felt at the same time. I knew I needed to change families, but I didn't think I would ever get over the feeling of failure.

There were three qualities that Adele Berg had that made it possible for her to have the affect on me the situation required. First, she had perception. She listened to *fru* Román, she listened to me (and didn't listen to me), and she perceived accurately what was happening. Second, she had a way of talking to me that got through to me. I was stubborn and I tended to argue with adults, but Adele talked to me in a way that helped me to listen to what she had to say. Third, she had the power to do. She was in a position to quickly make a decision and follow up that decision with appropriate action. At one level, everything happened so quickly that evening, that Adele made it look a lot easier than it actually was.

I Was a Teenage Norwegian

"*God aften*, Pete," *fru* Román wished me good evening as I took off my shoes and walked into the kitchen. "Adele called me while you were walking home, and told me of your decision to change families."

"Yes?"

"You should," she began in *norsk*, helping me make the transition from having talked in English with Adele, "have come to Norway thinking that everything would be fine and good, instead of coming to Norway unhappy."

"Unhappy?"

"You should give more of yourself," she continued. "You should think that everyone in the world is basically good. You should be more open and honest."

"Honest?"

"You should think less of yourself and more of others."

I was dumbstruck. How could this woman, this woman I felt I hardly knew and with whom I had hardly spoken, pick out just about every fault I had while hardly knowing me? Was I so transparent? I might have had more faults than the ones she listed, but those were probably the biggest and the worst. Maybe, if *fru* Román had helped me understand my behavior better, maybe if she had been both critical and supportive, maybe.... But Adele said I shouldn't think about this whole business for the next couple of days because it would be easier for me that way.

"I think I'll go to bed," I told *fru* Román. "*God natt.*"

"*God natt*, Pete," she said. I couldn't tell if she was happy to have gotten all that off her chest or just happy to have gotten rid of me.

-11-
Plukka Poteter

Oh, don't let it be morning, I moaned to myself, as my alarm clock rang. I didn't think I could manage another encounter with *fru* Román. She was damning the previous night, and I didn't need any more, even if there was a lot of truth to what she said. As I got out of bed and started to dress, the room appeared different: bigger, perhaps, or brighter? Everything felt a little more familiar, almost as if it were really my room. That was all I needed. I had finally made a decision and I was having second thoughts.

"*God morn*, Pete," *fru* Román greeted me, almost cheerfully, as I entered the kitchen.

"*God morn*," I responded, as cheerfully as I could. Early morning fatigue was mixed with an equal amount of apprehension.

"Don't worry, Pete," *fru* Román said, sensing my ambivalence. "You have made your decision. Don't worry about it."

"Come, have some breakfast. Have a glass of milk, some *geitost*, some marmalade. You must eat," she said, almost more of a mother to me that morning than ever before. That was an almost complete change from her attitude the previous evening, when she blamed me for the failure we both shared. I felt strongly that it was my fault to a great extent, but not for lack of trying. I certainly wasn't a completely upbeat and lively sparkplug of a guy. I didn't initiate conversations all that often. I was quiet and introspective. I didn't always share what was on my mind. I didn't ask Román about his work. I knew I was not the perfect son or brother and that I had many faults, but I still didn't feel that I accounted for all the problems; I still felt that I had never been fully welcomed into that family. The $64,000 question was: would it, or I, be any different the next time around?

"*Takk*," I said, breaking into my own reverie. "I'll be okay. It's just a little difficult, that's all. I'll be fine. I won't worry. I promise."

As I walked down the hill toward the *gymnas*, I wondered what my new family would be like. Would I feel more comfortable there? Would I have a real brother? Would I ever get to the point where I could call them *mor og far*, mother and father? *Nok*! Enough!

I Was a Teenage Norwegian

"*Hei*, Pete," Arnulf called out to me as I got to the *skolegård*. He and Pål waited just outside the entrance, having a quick smoke before school started.

"*Hei*, Pete," Jorunn greeted me and walked with me toward the door. "I hear you have made your decision about the Románs."

"How..." I began.

"This is Tromsø," Jorunn interrupted. "It's a small town, remember?"

"I don't think I'll ever be able to forget," I smiled, as we entered the building and started to climb the stairs.

"How are you feeling?" Jorunn asked.

"I'm relieved," I answered, "and I feel like a failure. It's the right decision, but I can't help feeling that I've failed, that it was my job to make it work with the Románs."

"At least you know it's the right decision."

"But that doesn't make it feel easier," I continued.

"*Hei*, Pete," Arnulf followed us into the classroom, "I hear you're moving from the Román's."

"It's not much of a secret," I responded. "I'm surprised I was one of the first to know."

"It's a ..."

"...small town," I finished the sentence Randi had begun.

"Don't worry about it," Randi continued.

"You sound just like Adele Berg," I said. "Don't worry; I won't worry. It's the right thing to do; it's just a little difficult. But at least I have all of you to let me know what is happening in my life. If you hadn't told me, I'm not sure I would have known."

I was an ambivalent teenage American with a strong will. I was a big junior high school student. I had started shaving in 7th grade and I was 5'7" and 150 pounds in 8th grade. So, I played football. When I arrived at Staples, I was committed to playing football there, too. Unfortunately, I had reached my peak in junior high school; in 10th grade I was 5'8" and 165 pounds (I ballooned to 185 pounds by the time I left for Tromsø). I wasn't much of a football player...not at that size. Football was what boys did, but I didn't really enjoy myself and I never got to play. I was on the team; I was a part of school spirit; I stayed on the team and then quit. An example of strong-willed ambivalence.

The next year, I did it again. I joined the team at the start of the school. I was welcomed back to the fold, by both the players and the coaches. But I was still the same size and I still didn't play that well and I still didn't really like the game. There on the locker-room walls was the famous locker-room message: Winners never quit and quitters never win. Was I a quitter? Yup. Two years in a row.

I joined the team because many of the popular boys in school were on the football team, and I desperately wanted to be popular. I quit the team because I really didn't like football and I didn't even like being on the team. I had the strength to quit but I didn't have the strength not to join.

I had clearly brought this strong-willed ambivalence with me to Tromsø. I probably would have "stuck it out," in my typically stubborn fashion. My friends were helping me feel good about taking advice and being more flexible. I probably could have bathed all day in their support if Riksheim hadn't interrupted us.

"*God morn*," Riksheim, the principal, said as he walked briskly into the room. I had never seen the principal in the classroom; I just figured he sat in his office and thought important thoughts. I didn't know whether I should have been happy or afraid. I wasn't the only quiet *russ*; silence permeated our cozy little classroom. With Riksheim standing up at the front, the small room felt even smaller than it was.

"As many of you know," Riksheim began, "the Holt farm on the southern part of the island is one of the last remaining farms in Tromsø. The season is just about over, but there are still some remaining potatoes in the ground and they need some help. You are invited to *plukka poteter*, pick potatoes, if you wish."

"What does this mean," I whispered to Arnulf.

"Keep quiet," Arnulf whispered back. "Don't spoil our chance."

"The Holts," Riksheim continued, "will pay each of you KR15 for the day, but they do expect a day's work."

Two bucks, I thought to myself. Plus we got the day off from school. I could see how Arnulf didn't want me to spoil anything.

"Don't forget," Riksheim said, "to take your books home and bring your *matpakke* to the farm. Enjoy yourselves, and work hard." He marched out of the room almost before we had a chance to stand up again. We might not always stand up for the teachers when they left, but we bolted to attention when Riksheim did. Especially after such good news.

"Well," Engelsen said, almost lost in the back corner of the room, "I guess that's it for today. I hope you have more luck with the potatoes than most of you are having with French grammar."

We all headed our separate ways back to our homes. Everyone was excited, but no one looked especially surprised. Although I didn't know about Iowa and Indiana, I wondered if getting time off from school to help out the local farmers happened there, too? There were times when I wondered if the difference between where I was and where I had come from had more to do with the difference between Norway and America or more to do with the difference between suburban Westport and rural Tromsø.

"What's the matter, Pete?" *fru* Román asked as I took off my shoes and walked through the kitchen. "Are you worried about moving?"

"*Nei*, everything's fine," I answered. Where had all this concern for me and my well-being been when I needed it? "We're off from school today. We're going to *plukka poteter*."

"At the Holt farm?" she asked.

"*Ja*," I answered.

"You'll want to wear your *gummistøvler*," she suggested.

I Was a Teenage Norwegian

The *gummistøvler* were still in the little entrance way, between the kitchen and the front door. When Arnulf suggested I buy them, I agreed mostly because I figured he knew better than I did what I would need. I was used to only two kinds of boots: ski boots and rubber boots. *Gummistøvler* were more like work shoes, but they were definitely boots. They were made of rubber and they were at least a foot tall. And I wore them *instead* of shoes, not *over* them. They were solid all around and I just stepped into them. Every day still brought new surprises and new ways of doing old things.

"I'm meeting Arnulf at school," I told *fru* Román as I pulled on the *gummistøvler*. "We're going to walk to the Holt farm from there."

"Do you have your *matpakke*?" *fru* Román asked.

"*Ja*," and I almost said *mor*. But it was too late for that, even if she finally started to act like one. Was that what it was like to make a decision? I finally decide and everything around conspires to make me feel I made the wrong decision?

I met Arnulf, Randi, Johnny, and Jorunn in the *skolegård*. We all walked up the hill toward the top of the island.

I had walked occasionally on my own past the cemetery toward the topmost point of the island, but I had never walked any further.

"You know Arnulf," I said as we walked. "I've been in Tromsø over two months, and I haven't really seen that much of Tromsøy."

"What do you mean?" he asked.

"The first day I got here the Románs drove me around the island, and even over to Tromsdalen to see the whale factory. Since that drive, the only places I've been to are Storgate, the Román house, and the *gymnas*."

"And Nyløkken Kafé," Randi chimed in. "Don't forget the first *russefest*."

Randi was a bit of a strange bird. She was tall and severe, her face sort of pulled in from grimacing too much. She would crack everyone up with her seeming naiveté; she feigned ignorance of sexual innuendos, but we (and especially Arnulf) knew better. Although she sounded flighty at times, she may have been the smartest in the class.

"And Nyløkken," I added. "But that's it. I don't even know where we're going today. I saw the farm when I drove around the edge of Tromsøy with the Románs but I've never actually been to it."

"Well," Arnulf explained. "We're heading west, up to the top of the island. Then we'll head down toward the water that separates Tromsøy from Kvaløya."

I always thought in terms either north or south on Tromsøy, because those were the two directions I could walk Storgate. And, Tromsøy was long and thin, with its length running north and south. To the east lay the mainland. Up until the previous year, the only way to get to the island from the mainland was a short ferry; now there was Tromsøbrua.

The mainland—or Tromsdalen—had a small strip of somewhat flat land along the water's edge...maybe a couple of hundred meters. And then came the small, but steep mountain, part of which I could see from the picture window in the Román's living room. It was only 600-700 meters high, but it loomed large, large enough that I could see it from almost anywhere between Storgate and the topmost part of the island. My friends said it was great to climb up and then walk around on top, but I had only taken the gondola car with the Románs.

"As we get to the highest part of Tromsøy," Arnulf proceeded with his lecture, "it flattens out a bit. It's not that much higher here than at sea level—probably 50-100 meters—but you'll see big differences in the Spring."

"What kind of differences?" I asked politely, pretending I was listening all the while.

"How quickly the snow melts. Sometimes the snow will be all melted near the water and there will still be half a meter of snow covering the ground up here."

"The only lake on the island—Prestvannet—is up here, too," Randi contributed. Randi had lived here all her life; she was less interested in the topography than Arnulf.

115

I Was a Teenage Norwegian

As we walked, I realized how used to gravel roads I had become. The few gravel roads I encountered growing up were really rough: real dirt and stones, huge potholes, really rugged. But these gravel roads were almost as smooth as asphalt roads. There were no big rocks and almost no pot-holes, just smooth gravel.

"Actually," Arnulf had never stopped his travelogue, "we have been walking on Holtveien for the past five or ten minutes. It's one of the major roads across the island, and it runs almost all the way to the water. It was named for Holt, same as the farm. We're only ten or fifteen minutes more walk to the farm."

There were fewer houses up there, but otherwise it wasn't that much different from the more familiar parts of Tromsø. We passed a fairly new elementary school on the right, with a large *skolegård*. The houses were not packed as close together as I was used to around the Románs and closer to the center of town. Some of them had quite a lot of property around them. There was one house we passed on the left with a chain-link fence in front, that had a yard almost as big as our acre in Westport, although there were a lot more trees.

By the time I saw the farm, the view was dominated by water and mountains. I hadn't seen that much water and those many mountains since the *hurtigruten* ride from Bodø to Tromsø in July. Island after island covered the horizon, as far as the eye could see: west, north, and south. Even from the deck of the *hurtigruten* I had never seen anything quite as crowded. And almost all of the islands were covered with snow, even though it was September and we didn't have any snow in Tromsø.

"Is that typical?" I asked Arnulf. Maybe Arnulf hadn't, but the snow definitely grabbed my attention.

"It varies," he answered. "It depends on the amount of snow in the winter and how warm the summer is. There are always a few mountains that remain snow-covered; this year there are a few more than usual."

It was so spectacular that I almost didn't notice the farm itself, which was big by Westport standards. Our house in Westport was next to a small farm, maybe eight or ten acres. The Holt farm must have been five times as big as that. By the time we arrived, everyone else from the class was already there, waiting in the yard around the house and barn. Both buildings looked old and weather-beaten and they were quite big. The feature I liked best about the barn was its entrance. A set of big double doors appeared to be on the second floor. There was a long, grassy ramp angling up to the big doors, and that was how people and animals got into the barn. It was still a kick for me to see objects that were almost the same as those I was used to, but where the differences stood out almost more because of the basic similarities.

"Pete," Pål shouted out. "You're the last one here. Now we can begin to earn our *kroner*."

"Take it easy," I responded. "This is the farthest away from home I've been in Tromsø. I might get homesick."

The kids laughed as we all walked toward the field. They were getting used to my being able to joke in *norsk*.

"I see you have your *gummistøvler*," Jorunn noticed. She didn't miss much, not where I was concerned, at least. "You're going to need them, that's for sure."

I could see what she meant. There was a small, fenced-in space around the house and the barn for the animals: cows, horses, chickens, goats, and a pig. But other than that, the entire farm appeared to be one huge field. Parts of it were planted with some kind of grain; at that point of the year it looked like long grass, but I didn't know much about grain. Large parts of the field looked completely empty; it was, after all, the fall. What I couldn't figure out was where the potatoes were. I couldn't see any potatoes and I didn't know what potato plants looked like: corn I knew, beans I knew, strawberries I knew, potatoes I didn't know. All I could see was dark, seemingly moist earth.

"Where are the *poteter*?" I asked Randi.

"That's what today is all about," she smiled.

All eighteen of us wended our way through the dirt, most of which was only moist, though some was already a bit muddy. A woman was waiting for us, and I saw a tractor near the barn, but there was no machinery in sight. I didn't know how they *plukka poteter* in Maine or Idaho, but I assumed all farming was done with big tractors, combines, and the like. None of that was in evidence here, however. No *poteter* plukker.

"*God morn*," *fru* Holt greeted us pleasantly. "I think we still have plenty *poteter* to keep all of you busy for a while."

We all stood around, shuffling our feet, as we listened to her. I got the distinct impression that everyone but I knew what was going on. I had given up on the tractor, and my original thought that some machine would dig up the *poteter* and we would walk behind picking them up; after all, "*plukka*" did literally mean "pick," and that was linguistically close enough to "pick up" for me. With the easiest route gone, I kept my eyes open for the tools we would use; maybe they would give me a better sense of exactly what we were up against.

"Most of the *poteter*," *fru* Holt continued, "have already been *plukka*. This part of the field is all that's left." She pointed to a couple of acres of apparently empty earth. "It's now about half ten; lunch break at half one."

That was it; she left. What the hell were we supposed to do? There were no *poteter* in sight. There were no tools in sight. Just a bunch of bushel baskets, although they were a little taller and more narrow than bushel baskets in the America. Yet I was the only one who looked at all concerned.

"Let's get started," Arnulf said.

"That's easy for you to say. What do we do?" I asked.

"Follow me," he smiled as he dropped to his knees and began digging in the earth with his hands. "Here's one," he smiled again as he pulled a *potet* out of the ground and dropped it—actually it was more of a toss—into the basket.

"What are you doing?" I asked, fear and disbelief covering my face.

"*Plukka poteter*," he said calmly.

"That's it?" I asked again, acknowledging the answer in advance as I, too, dropped to my knees. "By hand?"

"By hand," the rest of my classmates laughed in unison. Clearly, this was not a surprise to them.

"You're in Norway, now," Pål explained. "No tractors, no tools. We work with our hands here," he added as he plunged his hands into the ground, dug around for a bit, and found another *potet*.

I resigned myself to my fate and dug in myself. Three hours till lunch break, three hours on my hands and knees, digging in the cold, moist earth with my bare hands. I guess it was worth getting off school for that, but I withheld judgment. We continued on through small parts of what soon looked like a huge area, and getting bigger as the morning wore on. My fingers wore on, too; the dirt was cold and rough and I had long ago given up on keeping it out from under my fingernails. The work was hard, but our spirits were surprisingly high, even mine. We sang songs, although I didn't know the words. We talked and laughed continuously, and we passed the time more quickly than I would have imagined. On the other hand, the work was hard; lunch had never been more welcome.

"I hope you're ready for lunch," *fru* Holt shouted as she approached our little work grew. "I've brought you some milk."

Did she ever. No bottles for that milk. She had a large milk can in the back of a small, horse-drawn cart.

"Fresh this morning," she said, as she ladled the milk into some metal cups she had also brought.

Was it ever. That stuff was still a little warm. I had never had milk fresh from the cow before. Not homogenized. Not pasteurized. Fresh squeezed, so to speak.

We all opened our *matpakker* as *fru* Holt dumped the contents of our baskets into the cart.

"Slow down, Pete," Jorunn laughed. "Are you in a hurry to get back to work?"

"*Nei*," I smiled, too. "I can't remember a time in Tromsø when I have been this hungry."

"I can't remember a time," Randi said, "when you've worked this hard, either."

"The only time that's close," I said, "is when I concentrate for an entire class period, and understand ten words. That's as tiring, but it doesn't make me as hungry."

My classmates laughed again. One of the things I liked so much about being in Tromsø was that I had become a bit of a celebrity. Part of that was inherent in just being an exchange student; there was an inevitable visibility that went with the job. I had come out of my shell a little bit. I clowned around some, and made jokes, even in *norsk*. In a way, it all started on the SEVEN SEAS.

One evening, I sought refuge in my cabin. I was into one of my moods and I wanted to be alone. Chuck-going-to-Switzerland would have none of that.

"Have you seen my squirt guns?" Chuck asked, barging unannounced into the confined space of our cabin.

"Squirt guns?" I asked.

"Yeah," he said. "I brought a couple of squirt guns just in case this place got a little boring. It's getting a little boring. The party wasn't quite enough; we need a little water. What the hell are you doing here, anyway?"

"I needed to be alone."

"Bull," Chuck said, with all the assurance of a social director. "Get your butt out of the bunk. We've got some serious business to take care of." He threw me one of the squirt guns, we both filled ours up in the sink, and we were off.

We started in the corridors, opening the doors and squirting at random.

"Look, Pete," Chuck said. "We've got two choices: two together or one-at-a-time. What do you think?"

"Let's start with one-at-a-time," I said, as we each opened a door, squirted, and ran.

"And finish with two together," Chuck said as we opened a door, squirted in unison, and ran down the corridor.

Then I got an idea for a soap slide. We got our towels soaking wet and wrung them out on the corridor floor; a ship was a great place for this because the doors at the ends of the corridors were raised a couple of inches anyway. Next, we spread soap over the floor and the towels, and ran the towels all over the floor; we created one slippery surface. And finally, we watched kids get out of their cabins and slide all over, usually landing on their butts. What a night!

In Tromsø, it all started with my crazy sign the first day of school. Kids still talked about that over a month later. I liked it, the notoriety. I liked it a lot. I liked being something of a personality. I liked being known by everyone. Whether at the *gymnas* or walking up and down Storgate, I felt known and important because everyone knew me. I felt different; I felt as if I were important, even special. I like being considered something special. It was a far cry from my total lack of popularity at Staples. And happiness sure beat self-pity any day.

"Okay, guys," Johnny shouted, "time to get back and earn our 15 *kroner*."

"I think another two hours," *fru* Holt suggested, "will be *nok*. I'll be back at three o'clock."

If anything, the last two hours were even harder than the first three. We might have been strong young kids and all, but few of us were used to that kind of manual labor. Johnny, Knut, and Torbjørn appeared most at home with it, and were always a little ahead of the rest of us. My fingers were slowly becoming raw, and my back was already sore.

"At least you have your boots," Arnulf consoled me, seeing in my face what I felt in my bones.

At 3:00, *fru* Holt was back, with her horse-drawn cart and our money. We each received a ten- and a five-*kroner* bill, at this point most welcome. There were a lot of happy *russ* faces as the money was handed out. Allowances, if they existed at all, were small, and it was uncommon for kids—even *gymnas* kids—to work. Fifteen *kroner* was a big deal for those kids; it would buy a lot of *øl* at the *kafés* later that evening.

"So," Jorunn asked as we all headed up the hill toward town together, "what do you think of *gymnas* in Norway, now?"

"I think the *poteter* are harder than the books," I said.

-12-
Another New Family

"You did well," Arnulf said as we passed the *gymnas*, the point at which we parted ways. "Was it worth the 15 *kroner*?"

"When I heard we were getting 15 *kroner*," I admitted, "I was pretty excited. Now that I know how much work is involved, I don't know if I'd do it again."

"But it was a lot of fun," Arnulf laughed. "You probably didn't even realize how shocked you looked when you found out we had to *plukka poteter* with our hands."

"And look what that dirt did to my pretty hands," I said, showing off my dirty hands.

"You know, Pete," Arnulf continued, " I wasn't so sure about you before I had met you. I had talked to people who said you were quiet, even shy; people said you didn't know how to have fun. Even Jorunn was a little worried about you."

"How did you know anything about me?"

"Tromsø is a small town, Pete," Arnulf repeated that often-heard phrase. "What you did with the sign was great; it was a great statement to make. You weren't anything like your reputation. Then at the *russefest*, I was worried everything I had heard about you was true; I couldn't believe someone couldn't have fun at a *russefest*. But today: you pitched in, took our joking, made jokes of your own, worked hard, and had fun. You're one of us, Pete; this was a great day."

I still couldn't get over it, the experience of that day. Getting a day off from school to *plukka poteter*, who in Westport would believe that? Digging in the dirt all day, picking out *poteter* with my bare hands, working so hard I was about ready to drop the minute I got back to the house. And then Arnulf, Mr. Intellectual, sharing his feelings with me that way. Tromsø was different, all right. I began to feel a part of the place, and a part of the class. The kids treated me more like one of them, which made me feel best of all. Jorunn, now Arnulf...they were real friends.

I was jolted out of my reverie the minute I walked in the house and took off my boots.

"Adele called," *fru* Román said, putting the last plate of food on the table. "You are to leave here tomorrow. *Middag* is ready. *Værsågod.*"

Fru Román was even more abrupt than usual, I knew the move was coming, but so soon? And knowing *that* was different from knowing *when*. Knowing when made it all more real, and that reality threw me back into my sense of failure. How else could I have behaved? Could I have talked more? Could I have taken the initiative more?

"Do you know where I'm going?" I asked as we sat down to *middag*.

"Norbye," *fru* Román told me.

"Do you know them?" I asked.

"Of course," Román answered.

"You have to be here before 8:00 tomorrow evening," *fru* Román said, more like a demand than a suggestion. The reality of my leaving had struck her as hard as it had struck me. The almost motherly compassion of the morning was replaced by an almost motherly resentment.

"What's the family like?" I asked.

"They have two daughters," *fru* Román answered. Damn, I thought to myself. The one thing I wanted in a family was a brother. I had even told Adele and Jorunn that I wanted to live with Harald Larsen, one of the boys in the Mathematics Line, because I thought he would make a great brother. I wasn't devastated, but I was sorely disappointed. What did I need with two sisters?

Karl Arvid sat quietly through the entire dinner conversation. I couldn't imagine what he thought about everything that was going on. I wondered if we would be better friends after I left than we were while I had lived there? Wouldn't that be ironic? Elin looked down at her food; she looked embarrassed by my leaving and the conversation. Did she feel guilty that she had never been particularly friendly? Did she want me to stay or want me to leave? Bergljot, of course, merely acted her age.

"Why do you have to leave, Pete?" she asked. "Can't you stay here and play with me?" Everything was fine, as far as she was concerned. She had always made me feel at home, always talked with me, always played with me. She was probably the only one there who would genuinely miss me; who wouldn't miss a playmate?

"I think Pete," Román explained to her and, perhaps, himself, "will be more comfortable with the Norbyes. But perhaps he'll still come and visit you."

"*Ja*," I assured Bergljot. "We can still be friends. We can still play together even when I live with the Norbyes."

After *middag*, I went straight to my room and started packing. In that room, at that moment, I couldn't wait to get out of that house, to move on to the Norbyes, even if all they had were daughters. I didn't know where they lived, I didn't even know for how long I would be living with them, yet I wasn't as anxious about going there as I was initially about meeting the Románs.

Clearly, something had happened to me over the previous three months. Part of it certainly was that I felt more comfortable in Tromsø. I knew when *middag* was served; I knew how to use my knife and fork the Norwegian way; I knew how to eat *geitost*; I could speak some *norsk*. It may not have been a lot, but all those little pieces added up. But part of it certainly was that I was also more comfortable with myself, particularly my new Norwegian self. I was a little less judgmental; I pushed myself a little harder; I enjoyed myself more and had more fun; I was more willing to take part in whatever activity was on the day's agenda. I was apprehensive about my new family, but I wasn't anxious.

I finished packing early enough to write one final letter from Karl Pettersensgate. In spite of my dislike of Staples (or was it my dislike of myself at Staples?), I felt a sense of gratitude to the place. Staples had selected me as an AFS finalist and Staples was footing the bill for my year abroad. I had already written a short piece for *Inklings* and I wanted to write an open letter to the students. I wasn't ready to tackle my move and share the feelings which engulfed me, but I did want to share my thoughts of thanks.

October, 1961

An Open Letter to the Students of Staples,

    Even though it is difficult for me to pay all of you back for making my stay here in Norway possible, I feel that every now and then I can use some of the knowledge I have gained from this experience to possibly help you.

    Nothing could have pleased me more than to hear that Staples has four foreign teenagers this year, and the possibility of a fifth. We are now living in a world that is coming closer and closer to destroying itself. Many people feel that it is just a matter of time before we will have an Atomic World War III and blow ourselves up, and three or four months ago I would have agreed with them. It is now my belief that the world is not doomed to destroy itself, but that through love and understanding—and mutual friendship and cooperation between human beings—we can save the world from the dangers of war and see the world grow and prosper.

    We would all like to see this dream come true and this fantasy take shape, but how are we to make this mystical dream-world come true? I believe the answer lies in the foreign students at Staples this year. I believe the first step we must take for world preservation is to have an understanding of the world's people, and that this understanding can only come through personal contacts with the peoples of the world. Try to get to know these people, be friends with them, learn from them, and teach them or help them in whatever way you can.

    Nothing made me happier than when one of my classmates-to-be came to visit and talk to me the evening before school was to start. I was scared a little, and this visit helped to break the ice (an important part of life here in the Arctic North) and give me a little confidence. Because of the actions of

I Was a Teenage Norwegian

the students here in Tromsø, I have been able to learn and take, to teach and to give freely of myself and my opinions from the first week of school.

You are faced with the same problem as the youth here in Tromsø, to insure the happiness of the foreign students, and with the same reward: a chance to gain a world of knowledge that can help both you and the World to continue to live and be happy. Why not give these kids a chance...a chance to have fun and to explain their way of life? But always keep in mind that they may have trouble speaking English; you should speak slowly to them and not expect too much from them at the beginning.

I know that Ingegerd has a lot to offer you being from Norway (or do you think I am already prejudiced?) and I can be equally sure that there are priceless stores of information about Brazil, Kenya, Holland, and France in the heads of Invelise, Geoffrey, Mattias, and Monique. It is fine to be able to say, "I dated a boy from Holland," or "I dated a girl from Norway," but wouldn't it be better to be able to say, "I learned something about France," or "I think I know a little more about the Brazilian people now." Think it over.

Hilsen,
Pete Dublin

"Pete," *fru* Román yelled upstairs, for what she knew would be the last time on that, my final morning with her family. "Aren't you awake yet? You'll be late for school."

I couldn't believe it. It was already 7:30. I had slept more soundly than any other night since leaving Westport.

"Here's your *matpakke*," *fru* Román handed me my *smørbrød* as I quickly finished my breakfast (also *smørbrød*). "Make sure you're home by *middag*. Remember, you have to be at the Norbyes before 8:00 PM"

I couldn't figure that 8:00 PM business out. I still had a problem periodically figuring out whether something I encountered was a Norwegian custom, or a peculiarity specific to a person or a situation. Was there a Norwegian custom about moving from one family to another? Did the custom include getting to the new family before 8:00 PM? Was it like check-out time at a hotel? I hadn't encountered the sanctity of 8:00 PM in any other context; it wasn't even a meal-time, and there were enough of those already. I had a sneaking suspicion the Románs were ready for me to leave, or maybe they had a previous engagement.

"Are you ready to go *til byen*?" Jorunn asked me as the last class of the day got out.

"*Ja*," I answered, somewhat tentative because Jorunn sounded like she knew something I didn't.

"You haven't forgotten?" Erika smiled.

"Oh, right," I quickly realized. Erika and Jorunn had offered to go *til byen* with me to look for yarn for a sweater. Erika had offered to knit one for me and the two of them had offered to help find a pattern and the yarn.

"Are you sure you still want to do this?" I asked Erika as we walked *til byen.*

"Of course," she answered, still smiling. "It's fun to knit, and it takes my mind off the most boring parts of school."

That was a habit I had difficulty getting used to. At Staples, when we entered a classroom, we brought books and notebooks. In Tromsø, on the other hand, it was common to see girls knitting in class. Already, Erika had finished a sweater for herself, and she hadn't even started until the second week of school. What was so remarkable was that knitting wasn't in any way distracting, for the rest of the class or Erika herself. In fact, Erika was able to knit right through her own recitation. She just sat and knit and regurgitated four or five paragraphs from the history text.

"There's Anne," Erika said, as we got to Storgate. "I asked her to meet us, too. Her mother owns a yarn store on the other side of the street."

"Is it all right," I began, with some trepidation, "to walk on the other side of the street?" It was, after all, Erika's suggestion that we visit that particular store. And, there were a number of stores on *that* side of the street. I saw people going to those stores, but they were generally adults. They didn't have to be cool.

"Of course," Jorunn laughed. "Why do you ask?"

"Everyone always walks on this side of the street," I answered, somewhat embarrassed at my continuing cultural ignorance.

"Oh," Anne said. "We're not *walking* on that side of the street. We're just going to my mother's store."

As I pondered the distinction, we entered the store. It was a small store; Anne's mother and a young woman were the only two people behind the counter, and there was only one other customer. The walls were covered with shelves full of small packages of yarn of an almost unlimited number of colors.

"*Mor,*" Anne said to her mother, "this is Pete. I've told you about him, haven't I?"

"Of course," *fru* Marcussen smiled and shook my hand. "Anne has told me a lot about you. At least you have gotten the dirt off your hands from yesterday's activity."

"He's looking for a typically Norwegian pattern," Jorunn said to *fru* Marcussen.

"Do you have anything specific in mind?" *fru* Marcussen asked.

"Jorunn, do you remember that grey sweater Johnny wore yesterday when we *plukka poteter*? The grey sweater with the blue pattern across the top?"

Jorunn remembered and explained the pattern to *fru* Marcussen. *Fru* Marcussen found the pattern with surprising speed; she handed me the pattern to make sure it was what I had in mind.

"That looks like it," I agreed. Then the four of them consulted with each other to find the right colors, which they also accomplished quickly.

"The yarn is KR52 and the pattern is KR51," *fru* Marcussen said, "but I'll give you a special AFS discount to KR45 each."

"*Værsågod,*" I said as I handed her what amounted to my entire allowance for October. On the other hand, that was a hand-knit sweater for less than $15.

"*Takk,*" I said to the three girls as I headed back up the hill to the Románs. "I don't want to be late for *middag*. It's the last supper. I'll see you tomorrow."

It turned out that I was a little late for *middag*. When I arrived at the house, all of the Románs were already seated at the dinner table, waiting for me.

"Sorry I am a little late," I apologized. "I was getting yarn for a sweater. One of the girls in my class is going to knit me a sweater. We picked out the pattern and the yarn," I continued my chatter, doing my best to fill the silence.

"Where did you shop?" *fru* Román asked as she began serving herself some fish.

"*Fru* Marcussen," I answered. "Her daughter, Anne, is in my class."

"I know," *fru* Román said.

"We will drive you over the the Norbyes after *middag*," Román told me me.

"Does he really have to go?" Bergljot pleaded with her father, as unsuccessfully that last time as she had the first.

"*Ja,*" he said simply while Elin and Karl Arvid ate their food in silence.

"Are you all packed?" *fru* Román asked.

"*Ja,* I think so," I answered.

I went upstairs after *middag* to make sure I really had gotten everything. I looked around my room, for what I assumed was the last time. I remembered how disappointed I was that first day, when I found out that I was going to have a room of my own. Perhaps having this room to myself was a harbinger of things to come. At least having to change families gave me a chance to catch some of my mistakes and faults as they had been brought out into the open from this experience within an experience.

"Pete," *fru* Román's voice interrupted my thoughts. "Bring your bags downstairs."

"I'll see you tomorrow in school," I said as I shook Karl Arvid's hand. I shook hands with Elin, too, and give Bergljot a big hug.

"I'm sure everything will be fine," *fru* Román said as she shook my hand. "Don't worry." That was easy for her to say; she wasn't switching families nine months ahead of schedule.

Román helped me with my bags into the Volvo, and I waved limply to the others as we drove up the hill.

"Where do the Norbyes live?" I asked him as we drove past the cemetery toward the top of the Island.

"Holtveien."

"Holtveien? That's the road we walked on when we went to the Holt Farm, isn't it."

"I should think so."

"I wonder if I passed their house?" As we continued up the hill, I saw some familiar sights.

"This is Holtveien," Román said.

"I remember the school." I clearly remembered the house with the large yard and the chain-link fence in front, the house set off in the woods. "We walked by this house," I remarked, as Román slowed the car and pulled into the driveway through the opening in the chain-link fence.

"This is where the Norbyes live," he said simply. A man of few words, and none of them particularly well-chosen.

Now that I had to consider that house more carefully, I noticed that it was bigger than the Románs, and it was much more interesting. The driveway was a real driveway, like we had in Westport. The neighboring houses, as was also the case in Westport, were a distance away, and blocked off by trees. There was a sense of privacy not common among the houses closer to the center of town. There was a small VW parked in the driveway; the Román's Volvo was spacious by comparison. But the house and the yard—especially the yard—were much bigger than where I had lived for the previous few months.

All I knew about the family was that there were two daughters; I didn't even know how old. If I were lucky, they would both be Bergljot's age, or even younger. I got along well with the little kids.

As we parked the car, the front door opened and I saw Norbye and *fru* Norbye. They looked noticeably older than Román and his wife. I was looking for parents, not grandparents. Norbye looked somewhere between severe and formal...a really great continuum. He had straight, dark hair; he must have used the Norwegian equivalent of Brylcream, because the hair was pretty well plastered down. He was wearing a suit, a tie, and dress shoes. *Fru* Norbye was quite a bit shorter, and a little plumper. Unlike Norbye, she wore a big smile and looked a lot friendlier. She was wearing a plain dress and an apron, and she had her slippers on.

"*God aften, Norbye,*" Román greeted his counterpart. "This is Pete."

"*God aften*, Pete," Norbye shook my hand, with a firm hand and the hint of a smile.

"*Velkommen hit.* Welcome to our house," *fru* Norbye said, as she shook my hand, too. It sounded so trite and I was embarrassed to feel it, but she really did have a twinkle in her eye.

Román helped me in with the bags, at least as far as the entry room, and then hurried back to his car. Was he afraid he would catch something? Was it me or the Norbyes?" In a way, he was such a sad man. The whole scene was sad. My three months with the Románs had been sad. But the Norbyes didn't give me much opportunity to dwell on the past.

"Come in and meet our daughters," Norbye said as I took off my shoes.

"Perhaps you would like to *drikke kaffe?*" *fru* Norbye asked. It had taken me the entire previous month (when I knew enough *norsk*) to fully understand that phrase. The literal translation meant that they were offering me a cup of coffee to drink—*drikke kaffe* = drink coffee—but the phrase was deceiving. When Norwegians drank a "cup" of coffee, they "*drikke en kopp kaffe.*" But when they asked you to *drikke kaffe*, they are really referring to a fifth meal of the day, the coffee meal: coffee and cakes.

"This is our oldest daughter, Helen," Norbye introduced me to a tall, blond girl four or five years older than me. She had a slightly nervous, but firm handshake.

"And this is Torild, our other daughter," he continued formally. She looked to be my age or a little younger. Right age; wrong gender. She was even taller than Helen, and taller than me. She was full of smiles, energy, and enthusiasm.

"*Værsågod,*" *fru* Norbye asked us to the table. Norwegians didn't *drikke kaffe* at the dining table; instead, they used the coffee table, which had the *kaffe* and a large, beautiful, one-layer chocolate cake. The way to my heart may not have been through my stomach, but the way through my worrying certainly was; they started off on the right foot.

"*Værsågod, vil du ha et stykke kake?* Please, will you have a piece of cake?" she asked, handing me a piece of the delicious-looking cake.

"*Ja, takk,*" I answered, showing my pleasure. I kept saying to myself: make it work; enjoy yourself; they're pleasant people; they want you here; be appreciative. I wasn't used to thinking that way; I always wanted to just let the feelings flow. But I had failed once (whoever's fault it was) and I didn't want to repeat that performance. But two sisters?

"I have seen you at school," Torild ventured. "I am in 3rd English. Our class is off in the annex, so we don't mix as much with the rest of the school. But I have seen you there."

"I work at my father's office," Helen explained. "Peder Norbye is the name of the firm. You may have seen it?"

"I don't think so."

"It's on a small street off Storgate," she continued. "If you stand at the Wito corner store and look toward the harbor, you can see our sign. We are printers, and publishers, and stationers."

"We have a retail store," Norbye explained, "and a wholesale business."

"We also have a son," *fru* Norbye joined in the conversation. "Per. He's twenty-eight and he also works at the firm. He's married and he lives with Bodil, his wife, and his two young children. They live in the large apartment buildings."

"I didn't even know Tromsø had apartment buildings," I said, genuinely surprised.

"Of course," Norbye smiled. "Tromsø is the capitol of Northern Norway. We're not some small town, here." Everyone laughed, including me. Every time I did anything, I bumped up against Tromsø's small-townness. How else would Torild have known me without my ever knowing her, for example?

"Tell *mor* and *far* about the sign," Torild suggested. "I told them a little, even though I never saw it. But you tell them, too."

"I just thought it would help with my *norsk,*" I said more modestly than I felt. "It was a bigger success than I ever imagined."

"It certainly worked," Norbye smiled. "You really didn't know any *norsk* before you came to Norway?"

"*Nei.* But people are kind to me: no one has a problem telling me when I hide a mistake."

"That was clever," Helen said.

"It's difficult to make jokes in another language," Torild's energy level was infectious. "I've been studying English for years and I still can't say anything phony."

Our conversation continued in that animated fashion for a couple of hours. The family was interesting and interested in me. All of them were lively and full of fun; we even got Norbye to laugh...often. I was still holding my breath, but I was beginning to let myself believe that this family might be okay. At 8:00 PM the doorbell rang.

"It's Lund," *fru* Norbye said as she returned from the front door with a man I had never seen. "We were just about to have *aftens*, Lund. Would you like to join us?"

"*Takk*," Lund accepted her invitation.

"Oh, Pete, this is Lund. He works with my husband," *fru* Norbye explained. "And Lund, this is Pete, our new son."

My God, the magic words. In the three months with the Románs, *fru* Román never introduced me as her son; I always felt as if I were just a guest in their house. Karl Arvid didn't refer to me as "his brother" until the end of September. Clearly, I was still just a guest here with the Norbyes, but at least they were willing to think of me in a different way. I never had the guts to call *fru* Román "*mor*," but I thought, even on that first evening, I could call *fru* Norbye "*mor*" tomorrow morning, because it already felt as if I had a better relationship with her after three hours than was the case with the Románs after almost three months.

"Pete," *fru* Norbye called out the next morning. I had probably set my alarm, but the excitement of the evening ended with an unbelievably sound sleep. My room *hos* Norbye, at the Norbyes, was my own, as had been the case at the Románs, but *hos* Norbye I had two sisters instead of a brother, and my expectations were substantially different. The room was even smaller than what I had *hos* Románs, and plain: just a bed, a small dresser, and a window looking out through the woods and over the driveway toward Holtveien. Somehow, the size didn't bother me. Somehow, nothing that morning bothered me.

I quickly washed, shaved, and took off down the stairs. Torild was already sitting at the kitchen table. It was a small table, tucked away in a brightly lit corner of the kitchen, facing the back yard, which was mostly the woods surrounding the house.

"*God morn*," Torild greeted me.

"*God morn*," I said in return.

"Did you sleep?" *fru* Norbye asked.

"*Ja, takk*. I hope you won't have to wake me every morning."

"I guess he feels comfortable here," Torild said, really addressing both of us.

"I guess so," I agreed, truthfully.

"You're not used to school on Saturday, are you?" Torild asked, spreading some marmalade on a piece of bread. "We had another exchange student—Lois—a few years ago, and she wasn't used to school on Saturdays either."

My first warning flag went up. The Románs also had another exchange student living with them, just a few years before me. She was the same age as Karin and, according to *fru* Román, the two of them had gotten along fabulously. The student was, in fact, a fabulous student. They couldn't say enough good things about her. I got the distinct feeling that two exchange students *hos* Román, was one exchange student too many. I didn't want the Norbyes to be anything like the Románs. There was more conversation—at least conversation including me—at that brief breakfast than I think I ever had in three months of meals with the Románs, but any similarity was scary. I wanted everything to work; I didn't want to be compared to anyone's "fabulous" exchange-student sister.

"I'm getting used to it now," I answered, doing the best I could to wipe away my doubts. "It's been over a month, and it almost feels normal. Anyway, it's just half a day, and we always go to the newsreels and that's a lot of fun."

"I don't know how you did things at the Románs," *fru* Norbye explained, "but here *hos* Norbye we all make our own lunch."

Fru Román had made lunches for everyone. I actually preferred having to take care of at least some small part of my life. Here the task was especially easy, because lunch and breakfast were essentially the same. All I really had to do was make two breakfasts, and take one with me to school.

"So," Torild looked at me with a smile, "you like our *geitost*?"

"I love it, although it did take me a while to get used to it," I admitted.

"Are you ready to walk to school?" Torild asked.

"*Ja. Takk for mat.* Thanks for the food." Norwegians found an excuse to thank for almost everything. When Lund had left last night, he said: *takk for nå*; thanks for now. At the end of the first *russefest*, many of the kids said: *takk for festen*, thanks for the party. Everyone says "*takk for mat*" at the end of every meal.

"Have a good day," *fru* Norbye waved to us from the door, as we walked out the driveway and onto Holtveien. Torild and I had a much longer walk than I had from the Románs: at least twenty minutes. Despite my fears, things with the Norbyes felt different already that first full day. Having to make my own lunch made me feel a part of the family. There was a vitality in that family, more like what I was used to in Westport. They laughed a lot, and showed a great deal of affection for each other. I didn't get the feeling I would be lonely in that family.

"Are you all right?" Torild asked. "You are so quiet."

"Everything's fine," I answered. "I was just thinking."

"Well," Torild laughed, "just don't think too much."

-13-
Mor og Søster

Sunday was a day of rest and relaxation for Norwegians. Like the Románs, the Norbyes didn't go to church either. I didn't mind and loved the irony of everyone belonging, and no one going, to the same church.

"Pete," Helen asked after breakfast, "shall we *gå en tur?*"

"*Gå en tur?* Go on a trip?" I asked in return. I was a bit confused. What kind of trip could we go on Sunday afternoon?

"Shall we *gå en tur?* Shall we go for a walk?" she repeated.

I was constantly struck by the way different cultures used words in slightly different ways. At Staples, I remembered a teacher telling us that Eskimos had more than twenty different words for snow, and I remembered how that made no sense to me. But after four months in Norway, and over one month in *norsk*, I began to appreciate what that teacher had said. "*Gå*" meant to go: go to school, go *til byen*, go to church. So when Helen asked me if I wanted to "*gå en tur*," I translated that to mean: go on a trip. But, to Norwegians, "*gå*" implied to walk, even if it meant to go. So, when you go *til byen*, you walk *til byen*; when you go to school, you walk to school. If you get *til byen* by car, you don't *go* there, you *drive* there. I loved learning all those little differences and seeing the culture through its language.

"Oh, *gå en tur*," I said, now knowing what she was asking. "Sure, I'd love to."

"I don't think you'll need a jacket," Torild said, as she joined Helen and me at the front door. "Do you have a sweater?"

"Erika in my class is knitting me a Norwegian sweater," I said, "but it's not done yet. I'll get one of my American sweaters from my room. I'll be right back."

"Wait a minute," *fru* Norbye suggested. "What about that old one of Per's?"

"The blue one?" Helen asked.

"*Ja,*" *fru* Norbye answered.

"He could even have that one," Torild suggested. "It's too small for Per."

Helen sprinted up the stairs and brought back down a blue, V-neck sweater. "Try this on."

"It's not hand-knit," *fru* Norbye explained, "but it's all wool."

"This way," Torild examined the fit as I pulled the sweater over my head, "we can keep the sweater in the family."

"That looks great," Helen exclaimed, with genuine enthusiasm. "Now you have your first Norwegian sweater."

"*Takk*," I said, with genuine appreciation, both for the sweater and the comment about keeping it in the family.

"You kids have fun on your walk," *fru* Norbye bid us good-bye at the front door.

It was an unbelievable day. The sun was out, there was hardly a cloud in the sky, and it was warm. I had feared for the worse about Tromsø's arctic climate, but there was no snow yet, and it was already October. And that Sunday, as we headed out on our walk, it was positively balmy: a whopping 65°F.

We walked down Holtveien, away from town and toward the Holt farm. The weather may have felt like spring, but Tromsøy definitely looked like fall. The colors were spectacular, and just like New England. All the leaves had turned, and there were yellows, and browns, and reds, along with the green of the pine trees. We walked down Holtveien toward the water; the farm was on our right as we turned left along the coastal road. There were a few houses scattered along the road at the water's edge, and even fewer on the other side of the road. There were few houses but lots of trees.

We were not alone. The road was full of people, all out for their Sunday walk, while the weather permitted. There were families with small kids; what I would have expected. But there were older people, too, all out walking, some at a brisk pace. And there were kids, kids my own age, out for a walk by themselves.

"Isn't that Harald Larsen?" Helen asked her sister. "With the beautiful sweater?"

"*Ja*," Torild answered matter of factly. *I* was still taken aback by the fact that everyone knew everyone else, but people there took that for granted. Helen and Harald's older sister had probably grown up together.

"*Hei*, Pete," Harald greeted us. "I see you've got two new sisters."

The month before I would have been impressed that he knew I had moved, but not by October. I had been *hos* Norbye for almost two days; that was old news, now.

"*Hei*, Harald."

"You're not in Pete's class, are you?" Helen asked.

"Helen," Torild scoffed, as only a younger sister could. "Harald's in 5th *Mathematics*."

"Let me get a picture of my two new sisters and my old friend," I said.

I Was a Teenage Norwegian

I had taken a few pictures during the summer, but I hadn't taken many since school had begun; I hadn't taken any *hos* Román. I remembered about AFS students at Staples coming back with great slides to show off at a school assembly. If I didn't start cracking, the only thing I would have to show for my year abroad was a couple of Norwegian sweaters and my "*Unnskyld men jeg forstå ikke engelsk*" sign from the first day of school. Of course, I could dazzle them with my *norsk*, but they wouldn't appreciate how clever I was.

"Let's stop at the Lunds" Torild suggested on the way back home.

"Do they know we're coming?" I asked naively, getting to feel more and more like a stupid American.

"Don't be silly, Pete," Helen chided me. "I remember Lois had the same problem when she lived with us. We got the impression that no one in America goes anywhere without an invitation..."

"... or at least telephoning in advance," Torild interrupted.

"In Tromsø," Helen continued, "it's all right to just visit friends, to just drop in on them. You'll see."

And see I did. The Lunds greeted us at the door, looking for all the world as if they had expected us. Within ten minutes, *fru* Lund had set the coffee table; we would *drikke kaffe*. Along with the *kaffe*, there were two kinds of cakes, and bread slices with jam. It was as if people there were always prepared to have visitors. Well, maybe they were.

"Are you making lots of friends at school?" Torild asked me as we walked to school together the next day.

"*Ja*, lots," I answered. "Especially among the *russ*."

"I'm glad I'm at the *gymnas*," Torild said, "but I can't wait until I'm a *russ*."

"I never know whether the other kids think of me more as a *russ*," I wondered out loud, "or as an exchange student."

"As an exchange student, I think, especially the *småpiker*," Torild giggled.

"How...?"

"Sisters know these things."

Something was different, that was certain. It was either me, or the Norbyes, or a little of both. I had been *hos* Norbye for five days and Torild and I had walked to school together every day, just like brother and sister. I had been *hos* Norbye for five days and I felt more a part of that family in that brief time than I ever had *hos* Román. Was it simply that the Norbyes were different: more open? more accepting? more genuinely desirous of having me? Or had I somehow changed already: more open? more accepting? less judgmental?

"*Hei*, Pete," Gunnar greeted me as Torild and I reached the *skolegård* and she headed off to be with her friends.

"Who was the girl I saw you with, Pete?" Gunnar asked, ever curious and ever the ladies man.

"That was no girl," Franck answered. "That was his *søster*."

After school I walked to the USIS office and got my first look at the Paris Herald Tribune in a week. I couldn't believe I was so busy and pre-occupied that I had almost lost track of Maris. I made it just in time; he had made the front page with his record-breaking 61st home run. Who would have believed that anyone would ever break Babe Ruth's record? Well, maybe I could now put that little piece of America behind me.

With everything that had happened, I found it difficult to keep up with my letter writing. It was surprising how letters gave me a way of thinking about, and processing all that happened to me.

October 11, 1961

Dear Mom and Dad,

I'm sorry it has been so long since I wrote you last, but so much has happened, and I've found it difficult to write.

As you can guess from my new return address, I have finally moved from the Románs. I am living with a family called Norbye, and the difference is astounding. They're so much fun, laughing and making jokes, and making me feel right at home. It really feels like a family.

The first russefest got me started as being "one of the russ" and the icing was put on the three-layer cake of change as I was officially (through my own private ceremony in my own private mind) made "one of the boys." That is one of the many reasons I consider the first russefest so important.

This takes on even more importance when you realize that I was never this close to my schoolmates in Westport after eleven years...and it has been only a little over a month here in Tromsø. I have really found a home now with my schoolmates.

I can now joke around with everyone in school (even Engelsen) and I am a part of 5th English. These relationships now insure a great, fun-filled, happy, exciting, inspiring, serious, thoughtful, growth-filled, memorable, loving, broadening, eye-opening and, most of all, warm and wonderful year. All my fears are gone now—except my basic fears of people and myself that will take more work than a few weeks to exterminate—and I am both happy and relieved.

In order to make a venture such as this successful, one must get close to the people one lives with, and I believe the foundation for that closeness has been laid. There is one less burden for me to carry—and when there are so many—contrary to popular belief—one less makes all the difference in the world. For as one goes, so the optimist in me contends, so go the rest.

How can people become close to one another? By love and understanding. How can people love and understand one another? By being close. It's as easy as that, and much more rewarding.

All my love,
Pete

"Pete," Torild asked after *middag* on Saturday, "are you going to the *Bragefest* this evening."

"Of course," I answered. "I'm not one to miss a *fest*." If I were speaking English (and, therefore, still in America) that comment would have been completely out of character. But I was speaking *norsk*, and *fester* were a natural part of the new, Norwegian me.

"Will Karl Arvid be there?"

"I'm sure he will."

"Is that a problem for you?"

"*Nei*. We probably get along better now that I'm not living there than we did when I was. That's kind of strange, isn't it?"

Just as we finished our conversation, Torild headed upstairs and the telephone rang. I was the nearest one to the phone.

"Can you get the phone?" Torild yelled from the stairs.

My *norsk* had improved, but there was something about speaking on the telephone that was noticeably more difficult than speaking to people in person. Maybe it was not being able to see the speaker's face; maybe it was the hollow sound of voices on the telephone. In any case, I rarely spoke on the telephone, and never unless it was absolutely necessary; when I did speak, I always made it fast.

"Norbye, *værsågod*," I answered in my most polite telephone-answering voice, using the greeting I had most often heard and assumed was the most correct one.

"*Er fru Norbye inne*? Is *fru* Norbye in?"

"*Ja. Et øyeblikk*. Just a minute." I was now faced with my first family crisis with the Norbyes. The phone call was for *fru* Norbye and she was in the kitchen. I had told the caller to wait a minute, so I had a small amount of time in which to make my decision. I had two choices: I could walk into the kitchen and tell her the phone call was for her, or I could yell to her that the phone call was for her. Yelling was common—Torild had just yelled from the stairs for me to get the phone—so that wasn't the issue. The issue was what did I call *fru* Norbye? Was I ready to take the plunge? If I was, yelling from a distance was the safest, easiest way. I could do it without actually having to face her. What the hell; I would do it.

"*Mor*," I yelled out. "the telephone is for you."

God damn! I did it! I called her mother. I had made the transition. I had a real family now. Unbelievable! Amazing! I did it!!

After she finished with the call, *mor* stuck her head out through the kitchen door and simply said, "*Takk*, Pete." She took for granted what was so agonizing for me. She took for granted what I felt was the biggest step I had taken in Norway. She took for granted she was my *mor*.

Except for the Holt farm, everywhere else in Tromsø was a longer walk from the Norbyes than from the Románs, so I had to start a little earlier if I wanted to get to the *fest* by 8:00 o'clock. I had assumed Torild would be coming to the *Bragefest*; I forgot she wasn't in the *Bragerevy*. Now that I was going alone, I realized that maybe it was better that I went alone; after all, who wants to go to a *fest* with his kid sister?

It took me almost forty-five minutes to get to the *kafé* and the *Bragefest*. Kafé Syd was near the *badestrand* on the southern part of the island. The walk probably took me a little longer than necessary since I tended to stop and watch the fisherman unloading their catch as I walked along the shore.

It was my third *fest*, and my first since the *russefest*. I might have been "one of the *russ*" by then, but I also had to be one of the Brage people, too. There were a number of different kinds of groups in Tromsø—classes in school, political party youth groups, church youth groups, sports clubs—and there weren't any problems being associated with a number of different groups. There were a number of *russ* in Brage, Franck Pettersen, for example, and no one made fun of me for being involved.

"Pete," Karl Arvid greeted me at the door. He looked genuinely happy to see me. "Glad you could come. Did you come with anyone?"

"*Nei*," I said. "I walked by myself."

"Well, come in and meet some of the other kids." He walked with me to a bunch of kids off in a corner of the *kafé*.

"Why don't you sit with these guys," Karl Arvid continued. "You may know some of them already, since many of them are in Torild's class. You all know Pete. This is Anna Britt. This is Sonja. This is Mette. This is Pål. Franck, you know. You'll have to ask the others; I've got to get back to the door."

"Well, Pete," Franck began, "are you ready for another *fest*?"

"I hope so."

"You see," Franck explained to the others with a smile. "Pete doesn't drink. Not even our famous *Mackøl*. So, we all have to make sure that he can have fun, anyway."

"Do you like living with the Norbyes?" Anna Britt asked me. She had bright red hair and I'd seen her with Torild; I couldn't forget that hair.

"It's great," I answered. "Everyone is so friendly and full of fun. We laugh all the time."

"How long will you be there," the girl Karl Arvid introduced as Sonja asked. She was pretty, but I hadn't seen her before, at least not to remember.

"I really don't know," I answered truthfully. "I assumed it would be a few days or maybe a few weeks, but no one has told me. I don't know if anyone knows."

There were forty or fifty kids there, about the same size as the first *russefest*. Most of the kids were sitting at tables spread along the outside walls. The serving area was near one of the inside walls with a number of glass display cases, much like a bakery. That was the way the *kafés* in town worked, too. Because the Kafé Syd was closed to the public, that meant the tables could be moved against the outside walls to make a big space in the middle of the *kafé* for dancing.

"Do you want to dance?" Sonja asked as the music started.

"*Ja*," I answered.

"Is it common for girls to ask boys to dance in Tromsø?" I asked Sonja.

"I guess so," she answered. "I've never really thought much about it. Is it common where you come from in Connecticut?"

"Not at all. It's never even happened to me before."

"That's strange. How else can I make sure you know I want to dance with you unless I ask?"

The music was provided by a live band. In Tromsø, kids listened to records, especially American records, but at *fester* they didn't play records for dancing, only for listening. Some of the band's music was fast enough to dance fast to; lots of it was slow enough to slowdance to. Some kids were pretty good dancers, but there were many who weren't much better than I was.

"Do you have parties like this in Connecticut?" Sonja asked.

"Not really. Our parties are either at school—those are the big ones, like this—or at people's houses. There really is no place where kids can go off by themselves and have a *fest*, like you do at a *kafé*."

"We always have parties like this," Sonja said. "Especially the *russ*, but you've already had your first *russefest*, haven't you?"

We talked a while longer. Then, when the band started playing a tune with a fox trot beat, I said, "Do you want to dance?" I figured it was my turn to ask Sonja. After all, how was she going to know I wanted to dance with her unless I asked?

As a dance ended, most of the boys kept their arms around their partners' waists, and the girls did likewise. My biggest concern was that I would leave my arm around Sonja's waist and she would pull away from me. Rejection had always been my biggest fear. I would rather have done nothing, than have done anything that might have lead to rejection. But, what the hell; when in Tromsø, and so forth. I kept my arm around Sonja's waist, and she kept hers around mine. She didn't move away; in fact, she actually moved a little closer to me as we waited for the next dance to start. I might be able to get used to that closeness and those feelings.

Although Sonja and I danced with other kids throughout the evening, we came back to each other periodically. When the music ended each time we danced, we stood a little closer to each other than I stood to other girls. When we talked to each other, we laughed a little more at each other's jokes. When we slowdanced together, we held each other a little closer.

At about midnight, most of us were ready to call it a night, and we headed back toward town on foot.

"*Takk*," Sonja said as she reached the road where our paths parted. "I had fun."

"Me, too," I said, meaning every word of the two words. "I'll see you on Monday."

"*God natt.*"

"How was the *Bragefest*?" Helen asked me, as I took off my shoes and walked into the living room. I was not used to people in my family being up when I came home late at night; I liked the change.

"It was great," I answered. "We had a nice little band: a guitar and an accordion, just like the the *russefest*.

"Who did you meet?"

"I met one of Torild's friends, Anna Britt. And I danced a lot with Sonja Heim."

"Oh, Sonja. She has an older sister who is married to Kjell Hansen, who works in our warehouse. I don't think I've seen Sonja since she was little. I imagine," Helen said with a smile, "that she's not so little any more."

"*Nei*, not any more," I returned her smile.

"So, how are you finding the Norwegian girls?"

"Well, they are different from what I am used to. They're more friendly, and I find it easier getting to know them. It's probably because I'm an exchange student, at least in part. But I think kids here are different, as well. I really do feel more comfortable here."

"How do you mean?"

"Well," I decided to open up, "back in the States I wasn't too popular."

"Really?" Helen looked genuinely surprised. "I have always assumed all AFSers were popular."

"You're looking at one big exception. But things feel different here. Part of it is being different, being an American. But I feel different, too, and I'm sure part of it is that."

"How do you feel different?"

"It's difficult to explain. I'm not used to talking like this in *norsk*."

"You can talk in English, if you want."

"*Nei*, I want to be able to say everything in *norsk*. In America, I don't get close to girls. Ever since the first *russefest*, I've noticed that kids are different here. They get close to each other. Just friendly, you know. I never thought I could be that way, but tonight I did it and it was fine. It was great, actually. You know, I kept my arm around Sonja's waist after we finished dancing. It was just friendly, but it felt real nice. Does any of this make sense?"

Helen and I kept talking until 2:00 o'clock in the morning. All in *norsk* and all about those changes coming over me. I had never had a big sister before and I found it much to my liking. And I liked having a kid sister, as well. In fact, Helen and Torild had quickly become the brother that Karl Arvid had never been.

-14-
Family and Friends

I came to Tromsø wanting to have a brother my own age, but sisters were turning out to be just as much fun and just as supportive. I came to Tromsø wanting to have another family I could feel was a real family, and with the Norbyes I had that family. I came to Tromsø speaking hardly a word of *norsk*, and by October I spoke hardly a word of English. I came to Tromsø as the person I was in Westport, and I was beginning to feel I was becoming the person I could be.

By October, I was already on my second family in Tromsø, and there was still a third in my future. It wasn't until I moved in with the Norbyes that I felt a part of a Norwegian family. It may have taken me almost three months to have someone in Tromsø I could call *mor*, but when the time came, I was ready for it.

"*Mor*," I said as I ate Sunday breakfast, the word spilling out of my mouth as naturally as if I had called her *mor* for all of my life, "I have to go back to the Románs this morning."

"Oh," she said.

"I borrowed some money from *fru* Román before I left, and I want to return it, now that I have my monthly allowance from AFS."

"Don't forget, we are visiting Per this *formiddag*."

By October, I had come to the conclusion that time is a central aspect of culture, and the way a culture tells or describes time says a lot about the culture. Noon was the big dividing event in American time; *middag* was the big dividing event in Norwegian time. There was a morning there, and it more-or-less corresponded to morning in America. But there was no concept of noon and there was no afternoon in the American sense. After morning in Norway came *formiddag*, that is, the time before dinner time. After *formiddag* came *eftermiddag*, that is, the after dinner time. *Middag* was traditionally between 3-4:00 o'clock; *formiddag* preceded that time and *eftermiddag* came after it regardless of exactly when a family ate *middag*.

Telling time was, in a way, additionally difficult, because Norway had one other new concept for me. Norway had hours and minutes, but there wasn't a *half past* the hour; instead, there was a *half before* the hour, and it was referred to as half the hour. For example, I had that conversation with *mor* that Sunday morning at 9:30; in Norway, we referred to the time as half ten. I was often off by an hour, both in my head and in my actions, because of my continuing inability to understand the time.

The Románs' house was a 15-20 minute walk from the Norbyes, mostly down hill toward town, and I was anxious as I approached the house. One thing was certain: I saw that house differently that day than I had on the day I arrived in Tromsø over two months before. On that memorable day, I looked at that small, reddish house with its tiny parking space for the car and its walls without windows with awe and anticipation. That was my new house; that was my new family. On that fall Sunday in October, walking back to that house, it was just a Tromsø house, like so many others. The small number of the windows was no longer a curiosity; the lack of windows now made sense in terms of the harsh climate. The tiny parking space for the car instead of a real driveway, was no longer an oddity to be noticed; it was about average for Tromsø.

"*God morn*, Pete," *fru* Román greeted me at the door.

"I've come to return the KR10 you loaned me before I left," I explained as I took off my shoes and walked through the kitchen.

"*Takk*," *fru* Román said as she accepted the money. "Can you stay for a few minutes?"

"*Ja*," I answered, sitting down with her in the living room. "Where is everyone?"

"Elin and Karl Arvid are still asleep, but Román and Bergljot are up somewhere. How is everything going with the Norbyes?"

"Everything's fine," I answered, having dreaded the question for the previous few days, ever since my allowance had come from Oslo. How could I really tell her the truth, at least as I saw it? "They're all very friendly."

"We've known them for years. Román and Norbye are in Rotary together."

"Oh."

"I hope you are able to talk more with them than you did with us, Pete. I'm sure that will help. Maybe if you're happier there you will give more of yourself."

As *fru* Román and I continued our little talk, Román came down the stairs, nodded at me, and sat down in one of the living room chairs. He didn't join our conversation.

"Pete," Bergljot screamed, racing toward me, jumping in my lap, and giving me a huge hug. *There* was someone who missed me.

"*Hei*, Bergljot," I responded, without the scream. "*Kor det går?* How are you?" Now that I had grown and changed so much, it was appropriate to show off. What better way to show off than to show off my *Tromsøværing*.

"Are you coming back to live with us again?" she asked, always hopeful. From her point of view, there had never been a reason for my leaving; there was no reason why I couldn't just move back in with her.

"*Nei*, Bergljot. I'm living with the Norbyes now?"

"Why...."

"No more questions," *fru* Román interrupted. "Pete and I are just finishing our conversation. He has to get back to his new home."

I cringed at the way she said "his new home." *fru* Román would have made a good Jewish mother.

I don't care what she says, I said to myself as I walked back home. I don't say that I share no responsibility for what happened, but it wasn't all me. No matter what she says. It's only been two weeks since I left. I don't feel any different now; I don't feel I'm acting any differently with the Norbyes than I did with the Románs. But I sure notice a difference in the behavior of the Norbyes in comparison to the Románs. She's not going to make me feel any more guilty than I normally do. I wanted things to work out with the Románs; I really did. I worked harder at it than any of them did, that's for sure. In the whole family, Bergljot's the only one who genuinely misses me; that tells me something.

In spite of that conversation with myself, I was genuinely torn. On the one hand, I needed to feel that a large burden of responsibility for the failure with the Románs rested with the Románs. On the other hand, I needed to feel that I was changing, that I was learning from past mistakes, that I was becoming someone new and different. The fact that the truth lay somewhere in between didn't reduce my ambivalence and confusion, at least not at the time.

After lunch *hos* Norbye, we all piled into the VW and headed for Per's.

"If there's one thing I want, *far*," Torild said as she squeezed into the back seat, "it's a four-door car. Maybe now that Pete's living with us...."

Far just smiled, as he pushed the seat-back forward and got in himself. A VW was a bit small for this family without me. *Mor* was short, but not small. Helen was about my height—5'7"—Torild was a couple of inches taller than that, and *far* was taller still. With my addition to the family, the back seat of the VW felt quite cozy.

"How is it back there?" *mor* asked, knowing the answer already.

"I think a Volvo would be nice," Torild continued her original thought. "Maybe an Opel."

"I like this VW," I smiled. "It gives me a chance to get to know my sisters real well."

"How 'well' are you ready for," Helen traded glances with Torild, and they both started tickling me. I think they enjoyed having another brother as much as I enjoyed having two sisters.

Per lived in one of Tromsø's three skyscrapers, large apartment buildings that rested on the plateau that defined the top of Tromsøy. They were at least fifteen stories high, which, by Tromsø standards, was mammoth. Tromsø was essentially an island of small, single-family houses.

"*Velkommen*," Per greeted us at the door. "Pete, this is Bodil, my wife."

"*Det gleder meg*," Bodil said as she shook my hand firmly.

"That's quite a nice sweater you have on," Per said, winking at *mor*. "It looks familiar."

If there was such a thing as a "typical Norwegian," Per was probably it. He was well over six feet tall, with thick, wavy blond hair, an elfin smile, which on him was not at all in conflict with his substantial size, and a captivating warmth and friendliness.

"And here are my two children: Mette and Bente. This is Pete."

The women headed off to the kitchen to see what Bodil had prepared,and to get the *kaffe* made, or something. Per and I played with the children. Bente was content with her dolls, but Mette definitely wanted to check out her new playmate. She had an old-fashioned top, the kind you pushed down on a vertical handle to make the top spin. She definitely liked that, and couldn't get enough of my spinning it for her.

"*Igjen, onkel* Pete, *igjen,*" she squealed.

I'll do it again, and again, and again some more, I thought to myself, as long as you keep calling me *onkel* Pete. What a great way kids have of making you feel comfortable. It was amazing how I was brought immediately into this family.

"*Værsågod,*" Bodil said, as she brought the final plates to what appeared to me an already fully-laden coffee table.

It was apparent to me that I still had not gotten straight the rules and regulations around eating. Here it was still *formiddag* and we had this gargantuan spread of cake and waffles, with cheese and jam. And I knew there would still be *middag* when we got home, and there was always *aftens* to end the day.

"I hear," Bodil said, "that you like *sjokoladekake*, chocolate cake. At least that's what *mor* says. So I've made you my version."

"*Takk,*" I said, accepting a piece of the one-layer cake. I was still struck by all the *little* differences. *Smørbrød* used only one slice of bread. You were only supposed to put one topping on a *smørbrød*. *Sjokoladekaker* were only one layer. Bodil's cake was good, but *mor's* was better. I could eat *mor's sjokoladekake* every day.

"You appear to like kids," Per commented. It was a little difficult to understand the words through the *sjokoladekake*.

"I guess so. I never really think about it, but I guess I do. I do a lot of babysitting in America. I mean, I did."

"Pete," Helen asked, "did I tell you what I heard a girl from the *gymnas* say when I was waiting on her in the store yesterday?"

"*Nei,* but I guess you will now, right?"

"She said that everyone at school thinks you're *artig* and *søt*."

"Fun I can understand," Torild chides me, "but cute? Our brother, *søt*? Look at that face. Who is she kidding? I'm at school every day and I never hear anyone call Pete *søt*. Who were you talking to? No one in my class, I'm sure; we know better in Third English."

I got the feeling that being *artig* was quite important to the Norwegians. They liked the fact that I was fun, even a little playful at times, and that I could make jokes in *norsk*, even puns. I knew it was important for me to continue to be that way, rather than expose my more serious side. It was a source of tension, however, and I often felt there were important parts of myself which never got expressed. My serious, intellectual side was a critical component in my LRY friendships, which were my closest friendships.

Although the Unitarian church my family joined when I turned 13 was located in Westport, it serviced the entire county; there weren't that many Unitarians. LRY, then, drew from the entire county as well, and most of my LRY friends were from near-by towns. Although my inter-action with them was infrequent, it was intense. We were, for the most part, intellectually driven, and most of our time together was spent thinking about and discussing issues: comparative religion, existential philosophy, the difference between religion and morality...light, after-dinner conversation. The times we spent together were, for almost all of us, like being on an island. We all felt left out of our regular school/com-munity social life. LRY was a place where we felt a strong sense of com-munity and connectedness to other outcasts like ourselves.

LRY was a perfect place for me, and within its limited confines (meeting one evening a week) I thrived. I liked my fellow LRYers and I was liked by them. I was able to give expression in their company to many aspects of myself. My sense of humor developed and expressed itself without fear of being misunderstood. Although I was not at all religious, there was an element of spirituality in my personality and LRY was a safe and supportive environment in which to express that part of me.

Sometimes, I felt frustrated that those parts of me disappeared in Tromsø. The kids were fun, *artig*, but I often felt I couldn't talk to them. But, I thought to myself, I'm not here to satisfy just myself and my own desires; I'm here as much to satisfy the *Tromsøværing* and their desires. I could handle being *artig* if I really was *søt*, too.

Later in the evening, after *aftens*, Torild and I talked. Part of what was so exciting about being in Tromsø was that life so often contradict-ed thought. Torild and I sat together on the couch in the living room. It was a big room, much like our living room in Westport, but brighter because of the lighter and more colorful furniture and the shiny natural wood floors. In spite of its shiny appearance, it felt lived in. And I felt as if I were a part of that 'lived in' feeling. We talked as if we had lived together all our lives. And our conversation contradicted my feelings of the afternoon, because Torild and I talked as seriously and intimately as I had talked with any of my LRY friends.

That was one of the special parts about being a member of the Norbye family: the long talks I had with my sisters. Everyone talked in that family, and I talked with everyone. We always talked at meals, the whole family, just like the animated conversations we had at the dinner table in Westport. *Mor* and *far* talked to me all the time: about school, about my stay at the Románs, about my friends, about my life in Tromsø, about my life in Westport. But it was with Helen and Torild that I had really long talks. That evening, Torild and I talked for over two hours.

I thought a lot about the future and what I could do to prepare to meet it. That was one of the things Torild and I talked about, although I did more talking and she did more listening. I wanted to do something to help the World and its inhabitants, but what I wanted to do was still pretty nebulous in my mind. I felt there was something special about me (although I was not always sure what it was) and that it was up to people like me to take upon ourselves the responsibility of working toward world peace and understanding.

Luckily for me, Torild helped me translate those abstract thoughts into thinking about what I could actually do to begin. Naturally, she explained, I had the opportunity to start in on that job right then and there in Tromsø, although I had to insure I didn't overdo it and either make an ass of myself or make people angry with me. But my main task was to continue to live and learn, constantly working toward improving myself, so that when the time came for me to do my part, I would be a good enough human being to do it and to do it well.

"I don't know how you'll do in the future," Torild said, "but I think you're doing fine, now."

"You know, Torild," I responded, "I have really never had the freedom I have here. Here, with this family, I have a special freedom. *Mor og far* treat me like a son, but I don't sense they are as tough on me as they are on you and Helen. *Mor* asks me where I've been when I come home, but I can come and go as I please. I'm more independent than I've ever been; I make my own decisions and deal myself with the consequences. With my friends, I am accepted and I can act in just about any way I want. I can't always express myself, but I am always free to try."

"That's one of the advantages of being *artig* and *søt*," Torild continued.

"There are a lot of things I don't have here: my American friends, my American family, my ability to communicate any idea I have. That makes this new freedom especially valuable."

"I think it makes you happy, too."

"*Ja*, that too. But I'm also happy because I see so much happiness around me. The kids I meet are so full of happiness and I think it must rub off on me. There are times when I feel I could never be unhappy here, even if I wanted to."

"You always look happy, but is it difficult for you sometimes? I know it was difficult living with the Románs, but other things?"

"*Ja*, sometimes. It's still difficult not being able to say everything I want to in *norsk*. It's difficult eating seven meals a day. Sometimes I feel as if I am on stage. But I love it here. It's wonderful. And it makes me feel good that I'm doing what I am doing, that I am being an exchange student, that I am an ambassador for America. I don't want to give that up for a long, long time."

My year was settling down to a couple of main ingredients: family and friends. Torild was great because she was really a little of both. She was my *søster* and we had brother-sister talks, but we could also talk like friends. She was good *søster*, and she was a good friend, too. As much as I enjoyed her and the relationship, however, I still longed for a brother my own age. I knew I would eventually get a new, and third, family. As much as I liked my sisters, if I had to move on, I wanted to move on to where I could have the brother I had longed for right from the beginning of my journey.

"Pete," Torild yelled at me the next morning, "hurry up or you'll be late for school. I'm ready to go."

"I'm coming; I'm coming," I mumbled as I finally got into the kitchen. "I've got to make my *matpakke* and eat at least one *geitost smørbrød.*"

"I can't wait that long, "Torild complained. "I have to get to school early today."

"You can go without me," I said. "I think I can remember the way."

"But I like walking to school with you," she said. For my part, walking to school with Torild was my *kopp kaffe* in the morning: a great way to start the day. And it meant a great deal to me that it meant a great deal to her.

"Go on," I said. "We can walk together tomorrow."

Mor, as usual, was there at the door to wave good-bye to me as I finally headed off to school, *matpakke* in hand, *geitost* in stomach. *Mor* is a real mother, I said to myself as I waved back. As I walked to school, I realized how much walking I did every day: to school, back from school, *til byen*, back from town, sometimes to a friend's house. I probably walked four or five miles a day, which suited me just fine. It not only kept my weight down, but I genuinely liked to walk. I used to walk in Westport, but that was much less often and never out of necessity. I even liked walking to school, but I most enjoyed walking in the stillness and serenity of the night. When I walked home, either from school or town, I had 20-30 minutes all to myself, to think or not to think, to do whatever I felt like, but to be alone. In many ways, I liked walking and that time to myself almost more than anything else in Tromsø.

"*Hei*, Pete," Arnulf shouted as I walked right past the *skolegård*, deep in thought. "Are you with us this morning?"

"I was just thinking."

"Well, stop thinking." Gunnar smiled, "It's time for school."

During the second *friminutter*, most of us were standing outside, either in the *skolegård* or just outside of the gates, where only *russ* dared to tread. Even though we were well into October, the weather was still warm, warm enough that even the *russ* wanted to go outside during the *friminutter.*

I Was a Teenage Norwegian

All of a sudden, I noticed that everyone was looking back toward the school. In the middle of the building, on the second floor, was a small balcony with a railing. I had surely seen it every day, but I had never really noticed it. There was a large set of double doors opening up onto the balcony from the *rektor's* office. There was someone standing on the balcony, but it wasn't Riksheim.

"That's *Inspektør* Hansen," Bjørg answered my unasked question. "He's next in authority after Riksheim."

I had never seen this Assistant Principal—Hansen—before. He was much younger than Riksheim, and clearly more energetic. But he looked as if he had graduated from the same military academy; his erect posture and strong voice gave him away. He needed the voice; he was, after all, talking to some 400-500 kids outside.

"As you can all see," Hansen began, "this is one of our typically nice fall days in Tromsø: sun, warm weather, and the like."

"Where have you been all your life, Hansen?"

"Do you call this warm?"

"Would you vacation in this weather?"

The formality of the classroom was nowhere in evidence. The anonymity of the crowd brought out the boisterous in everyone. But it must have been acceptable behavior, because Hansen enjoyed himself, keeping as straight a face as he could.

"Personally," Hansen continued, "I think today is a terribly poor day to be stuck inside. Personally, I'd much rather be climbing a mountain, like the one I can see from my balcony. Take a hike." Hansen ended with a flourish, hands high in the air for emphasis, pivoted toward the doors, walked through them dramatically, and closed them without uttering a further word. He never looked back.

His talk startled me. I had never experienced such a thing: being allowed, actually told, to take off from school because the weather was nice...and to climb a mountain.

"You heard the man," Bjørg tugged at my arm. "Let's get going."

"Does this happen often?" I asked.

"Pretty much once a year," Johnny answered. "Just depends on the weather."

Some of the kids walked home to get different clothes on, but I didn't have anything else to wear anyway, so I joined Bjørg, Johnny, and Lillian from Fifth English and Franck and Gunnar from Fifth Math. I still spent most of my time with the kids in my own class, but more and more I divided my time with lots of other kids as well. I was often up in Fifth Math because it was right above our classroom.

We strolled down the hill into town and walked out Storgate toward Tromsøbrua. Everything was familiar to me as we walked north on Storgate, until we passed the *kino* on the other side of the street. The *kino* marked the northern edge of walking up and down Storgate. We

passed it and continued on a smaller street, lined with old shops and houses, all made of wood, taking us to the entrance to the bridge. I had driven across Tromsøbrua once or twice, with the Románs, but I had never walked over it.

"Tromsøbrua," Franck explained, "is a little over one kilometer in length. It's the longest all-concrete bridge in the world."

"Okay, Mr. Engineer," Gunnar chided Franck. "Pete isn't a tourist any more and you're too young to give us lectures."

It was, however, a beautiful bridge, with or without its world-record length. It sloped up to a high point in the middle of the sound to allow boats to pass under it and then curved down and around to Tromsdalen on the mainland. I still found it difficult to imagine what it must have been like when the only way to get back and forth was by ferry. I had only taken a ferry boat once in my life, when my family was on vacation in Virginia Beach. It was difficult for me to imagine what it would be like taking a ferry twice a day, just to get to school. And Tromsøbrua was finished only the year before I arrived on the scene.

We walked for over half an hour to reach the *fjellheis*, gondola car lift. I had taken the *fjellheis* only once before, when Román and Karl Arvid took me up the first day I was in Tromsø. Then, we stayed up for ten minutes and came right back down. There was already quite a crowd of kids waiting for the next car.

"How much is the *fjellheis*?" I asked Bjørg.

"Usually, it's KR5 up and KR5 back. But today, with the whole school going up, they have a special sale: KR1 each way."

We had to wait fifteen or twenty minutes to get one of the gondola cars, each of which held about fifteen people. We all jammed into the small cable car, which had windows all around so we could see out. I would have more thoroughly enjoyed it if I weren't so afraid of heights. That was something I had brought with me from America, and I couldn't shake it, no matter how much I changed in other ways. I had problems with ladders, let alone gondola cars, even if they never got up more than a couple of hundred meters off the ground. But I just held onto the railing and looked outside, and I didn't feel too faint during the five-minute ride.

The view made up for at least some of my fear. It was spectacular. As we started our upward ascent, I could see most of Tromsdalen, the community on the mainland directly across from Tromsø. Tromsdalen was actually a part of Tromsø; it was more of a neighborhood than a separate town. But people always referred to it as Tromsdalen, probably because it was separated from Tromsø itself by the sound and (recently) by the Tromsøbrua. Kids who lived there said they lived in Tromsdalen; they never said they lived in Tromsø.

The higher we got, the more of Tromsdalen we could see, and it stretched for miles each way, both north and south of the *fjellheis*. As we got up a little higher, perhaps about midway up the mountain, I could see the entire island. I could make out the weather station on the top of the island near Holtveien and the Norbye house; from that vantage point the apartment buildings where Per and Bodil lived stuck out like pimples. I could easily see the large, red-brick *gymnas*, just up the hill from the center of town; its *skolegård* was unusually empty. I allowed my eyes to follow Storgate from its northernmost point past the Grand Hotel and the Mack brewery; my eyes followed the coastal road south all the way to the southern tip of the island and the *badestrand*. For the previous months I constructed a map of Tromsøy in my mind: walking to the Holt Farm, walking along the western shore of Tromsøy with Helen and Torild, walking to Nyløkken Kafé for the first *russefest*. From up in the *fjellheis*, I could test the accuracy of that map.

The views were even better when we finally reached the top of the mountain. We were actually not that high up; Bjørg told me it was about

600 meters above sea level. But we were high enough to see for miles and miles and miles. I hadn't realized how many islands there were, both separating Tromsø from the Atlantic, and north and south of us. Many of the mountainous islands which separated Tromsø from the North Atlantic were still snow-covered, or snow-covered again...I didn't know which was more accurate. I began to see Tromsø in the context of northern coastal Norway: its beauty, its island nature, its isolation. Wow!

"Pete," Lillian said quietly. "If you're ready to close your mouth, maybe we can start our hike." Lillian was one of my classmates that I hardly knew, even though we sat next to each other in the back row. She was pretty enough, but she was as quiet in class as Karl Arvid was with me, and that kind of quiet I didn't need. But that day on the mountain she displayed a sense of humor that I had not encountered before in her.

For the most part, the mountain was reasonably undulating, although there was one large hill on top that we decided to climb. It was clearly more of a hike than a mountain climb, especially having taken the *fjellheis* up. But we walked for three or four hours and it was tiring.

"I have been wondering," Harald Larsen asked me on the way back to the *fjellheis*, "why you moved from the Románs to the Norbyes." Harald was tall and slender, with jet-black, close-cropped hair. He was good-looking (although not in a typically Norwegian way) and easy to talk to.

"I wasn't real comfortable *hos* Román," I answered. "We didn't talk much and I don't know if they ever really wanted an exchange student living with them."

"Didn't you get along with Karl Arvid? He strikes me as pretty outgoing."

"We get along better now that I'm not living there," I said. "He's much more outgoing here at school than he was at home or with me."

"You strike me as being pretty happy with your new family."

"*Ja*, they are really great. They are so much fun, they talk to me all the time, they...."

"What's it like having two sisters?" Harald asked. "You guys really looked like you were all part of the same family when I met you walking two Sundays ago."

"They really are sisters to me," I laughed, "even if we don't look much alike. They are great. We laugh all the time, but I can really talk to them, too. Sometimes I'll get back home late and I'll talk with Helen or Torild for two or three hours. It's great; it's really great. Of course, I wouldn't mind having a brother my own age, either."

"What do you like most about being here in Tromsø?"

"Two weeks ago I would have said 'friends.' Now, I thinks it's both family and friends. I feel liked by my family and friends. I think that's what I like best here. It's not bad getting a day off from school to *plukka poteter* or take the *fjellheis*, either. I like that a lot, too."

I Was a Teenage Norwegian

As we reached the *fjellheis* and waited for the gondola car, I wondered if I could ask Jorunn to find out if I could live with Harald and his family. He was a really wonderful guy. He could be as full of life as anyone I knew. I thought he would make a great Norwegian brother for me. I really loved Helen and Torild, but I still wanted to have a brother my own age.

As the *fjellheis* began its descent, I realized how surprised I was at being able to talk to Harald that way in *norsk*. To be able to share with my Norwegian friends—in *norsk*—my real thoughts and feelings was exciting. To be able to share with my Norwegian family—in *norsk*—my real thoughts and feelings was exciting. Family and friends; that had a nice ring to it. *Familie og venner*, even better.

-15-
Hyttatur

It was Saturday: party night in Tromsø. I had been at school for six weeks and this was my fourth *fest*, and the second *russefest*. The *fest* was at Prestvannet Kafé near the lake at the top of Tromsøy, and walking was the only way get there. It was a pleasant night—and dark at night, too—clear and not too cold, and I enjoyed walking and the time to myself.

I had left home four months ago to the day. It had been four months since I had seen Sue. I still thought of her as my girlfriend; did she still think of me in that way? How could I really stay "true" to her when I was so far away for a whole year? Was that what I wanted? She meant so much to me, but *which* me was it she meant so much to? Was I the same person who left Westport four months before?

"*Du*, Pete," Gunnar greeted me as I entered the *kafé*. "It's a shame you don't drink; you look like you could use a *Mackøl*."

"Well," I said, "I could probably do with a Solo." Solo was the Norwegian national soft drink. It was an orange soda, made with real orange juice. Unlike *geitost*, I loved it at first swallow.

"A Solo?" Arnulf repeated. "What kind of American are you? You want Solo when you can have Coca Cola?"

"For an American," Randi interrupted, "he looks pretty Norwegian to me."

"Do you realize, Pete," Jorunn joined in, "that we have the world's northernmost Coca Cola bottling company right here in Tromsø?"

"*Hei, dokker*," I finally got an opportunity to say something. "I'm not all that thirsty. Would you prefer that I drink nothing, so that no one gets upset at what I'm not drinking?"

"You have to drink to my birthday," Gunnar admonished me.

"How old are you?" I asked.

"Twenty. Today."

"And to think," I said, "you don't look a day over...nineteen."

Prestvannet Kafé was quite similar to the *kafé* where the first *russefest* was held. There was a kitchen off to one side, with glass-enclosed counters containing all different kinds of *smørbrød*, *vaffler* (the heart-shaped Norwegian waffles), and cakes. And all of the tables and chairs were around the outside edge of the *kafé*, leaving a large dancing space in the middle. I looked around to see what kind of a band we had, and it was exactly the same as the one we had at the first *russefest*: Johnny Kaspersen on guitar and Kåre Dreyer on accordion.

The music was fun, and I danced most of the time. Sometimes I asked a girl; often, girls asked me. I tried out my new style of "when in Tromsø..." and kept my arm around my partner's waist. I blended with the locals; it was satisfying to feel Norwegian.

I danced mostly with the girls in my class, in large part because there weren't many girls in the other two *russ* classes, Fifth Math and Fifth Science. And the prettiest of those girls—Bitten—had a steady boyfriend, anyway. Most kids danced around, but Bitten and Knut Aune stuck to themselves, a rarity among the *russ*. But there were plenty of girls in my class.

"*Du*, Pete," Erika said, "When you turn me to the left, go under my arm. Come on, try it."

"It's my turn, Pete," Elin complained. "You haven't danced with me all evening."

"It's not my fault that I'm so popular."

"I didn't know you couldn't dance," Elin joked as we waltzed around the *kafé*.

"Waltzing doesn't count?" I asked.

"We don't count in 5GE," she laughed, keeping her eyes focused on me as we turned. "They count in Fifth Math."

"You're having a lot more fun these days," Jorunn said during one of our dances. "You certainly look happier now than at the first *russefest*."

"I didn't realize I was so obvious."

"You're pretty obvious," Jorunn smiled, "and we Norwegians are pretty observant. I heard you had a pretty good time with Sonja Heim at the *Bragefest* last week."

"Why am I not surprised that you heard?"

"Anything special?"

"*Nei*. We're just friends."

"You know you can have a good time with a girl even if you're just good friends."

"I don't think I'm quite ready for that," I said with some embarrassment. "I appreciate the talk we had at the first *russefest*, but I don't think I can be that way."

"Don't worry about it," Jorunn said, smiling and holding me tight. "I understand. But you've only been a *russ* for a few weeks. We'll make a *Tromsøværing* out of you yet."

As the dance ended, Johnny and Kåre discussed what they would play next. Jorunn and I waited to see what the next dance would be, and I left my arm around her waist.

"My, my, Pete," Jorunn said, moving closer to me. "You're getting to be one of us sooner than I thought."

I instinctively removed my arm, we looked at each other, and immediately both broke into laughter. I put my arm around her waist again and walked her over to one of the tables.

"Maybe so," I said. "Maybe so."

As we sat down, I noticed Harald Larsen sitting by himself a couple of tables away. I was surprised, because he didn't look happy. I had found the fundamental happiness of the people in Tromsø to be contagious, and I now felt a little gloomy just looking at Harald. I asked Jorunn about it, because I knew she and Harald were particularly good friends.

"I don't know, Pete," Jorunn answered. "I'll talk to him."

"Has Liz found a new family?" I asked.

"I don't think so."

"You know, my dream is to have Harald Larsen for a brother."

"Are you unhappy at the Norbyes?" Jorunn asked, concern in her voice.

"Oh, no," I said emphatically, not wanting her to get the wrong impression. "I love the Norbyes. I couldn't be happier. Torild and Helen are great sisters. We stay up all night talking. But I had always wanted to have a Norwegian brother my age, and I feel as if I can talk to Harald. I think he would make a great Norwegian brother. Is that possible?

"I don't know," Jorunn answered. "I can certainly ask him what he thinks about it. I didn't realize you felt that way about Harald."

For the rest of the evening, the second *russefest* was quite a bit like the first. Lots of dancing for me and lots of drinking for the other boys. They drank a lot, but only enough to get high, not enough to be out of control. Most of the boys lurched a lot; I was astounded that so many of them remained standing. The girls were surprising tolerant; they were obviously used to that side of the boys. The boys were raucous and boisterous, but more fun than wild. Only Einar in our class drank so much he got sick. By the end of the evening I saw him lying on a chair, actually more on the floor than on the chair. He had thrown up all over himself and the floor; there was vomit all over his shirt and tie and he was completely out of it: looking like a drunk, sleeping like a baby.

After the *fest*, a small group of us walked over to Lars' house; Lars was one of the boys in the Fifth Math Line. There were only about ten or twelve of us. I knew Lars and Gunnar from Fifth Math, and Arnulf, Randi, Erika, and Lillian from my own class.

That second *fest* was completely different from the *russefest* we had left just an hour before. There was no music and no dancing; there wasn't much drinking, either. Instead, we sat around in a completely darkened room, talking. One by one (it was really two by two) the kids coupled off. I was left with Lillian, from my class: Lillian Ingebrigtsen. Thanks, guys, I thought to myself. You leave me with Lillian, the quiet one. Of all the girls at the *fest*, you leave me with the one who doesn't talk. Don't you serve the guest first? One by one, the couples started making out. What was I supposed to do? Lillian was so quiet I didn't even know if she liked me. There we were, sitting together on the couch. I felt as if we were posing for a Norman Rockwell picture of embarrassed teenagers. But this was not to be a scene painted by Norman Rockwell; Lillian saw to that. I may not have known what to do, but Lillian knew exactly what to do. She surprised the hell out of me: she put her arms around me and started kissing me.

That had never happened to me. My experience was that I always had to take the initiative, and most of the time I was rejected. I would put my arm around a girl, and she would move away or take it off. My fear of rejection was so great, I usually didn't bother to initiate anything; nothing ventured, no rejection. But with Lillian, I didn't have to take the initiative or even think about taking the initiative. I didn't have to think at all; she started and she led. I still didn't have any idea if she liked me; maybe she was just extending Tromsø friendliness. But how could Lillian make out with me if she didn't like me?

To be truthful, I no longer cared. I hadn't made out with a girl for over four months. I had subscribed to the *theory* of being "off," which provided me with a sense of intellectual satisfaction, but the *practice* of the evening provided equal satisfaction, albeit of a more stimulating kind. I was not an experienced make-out artist, and I had never done more than make out. Lillian was not only more assertive, she was way ahead of me. What surprised me most was the way she kissed. I had always heard about French kissing; apparently the style extended throughout Europe. That was certainly the way Lillian kissed and she sure as hell wasn't French. And she sure was good: her tongue outlining my lips, the tips of our tongues touching, the tip of her tongue exploring the bottom of mine. French kissing, or Norwegian kissing, was far superior to anything I had ever experienced.

I could hardly believe what was happening to me. Here I was, 200 miles north of the Arctic Circle, at a make-out party. Everyone had silently coupled off, taking care of their needs, leaving me with a surprisingly assertive, attractive girl. I was with a girl who was a great kisser, showing me things about which I had only fantasized. I got a huge erection and I was excited as hell.

The *fest* ended at about 3:00 in the morning and we all started walking together back to our various homes. At points along the way, kids headed off in different directions.

"I'll walk Randi and Lillian home," Arnulf offered as we neared Holtveien.

"*Takk*," I said, grateful that I didn't have to do it. I was a little tired and a lot confused.

"*God natt*, Pete," Lillian said as she kissed me. "*Vi sees imorgen*."

"I'll see you tomorrow, too," I repeated. "*Takk for nå*." I was getting into the Norwegian habit of thanking for everything.

I walked up Holtveien by myself at 3:30 AM. Lillian and I were just classmates, not even real friends. And making out didn't change the fact that we were just classmates, or that I still liked Sue pretty much. There were many ways to be true, but it was through the heart that counted in the end...not through the lips. I was happy at that moment in time and there was clearly no need to prevent myself from having a good time because of a worn-out philosophy or asinine idea. Maybe I was off being "off."

October 18, 1961

Dear Mom and Dad,

It seems like a lifetime since I last wrote to the two of you. I can't believe how much has happened. This past week has been one of the strangest since I have been in Tromsø. I went to the second russefest *last Saturday. I danced a lot, even getting asked often by the girls. After the party a smaller group of us went over to a boy's house for a smaller party. There was a mass production necking party, and even I took part. I necked with Lillian, a girl from my class at school. We're just friends; it's nothing serious.*

So, all this week, it was strange. Keep in mind, Tromsø is this small town and everybody knows everything about everybody. So, My friends knew I was going to move before I knew it myself, but nobody asks me about the party at Lars' house and nobody asks me about Lillian.

Lillian and I sit next to each other in class and we still talk and everything. She's exactly the same, friendly, somewhat quiet person, but I keep imagining she's looking at me differently. And I keep imagining everybody's looking at me differently. And I don't know what to say, and nobody says anything. Even Jorunn, who always talks to me about everything that's happening to me acts as if nothing happened.

And what's even stranger is that I don't even know myself how I feel about everything. I still think I like Sue. But I'm here now and I really like these kids and I want to be a part of everything that's happening here. I am more playful; I mess around more. I feel I can be anything I want to be, and act any way I want to act, and these people—both family and friends—will accept me.

So what do I do with this new me, if it really is a new me? What do I do about Sue? What do I do about Lillian? Tune in again next letter, and maybe I'll know something more by then.

Oh, one other thing. Tonight I did something quite strange, in a way: I prayed (and in norsk, *too). I used to say that I haven't prayed in such a long time because I didn't know if there was anything to pray to. I am such a thinking Unitarian, I have nothing resembling anything like God to believe in...and I feel this is not good. So I prayed and asked for God to help me help myself and not to help me unless I did help myself. It wasn't much of a prayer, I guess. I didn't even wish for the betterment of mankind or the abolition of war, but I did pray. I'm not even sure that it's important that I prayed, but I did...and in norsk, too.*

All my love,
Pete

I Was a Teenage Norwegian

It was the end of another week, and the beginning of another weekend. Weekends in Tromsø were special. We had a *fest* almost every other weekend since the start of school. The upcoming weekend loomed as even more special, because a group of *russ* were planning a *hyttatur*, an overnight trip to Gunnar's *hytta*.

When I first heard of the plan, I couldn't believe it. There was no way a group of 17 high school seniors in Westport would have ever been allowed to go off by themselves for a weekend without an adult chaperone. But in Tromsø, it was quite normal. That was what the *hytta* was for: people spending time relaxing with each other. And in Tromsø, *russ* were considered mature enough to take care of themselves. It was partly because *russ* were older than their American counterparts, but it was also that Norwegians gave their kids more freedom and assumed their kids would be more responsible.

I walked straight home after school and packed a small rucksack with my toothbrush, sweater, and a clean shirt. I said good-bye to *mor* and was off to school, where we all met.

"Do you need anything else?" *mor* asked me as I bounded down the stairs. "Are you supposed to bring food?"

"*Nei*," I answered. "They said I am on such a small allowance that I don't have to bring any food."

"But I can give you something." *Mor* looked genuinely hurt.

"It's a joke, *mor*," I assured her. "Gunnar said he and some of the others have everything taken care of."

"Who's going with you?"

"Gunnar, his *søster*, Per, Sverre and Olav from Gunnar's class, Lillian, Arnulf, Bjørg, and Erika from our class. There are more than fifteen in all, but I'm not sure exactly who the other kids are."

"The Brox *hytta* is nice; I'm sure you'll like it there."

"How..." I started.

"...Brox works at the weather station up here near our house. We've known the family for years. Their oldest daughter was a classmate of Helen's."

"It's..." I began.

"...a small town," *mor* finished.

"I had better get going," I said, moving toward the front door, putting my shoes on.

"Have a good *hyttatur*, Pete," *mor* said as she waved her usual good-bye. "*Ha det.*"

"*Ha det*," Torild yelled out her bedroom window, directly above the front door.

"*Ha det*," I yelled as I reached Holtveien and headed toward the *gymnas*.

I walked faster then, than I usually walked to school. Partly, I didn't have any strong desire to talk to myself, which I usually did when I walked. Partly, because I was in a hurry. I had looked forward to the *hyt-*

tatur all week, since Gunnar had suggested it Monday. It was a combination of being so completely different than anything I had done in America and sounding like so much fun.

By the time I got to the *gymnas*, everyone else was already there and the car and the delivery truck were packed. Gunnar and Per—both from Fifth Math—drove. Unlike Westport, *russ* in Tromsø did not have cars; in fact, no kids had cars. It was a special event for the kids to be able to drive, even though some of them had had their license for two years.

"Pete," Gunnar greeted me as I walked through the entrance way into the *skolegård*. "Why don't you come with me. Erika and Lillian are coming with me, and my *søster*. Have you met Anna?"

"*Nei.*"

"*Hei.* I've heard a lot about you from Gunnar."

"Anna graduated from *realskole* and doesn't go to the *gymnas*," Gunnar explained. "That's probably why you've never met her before."

There were five of us in the car and the rest were in the pick-up truck that belonged to Per's father. We pulled out of the *skolegård*, drove down the hill toward Storgate, and headed toward Tromsøbrua, with Gunnar in the lead.

It was easy crossing Tromsøbrua getting out of Tromsø because there was no toll; there was only a toll coming in, but not going out. The same money was collected but with fewer people needed to collect the tolls and less annoyance for the drivers.

The trip took me farther away from Tromsø than I had been since the three-day—that lasted three weeks—summer trip with Dr. Jenssen. Our caravan headed out the same road, because there was only one road out of

I Was a Teenage Norwegian

Tromsø. The road ran along the Tromsø Sound, on the mainland side, so we had a good view of Tromsøy to the west for the first few kilometers of the drive. I still couldn't get over driving along such a thin strip of land— no more than a quarter of a mile wide—separating the water from the mountains.

Gunnar's family *hytta* was only a forty-five minute drive from Tromsø, but that was far enough away to feel like another world. We were out in the country, even though we were just a hundred meters from the road. The *hytta* was like a picture out of a story book: log cabin, grass roof, set in the middle of a field, with a mountain on one side and the water on the other.

We all piled out of the parked vehicles, carrying our own things and the food into the *hytta*. The inside of the *hytta* was as rustic as the outside was picturesque. As we walked in, there were two bunk rooms to the right, along with the small bathroom. There was running water but no electricity. There was a tiny kitchen to the left, with the icebox, the wood-stove, and an opening to pass food through to the dining area of the living room. Gunnar had brought ice for the icebox and had told me that we would cook *middag* on a wood-stove. I was up for the experience. The rest of the *hytta*—almost half of the whole area—was the living room/dining area. There was also an outside area, through a door in the living room, that had a table and a few chairs.

"Pete," Gunnar asked, "could you get the wood-stove ready? We need to boil some water for the *poteter*.

"Sure," I said, with all the confidence of ignorance. Since when had I used a wood-stove before? How difficult could it be? We had a fireplace in our living room in Westport; I knew how to start fires; I knew about dampers. I was cool. I found some newspapers and kindling, and put that in the wood-stove along with some larger logs. That was the strategy I used in Westport to light a fire in the fireplace; I assumed Norwegian fires operated more or less like American ones. Gunnar gave me some matches, I lit the fire, closed the stove door, and opened the damper in the chimney. Mission accomplished.

For the next ten minutes or so, I helped Gunnar, Anna, and Lillian in the kitchen with supper. I noticed that the kitchen was getting a little stuffy. In fact, the whole *hytta* was getting quite smokey. Gunnar checked out the wood-stove. He could hardly stand up, he was coughing so much.

"Pete," Gunnar said, when he could get enough air to clear his throat and talk. "Let me tell you a little something about wood-stoves. They are built with a firebox, where you light the fire to warm up the stove. The firebox is connected by pipes to the chimney, to give the fire air and get rid of the smoke."

"I know, Gunnar," I said indignantly. "I opened the damper. *Æ e' ikkje så dum som æ se' ut.*" I'm not as stupid as I look, I said in my best, and most indignant, *Tromsøværing*.

"True, true," Gunnar began to smile, as the rest of the kids listened to his little lecture. "But you did make one little mistake: you built the fire in the oven instead of the firebox."

Middag was a great time, with all seventeen of us sitting around a dining table meant for eight. Those kids were lively and full of fun, joking with each other and having the best of times.

"Gunnar," Per teased, "do you remember the time you were so drunk you couldn't remember your name?"

"Who's this Gunnar you keep talking about," Gunnar asked.

"Per," Anna joined the fun, "Do you remember the time you were so drunk that you couldn't remember I was Gunnar's *søster*?"

"Since when did that happen?" Per asked.

"And what about the time *fru* Engelsen wouldn't let Bitten go to the bathroom until Knut Aune could conjugate "to pee" in French."

What was especially nice was that the mood of the group was set by the group, not one or two individuals. No one dominated; there was a sense of collective spirit. The closest situation from my past it resembled was with my LRY group, but the Norwegian version was more spontaneous and less cerebral.

After *middag*, some of the kids played checkers and the rest of us talked. Lillian and I ended up under the counter (beneath the opening between the kitchen and the dining area), which turned out to be a nice place to cuddle and, eventually, to make out again. After the previous week of not knowing exactly what was going on between Lillian and me and not knowing how I felt about us, we started again as if no time had passed since the previous Saturday night at Lars' house. And making out the second time was as exciting as it was the first time. Lillian was not only a great kisser, she was more into making out than the few American girls with whom I had made out. She enjoyed making out as much as I did, and there was no embarrassment. She was as assertive with me as I was with her. She was....

Oh my God. What the hell was that? I peed in my pants. *Nei*, that wasn't it at all. I was all relaxed. My erection was gone. What had happened? This wasn't in the travel brochures. This was serious. I wasn't used to this; in fact, I hadn't experienced anything like this in my life. What the hell did I do? What the hell did Lillian do? I hadn't a clue. This was serious.

I pulled away from Lillian, completely confused. Lillian was completely surprised. Lillian had a way of looking wise, like she knew what was going on but didn't have to talk about it. She looked that way—as if she knew exactly what was going on—but I didn't have the faintest idea what was going on and I didn't know what to do. I couldn't talk to her. Not about this. This was serious.

There was no one there I was used to talking to seriously; Jorunn wasn't there and neither was Arnulf. Gunnar was the closest one to a friend. We had talked a lot, but we had joked together more than we had talked, and we had never talked about anything as serious as the Common Market, let alone this.

"Gunnar," I said nervously, "I need to talk to you."

"Sure," Gunnar said, looking at me and then looking at Lillian. Gunnar had been making out with Erika from 5GE. I hoped I could talk with him seriously.

"Not here," I said, quietly.

"Let's go to the bunkroom. Lillian, do you want to join us?"

"*Ja.*"

There was so much going on, and the *hytta* was lit by so few kerosene lanterns, no one noticed the three of us sneaking off to the bunkroom.

"What's the matter?" Gunnar asked. "You two looked like you were having fun."

"This is getting too serious for me," I began.

"You were just kissing," Gunnar said.

"I know. But I don't think we can just keep kissing. I think we have to go all the way or quit. And I can't go all the way."

"I don't understand."

"It's difficult to explain. I've grown up feeling that I couldn't go all the way unless I loved the girl, and then even love might not be *nok*. When I left America, my father told me to "keep my pants on." He said it as a joke, but he meant it seriously."

"Are you afraid?" Gunnar asked. Gunnar and I did all the talking. Lillian sat on one of the bunk beds across the room, not saying a word, but listening to everything.

"I don't know. I don't think so. When we were making out, I really felt I had the guts to go all the way. But I can't afford for Lillian to have a child. AFS in Tromsø would be finished, and maybe even all over Norway, and it would be my fault."

"How do you feel about this, Lillian?" Gunnar turned to her.

"I have a rubber," she said calmly.

"I'm too confused," I blurted out. "This is just too much for me. I don't understand what's happening and I don't know what to do. I can't keep making out and I can't go any farther."

"Look, Pete," Lillian said. "It's okay, whatever you do. You'll know when you're ready. You'll know what's right for you. I'll be here when you're ready."

"*Takk,*" is all I could say. It was all I could do to comprehend that I was having that conversation at all, let alone in *norsk*. Thank God Gunnar was there and Lillian was who she was. I was enough of a wreck as it was; I could imagine how much worse I would have been if I hadn't had real friends there.

"Look," Gunnar suggested. "It's late, anyway. Let's go to bed and see how we all feel tomorrow."

"Sure," I said, since I was at the point where I could have accepted almost any solution that helped to extricate myself from the mess I had created.

"Why don't you and I sleep up in the attic, Pete," Gunnar lead me out of the bunkroom.

One question every AFS candidate always expected to be asked in an AFS interview was: "If they go skinny-dipping in the country where you are placed, will you?" That night, I got to answer that question, in a way. Norwegians didn't go around nude in mixed company, but for a guy to be seen by a girl in his underpants was not even given a second thought. Three of us slept in a small room up in the attic: Gunnar and I in one bed (in two sleeping bags) and Bjørg Wilhelmsen in the other bed. And when Bjørg came the room, I had just my briefs on. I hesitated momentarily. I was supposed to have an American outlook of modesty on those sorts of things.

"You can come in, Bjørg," I said, with all the self-assurance of a new convert experimenting with his newly-acquired customs.

After breakfast on Sunday, all different kinds of activities took place, none of which required any thought or reflection on my part. Someone drove to the nearest store and got a variety of newspapers, representing the variety of political parties reflected in the variety of *russ*. Some of the kids read the papers and discussed the new government, the cabinet choices, and whether or not Norway should join the Common Market. Three or four of the group borrowed fishing rods from Gunnar and headed toward the *fjord* to try their luck. Anna Brox was over in the corner of the living room making up Jan Hendriksen's face, and Bjørg was doing the same for Sverre. While I cleaned up after breakfast, I must have missed the explanation of that strange Norwegian *hytta* tradition, which concluded outside with Gunnar and Per proposing marriage to Jan and Sverre in their full female regalia. Everyone had great fun, but I could not for the life of me figure out the basis for that particular drama.

We drove back to Tromsø after lunch. On that trip I opted for the relative anonymity and emotional security of riding in the delivery truck with six other boys and all five girls. We sang almost the entire way home, mostly American songs—both popular and folk songs—all of which were fast and bouncy. It was definitely a great way to end the weekend and highlighted, once again, how full-of-fun these kids were. It was certainly a welcome change to be among people who were so thoroughly happy, but it meant that I had no outlet for my serious side. I got a chance the previous night, finally, to let Gunnar know that I had a serious side, too. I told him that I couldn't possibly be happy and lively all the time; I told him he should not think that I was unhappy when I got a little serious. I think he understood.

"So, how was it, really?" Torild asked me later that evening, after everyone else in the family had gone to bed. That was often the time when Torild and I had our brother/sister talks.

"It was great fun," I began, "but it was difficult, too."

"What do you mean?"

"It's difficult to explain, even in English, let alone *norsk*. Sometimes, when I have so much fun being with kids that are having so much fun, I forget my serious side. I forget that I need to be able to share my thoughts and feelings; I can't just keep them all inside. It's still difficult to do this in *norsk*, but I feel I can usually express myself now when I am with my friends; I even talked to Gunnar more seriously than ever before. Luckily, you've always been easy for me to talk to...all two weeks I've known you.

"But I am worried about my next family. What if I don't have anyone there I can talk to like I can talk to you? It's real important for me to have someone I can be close to. I need friends like that and I need family like that."

"So," Torild asked, "when are you going to tell me about the weekend? What was so difficult about it?"

"I guess I'm having trouble sticking to my topic, aren't I? The difficult part was Lillian, again."

"But I thought you liked her. Isn't that what you told me last Sunday?"

"I do; I do like her. But I'm confused. I'm not used to girls liking me. I'm certainly not used to a girl taking the initiative the way Lillian does."

"You're just going to have to get used to us Norwegian girls," Torild smiled. "We know what we want and we don't always wait to have it offered to us."

"I'm really beginning to feel the need for a girlfriend...."

"You keep telling me how difficult the weekend was," Torild interrupted, "and I'm getting more confused. You say you want to have a girlfriend, you like Lillian, she likes you...what's so difficult, then?"

"You make it sound simple and easy, and I feel confused. I'm afraid she may want more than I do."

"You want a girlfriend. She wants a boyfriend. Sounds to me like you both want pretty much the same thing."

"The problem is..."

"The problem is," Torild suggested, "that you think too much. Don't think. Decide, and then do it."

"Life isn't that simple."

"It is, here."

"I guess I have to decide about Lillian."

"I guess you do."

-16-
Lillian and Baseball

As my alarm went off at 7:00 AM the next morning, I slowly surveyed my room and my life before getting out of bed. I had an eerie feeling that it was getting to be a time of taking stock, of looking back over a part of my life that was beginning to fade into the past. As I looked at my room, I realized that I was less and less prone to comparing that small, second-story room in Tromsø with my slightly larger, first-story room in Westport.

Westport, Connecticut. I had lived there most of my life and I hated it. It was the people I couldn't stand. They were too rich and snotty for my taste. Everybody was into money and possessions, and they already had more of both than people really need. There were people in Norwalk or Bridgeport who didn't have enough money to feed their kids, and people in Westport were worrying about whether their sweaters matched their slacks or skirts.

"Are you awake, Pete?" *mor* asked sticking her head through the doorway into my room.

"*Ja, ja*," I responded, still somewhat groggy. "I'm awake. I'll be down in a couple of minutes."

It was impossible to stay groggy for long *hos* Norbye, even at breakfast. By the time I stumbled into the kitchen, everyone else was already there and everyone was in motion. I didn't need *kaffe* in the morning; that family was all the caffeine I needed to get going. Most mornings, we ate in shifts, since different people left the house at different times. That morning, everyone was in the kitchen at once. It was as if the family knew I was taking stock of my life and wanted to be there, all together, just in case I needed any help.

I was silent as Torild and I left the house for the *gymnas* after breakfast. I was used to silence when I walked alone, but silence was rare when Torild and I walked together. It was as if the silence was a part of the plan for that day; it afforded me an opportunity to see more clearly all the little familiar odds and ends of that walk to school. I noticed in greater detail the small *kiosk* on the right-hand side of the road.

The *kiosk* was a small, circular stand, with yellow-painted vertical clapboards and a single door; I would sometimes buy a candy bar on my way home from town if I thought I could sneak it in without spoiling my appetite for *middag*. I walked by the *kiosk* every morning, I knew it was there, but I hardly ever noticed it. That morning, I noticed it. That was a morning I noticed everything.

I noticed the *kiosk* on the right-hand side of the road, and the elementary school on the left. The *skolegård* was already full of kids, racing around, yelling and screaming, getting as much of their energy out before the bell rang. Not really much different from my own elementary school in Westport. And yet, the kids all wore rucksacks, where they carried their books and their *matpakker*. Their *smørbrød* were made of *geitost* and *Jarlsbergost*, instead of peanut butter and jelly. The *kiosk* was like stores in Westport, where the kids could stop and get snacks and the housewives could buy fruit on their way home from town. But the *kiosk* was a stand and the kids bought Freia instead of Hershey and the housewives were more limited in their choice of fruit: apples, oranges, and bananas.

I found Tromsø stranger and stranger the more familiar it appeared. Everything in my life there, was on the surface so similar to my life in Westport, but the subtle differences added up: walking to school, instead of taking a bus; walking everywhere, instead of driving; taking a *matpakke* to school, instead of buying lunch; taking shoes off inside houses, instead of leaving them on. Nothing in and of itself was a big deal; taken together, the differences in my life began to make both me and my life different.

"You working on your decision?" Torild asked, seemingly suddenly.

"What did you say?" I asked, half haltingly.

"Lillian, silly," Torild smiled, as if she had to coax me along. She was no more used to my walking silence than I was.

"Oh, yeah, Lillian," I said, still sounding distant and confused.

"You remember Lillian?" Torild asked keeping her smile. "You know, the girlfriend you've been wanting. The girl who wants to be your girlfriend. That one."

"I just don't know what to do."

"You know what you *want* to do. You know what *she* wants. You American boys are pretty frustrating when it comes to girlfriends."

"Look," I said as we approached the *gymnas*. "I understand what you said, but I still feel strange. I've got to let this all sit for a while, okay? It's only been one evening, you know."

"Well, just don't expect me to sit back and watch you make a mess of this," Torild continued, with a little more vehemence. "I may be your younger *søster*, but I am bigger than you are. And it appears I know a lot more about the world, too. You take your time, but I'm going to make sure you do what you need to do."

Even I had to smile. I may have had trouble with my relationship with Lillian, but I certainly wasn't having any trouble with my relationship with Torild. I had some experience with younger sisters; I had one in America. But I had never had a younger *søster* with the strength and perseverance of Torild. I respected her for that strength, and liked her for it, too. She was going to keep me honest. I wondered for a moment what life would be like when I moved in with my new family and didn't have a *søster* like Torild. Maybe she could still be my younger *søster*...from a distance; after all, it would be walking distance.

"I'll see you later," Torild chirped.

"Pete," Gunnar interrupted my mental wanderings. "*Takk for sist.* Thanks for the last time."

"Thanks to you, too," I answered. Thanking was one of Norway's national pastimes, and it had taken me a long time to fully appreciate and understand it. In fact, one of the few things I remembered from my stay *hos* Román was a story Román told me about *takk* and Norwegians. There were two friends who hadn't seen each other for thirty or forty years; one had stayed in Tromsø and the other emigrated to America. The one from America finally returned to Tromsø for a visit. He returned on the *hurtigruten* and recognized his friend waiting for him on the dock. As he walked down the gangplank to greet his old friend, the first thing both of them said was, "*Takk for sist.*" Then they greeted each other, talked, and caught up on old times.

"You ready for another week?" Gunnar asked.

"I guess so," I answered.

"Have you seen Lillian yet?"

"Why is everyone so interested in Lillian?"

"Who is everyone?"

"You. Torild. Everyone."

"What's the problem? She's a great girl. You're lucky she likes you. She's pretty choosy. I should know; I've known Lillian for years and she's never chosen me."

"I just don't know," I mumbled. It was a clear indication of modest growth in my ability to speak *norsk* that I could mumble in *norsk* as well as in English. In the midst of struggling with momentous issues of the heart, I took satisfaction wherever I could find it.

"Well I do know this, Pete. She likes you. Don't be crazy."

"We'll just have to see, okay? We had better be going in."

I was apprehensive about going to school for the first time since my first day of school. Then, I was apprehensive about the great unknown of the Norwegian *gymnas*. Now, I was apprehensive about the lesser unknown of my feelings for Lillian. How would Lillian respond to my own ambivalence? I didn't know Lillian well; that was one problem. The other problem was that I didn't know Norwegian girls at all. Throughout the previous few months, particular situations confused me because I didn't know whether the situation was typically Norwegian or typical of the people involved. I still laughed every time I remembered how I had thought all Norwegians carried toothbrushes around in their back pockets, until I found out that Geir's father was dentist. If Lillian was angry with me, how much of that would have been Lillian, and how much of her anger would have been typically Norwegian? If she were tolerant and patient, would that have been Lillian or the Norwegian in Lillian? Learning Norwegian, was easier than learning Norwegians.

I barely made it into my seat before I had to get up again when Andreassen entered the room.

"*God morn*," the class said in unison.

"*God morn*," Andreassen mumbled into his chest.

Learning *norsk* with Andreassen was a virtual impossibility for me, given that he was still completely unintelligible. I smiled quickly at Lillian, sitting next to me, but I didn't want to attempt a quiet conversation with her during the other kids' recitations. Not that day; not after Saturday night.

With nothing better to do, I dropped into one of my various "Learning-*norsk*-on-my-own" modes. One of those modes involved total concentration on the teacher for an entire class period; Andreassen made that mode fruitless. So, the mode for that day was memorizing verbs. I still had a grammar book from my stay at Trollvasshytta. Nobody in the class could quite figure out what I was doing. I was clearly not listening to Andreassen; I was clearly looking at a book; I was clearly not reading the book; I was clearly mouthing words. It must have looked odd to all my friends, but I was committed to learning *norsk* whatever I looked like doing it.

There was one way in which *norsk* was noticeably easier than English. *Norsk* verbs didn't change with person: I am, you am, he am, we am, you am, they am. As a result, there were really only four parts of each verb to learn: infinitive, present tense, past tense, and past particle. As if this wasn't easy enough, almost all *norsk* verbs ended their infinitive with "e," and the present tense was formed simply by adding "r."

infinitive	present	past	past participle
å komme	*kommer*	*kom*	*har kommet*
to come	comes	came	have come
å like	*liker*	*likte*	*har liket*
to like	likes	liked	have liked

Occasionally, I would add a couple of irregular verbs to my list, as they were always a little harder.

infinitive	present	past	past participle
å gå	*går*	*gikk*	*har gått*
to walk	walks	walked	have walked
å be	*ber*	*ba*	*har bedt*
to pray	prays	prayed	have prayed

I had always had a "good ear." Westport started foreign language instruction in ninth grade. Our choices were Spanish and French. I chose French because my mother spoke fluent French, both from her multi-lingual childhood (German, French, and English) and her year at the Sorbonne.

At the end of my first year of French, and my last year of junior high school, my mother made me an offer. If I would work hard with her over the summer, she would tutor me and guarantee that I passed out of French II and went right into French III at Staples. I was a kid with nothing to do in the summer except spend two weeks at camp. Sounded good to me.

It may have been good, but it was difficult. We spent 6-8 hours a day together working out of the French II book my mother had gotten from the Foreign Language Department at Staples. I learned grammar, I memorized verbs, I constantly used the dictionary to learn new words. That wasn't the worst of it, however. I was only fifteen, and too young to drive. Westport was a suburb, with great distances and no public transportation. My transportation choices were always to hitch-hike (which I did frequently) or to get my mother to drive me (which was always faster and more convenient). But that summer, there was a cost. Whenever we drove, my mother refused to talk to me in English; we talked in French or we didn't talk at all. And my mother liked to talk to me in French, and wouldn't take silence for an answer. Whether the ride was for five minutes or half an hour, we talked French, and I added conversation to my repertoire.

Neither my mother nor I gave up just because I went to camp. I was expected to write home from camp, and being the dutiful son I wrote. But I was cool. That was my French summer and I decided to write my letter in French: a whole page. I was so proud of what I had done: both the quality of letter itself and the fact that I had written in French. A few days later, I got a letter from my Mom. She had sent back my letter to her, corrected in bright red pencil. She was a tough Mom, but an even tougher teacher. I never had to wonder where the high standards I set for myself came from.

The day wore on and I avoided any contact with Lillian. Lillian was sensitive to my ambivalence and didn't push herself on me. By lunch time both of us, and the rest of the class, were ready for our *storefriminutter*.

"I think it's time," I suggested to my classmates, as we finished our *smørbrød*, "for me to teach you something American in return for all the *norsk* you are helping me learn." About half the class had eaten their lunch and departed for the great outdoors of the *skolegård*, where all the other students had to be anyway. "It's time *dokker* learned a little baseball."

Outdoor activities were quite popular in Tromsø—hiking, skiing, skating—but sports as such were limited essentially to *fotball* what the Norwegians called soccer. Baseball was something many of the kids had heard about, but no one really knew much about it or how to play it.

This was not the first time I took charge and let the more playful side of me loose in school. The first time was the day after we *plukka poteter*.

"What are you doing, Pete?" Bjørg had asked me.

"I have a little gift for Engelsen," I answered, walking behind his desk. "Stay in your seats, *dokker*. It's not for you anyway."

I just barely made it back to my seat in time to stand up when Engelsen entered the room.

"*God morn*," Engelsen said, as he walked into the room and plopped his briefcase on his desk. He pulled out the chair, and five or six dirt-covered *poteter* crashed to the floor. I had hidden them in my coat pocket when we left Holt Farm the day before.

"A gift from an anonymous admirer?" Engelsen asked.

"If you had cancelled the test for today," I responded, "I might have washed them for you."

"This isn't exactly the right place for baseball, is it?" asked Arnulf. Outside of Jorunn, who had lived in Michigan for a year as an AFS student, Arnulf was the most America-literate of my classmates; he watched the most American movies. That was his way of learning English; definitely more enjoyable than my total concentration method.

"That's true," I said, looking around the small classroom with its desks bolted to the floor, "but we'll manage. The teacher's desk can be home plate, Torbjørn's desk is third base…"

"What's third base?" asked Marit. "And what happened to the first two bases?"

"Is home plate one of the bases?" Bjørg asked.

"What's the difference between a plate and a base?" Randi asked.

"Why do you start at third base and not first base?" Pål asked.

"Hold all your questions until I get us set up," I said, showing just a hint of frustration. I had forgotten that what might be simple and obvious to someone from one culture might be unfathomable to people from another. "Forget what everything's called, okay? There are four bases that you have to run around, and you start at this home one here. In order to run around the bases, you have to hit a ball with a bat."

"I think there's an old *fotball* in the closet downstairs," Johnny suggested, "but I don't know what a bat is."

"Okay, okay," I continued. "Let's manage with what we have." I looked quickly around the room to see what I could find that would work. "Johnny, go pick up that meter stick. We can use that for a bat; it's close enough. Give it to me a minute and I'll show you how to hold it and swing it." I showed Johnny and the rest of the kids still in the classroom how to hold and swing the bat. It had been months since I had played baseball, but that was one thing I hadn't forgotten how to do.

"Bjørg," I continued. "Can you get that sponge near the blackboard, the one Andreassen is always using to clean the board? We can use that for the ball. A *fotball* is meant to be kicked around; it's too big for baseball. The sponge will work out just fine.

"Johnny, are you ready? I'll be the pitcher. That means I throw the ball—sponge—to you and you hit it with the bat—meter stick. Then you run around the bases. The other kids catch the sponge and—for this version of the game, at least—throw it at you. If they hit you with the sponge before you get to a base, you're out. That doesn't explain everything, but if we just get started, you'll catch on, and I can explain the finer details of the game as we play."

The game began and soon descended to the level of slapstick. Some of the kids would whack the sponge with the meter stick and start climbing over, or crawling around, the desks between one base and the next. Meanwhile, the rest of the class tripped over the desks, and each other, to get to the flying sponge and toss it at the so-called runner. The game continued on in this fashion for three or four batters—and three or four minutes of mayhem—until a modification emerged.

"The sponge is already a little wet. Why don't we," Lillian suggested, "fill it with water and then hit it?"

No sooner said than done. Leave it to the *russ* of Tromsø to sense a great idea when they heard it. The sponge was thoroughly soaked and then batted, chased, and thrown. The moderate mayhem descended into serious mayhem, much to everyone's delight.

"*Fanden*," Johnny swore as his next batted sponge sailed out the window into the *skolegård*. The rest of the school was used to having to live with the *russ* being able to stay inside during *friminutter*. What they were not used to, however, was the level of noise and laughter emanating from the second-floor room. They were even less used to sponges flying out of second-floor windows.

Arnulf raced outside to grab the sponge and threw it back up to Jorunn, who was standing in the window.

"Throw it back down," Arnulf suggested, which prompted a few minutes of catch before Jorunn kept it and we got back to our game. The sponge, unfortunately, kept flying out the window. By the second time, there were plenty of willing volunteers resigned to their place in the *skolegård* who were willing to retrieve the errant sponge and toss it back up to us.

By that time, we not only had the attention of everyone in the *skolegård*, but most of the 5th Math Class directly above us on the third floor were looking out the window, trying to figure out what was going on. Gunnar and Per Sparboe were halfway out the window trying to see in through our window.

"I've got another idea," I said to my classmates. "Don't say anything; just let it happen. When Gunnar comes down, start explaining the game to him. When I call him, let him go to the window. Gunnar," I shouted out the window to my friend upstairs. "Come on down and play baseball with us."

While Gunnar walked down one set of stairs to the second floor, I walked up the stairs at the other end of the hall to Gunnar's room on the third floor. And I had the sponge, soaking wet and dripping water on the floor. I walked over to the window and started to work the audience. I didn't say anything for a minute; I just showed my audience the sponge, and shook it a tiny bit so they could see how wet it was. I put my finger to my lips, hoping that was a pretty universal sign for keeping one's mouth shut.

"Gunnar," I shouted. "Gunnar!"

It was now obvious to the 300-odd kids in the *skolegård* what I had in mind. I worked my audience like a puppeteer with a small group of children. I almost had them shouting at Gunnar to watch out, but they were *gymnas* students; they were too old and wise to spoil such a good trick.

Gunnar came to the window and stuck his head out, expecting, perhaps, to see the sponge flying to the ground. There was nothing on the ground except the students, and they were all looking up at me in the window above. Gunnar followed suit, and I squeezed the water out of the sponge right onto Gunnar's face one story below. A howl went up, simultaneously from Gunnar and the 300-odd students. Even the bell signaling the end of the *storefriminutter* could not drown out the combined howls. For the kids, the incident was special. Something happened at school that had never happened before: a new kind of joke. It was great fun, for everyone, both those directly involved and the rest of the students who got to watch the event unfold before their very eyes.

The incident was as much fun for me as everyone else, but it was really something more. It was not just that the baseball game was an event; *I* was an event. The *gymnas* was a small school and literally every student was in the audience. My sponge antics that day marked me to everyone as someone quite special. At that point in time and in that part of the world, I was someone special, someone the kids at the *gymnas* would talk about, someone to make all the *russ* smile when they thought of him. I was slowly coming out of my somewhat self-imposed shell. I was able to integrate my sense of humor and my playfulness into my everyday life. Tromsø may have been a little pond, but I was becoming a big fish in it, and I liked that.

That evening, my new-found persona struggled with my new-found issue: Lillian. It was getting easier and easier for me to loosen up and have fun with my friends, but my questions surrounding Lillian were no easier for me to answer.

October 23, 1961

Dear Mom and Dad,

I have three thoughts of importance to share with you. It doesn't really matter when I thought of them, but I think they were all on Monday, after my weekend at Gunnar's hytta. *Lillian and I went at it again, and I got scared of where we were going. Let's say I felt we were on our way farther than I have ever been before.*

The first thought pertains to "going all the way" with a girl and why I cannot do it and I will write in the first person. I can't go all the way. I'm not afraid of doing it now, for when Lillian and I were going at it last Saturday I sure would have had the guts to do it. But I just can't afford it; I just can't afford for her to have a kid.

Number two thought. I am able to live without many things: happiness, my own family, even a typewriter. But there is one thing that I cannot live without, that I must have, that I need to live and I would be one of T.S. Eliot's "living dead" without: the freedom to think. The freedoms of feeling and expression are also quite closely related, for if one snuffs out these, one really cannot think freely, either. Taking all things into consideration, I have all of these freedoms now. I can usually express myself when I am with my classmates but, more important, I can talk with my youngest sister, Torild.

Number three is a little new. I see four kinds of love: love of an individual, love of one's family, love of an organization, love of a group. Here in Norway I have the latter two loves: I love AFS and all that it stands for and I love, in a mild way as of yet, my school-mates. I had (even in Westport) thought these two loves were enough; in Westport, both pertained to LRY. But now I feel that the first two loves are the more important. I feel a cavity in my heart and stomach for the direct love of a single girl, direct because she would be near me (at least nearer than Sue, 8,000 kilometers away). I never really felt this need for one person quite as strongly before. And now that I am away from my family and I cannot take my love for my own family for granted, I realize how important that love is, too. It is so very, very strange how that old, trite, hackneyed phrase that even AFS told me to forget about when I came abroad is probably the truest statement I can think of now: absence makes the heart grow fonder.

> *All my love,*
> *Pete*

I had received three letters from Sue since I had left home. Although my letters were full of emotion and feelings, bordering on the maudlin, Sue's letters were chatty and sparse. It was difficult to decipher from them what was going on for her in terms of our relationship, and I usually felt just as confused regarding my own feelings, no matter what I said in my letters.

"*Du*, Pete," Jorunn accosted me the next morning at school before I could even get my jacket off. "Have you talked to Lillian yet?"

"Why is everyone so interested in Lillian?"

"Who is everyone?"

"You. Gunnar. Everyone."

"Because we care about you and we care about Lillian."

"I don't know what to think."

"Stop thinking," Jorunn said, with a seriousness unfamiliar to me. "You think too much. Stop being an American and start being a Norwegian. Stop thinking and act. Talk to her."

On the one hand, I was completely frustrated with my inability to decide or to take any action. On the other hand, I was completely happy that my friends cared for me as much as they did. Jorunn stopped castigating me as the other kids wandered into the classroom. But as I looked into each of their faces—Arnulf, Bjørg, Randi, Johnny, Erika—I felt them all looking at me and telling me the same thing: talk to Lillian. And then Lillian walked in, as calm and at-ease as always. Her look, unlike the looks of everyone else, didn't say "talk to me." Her look went right through me, right through my veneer and deep into my psyche. It was as if she knew everything I felt, everything I was, all of my weaknesses and foibles. She understood everything, and everything was all right with her. I didn't have to talk to her that day. She would wait. Whenever I was ready.

-17-
An Unconscious Decision

"Where are you going?" *mor* asked me, one Saturday evening.

"*Til byen*," I answered, as I did with increasing frequency. In Westport, we never went to town in the evening. There was nothing to do there. Occasionally I went to town on Saturday mornings to shop. When I was younger, I used to go to the YMCA on Saturday mornings to play basketball or shoot pool. But no one ever went "to town" to meet people or hang out.

In Tromsø, social life was much more informal, spontaneous, and more group-oriented than in Westport. Here I was walking *til byen*. It wasn't that everyone came *til byen* every evening; it wasn't even that everyone came *til byen* at all, because a lot of the kids in my class never came *til byen*. But a lot of kids did; it was a dominant aspect of Tromsø social life.

I Was a Teenage Norwegian

I arrived in the middle of Storgate, leaving me two choices: right or left, south or north. The routine was to walk up and down Storgate for an hour or more on a given evening. There was a clearly prescribed route. I walked between the *kino* at the north end and the Grand Hotel at the south end...never farther in either direction. And, as I had learned so well the previous summer, there was only one side of the street on which to walk.

"*Hei,*" I said to Tordis as we passed each other.

"*Hei*, Pete," Tordis responded.

The choices were limited. You could say hello, as Tordis and I did or you could just nod as you passed each other. Once you had said hello the first time you met, you just nodded when you passed each other after that. It took no more than ten minutes to walk the entire length of the prescribed route, which meant that we passed each other a number of times each time we went *til byen*. The potential problems associated with having to say hello each time were obvious...hence, the nod. It allowed us to keep on friendly terms without having to say something each time we passed. A clever solution.

It was also possible to stop and actually talk, but this too, took place only once each evening.

"*Hei*, Pete," Andreas greeted me and stopped walking. If someone greeted me and stopped walking, I stopped walking, too. That was the way it worked in Tromsø.

"*Hei. Kor det går?*"

"*Bra. Det går bra.* And what about you? Was that Kristin I saw you talking to before?"

"*Ja.*"

"*Ei deilig jente,*" Andreas said with a genuine smile.

"*Deilig?*" I asked, never having heard the word before.

"*Deilig,*" Andreas repeated. It sounded like "daily" in English, but it certainly meant something different.

"*Ka deilig betyr?*" I asked Andreas what the word "*deilig*" meant. "Describe it in *norsk*," I asked him.

"*Søt, pen,*" Andreas explained.

"*Søt* " I knew meant sweet but I wasn't sure about "*pen*." But I came prepared.

"*Et øyeblikk.* Wait a minute," I asked Andreas as I fished into my right rear pocket. I reached for the orange-and-white pocket dictionary—*ordbok*—Karl Arvid had helped me purchase. I used it a lot. I needed it when I talked to people and couldn't understand what they said. If I couldn't get the meaning of a new word from context, and if I didn't feel I quite understood the meaning of the word when someone explained it in *norsk*, I just reached for my trusty pocket *ordbok* and looked it up.

I had used the *ordbok* for about six weeks and there definitely was a pattern. The first time I heard a word I didn't understand I looked it up in the *ordbok*. The next time I heard the word, I recognized it but couldn't remember its meaning, and I had to look it up again. The third time I heard the word, I remembered that I had already looked it up in the *ordbok*, the word was now familiar, but I wasn't quite sure what it meant. I still had to look it up in the *ordbok*, but I knew this would be the last time. And it was. The fourth time I heard the word, I knew what it meant and I didn't have to look it up.

"*Deilig*," I said out loud, but mostly to myself, as I moved from DA to DE in the *ordbok*. "*Deilig, deilig*...there it is. Delicious; wonderful; adjective".

"*Ja, deilig*," I said to Andreas, acknowledging his three-minute-old comment. It took people longer to talk to me than to their other friends, but they didn't give any hint of frustration.

There was the verbal greeting, the nod, and the once-an-evening stop-and-talk. But that wasn't all. One step up from stopping and talking on the sidewalk, was a decision to move from the street into a *kafé*. This move was always an extension of the stop-and-talk. I never went into a *kafé* by myself, and I didn't get the impression that anyone else did either.

"Pete, do you want to go to Sagatun?" Andreas asked me.

"*Ja*," I answered. Sagatun was one of the bigger *kafés*, in its own building just a block off of Storgate, closer to the Grand than to the *kino*; it was closer to the water, too.

"Hey, there's Elin and Geir and Anna Britt," Andreas smiled and waved as we entered Sagatun. "You want to sit with them?"

"*Ja*. That's fine." Kids didn't go to the *kafés* for privacy. Kids didn't go *til byen* for privacy. In fact, I didn't know where kids went if they wanted to be alone. It was inevitable that kids met other kids when they went to a *kafé* and it was common practice to sit down and join an already-existing group.

"*Hei*, Pete," they all greeted me.

"*Hei*." I knew everyone at the table, or at least I had seen them all before. They were my age, but they were in Third English, many in Torild's class.

"Do you want something to eat?" Andreas asked me.

"*Ja*, I think so," I said as I sat down.

"Don't sit down," Andreas laughed. "We have to order at the counter."

This was just another little part of Norwegian life I hadn't completely internalized. This was a *kafé*, not a restaurant. Food was ordered at the counter and paid for at the counter. Then someone brought it to the table. My instincts were still to sit down and wait for a waiter or waitress.

"*Øl*," Andreas ordered a beer, by far the most common drink, at least among the boys.

"Solo," I ordered my usual soda. Both the *øl* and the Solo were KR2, or 30 cents, about what I was used to paying at home.

"How about some *vinerbrød*?" Andreas asked.

"Definitely," I smiled. I loved the Norwegian pastries.

I Was a Teenage Norwegian

"I saw you at the *kino* today," Elin said as Andreas and I got back to the table. "Do you go to the newsreels every Saturday?"

"Pretty much," I said.

"He goes because they're in English," Geir laughed. "He won't let any of us speak English to him, but he sneaks in English at the newsreels."

Although a lot of the kids joked about it, and they all understood why I did it, many of them were disappointed I didn't let them speak English with me.

"I don't listen to the English," I said firmly. "I just read the sub-titles." They all laughed; none of them believed me. "Actually, going to the newsreels, or even the movies, is a good way to learn *norsk*. I can listen to the English and read the translation in the sub-titles at the same time. Really."

"Sure, sure," Geir said. "You don't need an excuse to go to the movies. You don't even need an excuse to listen to English."

"Is there a *fest* anywhere tonight?" Elin asked.

"I haven't heard of any," Anna Britt said. Some parties—*russefest* or *Bragefest*, for example—were planned. They involved a specific group of people and they generally took place at *kafés*, mostly outside the center of town. But other parties were more spontaneous; they happened as a result of conversations either in the street or in *kafés*. Saturday night was *fest* night, because kids had school six days a week. You could look for a *fest*, as Elin was doing, or you could just start one, if none were to be found.

"My mother has guests," Elin said, making it clear that her house was out. She looked at the others, and their houses were out, too.

"We can go up to my house," I volunteered.

"Great," said Elin, Geir, and Anna Britt.

"Is Torild home?" Andreas asked, with some clear self-interest.

"I don't know," I answered. "Probably."

As we walked along Storgate, we invited a few other friends to join us at the *fest* at my house before we got to the point where we left Storgate and headed up the hill toward Holtveien.

The *fest* itself was enjoyable and uneventful. A nice group of kids sitting around, listening to music, dancing, making out, and talking. Torild and Helen weren't at home and *mor* and *far* had greeted us when we arrived and then made themselves scarce. The dancing continued for an hour or two, and then everyone started to pair off. I was an experienced Tromsø party-goer by that time and I knew what to expect. The key was to decide with whom you wanted to be paired—and either boys or girls could take the initiative in this regard—and dance with that person. At the end of the dance, arms around each other's waist, the two walked over to one of the couches or simply sat on the floor. I chose Anna Britt (or did she choose me?) and we went at it along with the others.

Anna Britt made it easy for me to forget the dilemma I faced with Lillian. I knew there was something different about my relationship with Lillian, or what my relationship with her could become. With Anna Britt, we were just making out at a *fest*.

Although making out with Anna Britt may not have had any special significance, the *fest* itself did. It made me realize how much of a Norwegian I had become, and how much of a Norbye. When I offered my house for the *fest*, I did something Peter Dublin would have never done. I did something only the newly emerging Pete could have done. I was able to invite these kids because I felt like one of them; I was becoming a teenage Norwegian. Sure, I still had my *ordbok* in my pocket. Sure, they often treated me gently because of my cultural ignorance and naiveté. But this kind of pick-up *fest* was common in Tromsø, with its emphasis on kids making do with themselves for their own entertainment. I was developing that self-sufficiency, too. What would have made me uncomfortable only a month before was something I now took in my stride.

At the same time, I was able to invite these kids to my house because I was becoming a Norbye; it was *my* house to which I invited them. The Norbyes were not some people in whose house I was living. They had become my family. It was not Norbye and *fru* Norbye; it was *far* and *mor*. Helen and Torild were my sisters; we talked into the night and I tickled them when they were fresh. I could invite my friends to my house because it was my house, and it was my house because I was becoming a member of a Norwegian family.

Fester and the *gymnas* were the two places where I shined and came out of my old shell. At *fester*, it was the dancing and the making out. At the *gymnas*, it was the discussions with my other classmates.

"He's a good guy, that Engelsen," Arnulf remarked as Engelsen left the classroom after our fourth period class the following Saturday.

"I agree, I agree," I said, taking out my *matpakke*. "I like him, too. But I don't think his French class is as good as my French class was in America."

"We're reading Molière," Bjørg chimed in. "You can't get much better than that."

"I agree that you learn to read French quite well," I said. "And your vocabularies are large."

"That doesn't sound like criticism to me," Johnny put his two *ører's* worth in between mouthfuls of his peanut butter *smørbrød*.

"What I find difficult to understand," I continued, "is that after five years of French, most of you have trouble speaking the language. And your pronunciation is often so poor that when you do speak, I can't understand what you say."

"And how was your French class different?" Arnulf asked.

"From the moment the class began until we left the room—even including when we asked for help after the class was over—everyone spoke in French, both the teacher and all the kids."

"In my French class in Michigan," Jorunn objected, "no one ever spoke French. It was even worse than in Norway."

"I agree," I said, "but I was comparing my French class—which I consider was taught by one of the best American teachers—with your French class, which you consider is taught by one of the best Norwegian teachers. You learn grammar, you learn words, and you learn to read...but you don't learn to speak."

"How is Engelsen like an American teacher?" Lillian asked me.

"Well, he's on a pretty friendly basis with the class," I answered. "He's almost as friendly as the American teachers I have had. Of course, there are differences, too. There are no surprises. In America, we have surprise quizzes; here, we don't. Just the written essays and translations in French. And those stupid recitations."

"How do you mean, stupid?" Arnulf challenged. "How else do you expect a teacher to know whether or not we have read our homework?"

"But all you do is repeat what you read," I explained. "Take Andreassen, for example."

"You take Andreassen," Arnulf said. Everyone agreed that Andreassen was a hard worker, fairly intelligent, and thorough as a teacher. But no one could stand him. I was afraid to even talk to him. Part of the reason was that I still had trouble understanding him, with his dialect and habit of talking into his chest. Part of it was he just looked frightening.

"Take today," I continued undaunted. "He asked Marit a question about the novel we're reading. He asked her to begin at the beginning and tell what happened. It was as if Marit turned on the tape recorder. After a minute or two, Andreassen turned off Marit's machine and asked Bjørg to turn on hers."

"But the alternative," Torbjørn joined in, "is your stupid American discussions."

"But that's just it," I said. "Class discussions allow kids to think about what they're learning."

"They also," Jorunn interrupted, "allow kids to cover up the fact that they don't know anything. It's easy for kids to weave nonsense into fairy tales that sound good."

"Recitations," Randi agreed, "are the only way to insure that students have read and understood their lessons."

"I disagree," I disagreed. "Recitations make memorization the key to success in school."

"Which is exactly what is true in America," Jorunn continued. "You get to talk in class, but tests require memorization. If you can't memorize what you are taught, you fail...whether you are in Norway or the United States."

I had wanted to leave America so badly I could taste my departure for years. I got to Norway, and I began defending the place I hated. *Pussig*, as we said in *norsk*: funny.

"Are we going to the movies?" Arnulf asked as we walked down the hill from the *gymnas*.

"Sure," the rest of us answered.

We had already by the end of October developed a 5GE tradition. Almost every Saturday since the beginning of school, we went to the movies right after school. To the *kino*, but not exactly to the movies. What we saw were newsreels, the movie version of the News of the Week in Review. Our tradition was to sit in the front row, usually about half the class, eating Freia milk chocolate, and looking straight up at the screen.

"It's so dark," I mentioned to no one in particular as we got walked out of the *kino*. By that time of year, we were midway between the end of the Midnight Sun and the beginning of the Darkness. It wasn't that it was really dark at 2:00 o'clock in the afternoon, just that it was getting progressively darker—literally day by day.

"I've got to get home," Arnulf waved as he headed north toward his *hybel*, a rented room. Arnulf wasn't from Tromsø originally; he had grown up in Lyngseida, about sixty kilometers away, and had gone to elementary school there."

"You don't live with your family?" I asked him when I first heard he lived in a *hybel*. After all, this was *gymnas*; it wasn't university.

"No," Arnulf smiled, sensing my disbelief. "We don't have any *gymnas* where I grew up. I took the same exam as kids in Tromsø. When I passed, I got a place here; Tromsø was the nearest town with a *gymnas*. When I came here, I got a *hybel* and that's where I stay when I'm at school. I go home at Christmas and during the summer. It's not so bad; it's easy to have a *fest* there because I don't need to ask my parents' permission."

"It may be easy to have a *fest*," Johnny had responded, "but your *hybel* is so small it's difficult to have anyone attend the *fest*."

"See you tonight," I called to no one in particular as most of the others left, too.

"Do you want to walk once or twice up Storgate?" I asked Lillian, who was the only one still with me.

"Sure," she fell in step as we walked away from the *kino*.

I never planned what occurred during those next few minutes. In fact, I didn't really even think about what I was doing at the time. We walked about half of the way between the *kino* and the Grand Hotel. By the time we passed the Tromsø Cathedral, we were holding hands. It just happened. Here I had struggled with myself, unable to explain my feelings to my parents or Torild, unable to explain them because I was so confused and ambivalent. And in those few moments, I just let those feelings control my actions.

Lillian was sensitive, she just took my hand and said nothing about it. We continued to talk as we walked, but not about what was happening. Holding hands was a big deal; it was as close to commitment as I could manage.

"I've got to go up and see Liz Arnett," I said to Lillian as we got to the middle of Storgate on our way back toward the *kino*.

"I'll see you tonight?" Lillian asked.

"*Ja*. I'll be here."

"*Ha det*."

"*Ha det*." Just like that. It was done. As I walked up the hill toward Liz's apartment, I could hardly believe what had happened. I had done it; I had a Norwegian girlfriend. I held her hand, and she held mine. She didn't reject me. I went public. Now I had told people that Lillian and I were an item and it felt fine. It felt great, in fact.

Liz lived in a *hybel*, just like Arnulf. When Adele Berg left for Germany in September, Liz took her place as the head of the Tromsø AFS committee.

It took about fifteen minutes to walk from Storgate to Liz's *hybel*. I didn't see her that often, but every now-and-then she liked me to check in with her. She had called me during the week and asked me to come by on that Saturday.

I stopped at her front door. Her *hybel* was really more like half of a two-family house. Except for the set of buildings where my brother Per lived, all the other apartments were in people's houses.

"*Stig på*, Come on in, " Liz said as she opened the door, literally seconds after I rang the bell.

I had barely gotten my shoes off and made my way into the living room, before I got another of those reminders about the size and nature of my new home town.

"So," Liz started, "who's your new girlfriend?"

"What?" I asked incredulously.

"Who were you holding hands with as you walked Storgate?" Liz asked.

"Oh, that," I fumbled for a moment to fully appreciate what had happened. From the time I had started holding hands with Lillian until the moment I hit Liz's doorstep, no more than twenty minutes had elapsed. No more than twenty minutes. In that time, someone had seen the two of us and reported to Liz. "Reporting" wasn't quite the right word; "sharing" was perhaps more accurate. I knew I hadn't done anything wrong; Liz wasn't going to reprimand me. The incident wasn't "reported." People didn't "tell" on each other; they were simply curious, and they had a strong need to satisfy each other's curiosity as well as their own. That was why someone called. I didn't feel my privacy was invaded; after all, I had held Lillian's hand in public. I wasn't in any way annoyed or upset, just reminded of the speed with which information traveled in that town.

"Lillian," I replied. "Lillian Ingebrigtsen. She's in 5GE," I continued, as if Liz didn't already know that, along with her height, hair color, mother's maiden name, and God knows what else. In fact, there was no question in my mind that Liz probably knew much more about Lillian than I did. That was the way things worked in Tromsø even for someone like Liz who wasn't a *Tromsøværing*.

"I know," Liz smiled. "You were with her at Gunnar Brox's *hytta*."

Damn! I hadn't even told Liz about anything that happened on that *hyttatur*. I had to get her permission to go because AFS students weren't allowed to travel without their parents, unless they got special permission from AFS. But I never talked to Liz about that weekend afterwards. How did she know? Actually, that was the wrong question. Was there anything she didn't know about me?

"It's been a little difficult," I decided to talk for real, given how much she knew anyway, "figuring this all out."

"In what way, difficult?"

"Sometimes I feel she wants more from me than I can give," was the way it came out that time.

"Does she ask for more than you can manage?"

"*Nei.*"

"Does she put pressure on you?"

"*Nei.*"

"Does she make demands?"

"*Nei.* In fact, she's really nice that way. I don't feel she pressures me at all."

"So," Liz continued, smiling, "where's the pressure coming from?"

"Me?" I asked both of us.

"Sounds like it."

"I've felt confused," I continued, "but I never felt like I was putting pressure on myself. That's a strange thought. I've never thought of that before." It would have been difficult enough talking about it in English; it was even more difficult thinking about it in *norsk*.

"Keep in mind," Liz kept the conversation moving, "that everything is going to be somewhat new and difficult for you. You were used to living in a family in America, but living with a Norwegian family was just different enough to be difficult. I'm sure you've had girlfriends before, but having a girlfriend in Norway will also be a little different."

"How?"

"I don't know how," Liz answered, "I just know that it will probably be a little different from what you're used to. The less you worry about it, the better off you'll be. It's different from living with a family. That you *have* to do. When the Román family didn't work out for you, you needed to find another family. If Lillian works out, that's great. If she doesn't, you can live without a girlfriend."

"But I just started...."

"I didn't mean to imply it won't work. I meant that you should enjoy her and your relationship with her. Don't worry so much. You'll do fine. It will be fine."

"Well," I acknowledged, again to both of us, "I do like her. She's special."

"Now get out of here before you're late for *middag*."

"Are you getting anywhere with my new family?"

"Not yet," Liz didn't indicate any more concern about that issue than she did about Lillian. "Get out of here. I'll let you know when I know."

As I left the *hybel*, I encountered my second shock of the afternoon: snow. It was October 28, 1961, and it was snowing. Not little flecks in the sky; real snow, with real, larger-than-life snowflakes. It must have started while Liz and I talked, because by the time I was outside, it was coming down fast and furious.

I didn't know why I was surprised. When I first heard about coming to Tromsø I assumed it would snow in the summer. Perhaps being in Tromsø for so long, having experienced the midnight sun, having sunbathed on the rocky *badestrand*...perhaps all of those experiences lulled me into a feeling that my new home was going to be normal, at least by my American standards. But a snowstorm in October was not normal by my standards.

-18-
From Pete to Pipe

As an AFSer, I had permission to spend time in classes other than the 5GE class I usually called my home. One Wednesday, for example, I spent most of the day with Gunnar Brox and his 5th Year Mathematics Line class. Gunnar's class was directly above our classroom. It was from their window that I squeezed the ball-sponge full of water onto Gunnar's face as he looked out the window of our classroom. Except for being on the floor above, the two classrooms were almost identical. The only real difference was that Gunnar's class had twenty-six kids to our eighteen and the room was also a bit bigger. I found an empty desk toward the back of the room.

"*God morn,*" the class said in unison as it rose to greet Aschim, the history teacher.

"*Morn,*" Aschim responded as he walked toward the desk, put his books down, and seated himself in the chair. "I realize that yesterday's discussion of the Common Market was of great interest to you, but we will have to get back to our discussion of Norwegian History."

"But it's so difficult remembering, "Gunnar complained.

"Particularly for someone as old as you, Gunnar," Aschim responded. "Steinar, I would very much like to hear your thoughts on Ibsen's political views."

"He was definitely against the Common Market," Steinar was quick to point out.

It was a remarkable situation for a number of reasons. First, the Common Market was a hot political topic. All of these kids were born during the German occupation of Norway and there were still strong feelings in Norway about the Germans, feelings that ranged between distrust and hatred. The ability of Norwegians to joke about an issue with as much emotional content as the Common Market was a testament to their good nature. Second, it was remarkable that such a conversation even took place in school. Current events were not a part of the curriculum; they were not covered in the exams. Finally, It was remarkable that Aschim thought the joke as funny as the rest of us did.

I Was a Teenage Norwegian

Eventually, Aschim was able to get back to the topic at hand: the Second World War. He was talking about the war between the Soviet Union and Finland, most of which took place during an intensely cold winter.

"How," Aschim asked a boy named Wiggo, "did the winter battle go between Finland and the Soviet Union?"

"Finland lost," Wiggo answered.

"2-0," Bengt chimed in.

The Norwegian instructional system combined teacher lectures, questions asked of students, students reading parts of the text, and recitations.

"Ragnhild," Aschim asked one of the few girls in the class, "will you read please." A rather lengthy silence followed his question.

"I don't know where we are exactly," Ragnhild responded, rather quietly.

Odd Johnson was sitting next to Ragnhild. He leaned toward her and whispered, in a voice loud enough for all to hear: "Norwegian History, Volume I."

Toward the end of the class, Aschim looked toward Gunnar. "Gunnar Brox, can you tell us...."

"Wait a minute, Aschim," Gunnar interrupted. "You ask me to recite so often I should get a monthly pass, like I do for the bus."

Everyone laughed, but it didn't get Gunnar out of his recitation. Only the bell ringing for the end of the class managed to do that.

The bell got rid of Aschim, but it only brought *fru* Engelsen. In the 5th Year English Line we had English with Engelsen six or seven times a week. The 5th Year Mathematics Line had English only three or four hours a week and they had it with Engelsen's wife. They were clearly not as far along in English as we were, but they were a lot funnier.

"*Morn*," *fru* Engelsen greeted the class as she passed Aschim on his way out of the room.

"*Lykke til*," Aschim mumbled to her. Good luck.

"Let's hope it doesn't come to that," *fru* Engelsen said to the class. "Perhaps we need to start with something simple, then. Gunnar Brox, what is the plural of boot?

"Bits," Gunnar responded proudly.

"It's pronounced boots, Gunnar," *fru* Engelsen corrected him.

"Sorry. Butts."

"Gunnar Brox. Listen to me. Boots. Boo. Boo. Boo."

"You can't scare us, *fru* Engelsen," Franck warned her.

"Perhaps we can see an improvement if we involve someone else. Arnulf, can you give me an example of how the word 'perhaps' is used?" As she asked the question, *fru* Engelsen noticed Arnulf chewing gum.

"Arnulf," *fru* Engelsen admonished, "this is English class. Are you chewing gum?"

Arnulf nodded his head, unable to speak.

"Out in the hall this instant and spit it out," *fru* Engelsen ordered.

Arnulf stood up and said in somewhat garbled English: "PER-HAPS I could get one more chance?"

I couldn't tell whether I was in English class or watching a Dean Martin & Jerry Lewis movie. The class settled down for the rest of the hour...until the last minute or two. All of a sudden Gunnar began to laugh.

"What's so funny, Gunnar?" *fru* Engelsen asked.

"This question you gave us."

"How so?"

"You asked 'Why did it take Henry so long to throw up?' when I think you meant 'Why did it take Henry so long to grow up?'"

Needless to say the class roared with laughter.

"I hope you'll find the test as funny," said *fru* Engelsen.

"We will," Gunnar responded, "if you give us the same question."

I returned to my own class for French, with Engelsen the husband. If Engelsen had talked to his wife during the short *friminutter* he gave no indication. He walked in all business, as usual.

"Well, then," he began. "Let's see how your French is this morning, Knut. Please say the following: I have forgotten my book."

"Not me...I have mine right here!"

"That's it for French today," Engelsen said as the end of class approached. Arnulf had been reading one of his French stories.

The whole class moaned. "Can't we please hear some more of Arnulf's story?"

"*Nei,*" Engelsen said. "We can do that on Monday. Or perhaps you'd rather play records."

"With dancing afterwards?" Jorunn asked.

"Jorunn," I said, "that doesn't sound like you."

"Well, Pete," Jorunn smiled, "I guess there's still a few things you don't know about me."

"This has been my strangest day in school so far," I said, "and I'm still supposed to go back to Gunnar's class."

"What classes did you have this morning?"

"History with Aschim and French with *fru* Engelsen."

"And what's next?" Jorunn asked.

"Math, with Hansen."

"That should be more serious, then," Jorunn said, but I couldn't tell how serious *she* was.

"Back for more?" Per Sparboe asked as I got back into the room just in front of Hansen.

"I'd like to see what you can do with Math and Hansen," I whispered as we all rose to greet Hansen.

"You won't have long to wait," Per whispered back.

Hansen provided problems for the kids to work out and invited them to the board, often two or three at a time. It was in the middle of one of these problems that Hansen yelled out.

"Steinar, what is it you're doing up at the board? I've never seen you destroy an equation the way you're doing now.

"It's the National Speedskating Championships, Hansen."

"What about them?" Hansen asked.

"They're in Harstad," came the reply from Steinar.

"I know they're in Harstad, Steinar. I think we all know they're in Harstad, Steinar. What's the point?"

"I have a bad case of travel fever, that's the point."

"What's her name?" Odd asked.

Funny as my Norwegian friends were, I too, had a few jokes up my sleeves: my sweater sleeves. Westport was cold and I was used to sweaters, but the Norwegian sweaters were different. Norwegian sweaters tended to have a pattern across only the top of the sweater. Big star-like patterns were the most common; reindeer patterns were common, too. On any given day I could look around my own 5GE class and probably see fifteen sweaters on the eighteen kids.

Erika had already knit me one sweater, but I wanted more. How was I going to get more hand-knit Norwegian sweaters? I had never seen either Torild or Helen knitting, so I didn't feel I could ask them. *Mor* knit, but I was uncomfortable asking her, especially since I could be leaving for my new family at any time. But I had an idea.

"Jorunn," I said one day. "I need to buy some more *garn*, more yarn." Anne, Jorunn, and I went back to Anne's mother's store after school.

"So, Pete," *fru* Marcussen said, "you weren't satisfied with only one sweater? You want more?"

"*Ja.*"

"We have a few already knit," *fru* Marcussen pointed to the sweaters on the wall.

"*Nei*," I said, "I have a particular pattern in mind. "You know the sweater Knut wore today?" I asked Jorunn.

"*Nei*, I don't think so." Clearly sweaters were not as memorable for Norwegians as they were for me.

"Sure," Anne said, "he was wearing his *Norlandskofta*." Anne sat next to Knut and had probably seen that sweater for the last three or four years.

"That's the one," I agreed

"That's a problem," *fru* Marcussen explained. "I can get you the *garn*, but I can't give you the pattern. "It's a special Norwegian pattern and we can only sell it to specific women to make sure the pattern is adhered to exactly."

"Pete is an AFS exchange student," Anne argued.

"I wish," her said, "we could make an exception."

"*Takk*," I thanked *fru* Marcussen as I paid her.

"Come back again," she smiled, "and let me see it when it's done."

"How are you going to get the sweater knit," Jorunn asked me as we walked across the street and headed south on Storgate.

"I have an idea," is all I said.

The idea depended on Knut wearing the same sweater again the next day, but I felt I could count on that. At Staples, I never saw anyone wear the same clothes two days in a row. I never even wore the same pants two days in a row, let alone the same shirt or sweater. What was true in America for a day was true in Tromsø for a week. I never changed my pants more than every week, and sometimes longer. I would sometimes wear two shirts during a week, but it was more likely that I would wear the same shirt for the entire week. That was why I was confident that Knut would be wearing the same sweater the next day.

"Knut," I said, sitting on Anne's desk before the first class started. "I'm going to need your help today."

"Sure," Knut said. "Now?"

"*Nei*," I answered. "During the *storefriminutter*."

I wanted a sweater and I had the *garn*. I needed someone to knit it for me and it had to be a girl, because I had never seen boys knit. I was always on the lookout for new friends, especially *småpiker*. My idea combined those two needs.

During the *storefriminutter*, Knut and I went outside into the *skolegård*. I carried the *garn* behind my back in the bag *fru* Marcussen had given me.

"Do you knit," I casually asked the first pretty girl I saw.

"*Nei*," she smiled. "*Desverre*. Unfortunately.

"What are you doing?" Knut asked, genuinely curious.

"You'll see," I said. "Do you knit," I asked another girl.

"*Nei*," she said sweetly.

By this time, celebrity that I was, I had attracted some attention, and other kids were following in my wake. Third time was the charm, I thought to myself.

"Do you knit," I asked another 15-year-old girl, knowing how honored she felt just being asked a question by the strange American AFS student.

"*Ja*," she said the magic word, probably thinking my question was a result of simple curiosity not blatant self-interest.

"Could you knit me a sweater?" I asked directly, taking full advantage of my celebrity status. I didn't know her at all, but I could count on her knowing me, the funny American who squeezed water out of a sponge onto Gunnar Brox's face. I got a lot of mileage out of that prank.

"I guess so," she said, somewhat hesitantly.

"*Værsågod*," I responded immediately, taking the *garn* from behind my back and handing it to her.

"What is this?" the poor girl asked.

"The *garn*," I answered.

She opened the bag, feeling the *garn* and noticing the three colors. "What about the pattern?" she asked, noticing its omission in the bag.

"There," I said pointing to Knut. "Just like that one."

And that was how I got my second sweater. The girl, Mette, turned out to be a great knitter, and fast, too. I had the sweater in less than two weeks. I had my *Norlandskofta* and Mette had enhanced her reputation at the *gymnas* beyond her wildest imagination. Mine hadn't suffered much, either.

"I'm sorry it took so long," she apologized. "I could only knit in school."

I loved the sweater and wore it frequently throughout the year. I loved just as much the process of getting the sweater, which I used it eight more times throughout the year, for myself and my entire family. Great sweaters at a great price, and a great way to meet new people. And a great way to show my *russ* friends I could be as funny as them.

"Pete," Gunnar stopped as we met in Storgate a few weeks later. "Nice sweater. I was impressed when I heard how you got the pattern."

"*Æ e' ikkje så dum som æ se' ut*," I answered, like the good *Tromsøværing* I had become."

"*Du* Pete," Gunnar continued. "What are you doing in town? Didn't you go to the *hytta*?"

A number of kids from school had gone off to a *hytta* the afternoon before, but I had decided not to go. I didn't know exactly why, but I had felt a little down the past week. My time in Norway included lots of ups and lots of downs: getting down at the Románs and up at the Norbyes; getting down at not understanding a word of what Andreassen said and getting up as I understood more and more of what Engelsen said; getting down when I thought excessively at parties and getting up when I danced; getting down when I worried about Lillian and getting up when I enjoyed being with her. Most of the time, up or down, I felt as if I were on stage, and periodically I opted to be off stage, by myself. The day before I had made one of those choices.

"Well," Gunnar went on, "I'm driving out there this afternoon. You want to join me?" Gunnar was one of the few kids at school who had access to a car.

"I don't know, Gunnar," I said.

"*Du* Pete, *du* Pete" Gunnar said. "You can't hang out with *småpiker* in town all the time."

"I only talk to *småpiker* because they are so fond of me," I smiled. "You can understand that, can't you?"

"Are you coming with me or not?" Gunnar persisted.

"Okay, I'll come. I have to go home and get my stuff."

"I'll pick you up at Tromsøbrua at half two."

As we drove to the *hytta*, I thought about Gunnar Brox, since I had come along as much because *he* asked me as that I was *asked*. Gunnar had become my best friend, along with Jorunn. He was a real card, a jokester. His humor was clean and fresh, pointed at no one in particular, and without either sarcasm or cynicism. He was a class clown, in a way, but a class clown in a class full of clowns.

He wasn't a genius but he was bright. He got average grades, but the *gymnas* was so selective that kids had to be pretty intelligent just to get average grades. He was elected *russefestformann*, the social chairman of the *russ*. His election stemmed in part from the respect his classmates had for him, and in part from his great love of *fester*. He was a big drinker, but when he drove to one of our *fester*, he had one quick swig of *øl* and that was it; no one drank and drove in Tromsø.

We became good friends partly because of his fun-loving nature and partly because he had a serious side, too. Ever since I had come to Tromsø I longed for a way to express the serious side of myself, the side of myself that found its greatest expression with my LRY friends. I wanted to talk about politics, world events, religion, philosophy, morality, and virtually any heavy topic I could imagine. That was an important side to my personality, which is why I valued that side of Gunnar. There were times when he acted unbelievably immature, and then other times when he appeared to be much more mature than I. That made some sense, as he was already twenty...three years older than me. He was a good-looking charmer, with a way with both words and girls.

"Speaking of *småpiker*," I interrupted the silence, "you are hardly one to talk, my good friend. You certainly spend more time with *småpiker* than I do."

Gunnar just smiled. What I said was true, and he took no offense at it. He may have been my friend, but he was a ladies man, too, and quite proud of it.

"Is Lillian going to be at the *hytta*?" I asked.

"*Ja*," Gunnar answered. "Are you glad?"

"I guess so."

"I've never seen anyone so disappointed that a girl liked him. Do you have a girlfriend in America?"

"I think I do," was the most affirmative response I could muster. "I mean, I think of Sue as my girlfriend because that's the way I feel about her and that's what she said...sort of. She was generally open and honest with me—and beautiful—but she never exactly told me how she felt; she only sort of told me how she felt."

"Is that what you think of as a girlfriend in America?"

"I guess I wanted a girlfriend so badly that I would accept anything close. That's why I have her picture in my bedroom and I write her letters all the time. But she doesn't write me often and she never exactly says how she feels and she never exactly says I am her boyfriend. So, whatever there is between us, that about sums it up...except that I sort of feel she is my girl friend."

"Sounds confusing to me," Gunnar said.

"If that's not confusing enough," I said, "it makes everything with Lillian even more confusing. I've never really had a girlfriend; Sue is about as close as I have gotten. I feel Lillian likes me, and I enjoy being with her."

I Was a Teenage Norwegian

"I've never met an American before," Gunnar said. "I never knew you could make simple things so complicated. You have a girlfriend in America who doesn't write you letters, who doesn't tell you how she feels about you, and who doesn't say you're her boyfriend. Sounds simple to me: you don't have a girlfriend in America. You *want* a girlfriend in America, but you don't *have* one. I can't even figure out why you want to have a girlfriend in a country 8,000 kilometers away from where you are.

"Now, here in Tromsø you find a girl you like. She likes you. You don't have to be a *russ* to understand that; that one is simple. How can you be confused? You think too much. Just kiss her. You'll feel better."

That second *hyttatur* was noticeably less eventful than my first one. There were fewer kids and they didn't do as much together as a group. That left Lillian and me by ourselves a lot, particularly on Saturday evening when all the kids began to pair off. But we didn't make out all evening, like everyone else. We did make out, just not all evening. What we did for most of the evening was talk, almost more like friends than like girlfriend and boyfriend.

"Why did you want to come to Norway?" Lillian asked.

"I didn't really want to come to Norway exactly," I answered. "Mostly I wanted to get away from the town where I lived."

"Why? Were you unhappy?"

"I wasn't popular," I answered, surprised at how much she knew from how little I said.

"Which part of you wasn't popular?" Lillian asked. "The quiet part or the funny part?"

"The quiet part. I never showed anyone the funny part. You never show anyone anything but your quiet part."

"Are you saying I keep my funny part quiet?" Lillian joked. "My friends know who I am; they're the only ones I care about anyway."

"I wonder if I'll feel that way now that I have some real friends?"

"How do you feel about all the *småpiker* who are falling all over you?" Lillian asked me, with a smile.

"How do *you* feel about them liking me?" I asked her, with a similar smile on my face.

"I don't mind how much they like you," she said, kissing me, "as long as I get to kiss you."

Lillian was quietly assertive; she never raised her voice but she always got her way. She was self-confident without a trace of arrogance. She understood me, even without my saying much; I often thought that she understood me better than I understood myself. Her sense of humor was so different than mine. Her sense of humor grew out of her wisdom; my sense of humor grew out of my need to perform and be noticed. Perhaps more than anything, Lillian had the strength to help me change.

There were a lot of changes taking place in me in early November, and actually a lot of changes in Tromsø, as well. The most noticeable

change in Tromsø was the amount of daylight. The sun was rising somewhere between 8:30 AM and 9:00 AM and setting again between 2:00
PM and 3:00 PM. People had told me ever since I got to Tromsø that it
would be getting dark pretty early by November, and now that it was
early November, I could see that everything they said was true. We were
losing about 10-15 minutes of sunlight every day; by the 21st of
November, the sun would be on vacation for two months. It was unnerv-
ing already; I wondered how I would feel in a few weeks?

The weather was also changing, although not as dramatically as the
amount of sunlight. It had snowed already back in October. In mid-
October the temperature had climbed to a whopping 55°F, close to a
record for October in Tromsø. That kind of Indian summer was rare
there, and it didn't last more than a day or two. Since that time, the temperature had dropped to the winter temperature: between 25°F and 30°F,
or -5°C. Once the temperature hit that level, it stayed there all the time:
every day, day or night. I was used to wider temperature variations from
day to day, and usually between the daytime and the night-time. But in
Tromsø, winter temperature apparently meant *the* winter temperature.

I Was a Teenage Norwegian

But there were changes in me as well as changes in Tromsø, and the changes in my dreams were among the most noticeable. I had never thought much about my dreams growing up (one of the few aspects of my life I didn't think to death). Some of them were fun, some were scary, and some were sexy. In Norway my dreams began to change.

I began to integrate some of my Norwegian experiences into my dreams. I remember vividly the first time this happened. I was talking to my parents, explaining something about Norwegian beach habits. All of a sudden, Román was in the dream, at the stone-covered *badestrand*, in his underpants, which was what I was explaining to my parents. It wasn't fun, scary, or sexy; it was just weird.

But that was nothing compared to the first time I integrated *norsk* into my dreams. It involved Mrs. Destino, my American neighbor and mother of one of my few friends in Westport, Dave Destino. The dream took place in English and involved just Mrs. Destino, my American mother, and myself. I was talking to my mother; I can't remember what we were talking about. Mrs. Destino was across the street at her house. At some point, I can't remember why, I looked up and saw Mrs. Destino. She waved to me and yelled out, "*Heia.*" That phrase was definitely not English; it wasn't even Italian, Mrs. Destino's native language. *Heia* was an informal *norsk* greeting, somewhere between "hi" and "hello." I didn't know too much *norsk* at that time, and my dream reflected the influence my newly emerging *norsk* had on me.

From September to November my dreams changed and reflected many of the changes that were going on in me. First, the content of my dreams changed rather dramatically. In the summer, I was still dreaming of America; by September, I had integrated (or was it that I had confused?) my American and Norwegian lives. I dreamt of situations in which characters from both lives intermingled, as if they were all from the same place. By early November, the confusion resolved itself; almost all of my dreams were situated in Tromsø, with my Tromsø friends and family as the cast of characters.

Second, there were linguistic changes in my dreams as well. Even by November the dreams were primarily in English. That was strange enough: dreaming of Tromsø in English. But more and more *norsk* words entered my dreams and by early November, my dreams were a mixture of English and *norsk*. There was one dream in which I was explaining to Gunnar why I didn't want to go out with Lillian. I explained to him in *norsk*, but I thought everything out in English and translated it into *norsk*...all in my dream. I was conscious of talking to him in *norsk*, thinking in English, and translating my English thoughts into *norsk* out loud...in the dream.

The weather had changed, my dreams had changed, and my social life had changed. There was more snow than I could measure, my dreams were in *norsk*, and I had become a party guy.

The third *russefest* demonstrated that music and dancing were at the core of Norwegian parties. All of the kids danced, even the most studious at school, even those I wouldn't have thought were in the least social. They danced a lot of swing and rock-n-roll, a less acrobatic version than the American one, but with a lot more turns and swings. My favorite was the slow dance, and that was as popular in Tromsø as it was in Westport.

"Why aren't you dancing?" Jorunn asked me early on in the *russefest*.

"I learned all of these dances when I took ballroom dancing in fifth grade," I answered her, "but I don't remember any of what I learned."

"Come on, then," she took my hand and pulled me out onto the dance floor, "you'll just have to follow while I lead."

There was even something they called the "polonaise," which I had never seen before. The band started playing a marching song, of all things, and everybody got up and began marching two-by-two around the entire *kafé*.

"If you think this is something," Gunnar shouted as we passed each other, "you should have seen the time we did this throughout..."

"...the whole school," Arnulf had to complete Gunnar's sentence because the latter was already out of earshot. "That was something!"

A *russefest* was difficult to compare with American parties because it was a mixture of what we called a "school dance" and a private party. There was no making out at a *russefest*; making was reserved for private parties or *hyttatur*. I hadn't observed much dating in Tromsø. There were a few couples who were clearly couples; they went everywhere together, although they didn't necessarily stay with each other throughout a *russefest* and they always danced with other kids part of the time (even slow dances).

"Gunnar," I asked, "what if I bring a date to the next *russefest*?"

"She's yours for the evening," Gunnar answered.

"That's one of the reasons we don't like dates," Erika answered. Erika and Gunnar weren't exactly going steady, but they saw a lot of each other. "If we go as a date, the boy thinks we're his property for the evening."

"If I bring a date," Gunnar continued, "you're not supposed to try and 'get' her."

"But I see everybody dancing with everybody else," I said, "even with people's dates."

"Dancing is allowed," Arnulf said. "But that's it."

"Unless," Jorunn chimed in, "I decide to leave my date, which I can. I'm not supposed to, especially if he's paid for me."

"That's why," Erika interrupted, "I never let anyone pay for me: for parties, movies, anything. I don't want to owe a boy anything."

"If I decide to leave my date," Jorunn continued, "then another boy can make a play for me. Then it's okay."

"How does someone know," I asked her.

"You know," Gunnar smiled, knowingly.

"I can see *you* know," I smiled back.

"You will too, my friend," he said as he put his arm around my shoulder. "All you need is a few lessons from the master."

After the *russefest*, a group of us walked home together. Gunnar was in the group, and he was drunk.

"*Hei*," he stumbled toward me, "I want to have a word with you."

He grabbed my tie. All the boys always wore coats and ties to their *russefester*. Kids in Tromsø wore just as informal clothes at school as the kids at Staples, but they always dressed up for their parties.

"What happened?" he asked me, holding my tie in his hands. "Did I break it?"

I was wearing a clip-on tie. Gunnar had never seen anything like it and he thought he had ripped the tie and broken it. Being drunk merely added to the illusion.

"Say it in English," Gunnar switched into English. "I am a good English speaker, you know." He actually did speak English pretty well.

"You know," I insisted in *norsk*, "I don't speak English."

"Well I do," Gunnar continued in English. "I speak it wery good. And I want to speak English with you, understand you?"

"*Jeg forstår*," I said in my most formal and polite *norsk*.

"You can speak English with me," Gunnar slurred his words, still speaking English, "because I can speak English. And know you what, my American friend?"

"What, Gunnar?" I asked. I was still speaking Norwegian and he was still speaking English. Talk about role reversal. By that time we were walking behind the group we had started with, and we were by ourselves.

"I'm going to call you 'Pipe.' That's what I'm going to call you."

"And what does that mean," I asked, still thinking he was talking in *norsk*. The entire interaction constituted one of my more linguistically-confusing conversations.

"It's just Pipe," Gunnar continued in his drunken English. "It's that what I'm going to call you. Pipe."

"Why are you going to call me that?" I thought I was humoring him.

"Because that's your name now. Pipe. It's that what I'm going to call you because it's that what I'm going to call you."

All the way back *til byen*, Gunnar kept referring to me as Pipe. Eventually we caught up to the other kids in our group, and Gunnar told all of them he was going to call me Pipe. None of us could figure it out, and Gunnar certainly wasn't able to explain it any better.

When I got to school the next Monday, Gunnar still called me Pipe. He couldn't remember what had happened with the tie, but he remembered christening me Pipe. He didn't remember why or any of the particulars, just that my name was now Pipe and that was what he wanted to call me. And damned if everybody didn't start calling me Pipe, too, and damned if the nickname didn't stick. I was still Pete to my family, but I was now Pipe to all my friends. I had finally arrived; I had a nickname.

-19-
Family

By the middle of November I had been living with the Norbyes for almost two months. Although I spent most of my time with my friends, my relationship with the Norbyes was the backbone of my experience in Tromsø for those two months. Everything went so smoothly with them; there was none of the tension that I had so often felt while I was with the Románs. This stability and security made it easier for me to enjoy all the other aspects of my life. Adele had said that my year in Tromsø would be difficult enough without family problems; now I realized that it was as easy as it was because of just that lack of problems with my family.

So what was my family like? Who were those people who had done so much to help me become a teenage Norwegian? In that playful family, *far* was the closest thing we had to formal. He was tall, dark-haired, and stern-looking. He ran his own family business in Tromsø. The business was a little of a lot of things, as was necessary in a small town: part publisher, part printer, part stationary wholesaler, and part stationary retailer. He came home every day between 3 and 4 PM for *middag*, his hair slicked back and his suit always neatly pressed. He sat straight up at the dinner table, and asked me direct questions almost as if he were a teacher asking me to recite. But then he would laugh—somewhere between a chuckle and a giggle. He wasn't teasing me; the formality was a part of who he was. Along with it was a caring sensitivity and a genuine sense of humor.

Mor was, on the other hand, all mother. She was shorter than *far*, although not short, and looked much older, although I am sure she was not. It was her warmth and care-taking manner which made her appear older. I felt I never had a worry or concern when I was with her. After I made my *matpakke* every day, she put it in my hand in such a way as to make me feel she was always giving me a gift; she and everything she did felt so special. Periodically she pretended severity, but it never really worked. She was too happy and good-natured to pull it off. They were quite a pair, *mor* and *far*, and they obviously went well together, which simply added to the strength and appeal each had as individuals.

I Was a Teenage Norwegian

My brother Per was the good-looking nordic type that all the Westport girls talked about when I told them I was going to Norway. He didn't look much like *mor*, but I always thought of him as being her son. He had the same warm disposition, the same sense of humor. He was lovely with his kids; he was able to mix firmness with playfulness.

If Per was *mor's* son, Helen was *far's* daughter. She had his posture and his same apparent severity, but she was as inconsistent about it as he was. Helen was my older sister and she loved giving me older sisterly advice. But if she got too extreme about it, I just tickled her, as any younger brother would.

Torild wasn't anyone's kid; she was her own person. She was not exactly a blithe spirit because she was terribly organized and efficient; but she was a wee bit crazy at times. She would sometimes race about the house like a chicken with its head cut off. She talked a mile a minute; even *mor* couldn't always understand her. She always calmed down, but she always got excited again, too. She was as caring and sensitive as she was nutty. We talked for long hours into the night. She was what I had always hoped for in Karl Arvid as a brother, even if she was my sister.

What was so nice about our family was that it was as much a nice family as the members within it were nice people. There was love, affection, and genuine respect throughout our family. I wasn't exactly a member of the family, and I always knew that. But except for that minor fact, I was a Norbye and I was treated like any other child by *mor* and *far*.

"Pete," *mor* called up from the living room.

"*Jada*," I yelled back.

"*Per* and *Bodil* are here."

I liked it when Per and his family came over; we had gotten together three or four times since I had moved in with the Norbyes. Per was so fun-living and had such a great sense of humor. I usually played with Mette.

"Pete," Mette screamed when she saw me coming down the stairs. "Will you play with me? We can play with this toy," Mette said gleefully, showing me her top, which I had come to understand was her favorite toy. We had played with it the first time I visited Per and his family in their apartment and every time we had gotten together since then. We even had a routine surrounding it.

"It's nice," I said. "I'll watch you play with it."

"*Nei, nei*," she saw through my ruse. "You do it."

"Oh, no," I said, shrugging my shoulders. "It's your toy, Mette. I'll watch and you can play."

"*Nei, nei*," she squealed again. "You do it."

"Do what, Mette?"

"Push, push. Here, push," she pointed emphatically at the handle on top of the plunger. Mette was no dummy, just because she was only three years old. She knew what had to be done, even if she herself couldn't do it.

"Like this?" I asked as I pushed hard down on the plunger, starting the top on a long spin across the floor.

"*Jada,*" she responded, with obvious pleasure.

"I don't know," I heard a female voice say, "which of the two children is having more fun."

"Liz," I said, looking up from the top, "I didn't know you were coming."

I had forgotten that Per and Bodil and the kids were coming, but no one told me about Liz. At first, I figured she had come on official business...with some news. But she made no mention of anything except how clever at top-spinning I was and I figured she had just come to visit. After about forty-five minutes, Liz wanted to "talk" to me.

"Pete," she began after we found a place by ourselves at the table in the kitchen, "*vi har fant en familie til deg*: we have found a family for you."

"Do I get a brother my own age," I blurted out, without thinking. It was what I cared about most, or at least what I thought I cared about most. It wasn't surprising it was the first thought out of my mouth. "Is there a brother that can be a real brother, and a close friend, too?"

"Well, Pete," Liz said deliberately, "you will get a brother...in fact, you'll get three brothers. Two of the brothers are living at home: Tom, who is 13, and Olemann, who is 28. There's also a brother living in Kjøbenhavn; Paal is 25 and he was an AFSer in Arizona the same year as Adele Berg was in America. And there is a married *søster* living in Oslo, Astrid, with two children, about the same age as Mette and Bente here."

It wasn't exactly what I wanted, and Liz could see the disappointment on my face. I was never particularly adept at hiding my feelings.

"I know," she began, "that you think you're not getting what you wanted, because you think you wanted a brother your own age. But you are getting something else you want, even if you don't always understand it."

"What do you mean?"

"All you ever hear yourself asking for is a brother," she continued. "But I hear you asking for a mother and father as well."

"But *mor* and *far* Norbye are like parents to me," I objected.

"I know that," Liz said, "but haven't you often said you wished you had parents you could "talk" to?"

I had to admit she was right about that. I felt completely at home with *mor* and *far*, almost from the first. But they were so unlike my parents because I never felt I could "talk" to them, and get close to them in the way I was used to with my parents. I must have, in some way, conveyed that to Liz. I may have said very little, but Liz always read me like a book. I could never completely figure out whether she was especially clever or I was especially transparent.

"I don't know the Thyholdts that well," Liz said, referring to my new family. "They are a little quieter and less lively than the Norbyes, but they strike me as more like the parents you are looking for."

"That's fine with me," I said. "I have enough fun at school. A quiet, close, and warm home-life would be fine with me."

"Have you been dissatisfied with living here?" Liz asked.

"*Nei*," I answered immediately and without equivocation. Even I was a little surprised by the vehemently positive response.

"I didn't expect any other answer," Liz continued. "I think the Norbyes have been a great family for you for these past two months. I have seen some real changes in you, many of which I think can be attributed to them. You've come out of your shell a great deal, and I think this fun-loving family has been perfect for you."

"They sure have."

"And I think the Thyholdts will be good for you, too, but perhaps in a slightly different way."

"You know, Liz," I said, "I waited so long to be able to call the people I live with *mor* and *far*. I don't know if I can do it again. I don't know if I can have two sets of Norwegian parents, to go along with the one set of parents I inherited at birth."

"Don't even think about it for a while, and don't worry about comparisons. I'm confident that you'll do just fine. Just let everything happen as it needs to happen, and you'll do just fine."

"When do I move?" I asked, somewhat anxiously.

"Tomorrow," Liz answered, "if that's okay with you."

November 21, 1961. The day was memorable for a number of reasons. It was the last day of sun in Tromsø until January 21, 1962. I had listened to the radio reports indicating the amount of daylight each day, and I figured there was still a day or two of sun left. But the radio didn't take into consideration the mountains that surrounded Tromsø. The sun peeked out at us for a few minutes on that day, and then hid behind the horizon.

Second, that was the first day with my new, and third, Norwegian family. Saying good-bye to the Norbyes was much easier than I would have imagined, given how close I felt to them and how happy I was with them, certainly easier than saying good-bye to the Románs. There was no Bergljot wanting me to stay and not understanding why I was leaving. There were no adults wanting me to leave and saying nothing. I knew I would be coming back to visit; I knew I would be seeing Torild every day at school. I wasn't really leaving the family; I was simply moving out of the house. That was a huge distinction.

Liz drove us down toward the center of town and then south for perhaps a kilometer.

"That's the *sykhus*," Liz pointed out as we turned right after the hospital. We took the first left-hand turn and drove down Balsfjordgate itself. "You'll be living at Balsfjordgate 43, almost at the end of the road."

Even though it was dark, I could still see the differences between Balsfjordgate and Holtveien. Although the two houses were barely a five-minute drive from each other, the neighborhoods were completely different. The Norbyes had an acre of land and only a few neighbors. The houses on Balsfjordgate were smaller and much closer together; it was difficult to imagine that any of them had a yard at all. We parked the car in the tiny driveway and carried the suitcases to the front door.

"*God dag*," Thyholdt said as he opened the door.

"*God dag*," Liz and I answered in unison.

"Please come in," he said. "You can put your things in this room on the left. That's where you'll be sleeping. Then we can go upstairs."

I took off my shoes and carried my suitcases into the room Thyholdt had pointed out. I was already feeling a little uncomfortable, because the house was upside down. We walked in the front door but we walked into the bedrooms; all the bedrooms were on the first floor. They were small and there were four of them. It appeared I had my own room again: three for three, on that score.

So, if the bedrooms were on the first floor, where was the living room and the kitchen? On the second floor, naturally. We followed Thyholdt up the stairs through the dining room into the living room. It was like a scene out of a Bergman movie...the three of them sitting on the couch, waiting for me.

As *fru* Thyholdt stood up to greet me I could see she was short and heavy. She had dark brown hair and a big smile.

"*Velkommen*, Pete," she said as she shook my hand. "These are our two sons, Tom and Olemann." They each stood up and shook my hand. Tom was only thirteen years old. He was about average height for his age, which made him shorter than me. He had light brown hair, in a crew-cut. Olemann was as tall as Thyholdt himself, and a bit heavier. He had lighter hair, and his was also in a short crew-cut. His smile wasn't as big as his mother's, but it was noticeably more mischievous.

"*Vil du drikke kaffe?*" *fru* Thyholdt asked.

"*Ja, takk*," I answered.

There were two types of invitations for drinking *kaffe* in Norway. The first was when someone asked you before the *kaffe* was made. You were supposed to say yes, but it was possible for you to refuse. The second was like that evening; the *kaffe* was already prepared, and the table was already set with cakes and *vaffler* and jam and cheese and on and on. I had learned that one never refused that second kind of invitation.

Five of us drank *kaffe* (Tom had milk) and chatted for a while. We didn't really talk about anything and the conversation was stilted and more formal than I was used to in Tromsø. After half an hour Liz said she had to go, and I walked her downstairs to the front door.

"I'm afraid, Liz," I said to her at the door, "that it might be a little more difficult to get into this family than it was *hos* Norbye."

"I did tell you," Liz said, "that they might be a little afraid that you won't like it with them."

I Was a Teenage Norwegian

"I guess I'll just have to work a little harder than I had to with the Norbyes."

By 10:00 PM *fru* Thyholdt, Tom, and Olemann had gone downstairs to their rooms, leaving me alone with Thyholdt. I was apprehensive. He didn't appear to be as severe and stern as Norbye, but I sensed the same degree of formality.

"Your other son was an AFSer?" I asked, doing my best impression of an ice-breaker.

"*Ja*, Paal was in Arizona," Thyholdt answered. "He went to a boarding school; he even rode horses. My son the cowboy. You'll be sleeping in his room and you'll see some of his pictures on the wall. Paal is studying in Kjøbenhavn this year. He's studying insurance. Did Román tell you that Paal used to work for him at Tor Life Insurance?"

We talked, and talked, and talked. The time went by amazingly quickly; we talked for over two hours. My apprehension melted away. We didn't talk about anything especially serious: American football, the Norwegian language, my Norwegian language, the typical Thyholdt day. But I felt the fears begin to disappear from both sides: his and mine.

The Thyholdts were not as lively a family as the Norbyes (and there were no perky sisters in the house). I could already tell that the relationship would be different and probably less fun, but I was equally certain that a good, strong relationship could eventually evolve. Thyholdt talked to me more in that one evening than Román had talked to me in my entire two months with his family. I knew I had much to do to help build the relationship, and that I couldn't stop working hard toward that end, but it sure as hell was a damn good and encouraging start! The question was not if I would become their son, but how soon; not if I would like it *hos* Thyholdt, but how much.

"Pete," *fru* Thyholdt banged on my door the next morning, "It's time to wake up." At least that part of my family life hadn't changed. As I fell out of bed, I wondered if I would ever get used to the darkness, ever get used to having it just as dark when I woke up as when I had gone to bed, no matter what time I woke up.

My new bedroom was small, as had been the case *hos* Norbye. I didn't exactly have a bed; it was more like a couch-bed. Norwegians didn't sleep with sheets and blankets the way Americans did. I slept with a single sheet and a down comforter, a *dyne*, which I wrapped around myself to keep warm; it was different, but it was cozy. My sheet and *dyne* were hidden behind the back of the couch. *fru* Thyholdt had shown me the night before how to pull out and lift up the back of the couch, revealing the sheet, pillow, and *dyne*. In the morning, I simply reversed the process and hid everything again. The most interesting—and unusual—part of the room was that there was a small alcove in the corner with a sink. That was cool. I could wash my face, shave, and comb my hair each morning right there in my room!

The upstairs was different from any house I had ever been in, in Norway or America. It contained the dining room, living room, and kitchen. There was a little veranda off the dining room and a large picture window in the living room. But it was too dark to notice the nature of the view through the window; I would have to wait until January for that. By the time I got upstairs for breakfast, Thyholdt and Olemann had already left for work. They worked together in the family-owned business. Tom was sitting at the small table in the kitchen and *fru* Thyholdt was cutting some more bread.

"*Værsågod*, Pete," *fru* Thyholdt said. "What would you like for breakfast?"

"*Geitost* would be fine," I said.

"So," she smiled. "You like *geitost*?"

"*Jada*," I smiled, too.

"I like honey," Tom said, finishing his *smørbrød* and gulping down his milk. "We can walk to school together, if you want. It's on the way, anyway. My school is just beyond the *gymnas*."

Tom was clearly eager to walk with me. I got the sense that my living with his family was a big deal for him.

"Let Pete finish his breakfast," *fru* Thyholdt said. "Here, Pete, you'll need these *vitaminer*."

"Vitamins?" I asked. I never took them in America and I had never taken them in Tromsø, either.

"Yes, *vitaminer*. We always take them during *mørketida*, during the darkness. We get a lot of *vitaminer* from the sunshine, and when there is no sun, we take pills instead."

"*Takk*," I said taking the pills. There were three of them and I couldn't imagine they would do me any harm.

"And *tran*," *fru* Thyholdt continued, still smiling.

"*Tran*?" I asked.

"You need *tran*, too. *Tran* is best during *mørketida*. It has a lot of Vitamin D."

"Is that another pill?" I asked innocently.

"*Nei*," she said. She was still smiling and so was Tom. They clearly knew something I didn't and I wasn't sure I liked the situation. "You drink it," *fru* Thyholdt said, handing me a spoon.

I figured it was like the *geitost*; it was something I had to get used to. How bad could it be? It couldn't taste worse than the *geitost* when I started eating that. I held out the spoon, just a regular spoon, and she poured this oily-looking, thick liquid into the spoon. I looked at the spoon and then at *fru* Thyholdt. There was nothing I could do but drink it. How bad could it be?

Words were inadequate to answer that question. My first bite of *geitost* was like eating candy compared to that stuff. It was the most foul-tasting substance I had ever let into my mouth. The odor was obnoxious and the texture was repugnant. I must have made a king-size face, because both *fru* Thyholdt and Tom laughed out loud. They weren't malicious or mean. Norwegians were always laughing at themselves and each other, and they were never malicious or mean.

"You will get used to it, Pete," *fru* Thyholdt said, replacing the laughter with more motherly compassion.

Up until that moment, I had managed in the Thyholdt house, without having to use my trusty pocket *ordbok*. I obviously had to take that stuff, but I wanted to at least know what it was. I whipped the *ordbok* out of my back pocket, much to the surprise of *fru* Thyholdt and Tom (word of it had obviously not traveled as far as Balsfjordgate), and leafed quickly through the pages, with my mouth still obviously screwed up in a look of disgust. *Tran.* There it was: cod-liver oil. And I had two more months of that stuff!

"Come on, Pete," Tom smiled. "You've had your desert; now it's time to go to school."

"Have a good day at school, Pete," *fru* Thyholdt said as we walked downstairs.

I never really got used to *mørketida*. On the first day, I was walking to school from my new house I couldn't see much of anything.

"That's the *sykhus* over there," Tom pointed as we reached the end of Balsfjordgate. All I could see was the outline of a huge building; it was too dark to make out any details. We headed up a little hill and then turned north again, heading toward the center of town.

"This is the oldest church on the island," Tom said proudly as he pointed toward a much smaller shadow.

There were tons of kids walking to school. I didn't notice any of my friends; most of the kids walking were even younger than Tom. The neighborhoods we walked through were much denser than my Holtveien neighborhood. But it was too dark to see what the houses actually looked like.

"I'll see you at home after school," Tom said as we got to the *gymnas*. He enjoyed saying good-bye to me in front of all these older kids. Kind of like a younger brother.

"*Du* Pipe, *du* Pipe," Gunnar greeted me coming from this new direction. "No more walking down the hill to school for you."

"Think, Pipe," Franck added, "if you had stayed with Torild for just another week or two, you could have skied down the hill to school."

"*Hei dokker*," I chimed in.

"Who's your new brother?" Gunnar asked.

"Tom. He's at the elementary school."

"So, Pete," Jorunn was one of the few friends who refused to call me Pipe to my face. "How was your first night with your third family?"

Jorunn had a sensitive way of joking about my situation. She, more than most others, understood what I was going through, having been an AFSer herself and she had a way of talking that enabled me to laugh at it and myself. Maybe that's why we were such good friends.

"They're not as lively as the Norbyes," I said, "but they really want me to feel at home. I think it's going to be fine."

"It had better be fine, Pipe," Gunnar joked. "Otherwise we might run out of families for you."

Two nights later, I wrote my parents a Thanksgiving letter.

November 23, 1961

Dear Mom and Dad,

I almost forgot what day it was today, since the Norwegians don't celebrate Thanksgiving, but I certainly do have a lot to be thankful for.

Let's forget that my family and I are are both "feeling each other out," for today I wasn't served first, meaning my guest status was replaced by that of a family member.

There are so many things I am trying to forget...one being my pessimism. Til helveta (to hell) with all this junk. Takk for livet (Thanks for life)! I'm pretty lucky, and I'm aware of that. I just hope I can pay the world back for the goodness it has given to and done for me. A year ago I would have said the world is shit. Now I realize that if it seems thus, a great deal of the fault is my own. For those who say the world is lousy, maybe they don't deserve to be happy. All of us should be pretty grateful for what we have. If everyone isn't, at least I am.

It's now been 24 weeks: 15 hos Román, 8 hos Norbye, and less than 1 hos Thyholdt. Life is not as much fun or as lively hos Thyholdt as it was hos

I Was a Teenage Norwegian

Norbye, but I am quickly becoming a member of the family. I believe also that I am profiting by some of the earlier mistakes I made and, therefore, I am making a much more conscious effort to make things work: speaking to my parents, saying god morgen, god dag, *and* god natt *to them all the time, helping a little with clearing the table (not a "man's" job here in Tromsø), and getting to be Tom's "big brother." It's a nice, warm, friendly, and happy family, in its own more quiet sort of way and I am happy to be slowly becoming a part of it.*

Love,

Pete

Now that I had moved and spent my first few days with my new family, I figured I had better stop by the post office on my way home from school. For all of my becoming a teenage Norwegian, I still looked forward to my mail from America and I didn't want it sitting at the post office or at the Norbye house.

The post office was one of the biggest buildings in Tromsø: four or five stories high and took up half a block. Although it was a post office, it functioned as a bank, too. I deposited my monthly KR100 check from AFS there, and went there once a week, at least, to take money out.

That Friday afternoon I walked by the *Postsparebank* part of the post office, and went to one of the windows where they sold stamps.

"I would like to change my address," I said somewhat awkwardly. I could always make myself understood, even if I didn't have the exact *norsk* expression.

"I know," said the woman behind the counter. There were a number of different people who worked at the post office and I couldn't remember if I remembered this one.

"*Nei,*" I said firmly, "I want to change my address."

"I know," she repeated.

"I mean I live with a different family."

"I know," she smiled. " You live with Ole Thyholdt. Balsfjordgate 43."

"How do you know?" I asked stupefied. "I just moved there Tuesday."

"We've already sent your mail there today. There were two letters and your weekly newspaper. They should be there by the time you get home."

Here I had waited for two months for my third family, every day wondering when I would move and what the family would be like. I asked Liz all the time and all she ever said was she was working on it. When the move came, it came quickly: I moved to the Thyholdts within a day of when she told me. But news in Tromsø moved even more quickly. It took less time for the post office to know about my move than it took me to move!

-20-
College

I had been in Norway over four months. I lived with my third Norwegian family. I spoke only *norsk*. I was becoming a teenage Norwegian. But there were still some remnants of my American life and my American self that were not destined to disappear. I wrote to my parents every week, and I had to write to them in English. I still wrote to many of my friends, especially my LRY friends. And then there was college.

I was programmed from birth to go to college; I never even considered the possibility of not going to college. By tenth grade at Staples, it was something I had begun to think about; by my junior year, college was a major topic of thought and discussion.

College was one of the few American issues that stayed with me during those first months in Norway. I had to figure out where I was applying, and what my first choice might be. And I had to do it on my own. Somehow, between October and December, I managed to complete a process—from deciding which colleges I wanted, to writing applications, to taking College Board exams—that American kids did in their home towns with the support of their parents and their school counselors. I wrote my parents and shared my thoughts with them, and they wrote back and shared their thoughts with me. But there was no one in Tromsø I could talk to about it.

In America, particularly at a school like Staples where over 90% of the seniors went to college, thinking about college, visiting colleges, applying to colleges, and worrying about getting into college was a major agenda item. For my Norwegian friends, the process of going to university was quite different. First of all, there were only three universities in the country; choice wasn't the issue. No one talked about which college he or she was interested in, and no one wondered which extracurricular activity would look best on the application. The only issue was getting in; that was entirely dependent upon grades. There was no SAT to take. The system might have been less flexible than its American counterpart, but it was much simpler.

I Was a Teenage Norwegian

Although the issue of college loomed small, it was complex and confusing. I had no one else to talk to about it, and I had not given it a whole lot of thought before I left. Miss Barrie had told me that I could consider Earlham my safe school and that she recommended Oberlin.

I had some friends going to college who were giving me advice by mail. But I had more pressing issues—when would I learn to ski, learning intransitive verbs, my relationship with Lillian—which put college in an almost un-Norwegian perspective.

There were two big issues concerning college for me at that time. First, I had to decide to which colleges I would apply. That task had to be completed by November, to make sure the applications made it to the schools by their deadlines in December and January. The second college issue after college applications was that I had to take the College Boards, both the SATs and three achievement tests. I described my thought process regarding the first issue in a letter to my parents.

October 1, 1961

Dear Mom and Dad,

In your last letter, you asked me to speak about my preferences for college. I have (or will soon) made applications to four colleges: Lawrence, Oberlin, Earlham, and Harvard.

I applied to Brown because you, Dad, think I should. I have no intention of going there and I know nothing about it (and I don't care to know anything, either). Dad wants me to apply to an Ivy League College; I am committed to a small, mid-western college away from the East. I applied to Earlham mainly because Miss Barrie said Earlham was my "safe" school.

The difficult decision that I will have to make next Spring will be if I am accepted at both Lawrence and Oberlin (and this is a pretty big IF). I have been to Oberlin, I have seen some classes, I have seen and talked to some students, I have interviewed with some man from the Admissions Office, and I was impressed. The only knowledge I have about Lawrence is that it has a good academic rating, and the few people I have talked to about it love it. Even though it is not much to go on, I feel that I will be more at home at Lawrence than I would be at Oberlin.

This presents a problem because Dad and Baba want me to go to Oberlin (and do not argue with me because I am pretty sure about that). I do realize that you want me to make the choice for myself, but your influence and wishes must still play an important part in this decision. As of now, I still have my heart set on Lawrence (and Lawrence, being in Wisconsin, is in a heavily Norwegian-populated part of America). But my mind can easily change, because nothing is definite yet.

All my love,
Pete

October was the month for thinking about college. Even before I left the Norbyes, however, I got a letter from my Dad. Usually, my Mom wrote for the two of them, with my Dad sometimes adding a little note at the end. Talk about a lecture. All he wrote about was that I study like crazy for the SATs and Achievement Tests, so I could get great scores and get into all my colleges.

His letter reminded me of my grandfather's comment to me before I left. Baba was a self-made man. Although born in Lithuania, he grew up on the Lower East Side of New York City in the 1880s and 1890s. He was the only boy in his family and, according to tradition, the only child to receive much education. He graduated from college before he was twenty and went right on to get his doctorate in Mathematics.

My grandmother had died the year before I left for Norway and Baba lived with us between the time of her death and the time of my departure.

"So," he said with that mixture of criticism and impishness in his voice and eyes, "you're going to Norway. You've decided to give up a year of learning for a year of play."

As I composed my answer to my Dad, I felt I heard a little of Baba in my Dad's letter.

November 3, 1961

Dear Dad,

Well, you sure did give me a lecture, didn't you? First comes my lecture to you, Dad. I came here to be here, to learn, to give, to teach, to take, to change and be changed, to love and to be loved, to understand and be understood, to represent one people to the representatives of another. Everything has to revolve around my stay here in Norway, and nothing that you will ever say will change that, Dad...nothing. You hit me with about everything you had in your last letter, but I still stand fast on that which I hold most dear.

My mind has drifted away from college and every application made me more and more disgusted with this whole mess. I'll be damned if I want this stay to hurt my chances of getting into Harvard.

See, Dad, I just haven't completely adjusted yet. And until I can speak norsk fluently and can think in norsk, I won't have adjusted. Damn it: nothing must be allowed to stand in my way to learning and thinking norsk... nothing. It's my first concern; it has to be.

For the first time, one of your lectures didn't get me down; it inspired me. It inspired me to work harder, FIRST to make it here in Tromsø, and THEN on my own mind and study habits. It also polished off my decision concerning my choice of college—the necessity for a top-notch college with a stimulating student body rather than a college where I will be happy and "feel at home." Therefore, I wrote an "inspired" letter to Oberlin (and edited it, too) asking for an early evaluation, etc.

In a way, you accomplished your purpose of "waking me up and getting me off my ass," but I hope to God you can understand the way I feel. It's sad

I Was a Teenage Norwegian

in a way to completely leave behind my old way of life, but I feel that (at least for a while) it is the best way of making one's new life most valuable. You can try to change my mind, Dad, and I'm open to suggestions and criticism, but this time it's not just my stubbornness: it's a firm belief that you must try to change, and that's quite a task.

That's all I can think of for now. Please bear with me and my faults. But continue to criticize, for that's the best way to help me help myself.

> *Much, much Love,*
> *Pete*

That did it for my thoughts about college applications. I viewed the second college issue—the College Boards, both the SATs and three achievement tests—as the culmination of the college application/admissions process. It meant that I was finished thinking or worrying about college, and I could get back to becoming a teenage Norwegian. I had made arrangements to take the tests on December 2 at the *gymnas*. Now all there was left to do was study.

Theoretically, kids were not supposed to have to study for the SATs. I certainly hadn't studied for them when I had taken them the previous spring. But being in Tromsø changed my view of studying for these tests. I had spoken *norsk* almost 100% of the time for three months. With *norsk* creeping into my journal and my letters home, I feared it might creep into my SAT tests as well. In addition, I hadn't done much math of any kind since May. And my French was on the verge of disappearing. Those problems would pretty well take care of the Achievement Tests, and the SATs themselves could just as easily follow suit.

I didn't know exactly what had gotten me so all-fired-up over my father's letter lecture earlier in the month. It probably had more to do with not wanting to speak English and getting adjusted to Norway and *norsk* than with studying for the College Boards. Even though I revolted against studying, I certainly put in more time studying for those tests than for any of my work at the *gymnas*. I had brought some study aids with me from Westport. I had, for example, a grammar handbook of about 100 pages. And I read that book from cover to cover more than once during those last two weeks in November; it took about six hours each time.

The Friday before the tests, my focus was how to think about, plan for, and take the College Board exams themselves. I worked on the kinds of questions I could expect, the skills needed to answer those kinds of questions, and the reasoning behind the answer strategies. Then, I went to see a movie and got to bed early.

By 9:00 AM the next morning, I was closeted in a small room next to my real classroom. It was a different feeling from the previous spring, where I took the exam in the gym with almost 200 other kids. In

Tromsø, I was all alone, except for the teacher. Norwegian test-taking standards made it necessary for the teacher to be with me in the room at all times. If taking the tests wasn't a fun experience for me, think how boring it must have been for my guard.

I got an hour break between finishing the SATs and starting the Achievement tests later that afternoon. 5GE wouldn't get out of school until 1:15 and by then I would have to be back in my closet. So I walked to Storgate myself.

"How did the test go?" *mor* Norbye asked as I got to the bottom of the hill and turned right on Storgate towards the *kiosk*.

"Fine," I answered somewhat surprised. How had she known I was taking the test? I didn't remember talking about it much when I lived there. She may have called *mor* Thyholdt, or Torild may have asked one of my classmates. For all I knew, it was on page 17 of *Tromsø* or *Nordlys*, the two daily newspapers.

"Did you have any lunch yet?" *mor* asked. as we started walking.

"*Nei*," I answered. I felt her hand drop something in my pocket. *Mor* didn't say anything, and we just kept walking.

"I have to do some shopping here at Figenschau," *mor* said to me. "I hope everything goes well with your test." And she was off.

She had slipped me a Freia *melkesjokolade*, milk chocolate candy bar, slipped it to me as if no one else was watching, or could see what she was doing; it was little, secret communication between *mor* and me. The chocolate bar was much more than just a chocolate bar; it was a symbol of our relationship. I had become a teenage Norbye. It was easy to leave the Norbyes because I had known from the beginning with them that I would have to do it. I never really thought about the process, the way I had agonized over leaving the Románs. But I realized then how much a Norbye I had become. I realized how lucky I was to have two "families" in Tromsø.

By the end of the day, I was glad I was done. All I had to do was wait until April, when I would have to begin to think about college again. Until then, I had a four month vacation from that particular issue. Or so I thought.

As was so often the case, I was wrong. On December 5, I received the following letter:

OBERLIN COLLEGE
Oberlin, Ohio
Office of the
Director of Admissions

November 30, 1961

Dear Mr. Dublin,

An early evaluation of your application for admission to the College of Arts and Sciences of Oberlin College has just been completed and I am very happy to be able to tell you that the Committee on Admissions has voted to approve your admission to the Class of 1966. Please accept our congratulations for the outstanding record you presented and the fine recommendations which were submitted in support of your application. We are looking forward with great anticipation to next September when you will arrive on the Oberlin campus.

Enclosed herewith you will find a printed statement concerning the Promise of Admission, and an information card to be completed by you. Please note that the card is to be returned to this office within three weeks, but that no payments are required until you receive your term bills next September.

Since your Promise of Admission has been granted earlier than is customary, on the basis of your declaration of Oberlin College as your first choice, we will expect you to write at once to the Director of Admission at any other college to which you may have applied, withdrawing your application.

We hope that this early decision on your application will free you from the anxieties about college admission common to high school seniors, and will enable you to better concentrate on your studies and activities during the remainder of the school year.

Until you are enrolled at Oberlin next September you may be sure we will be delighted to be of service if you have any questions.

Sincerely yours,

Robert L. Jackson
Director of Admissions

I had just taken the College Boards and started my vacation from thinking about college. Oberlin was my first choice, but I had never imagined early admissions as a realistic possibility.

The letter was exciting, but it raised as many questions as it answered. It prompted an immediate letter home to my parents.

December 5, 1961

Dear Mom and Dad,

As you can well see for yourselves, I have just run into a streak of good luck. I had figured an early evaluation meant that they would tell me what my chances of acceptance were and just that. I had never expected that an early evaluation would mean a definite yes or no answer...and I certainly did not expect a yes answer.

It now seems funny that you yelled at me and told me to get off my ass and work. It seems funny that I studied and studied for those silly College Boards. It seems funny that I worried about not studying and not doing well. Those damn tests were not even necessary.

You should notice that I must answer this decision of acceptance within three weeks and there is something else: Harvard.

If I was given a choice of going either to Harvard or Oberlin, I would take Harvard. I believe it is a better school and I would have the opportunities, facilities, and "inspiring student force" to get more out of Harvard than Oberlin. Therefore, I am asking you for help...and you must write back immediately. The question is whether or not to write to Harvard. If I write and they say they cannot give me an immediate evaluation, I must withdraw my application from that school (I will immediately withdraw my applications from Brown, Earlham, and Lawrence, in accordance with Mr. Jackson's request). I have a duty now to Oberlin and it must be fulfilled in the shortest possible time. If I write to Harvard and they accept me, I will then write to Oberlin and turn down their offer. If I do not write to Harvard for an immediate evaluation, I will send them a letter withdrawing my name from the list of candidates.

You are surely aware that I will most probably accept your advice and follow through on it: I'll write to Harvard if you say so and to Oberlin if you say no to Harvard. I guess I might as well tell you the answer I expect to receive: to hell with Harvard; take what you've got. I've said this to myself, too, of course, but I was not 100% sure and I figured it was better to check with you before I did anything.

Thanks for all that you have done and will do to insure that my future life is both happy, rewarding, and prosperous; it has been appreciated.

Much anxious love,
Pete

I Was a Teenage Norwegian

On December 13th, I received a telegram from my parents. They had decided, after talking with Miss Barrie, to contact Harvard directly. Harvard was completely inflexible about even-earlier-than-early evaluation; I would have to wait until they were ready to make their decision. All of which prompted my final letter on the subject.

December 13, 1961

Dear Mom and Dad,

Thanks for the telegram about Harvard. It's a shame that I cannot wait to hear from Harvard, but Oberlin did something special for me and they should expect me to do a little something for them.

Oberlin is a good school and the only thing it lacks is norsk. Oberlin is a little far from home, but I should get a chance to be home three or four times a year—which, although not good, is a step better than the situation now. I can't say it will be easy at Oberlin, but I'll pull through.

No, I couldn't say I wasn't pleased, and "Look, Ma, no four month WAIT!" I believe the usual procedure is to notify Staples of all acceptances and possibly the newspaper, too. Perhaps you, Mom, could give Miss Barrie a ring?

All my love,
Pete

I went to Oberlin and it proved to be the best possible college for me. I cannot, now, imagine having gone to Harvard. I cannot even imagine that I ever gave it serious thought at that time. But I did. The folly of youth. At least, in this case, Harvard really did me a favor.

-21-
Mørketida

With college taken care of, I could concentrate a bit more on my *new* family, although it wasn't all that new any more. My new family was not quite as outgoing or talkative as the Norbyes, but everyone in it was full of life and cheerful, and each had a good sense of humor. Two didn't live at home. Astrid, my only *søster* and the oldest of the children, was married and lived near Oslo. There was a good chance I might never see her, unless she visited us sometime...perhaps at Christmas.

Paal was the middle brother; he was around twenty-five and had been an AFSer in Arizona. I was sleeping in his room and he had various pieces of memorabilia on the walls: pictures of his classmates in Arizona, his American high school diploma, and stuff like that. At the time I moved into his room, he was studying insurance in Kjøbenhavn, Danmark. *Mor* and *far* told me that Paal would be home for almost a month at Christmas.

Olemann was twenty-eight and worked for *far*. He had married a woman about eight years younger than he and they had one child, but the marriage didn't work out and they were divorced. She kept the son and eventually remarried. Olemann was quiet, but full of life at home and when dancing, with a good sense of humor. He and I were not as close as "real" brothers, but this was probably due as much to the differences in our ages as his character. He had to watch his weight—something in which he took no great pleasure—and usually didn't.

Tom was a real mainstay of the family and myself. What I particularly liked about him was that he provided support even without my "needing" it. He was a tall, well-built, short-haired, good-looking thirteen year-old. He was fond of food and was willing to let everyone know it—although he didn't eat as much as he talked. He was restrained, the epitome of good manners, always good-natured and pleasant, as was the rest of the family. There had never been a sullen, gloomy, unpleasant moment in this house since I arrived...not a one! Tom had a fantastic sense of humor. He was funny and in the best of ways: never critical, always restrained. *Far* and *mor* were not strong disciplinarians—they never, for example, said I had to do my homework—but they did an amazingly fine job with Tom.

A part of family life that was different from what I was used to in America had to do with family chores. In America I was used to clearing the table every night and washing the dishes. I did this with Tom and Peg and it often was more like a time to squabble than a time to work, but it was part of my family responsibility. I was also responsible for making my own bed, for vacuuming the living room and the study (what we called our family room), and doing the seasonal yard work: mowing the lawn, weeding the garden, raking the leaves, shoveling the snow, and so forth. I wouldn't say I was overwhelmed with work, but family chores were clearly a part of family life.

Life was different at the Thyholdts. *Hos* Thyholdt there were almost no chores I *had* to do. I did have to make my bed, but that was hardly a chore since all I had to do was store the *dyne* and sheet behind the back of the couch. And that was it; *mor* did everything else. She set the table and she cleared the table. She did the dishes and she did all the housework. I quickly learned that even helping with clearing the table was looked down upon (especially by Tom and Olemann). The back yard was about the size of the living room, and the driveway was the front yard; not too much outside work, either.

After a particularly extensive snowfall one day in early December, *far* asked Tom and me to go outside and shovel the snow. It was surprising how rarely we were asked to shovel snow, given how much snow we had. The snow in Tromsø tended to get packed down rather than shoveled, but that most recent snowfall was over the pack-down limits, and out we went.

Tom and I started shoveling in what I thought of as the normal pattern. We would use our shovels to pick up the snow, carry it out of the driveway, and heave it wherever we could. By that time in December, there was already a substantial pile of snow bordering on the narrow driveway leading from Balsfjordgate to the small garage attached to our house. For a while, Tom and I kept heaving the snow on top of that already-existing pile.

"How about," Tom said, with that gleam in his eyes I had already come to recognize, "we hide you, Pete?"

"Hide me?" I asked. That might have been a special Tromsø expression; I had learned not to take everything I heard literally.

"*Jada*," Tom said with great enthusiasm. "Sit up on that pile of snow."

"Sure," I said and I did. That was easy. Sitting down had the extra added benefit of making it impossible for me to continuing shoveling, and I had no problem with that.

"Just sit there," Tom laughed, "while I hide you." Tom proceeded to shovel the snow onto and around me. It wasn't all that cold to begin

with, and I didn't feel any colder with snow all around me than I had felt with snow all around me. Slowly, Tom covered almost all of me. He heaved snow up on the pile behind me, providing me with a natural backrest. He covered most of my body, allowing my feet and my hands to protrude out of the snow. He covered the rest of me up to my head, allowing that access, as well.

"*Mor, far,*" Tom yelled upstairs to the picture window in the living room. *Mor* and *far* looked out. "*Kor e' Pete?* Where's Pete? Come down quickly and help me find him."

I couldn't tell if this was a family tradition or something that Tom had just invented, but *mor* and *far* obliged their youngest son, came downstairs and outside, and stood in front of me.

I was completely immobile. I was covered in snow, with just my reindeer boots-covered feet, mitten-covered hands, and red hat-covered head sticking out of the all-white snow.

"Tom," *far* said, ignoring me. "You have done an excellent job. Olemann and I will have no trouble getting the cars out of the driveway. *Takk.* You can come in now."

And the three of them started for the house.

"*Du* Tom," I cried out.

"*Kor e' Pete?*" *far* asked Tom, somewhat casually.

"I hid him, *far*," Tom answered, overly politely. "I can't remember where."

They all three walked into the house, leaving me to break myself free from Tom's hiding place. It was the kind of joke my father would have played on me; now it was a joke *far* played on me. *Far* may not have looked like my father, but he had begun to act like him.

Far's light-colored hair had begun its backward journey and was already fairly thin. He was the only light eater in the family, and the only thin one, too. Like Román and Norbye, he was also an executive and an industrious worker. *Far* was quiet, but he constantly helped me (correcting my *norsk* mistakes, for example) and we always discussed various aspects of Norwegian life. I learned a great deal from the man and I had an enormous amount of respect for him.

Mor was completely different. She was much more lively (without being at all loud) and full of fun. She was thick and round, but I never really noticed that; to me, she was a real DOLL! We talked every now and then, but we joked almost always.

I would sometimes be the first one home in the afternoon and sit in the kitchen while *mor* prepared *middag*.

"Who were you walking in Storgate with today, Pete?" *mor* asked, clearly already knowing the answer.

"Lillian," I answered.

"Lillian Ingebrigtsen?" *mor* asked.

"*Ja.*"

"Do you see a lot of her?" *mor* asked.

"*Ja.*"

"You know," she said, "you can bring her over here if you like."

"Really?"

"Certainly. Any of your friends are welcome at our house. We're thinking about building a room in the basement where you and Tom can bring your friends. Until then, you can use your own room."

"*Takk*," I said. Not only was this a generous offer, but it reflected a socially liberal attitude I had never encountered in my politically liberal parents. I saw Lillian every day at school; it was difficult to miss her when we sat next to each other. We would go *til byen* after school sometimes, but we rarely met in Storgate in the evenings; Lillian didn't go out much during the week. I remained completely ambivalent about my feelings for Lillian. Either I was noticeably transparent or *mor* was exceptionally clairvoyant.

"If you're not too embarrassed," *mor* winked at me, "you can even bring her upstairs and introduce her to us."

I talked to *mor* a lot about Sue, but I rarely received a letter from her. I still thought of her as my girlfriend, but it was as if the only advantage that such a thought had was allowing me to avoid having to confront my feelings about Lillian. Lillian always demonstrated that she knew me better than I knew myself. As we spent more time together, she still never pressed me, never asked me the questions I couldn't answer, never confused me more than I confused myself. At the December *russefest*, we danced with each other and we danced with everyone else, as was the Tromsø habit. One minute, we'd be slow-dancing, with her head nestled into my neck, the next minute she'd be glaring at me because of a particular bad joke, and then she'd be off dancing with Arnulf or Johnny or Gunnar; happy as a lark with me and happy as a lark without me. But she always came back to me and I always came back to her.

I came to feel close to *mor* in large part because she helped me better understand who I was, but also because we simply saw much more of each other than did *far og jeg*. She was almost as lazy as I; that probably helped us get along well, too.

I was hardly ever *serious* with my new parents in those first few weeks (certainly not like my "talks" with Dad), but we had a surprisingly good and strong relationship almost immediately. My love for my Balsfjordgate family was much different from my love for my Red Coat Road family, but the love was there and I felt it was reciprocated. It was often cute the way in which it showed itself.

"Pete," *mor* said to me one morning in early December, "I hope you get that letter (from Sue) soon. I'm terribly excited each time I go to get the mail and disappointed when the letter still isn't there."

What greater demonstration of a mother's love could I have asked for?

A week later, I had a memorable family experience. One of my new cousins—Grete Maria—had her confirmation. In Norway, no one took their religion seriously, but everyone was confirmed. On that Saturday, all of the Thyholdts went to the confirmation ceremony at church. I didn't go, but I did go to the confirmation *middag/fest* after the church service. There were over twenty of us at *middag*...a true family event.

I expected Grete Maria to shed a few tears on such an occasion and it didn't surprise me that she did. But the highlight of the *middag* was when her father began to talk about Grete Maria. He talked about what she was like as a little girl. He recounted a number of stories both about Grete Maria and his relationship with her. He talked about how she had grown up and the kind of girl she had become. He was eloquent, but simple; I could understand everything he said. And he couldn't hold back his own tears.

I Was a Teenage Norwegian

My father was an emotional guy, and I had seen him cry before, both out of sorrow and out of joy. But I still wasn't prepared for Grete Maria's father. The love between a father and child that came gushing out of his heart like the water tumbling from his eyes was something I had not seen since coming to Tromsø. I had trouble holding the tears back myself.

"*Du*, Pete. *Du*, Pete." *Mor* knocked at my door the next morning. "*Er du våken?* Are you awake?"

"*Nesten*," I told her. "Almost."

It wasn't often that I slept through my alarm clock, but I was having more and more difficulty getting myself up.

Even when I first heard from AFS that I was going, I never pretended to know more about Norway than I knew and I knew very little. I associated Norway with *fjords*, even if I didn't know exactly what a *fjord* was. Vikings, of course, were included in my image of Norway, even though they hadn't existed for hundreds of years. And I thought of Norway as the Land of the Midnight Sun.

As I look back now, I am embarrassed by my inability to understand the consequences of the midnight sun. It sounded intriguing: seeing the sun at night. And it was. What I didn't appreciate was that the Midnight Sun came at a cost; the cost was its opposite, which was not referred to as the Midday Moon. Norwegians were more honest than that (although their ancestors, the Vikings, did come up with the name Greenland, in perhaps the world's first example of a public relations gimmick). For every month the sun never set in the summer, it never rose in the winter.

Mørketida. The darkness. It was so obvious and so completely unanticipated. I came to Tromsø in July, just toward the end of *midnattsolen*, the midnight sun. Everything was so new to me that I really hardly noticed the *midnattsol*, let alone appreciated it. After the middle of my first Norwegian July, the sun began to set and the days became shorter, even though there was still nothing approximating night.

On July 21st, Tromsø had 24 hours of daylight. On November 21st, Tromsø had no daylight whatsoever. Tromsø lost those 24 hours of daylight in four months; it lost about one and one-half hours of daylight every week from the middle of July until the middle of November. But it was usually—unless the sky was full of dark clouds—light for almost an hour after sunset and an hour before sunrise, so even after a week of sunsets, it was difficult to tell the difference.

By August and the start of school, there were real days and nights, enough so that I really didn't pay much attention to those kinds of changes. Every week, another one and one-half hours of darkness came unnoticed, every day another fifteen minutes. By early November, I had begun to notice some of the changes that had come over Tromsø. When I walked to school in the morning, or even when I walked *til byen* during the *storefriminutter*, all the cars had their headlights on. When I walked home for *middag* after a stroll up and down Storgate after school, I noticed the huge lights that lit up construction sights at 3:00 in the afternoon. *Mørketida* was clearly on its way.

Throughout the fall, I derived a great deal of pleasure from hearing when the sun rose and when it set (that was a highlight of the daily weather report on the radio) and constantly computing the hours of sunlight we had and how much less of the precious substance we had that day than we had the day before. Soon, however, I realized it was not all the appropriate to use even a phrase like "the day before," for by late November the sun took its last look at us and we got our last glimpse of it, and all of a sudden it was there no more; it had dipped behind the mountains for the last time (for that year, at least) and its two-month hibernation period had begun. The result was that I woke up to the same amount of darkness I thought I had left behind in slumber. I learned to live with the same degree of "pitch-blackness" from one in the afternoon until eleven the next morning; our treat each day was two hours of dusk.

Mørketida was probably the low point of the entire year. It was as strange as it was dark. It was as disconcerting as it was dark. We would go to the newsreels Saturday afternoon after our half-day of school. We stumbled out of the movies at 2:00 in the afternoon and I would be shocked by the darkness.

For many people in Tromsø, *mørketida* brought on depression. There was certainly a lot more drinking in winter than in summer. For me, the issue was sleep. I remembered the *hyttatur* I went on with Karl Arvid, Geir, and the others. We would be up to all hours of the night. It was nothing to be eating *aftens* at 11:00 o'clock at night. We would go out for a midnight canoe ride in broad daylight, and think nothing of going to bed at 2:00 in the morning. *Mørketida* changed all that for me. I felt as if I was sleeping all the time. I went to bed early, a lot earlier than in the summer. I probably slept 2-3 hours per day more during the winter than I did during the summer. Even so, I was always more tired during the winter than the summer.

Tran. Cod liver oil. That was a part of Norway no one had warned me about. I was always tired in the winter and I needed more sleep. The lack of sun was both psychological and physical. Sunlight—I was often told by *mor*—was a major source of Vitamin D. No sun, not as much Vitamin D. Unfortunately for me, and millions of other Norwegian kids, the single best source of Vitamin D after sunlight was *tran*.

I had never tasted anything that tasted as disgusting as *tran*. Within a day of moving in with the Thyholdts, *mor* explained to me about the sun and the need for *tran*. She also suggested a way for me to gradually build up my resistance to the taste—overpoweringly vile—and a tolerance for the texture—disgustingly oily. The first week, I took a mouthful of milk and swallowed it; I took a second mouthful of milk and kept it in my mouth; I coated a teaspoon with milk and filled it with *tran*; I held my nose with one hand, tipped my head back, dumped the spoonful of *tran* into my mouth, and swallowed. The taste was awful, but the experience was manageable.

Over the next few weeks, little by little I would drop one of the rituals. First, I didn't have to coat the spoon with milk. Next, I didn't have to have a mouthful of milk. Then I didn't have to drink milk at all with or before the *tran*. Toward the end, I didn't even have to hold my nose. Finally, I could simply and quickly fill up a tablespoon with *tran*, gulp it down without a grimace, and move on to *frokost*, to breakfast.

"Now," *mor* said proudly to me, "you are a real Norwegian."

All thought that this was some special practice to protect the weakling American from the harsh realities of a Norwegian winter disappeared when I went to visit an elementary school in early January. I was always curious about Tromsø and took whatever opportunity I could to visit different places. The elementary school Tom attended was just down the street from the *gymnas* and I asked *Inspectør* Hansen if I could spend a day there, to see what it was like. The most startling experience there occurred at around 10:00 in the morning. I was sitting at the back of the room watching the students finish with their writing lesson.

"*Nu er det tran*," the teacher said calmly. Now it's time for cod liver oil.

While he went over to a cabinet at the front of the room, the kids calmly put their writing books away in their desks and sat silently. The teacher took a bottle of *tran* and a spoon out of the cabinet and walked to the back of the room. He opened the bottle and poured a spoonful of the slimy liquid. In unison, the kids whipped their heads back and opened their mouths. The teacher walked up the aisle, dropping a spoonful of *tran* into each mouth. Up and down the aisles he went, dropping the *tran* into the mouths in a scene reminiscent of a bird dropping worms into the outstretched mouths of her babies. When he was finished, he put the *tran* and spoon back in the cabinet, the kids opened their desks and took out their books for geography, and the day proceeded as if nothing out of the ordinary had happened.

Weather always is a major aspect of life anywhere, and Tromsø was no exception. *Mor*, for example, always turned the volume up on the radio whenever the weather report began. For me, *mørketida* was the dominant aspect of winter weather. But just because it was difficult to see didn't mean that we had no snow. We saw our first snow in October and the snow began in earnest during the first week of November. It snowed at least once a week after that. By early December, we had about half a meter of snow, although there were drifts between one and two meters. That was pretty impressive by Connecticut standards, but the amount was not really what distinguished the Tromsø snow from the Westport snow: the real distinction was duration.

By early November, the temperature had settled into the 20s (Fahrenheit). Sometimes it got as warm as the upper 20s; sometimes it got as cold as the lower 20s. Night or day (or as we said in Tromsø: night or night). From what people had told,me that was the temperature I could expect until April. So the real difference with Tromsø snow was that the snow didn't melt...until April. The roads didn't exactly get plowed; it was more that the snow just got packed down. Sidewalks in town were shoveled, but they also tended to elevate during the winter. As I walked to school each day, I often wondered what I was walking over. And I couldn't wait until we got some daylight to see the snow because it was so clean...at least that's what all my friends told me. The surrounding mountains with their wintery coat of newly fallen snow and the glistening ice-cold, ice-coated water made as romantic a fairy-land scene as one could hope to see; it was a shame that it was too dark to see it.

I had one experience that, more than any other, brought the point of *mørketida* home with a memorable jolt. It was about 11:00 one night in early January and *mor*, *far*, and I were sitting on the living room couch.

"Would you like a little something to drink?" *far* asked *mor*.

"We like to have a little something before we go to bed," *mor* explained to me as *far* went into the kitchen to get the drinks. "It is good for our circulation."

I used to joke her about it, but I think she spoke the truth. Every night, the two of them each had a tiny glass of something. Otherwise, they never really drank. They didn't have cocktails, either when *far* came home from work or when they entertained. They never had wine for *middag*; such a custom was unheard of in Tromsø. *Far* and Olemann would have small glass or two of *øl* at *middag*; that was all.

"I guess I'll go to bed," I said, getting up.

"Are you all finished with your homework?" *far* asked. He knew I didn't do much homework, but he was my *far*; he cared about me and he always asked.

"We didn't really have much," I answered in as noncommittal a way as possible. "*God natt.*"

"*God natt, da,*" *mor* said.

"*God natt,*" *far* echoed.

I walked down the stairs toward my bedroom. I slept on a couch, with my *dyne* hidden behind the back of the couch. All I had to do was to lift up the back of the couch, pull out the *dyne*, drop the back of the couch back down, and place the *dyne* on the couch...and my bed was made. And as soon as my bed was made, tired as I always was during *mørketida*, I was in it. And as soon as I was in it, I was fast asleep.

When I woke up, it was still pitch black outside. I had a sink in my room and I washed my face and shaved. I had been shaving since I was thirteen years old, and I shaved every day, even at seventeen. I dressed, packed my books in my book-bag, and walked upstairs for *frokost*.

Mor and *far* were sitting on the couch, talking. They didn't have their coffee cups, which was what they usually drank for *frokost*. I noticed that, but it didn't register.

"So," *far* said, "what are you doing?"

"I'm going to get some *frokost*," I said.

"Why?" he asked.

"I always eat *frokost* before I go to school?" I answered tentatively. I had lived in this house for almost two months and felt myself a member of the family. But there was always the fear that I would not understand some convention or ritual, and that I would make some mistake. I wondered if that time had finally come.

"Do you know what time it is?" *far* asked again.

"*Nei.*"

"Why don't you turn around and look?" he smiled.

The clock was on the stairway wall. I saw it every time I went down the stairs. I had seen it when I went to bed a little after 11:00 PM. I walked over to the stairs and looked again: 11:30. I was confused. I couldn't have slept that long. I looked at *mor* and *far*.

"You didn't," *far* answered my unasked question.

My confusion disappeared, but not my embarrassment. *Mørketida* made it impossible for me to tell what time it was. I had, in fact, slept for about ten minutes.

-22-
Jul

Jul. Christmas was harder to notice in Tromsø than it had been in Westport. In Westport, Christmas began to advertise itself just after Thanksgiving: the town put up its decorations, the store windows displayed their Christmas gifts, and the newspapers—both the *Town Crier* and the *New York Times*—were full of nothing but Christmas advertisements. It may have been the season to be jolly, but it was clearly and obviously also the season to be buying.

My parents constantly talked about the ways in which Christmas had changed since their childhood. We talked, as kids, about the presents we wanted; we made our list for Santa. There was little question that Christmas in America had been redefined from its religious roots to its new status as the season of gifts.

In spite of this more general social transformation, the commercial aspect of Christmas was not the image of Christmas I took with me to Norway. For me, the dominant memory of Christmas was the Christmas tree. We lived next to the Burchee farm, where we could still buy fresh-picked corn every day during the summer. The Blue Ribbon Dairy in Westport still had its own cows and processed its own milk. And within a ten-minute drive, our family could trudge through snow-covered woods in December to select and cut down our own Christmas tree.

We would pile into our car on December 24th and head for the tree farm in Wilton. We would walk and walk, surveying thousands of trees, until we found just the right one. We always found an especially nice one for our high-ceilinged, relatively large living room. We cut it down, dragged it back to the car, tied it to the roof (always in an amazingly elaborate fashion), and drove it home.

I didn't know why, but we always got our tree on December 24. And we always put it up that evening. And we always put it up together, as a family. And we always overloaded it with every ornament we had, from the red spire at the top to the family heirlooms to the enormous amount of tinsel we had with infinite patience saved from the year before. It was that ritual that formed the strongest image of Christmas for me.

I Was a Teenage Norwegian

Christmas was a time for the family to be together. Although for the rest of the country Christmas began the day after Thanksgiving, it began for me on December 24th.

Jul in Tromsø started earlier than December 24th in a less commercial way than it did in America. On December 16th, *Brødrene* Thyholdt had its annual Christmas party, a *julefest*. *Brødrene* Thyholdt was the name of *far's* company: Thyholdt Brothers. He and his brother, *onkel* Edvard, had started the company years before and had named it after themselves. It was not an office party in the American sense: starting at 3:00 in the afternoon, at the office for those working in the office, with everybody getting silly and tipsy. As with so many other aspects of life in Tromsø, a *julefest* was a family affair.

First of all, the *julefest* was held on a Saturday evening: prime social time in Tromsø. Second, the event was held at the Grand Hotel, the most prestigious locale for any social gathering. Third, there was much more food at this *julefest* than there was alcohol. Fourth, the *fest* included not only the spouses of the employees but their children as well.

I had been to four *russefester* but they didn't really prepare me for the *julefest*. What dominated that *fest* was the generational guest list. When the employees brought their families, it meant (in some cases, at least) both their children and their parents. There were sixty or seventy people at the *fest*, ranging in age from three or four to well over eighty. And everyone danced, and everyone danced with everyone else. Kids danced with their parents and even their grandparents. Believe it or not, the parents and grandparents had as much fun as their kids.

A small band—guitar, bass, and accordion—provided spirited music and the people themselves provided the needed energy and happiness to set the whole room ablaze with the glow from their hearts. Even I was dancing up a storm with partners of all ages: *mor*, *bestemor* (my grandmother), office-workers I had never met, and kids of varying ages. The spirit was captivating; it completely engulfed me.

The *Brødrene* Thyholdt *julefest* was just one manifestation of *jul* during the *juletida*, the Christmas season; the *russ* had their own way of adding their contribution to the celebrations. On the Saturday morning of the *Brødrene* Thyholdt *julefest*, Jorunn had mentioned that the *russ* would be meeting at 4:00 on Sunday at the *gymnas*.

"What for?" I had asked her.

"We *russ* have a special part to play in *juletida*."

"What are we going to do?" I asked, knowing I probably wouldn't get an answer until Sunday. Both Jorunn and I liked giving, and getting surprises.

"Why are you always in such a hurry to know everything in advance," Jorunn smiled. "Pretend you're not an American."

"Do I have to bring anything?"

"*Nei*," her smile still in evidence. "We'll take care of that."

When I got home after the newsreels, I shared with *mor* my conversation with Jorunn.

"Do you know anything about this?" I asked *mor*.

"*Russetog,*" was all she said.

Russ train? That was, at least, the literal translation of "*russetog.*" I was getting pretty fluent in *norsk*, but I had never heard that expression. Since the trains in Norway didn't extend farther north than Fauske (except for the Swedish iron-ore train to Narvik), I assumed the expression didn't relate to the railroads, but I didn't have a clue.

By the time I trudged up the hill to the school at 4:00 o'clock, all sixty *russ* were there. I hadn't ever seen the entire group of *russ* together at one time before. The entire group was gathered in the art room. Everyone was spreading make-up over their faces, both the boys and the girls. A few were putting on masks, but most were using lipstick, charcoal, cotton and crayons to make their faces into festive and colorful configurations.

"What's going on?" I asked Gunnar Brox, as I watched him coloring his face with red and black lines and circles.

"We're preparing for the *russetog,*" he laughed.

I was standing in the art room with fifty-nine other *russ*, all of whom were painting their faces or putting on masks. And costumes, of sorts. It wasn't Halloween, and there weren't any formal, store-bought costumes, but the floor was strewn with burlap sacks, dirty cloth and rags, an occasional robe, and red sweaters. Some of the *russ* were already wearing rag-tag costumes brought from home; I could see the pins that held them together. The girls with long hair had already let it down and added sticks and twigs to liven it up. Others had made long, blond pony-tails made of rope, and still others had made elaborate head-dresses out of straw, also decorated with twigs. Bengt Mikkelsen stole the show: he had created his own head-dress out of reindeer antlers. He was the biggest boy among the *russ* anyway; the antlers just extended his reach, so to speak.

"What do I wear?" I asked Lillian.

"Your *russelua* is fine for a start," she said, pointing to the *russ* hat I always wore. Earlier in the winter, the *russ* girls had decided that all the *russ* boys needed *russ* hats, and they proceeded to knit them for us. By November, each of us boys was sporting a knit red hat with our name and our class on it; I got my nickname—Pipe—on mine. I was wearing it that day.

"Then just add some straw and sticks," Randi suggested. "You'll look great."

We were quite a sight by the time we were all finished: sixty teenagers with painted faces, cotton beards, pigtails and straw hair, rein-deer antlers, and burlap sacks. We walked outside into the *skolegård*. I still hadn't figured out what the "train" was or what we were doing.

"Photograph," shouted Gunnar Graf, barely audible above the din of voices from the sixty *russ*. Gunnar always had his camera handy, hence his nickname: Foto.

Years later, I came across that color photograph (from Foto Graf) and found it truly remarkable. Everyone had some sort of red hat: a *russelua*, a pointed knit hat, a stocking cap, some with tassels. And everyone was wearing red of some sort: dresses, blouses, shirts, vests, shawls. Half of the kids were wearing burlap sacks. Ragnhild Johansen was dressed up as a mouse: black pants, black blouse, black cap, black mask over her eyes, and beautifully hand-drawn black whiskers. Half of the boys had beards: some drawn with charcoal, some made up of glued-together pieces of cotton, and a few constructed out of woven white cord or string that dropped to their waists. Bengt was the centerpiece, towering above everyone else with his red shirt, black vest, painted black beard, burlap sack hat, crowned with the antlers.

The costumes were remarkable enough, but the background—pure black—made the photograph. It was 4:30 in the afternoon and these cos-tumed figures were silhouetted against a completely black background. That was what turned a remarkable composition into a stunning photograph.

A number of *russ* had left the group while the rest of us were hav-ing our pictures taken. As we finished, they returned in three groups. The first group, ten in all, carried a throne-like contraption on their shoulders. In the midst of all the red-colored outfits, makeup, and beards, I hadn't noticed that Per Sparboe had dressed up like Santa Claus: completely red outfit, white beard, and huge belly (which, in his case, he had to fabricate). He was handed a burlap sack stuffed full of old clothes, threw it over his shoulder, and was hoisted up onto the platform by some of the other *russ*. Father Christmas!

The second group led a horse into the *skolegård*. A horse! In the midst of the excitement, I hadn't noticed that one of the *russ*—Bitten Brigtsen—hadn't dressed in red. Instead she was dressed all in white: a long, flowing white (sheet) gown covering her entire body from the neck down. A golden (paper) crown was placed on her ever-so-blond hair and she, too, was hoisted up by some of her fellow *russ*, this time onto the horse.

"I understand Per," I said to Gunnar Brox, as he smeared his beard and tilted his *russelua*, "he's Father Christmas. But who is Bitten supposed to be?"

"*Jomfru*," answered Gunnar instantly. The Christmas Virgin. The Norwegian culture may have had such a character within it, but Bitten was an amusing choice. She *looked* the part better than anyone else in our class, but based upon her passionate relationship with Knut Aune, I doubted she *fit* the part.

The third group returned pulling a small wagon in whose center stood a huge, black iron pot. I was mystified.

"In a way," Gunnar explained, "Bitten is the Queen and Per is the King..."

"...and you, Pipe, are the Prince," Jorunn laughed.

I hopped into the wagon with few complaints.

"Let's go," Per shouted from his regal position. And go we did. With Bitten and her majestic horse in the lead, we headed down the hill from the *gymnas* toward the *sentrum*. We walked along a street parallel to Storgate until we got to its northern end, and then marched the entire length of Storgate.

"This is the *juletog*," Jorunn shouted to me, as she had to for me to hear her over the noise, both from the *juletog* itself and the throngs of people on the sidewalks watching us. I had taken the expression "Christmas train" too literally. In this instance, "*tog*" hadn't meant train; it meant parade.

And what a parade it was, all sixty of us marching down Storgate with our Christmas Virgin and Father Christmas, our Queen and our King. And what of the Prince? I was pulled along, perhaps a little less luxuriously, pretending to eat porridge out of the cast-iron pot with a royally oversized spoon.

We were not unexpected. There were hundreds of people lined three or four deep on both sides of the street to watch the parade and cheer us on. Especially children. And, of course, there was no need for police to block off the streets from traffic.

We arrived at the *torvet*, a kind of town square, decorated by a huge, well-lit Christmas tree that must have been almost ten meters tall. All of us, *russ* and children alike, made a series of concentric circles around the Christmas tree, each dancing in the opposite way: the inner circle to the left, the next-most outer circle to the right, the next circle to the left and so on for the seven or eight circles it took to accommodate all of us. There were so many people we barely fit inside the *torvet*. We sang and danced around the Christmas tree to the tune of a small band: one guitar, two trombones, and the ever-present accordion. Then we marched to the Grand Hotel and back up to the *gymnas*. I could not remember having had more fun!

"Did I tell you," Jorunn asked me as we changed into our "real" clothes in the art room, "that we're meeting back here at 11:00 PM tonight?"

"Another surprise?" I asked.

"Another part of the *russ* contribution to *jul*," she said simply.

I returned to the school a few minutes early that night. By 11:00 o'clock, about fifteen *russ* had assembled. We cut red letters out of the old red dresses and rags we had worn in the *juletog* earlier that day. Once they were cut out, we sewed them onto a sheet eight meters long and almost a meter high.

GOD JUL FRA RUSSEN-62

We worked steadily from 11:00 to almost 1:00 AM in the morning. When the "middle of the night" is the entire month of December, 1:00 in the morning doesn't feel so late. Jorunn and Lillian were the only two girls so we boys did most of the sewing...and a damn good job we did, taking everything into consideration.

From about 1:00-3:00 AM we hung up our sign. We walked down the hill into the *sentrum* and up and down Storgate until we found just the right place for it. Gunnar climbed up a light pole on one side of the street and Per a light pole on the other. They pulled the banner tight and tied it securely. It looked pretty wild rustling in the slight breeze, proclaiming our best wishes to the entire town...which still had to wait a few hours to appreciate it.

Juletida in Tromsø was both uncommercial and festive. Even in school. We had school during the entire week preceding *jul*, including a half day on Saturday, December 23rd. But it was school with a difference. Throughout the week, every class had its own *julefest*. In 5GE we pushed all the desks to the sides of the room, opening a large space up in the center of the room. We filled that space with a Christmas tree that Knut had brought in that morning.

We decorated the tree simply, with electric lights and small Norwegian flags. The Norwegians were quite patriotic, but in a way that never bothered me. I had always felt uncomfortable with American patriotism; it had always felt parochial, insular, and obnoxious. I would never have put an American flag on anything I owned; I wouldn't even salute it. But there was something different about the Norwegian flag. It flew over virtually every *hytta*; many people had a flagpole at their house; people decorated some kinds of cakes with little paper flags; it was natural to hang those same small flags on the Christmas tree. Perhaps it was that Norwegians could be patriotic without being arrogant; they never flaunted their nationalism. Perhaps it was that I had become more Norwegian. We covered the overhead lights in the room with colored paper. There was music: Johnny on the guitar and Arnulf on the accordion. And we danced. For the most part, we danced around the Christmas tree, holding hands in a large circle and singing Christmas songs. We had some cakes and Solo, too, but it was the dancing—always the dancing—around the Christmas tree that most typified the *julefest*. First in the *torvet* during the *juletog*; now at the *julefest* at school.

First the *juletog*: the Christmas parade. Then the *julefest*: the Christmas party. And then the *julebord*: the Christmas table, or Christmas *middag*. It happened the Wednesday evening before Christmas.

"Pete," Tom said excitedly as I returned from my Storgate walk after school. "It's *julebord*."

Christmas table. Even if the expression was not meant to be taken literally, that didn't mean I knew what it meant. My confusion must have shown.

"We're not eating *middag* at home today," Tom explained. "We're going to have *julebord på* Grand."

"*På* Grand?" I asked, making it sound as if I knew more than I did. I understood that whatever we did we did it at the Grand Hotel. And I knew that whatever we did, it took the place of eating *middag* at home, so I figured that we were having *middag* at the Grand Hotel. And my powers of deduction told me that it was a Christmas *middag*, or at least it was being served at a Christmas table.

"*Ja. Julebord på* Grand," he repeated. He demonstrated the same linguistic bias I had noticed in Americans: the way to get someone to understand something you said that they didn't understand was to repeat what they didn't understand...again. At least he didn't raise his voice and repeat, assuming that volume (along with repetition) overcame ignorance.

"So," I ventured, throwing caution to the wind, "we're having *middag* at the Grand." How far off could I be? It was December; I was an almost Norwegian.

"*Nei*," Tom said, with stubborn teenage emphasis. "*Julebord. Smørgåsbord*."

I was in big trouble. I thought I had it—and maybe I did—but that new expression threw me, at least momentarily. Butter-something-table I translated mentally. The hell with it, I thought.

"Great!" I said, smiling. It was food; it was going out; Tom was excited; it was bound to be something I would enjoy; I would figure it all out when we got there.

We drove to the Grand, a real treat for me; driving signified a special occasion. Paal was already home for the holidays so there were six of us: *mor*, *far*, Olemann, Paal, Tom and me. We walked into the smallish dining room and we were immediately confronted with a huge table taking up 20-25% of the entire room. And was it ever laden with food!

I had never seen anything like it, in Tromsø or in America. I had heard the word "smorgasbord" in America, but buffets were not especially common and I had never eaten at one.

First, there was the meat: the chicken and roast beef, a huge ham, roast pork, and pork chops. Then there was the *fisk*: salmon, halibut, herring, and shrimp (no cod, thank God). And the cheeses: *geitost*, *nøkkleost*, *jarlsbergost*, *gaude*, and *primula*. And the vegetables: *poteter*, *carrot* and raisin salad, *surkål* (the *norsk* equivalent of sauerkraut), cauliflower, and beets. And the deserts: 8-10 different kinds of cakes, all decorated with small paper Norwegian flags. And even fruit: oranges, apples, bananas, pineapples, and grapefruit. It was heaven to all of us.

We ate for about two hours: four times up for meat, *fisk*, vegetables, and pickles; five times up for cake, fruit salad, nuts, cheese, and crackers. And that included everyone: *mor*, too, not just "us boys."

"Do you know what we say about a *julebord*?" *far* asked, when he had a moment free for talking.

"*Nei*," I said, between chews.

"You can eat yourself full at a Norwegian *julebord*."

No kidding, I thought. I didn't eat again until *middag* the following day, and only then to be polite.

First there was the *julefest*. Then there was the *juletog*. Followed by the *julebord*. And, finally, *juleaften*.

Christmas in Norway wasn't celebrated on December 25th; it was celebrated on *juleaften*, or Christmas Eve. When I awoke that morning, I experienced the Norwegian version of a Christmas stocking. It wasn't the familiar elaborate, red stocking, with my name lovingly embroidered into it; it was a knee-sock, just a plain old knee-sock. I found the knee-sock wrapped around the standing lamp near my bed. It wasn't stuffed with enough presents to constitute *jul* in and of itself; it contained a banana and a marzipan pig as big as the banana! It turned out the differences between Norwegian and American stocking traditions were even greater than I experienced, since most Norwegian families didn't include stockings at all in their *jul*.

"Did the *julenissen* leave you something?" *mor* asked as I wandered upstairs already nibbling on the marzipan pig.

"My favorite," I managed between bites. "Is the *julenissen* like our Santa Claus?"

"Not really," *far* smiled. "They're more like elves."

"Santa Claus isn't really part of *jul* for us," *mor* added.

"In America, Santa Claus is the most important part of *jul*, at least for young children," I explained.

"Do children really believe in Santa Claus?" Tom asked.

"Definitely," I answered. "I would say most American children believe in Santa Claus until they are at least six or seven years old...sometimes older." I said this with a certain degree of pride, and a great deal of personal experience.

"How stupid can kids be?" was Tom's only remark.

"But what about *julenissen?*" I asked.

"That's different," Tom answered without hesitation. "They're elves."

Although *juleaften* translated into "Christmas Eve," the more literal translation was Christmas evening. And the Norwegians took that more literal definition seriously, meaning they didn't open Christmas presents until *juleaften aften*. So all of us (except *mor*) spent from 11:00 AM to 5:00 PM (when we had *middag*) killing time. That was not easy in Tromsø in 1961. There was no TV, let alone videos. And we had no gifts to occupy us; we hadn't opened them yet. We listened to the radio and played cards. We went outside and threw snowballs. I walked *til byen* and up and down Storgate; no one else was there but I was used to doing it. We decorated the tree, but the decorations were much sparser than what I was used to in Westport—basically lights and paper Norwegian flags—and decorating the tree was clearly not the central focus of *jul*.

Finally, 5 o'clock and *middag* arrived. *Mor* had prepared a "Sunday" or "treat" *middag*: pork roast and drippings, boiled *poteter*, and *surkål* (my favorite vegetable). Paal, Olemann, and I served ourselves three times to the pork!! It was that good. And, being *jul*, we had dessert...for only the second time since moving in with the Thyholdts over a month before. Like the first dessert, it was based on fruit: canned peaches with fresh bananas. The men (and especially the big eaters) tried to give their stomachs some digesting time while the women (*mor* and *bestemor*) did the dishes. I never felt completely comfortable with that division of labor, but I never rebelled against it, either.

Then came the time that (almost) everyone had been waiting for: gift opening. But first we all sang and danced around the Christmas tree (with all of its presents still under it). There was something special about singing songs and dancing around the tree. We did it at the *Brødrene* Thyholdt *julefest* and at all the *julefester* at school. We interrupted the *juletog* to dance around the tree in the *torvet*, all 200-300 of us *russ* and on-lookers. And we did it again at home, just the family.

The opening of presents followed a similar procedure to what we employed in Westport: one at a time. I had always preferred that approach, with its emphasis on everyone caring about everyone else and what everyone else received. The main difference was the frequency of the expressions "*skynd deg*" (hurry up) and "*neste, neste, neste*" (next, next, next). There were eight of us and the process still took three full hours. I, in particular, really cleaned up. I got presents from all of the Thyholdts there, all of the Norbyes, and three or four aunts and uncles in the Thyholdt family. *Mor* and *far* gave me a beautiful watch, the kind of gift a son might expect from his parents. The most popular gifts: cigars and pre-rolled cigarettes (most people ordinarily bought tobacco and wrappers and rolled their own), puzzles, silverware, candy, clothes, toys, and books. Candy was the "when one has nothing else to give" gift; in America, it was money...a completely non-existent gift at the Thyholdt's *jul*.

desember, *1961*

Kjære Venn,

Literally translated that last phrase would mean "good jule," but most Americans would probably be accustomed to it in the form of MERRY CHRISTMAS. That time of year that is set aside to commemorate the birth of Christ, eating oneself to an almost uncomfortable plumpness and, now, watching a "goodole American football game" is now here...both in America and Norway, although without the football here in Norway

But this lack of football is just one of the many differences between an American Christmas and a Norwegian jul. *When one thinks of Christmas, one thinks of December 25th. Although the converse of this statement is also equally true in America, such is not the case in Norway: December 25th is the first* juledag, *or Christmas day. But this is just a start, for all in all there are thirteen such* juledager. *So, instead of hearing the phrase, "December 28," for instance, one hears "the fourth* juledag *instead. It is not until the thirteenth* juledag *that Christmas is officially over, as the heart-breaking process of "burn the Christmas tree" begins.*

The gifts are opened on juleaften, *Christmas evening: December 24. The big Christmas Dinner "with all the fixins" is pretty big, but there is no traditional menu. And even though most Norwegian families have some sort of meat for this festive occasion, many a table will be decked with what such a great number of Americans dread: fish.*

Stores set up their Christmas displays and the town's main street storgate *(the big street) receives its wreath of colored lights and its brand new, but only temporary, name of* julegate. *But the one dark spot in the Norwegian Christmas is that although most people realize there is such a thing as Santa Claus, very few people really believe in him.*

My days are busy and full. I often study for school, read the International Herald Tribune or a magazine, or take out my last year's American History book to help me when I give one of my many talks on that subject. And as my norsk *gets progressively better and better, I will slowly be able to understand the Norwegian newspapers and follow the news in them. I have had many chances to get and listen to Radio Moscow. It is very interesting to hear the Russian version of their Communist Party Congress. Of course, there is hardly ever a chance where I can agree with what they say, but it has been interesting never-the-less.*

But it is a gay time, not one for serious "thought and meditation." The snow has begun to fall, the temperature also. If ever you, or I for that matter, think it is cold, it was -40°F inland from Tromsø last night. But it is beautiful here, even the weather, and I can only hope your Christmas will be as white and happy as mine. Is it not at times like this that one realizes how right the Greeks were: everyone is basically the same, and the quest for life is to find how people differ from one another. An atmosphere of love, warmth, and happiness is beginning to engulf Tromsø and, as it begins to make its way to America, I send with it my best wishes and sincere love.

Hilsen
Pete

-23-
Taking Stock

I had established a daily pattern in my life as a teenage Norwegian. School took up most of each day, starting at about 8:00 in the morning and ending around 2:30 in the afternoon. My school schedule was unique among *russ*, since I had dropped so many of my ordinary classes: Biology, because I had taken it at Staples; *nynorsk*, because one Norwegian languages was more than enough, thank you; English, because that was the one language I needed to forget. Even so, I always came in at the beginning of the school day, which gave me the opportunity to visit other classrooms when I didn't have anything with my own class.

Most afternoons, I walked into town, as did most of my friends. It was a two- or three-minute walk, and all downhill. The center of town—*sentrum*—ran along the water's edge facing the mainland. From the *sentrum*, the island rose up noticeably, all the way to where the Norbyes lived on top of the island, 100-150 meters above sea level. The school was situated just a bit above the *sentrum*, overlooking it and the water between Tromsøy and the mainland.

I often walked *til byen* with Lillian. And we always held hands when we walked Storgate. Holding hands was a symbol of a certain kind of relationship. In America, holding hands was a symbol of two kids "going steady." Holding hands in Tromsø also indicated that the pair was an item, but being an item did not imply quite the same degree of possessiveness that going steady implied in America. We could still talk to other kids, we could still dance with other kids, we could even "go out" with other kids (although Lillian never did). But holding hands was significant; it meant a special relationship. Besides, holding hands was something I genuinely liked. I liked what it said about my feelings for Lillian—ambivalent as they were—and I liked the feeling of holding hands. I liked the connection it forged between us.

"What will you do before *middag*?" Lillian asked as we walked north on Storgate.

"I'll probably go to the USIS office," I said.

"*Hei*, Pete," Arnulf and Randi both said as Lillian and I passed them.

"*Hei, dokker,*" I said in return.

"Have you gotten any mail recently?" Lillian asked, as we both kept walking.

"Not this week. I'll probably stop by the post office, too."

"How many letters do you get?" Lillian asked.

"I get a few every week: always from my parents, sometimes from my friends."

"Do you still write your journal?" Lillian had always found it a bit odd that a boy wrote a journal and, even more odd, that I sent it home to my parents.

"I still write it, but not as often as I used to. I'm enjoying myself more and writing about it less."

"And thinking about it less, too?"

"Not yet," I laughed.

"I'm impressed that you can laugh at yourself," Lillian remarked.

"*Æ e' ikkje så dum som æ se' ut,*" I said proudly. I'm not as stupid as I look.

"I'm going to walk home," Lillian said, dropping my hand as we reached the *kino.* "I'll see you tomorrow."

"*Ha det,*" I said simply. Holding hands in Storgate was acceptable; kissing good-bye wasn't.

Up and down the street I wandered, along with half of the school and much of the town seeing mostly the same people and always the same stores. Wito—the corner store—was literally on the corner of the hill coming down from the *gymnas* where we bought magazines and candy. Knut Følstad's parents' photography store where I purchased my film and sent it off for developing in Oslo. Peder Norbye on a side street, where *far* Norbye, Per, and Helen worked. Figenschau, with its polar bear, waiting for the tourists. There was hardly a trip up or down that didn't involve stopping and talking to someone. There was never anything special to talk about, but that never prevented us from talking.

For me, that kind of social activity was a growth step. It had always been difficult for me to make what I considered small talk; in Tromsø I had to do it five or ten times an afternoon and again most evenings. All the anxieties I had felt in Westport, all the insecurities that plagued my entire teenage years in America, were absent in Norway. I had to learn to act differently in Tromsø, but at least everyone there made it easy for me to be different.

I continued walking Storgate on my way home, stopping at Pedersen's *bakeri*, Pedersen's bakery. It was often my last stop before leaving the *sentrum*.

"*Værsågod*," one of the women behind the counter smiled at me. "*Skillingskaker eller halvmåner?*"

"2 *halvmåner, takk*," I answered. I was particularly fond of those "half-moons," crescent-shaped pastry with an apple filling. I was also particularly impressed that the woman behind the counter knew my taste, because I didn't recognize her.

I never talked to *mor* about my snack habits; I had always been embarrassed to tell my Mom about my snacks, too. But one day, I didn't eat as much *middag* as usual, and *mor* obviously noticed the change.

"Did you have too many *skillingskaker* from Pedersen's after school?" *mor* asked with her usual knowing smile.

"*Kem, æ?*" I answered, in my best, or at least most exaggerated, *Tromsøværing*. Who me?

"Oh, Pete," *mor* lamented, "Don't use such ugly language."

"*Kem, æ*" was pure, unadulterated *Tromsøværing*. It substituted for the more pleasing "*Hvem, jeg?*" a harsh and, to many Norwegian ears (especially those of parents), grating expression. I used the expression to show off my *Tromsøværing* and to annoy *mor*, especially when she had caught me.

How did she know about Pedersen's? How did she know I loved *skillingskaker*? Why did I even bother pretending I could keep a secret from her?

Middag was the big meal of the day and we ate anywhere from around 3:30 (at the Románs) to 4:30 (at the Norbyes) or even 5:00 (at the Thyholdts). In America the usual fare was "meat and potatoes;" in Tromsø it was *fisk og poteter*, fish and potatoes. Four or five times a week, we ate *fisk og poteter*. There were two choices for the *poteter*: (1) boiled in the skin and the skin peeled after boiling or (2) peeled first and then boiled. On Sundays, we got melted butter for our *poteter*. The *fisk*, too, was almost always boiled (the exception: once a week we got leftovers, which were pan fried in butter). My French aunt once described to me her view of Norwegian cooking. "I have never seen so little done with so much." And she was right. The raw ingredients were fabulous. I had never particularly liked fish before I came to Tromsø and I could never have imagined liking anything that was just boiled. But the *fisk* was so fresh and tasty that I loved eating it. Once a week we had *pølser* (hot dogs) or meat cakes (hamburgers), on Saturday we had fried egg and bacon (piled on a piece of bread and eaten with a knife and fork), and on Sunday we had pork chops or roast pork. But otherwise: *fisk og poteter.*

After *middag* Olemann usually went back to work at the office, Tom did homework, *Mor* stretched out on the living room sofa and closed her eyes, and *Far* and I slept. We *sove middag*: slept dinner (literally) or had our after-dinner nap. We both (and thousands of other Norwegians) went to bed and slept. To *sove middag* was an all-year phenomenon. It was a bit difficult in the summer, because it was broad daylight (that was true at "night," as well). I accommodated by developing my own version of a sleep mask. The technique I developed required that I sleep on my back. I covered my eyes with my left arm. I then placed my right arm under my neck and grabbed my neck with my right hand. Finally, I grabbed my right arm with my left hand. Voilà: I was locked in and the light was locked out. So effective was that technique I used it throughout the year and have used it throughout my life. I still sleep on my back and lock my arms around my face.

Juletida broke that routine. *Jul* was the most festive stretch of time I had in Norway: *julefest, juletog, juleaften,* and more *julefest.* Although the *førstejuledag*—December 25th, the first day of Christmas—was technically the beginning of *jul,* it marked the end of the festivities and the beginning of a more quiet and reflective time…at least for me. The week between *jul* and New Year's was a time to reflect upon my time in Tromsø and take stock, in a way, of everything that had happened to me and everything I had become.

More than anything else, *juletida* was a time for visits, the first of which was to the Románs. That was not a visit I relished; I had not seen much of the Román family since I left, except Karl Arvid, whom I saw at the *gymnas* almost every day. Karl Arvid was the "master of ceremonies" for the *Bragerevy,* the school revue that took place each year in the Christmas vacation. We got along much better after I moved out of the house. He was a truly funny guy.

I felt some responsibility to return to Karl Pettersensgate, at least one more time. Maybe I needed to make sure I had done the right thing in leaving. Maybe I wanted to see if the hatchet had been buried (on both sides). Maybe I just wanted to be polite and sensitive (two new traits of mine).

I had asked my parents to send me a variety of "family" gifts: Parker pens for the teenagers and adults and Snickers candy bars for the kids. I stuffed everything into a "stocking" (a knee-sock I borrowed from *mor*), put on my boots, and walked past the *gymnas* to Karl Pettersensgate. The house looked different. I could still remember the wide-eyed view I had the first day I set eyes on it. Coming back after so many months and so many families and so many visits to friends and their families, Karl Pettersensgate 37 had shrunk in stature as a regular Tromsø house.

"*God dag*, Pete," *fru* Román hugged me as she opened the door. "*God jul og velkommen.*" Who was this woman? She appeared genuinely pleased to see me.

"*God jul*," I said as I took off my boots in the hallway.

"You don't have to take off your boots," *fru* Román said. All Norwegians took off their boots, shoes, even sandals when they entered a house. When I visited a stranger's house, I was treated as a guest. I was always told, "You don't have to take off your shoes." I always took them off; after all, I was becoming a teenage Norwegian. *Fru* Román may have been genuinely pleased to see me, but I was a guest.

"Oh, Pete," Bergljot squealed as she saw me. She raced toward me and threw her hands around my neck as I knelt down to greet her.

"*God jul*," Román said to me as he shook my hand when I stood back up, Bergljot still hanging onto my neck. He may have remained cool to me, but he was talking and that was a significant improvement over my visit the previous September.

"*God jul*," I said, too. "I have some presents for you."

"Can I open them?" Bergljot said excitedly.

"Of course," *fru* Román said to her.

Bergljot loved the candy and everyone else enjoyed getting the pens. We had a little to eat after opening the presents; eating on visits was one of the main reasons for the visit, and eating at *jul* (even on the second day of Christmas) even more so. We played Bingo for a while and I took some pictures.

On the third day of Christmas I made a similar family visit to the Norbyes. Visiting the Norbyes was even more fun than I had anticipated. I felt a part of their family, and they obviously continued to feel that I was a part of it, too. I was a member of the Thyholdt family—in their eyes and in mine—but I still called Norbye and *fru* Norbye *far* and *mor*. And I still felt that Torild and Helen were my "big" (Helen because she was older, Torild because she was taller) sisters.

"*Du*, Pete," *mor* asked, after I polished off my third piece of cake "aren't you going to have another piece of *sjokoladekake*?"

"Pete," *far* asked, "haven't you learned to ski yet?"

"Pete," Helen asked, "how are you getting along with your *småpiker*?"

"Pete," Torild asked, "how are you getting along with Lillian?"

"Pete," *mor* asked, "where did you go for your *julebord*?"

"Pete," *far* asked, "how is your dancing coming along?"

"Pete," Helen asked, "who are you inviting to the Student Ball?"

"Pete," Torild said, starting to tickle me, "I'll kill you if you don't invite Lillian."

My last *jul* visit was to Adele Berg who was home for the holidays. Even though I didn't "report" to her now (I did that to Liz), Adele still felt a degree of responsibility for me.

"I've decided," I mentioned, "that I want to begin reading my Staples textbooks."

"What do you mean," Adele asked.

"I'm missing my senior year and I think I had better read the textbooks from those classes. And I'm planning to write compositions and send them to Mr. Arciola, my English teacher from last year. He helped me with my writing, especially my grammar."

"I don't think that's a very wise idea," she said. "Do you remember when I told you last summer to stop reading those textbooks?"

"It's difficult to forget when you give me advice, Adele."

"It's as important now," she continued, "as it was then to forget about your school in America."

"But I need to get ready for college," I explained.

"Even if you took only a couple of hours a week, it would hurt you more than it would help you. Read more *norsk*, if you want to read; don't worry about English. It would be much better for you to try and make up the 'lost' ground at college than here in Norway."

I had never seen Adele as firm in her convictions and as tough on me. Even when she had talked to me about moving out from the Románs she had been more open, understanding, and sensitive. In that Christmas conversation, she was a tiger.

"If I could, Pete," she continued forcefully, "I would *forbid* you to do this work. The question is that serious, as far as I'm concerned."

My parents (especially my Dad) had urged me to begin preparation for college; Adele said it was mandatory that I didn't. My personal feelings were ambivalent. Who were the authorities? On the one side were my parents: I loved them, they generally knew what was best for me, and they were both smart. On the other side was Adele: she had been in America as an AFSer, she had worked as Secretary of the Norwegian AFS for 3 or 4 years, and she had seen people do too much.

As much as I valued the judgment of my parents, I decided to stick with experience. Adele knew a lot more about the subject, both in general and particularly as it related to me, and I valued her advice; her first advice had proven to be priceless. Therefore, I said to hell with Oberlin and I decided to put everything I had into Norway, Norway, Norway (and Tromsø, too)!!!

There were other memorable events during *juletida*. The first was the Student Ball. It was not simply another *fest*; it was a real ball. It resembled more what we would have called a "prom" in America. I had never gone to any in the U.S. I thought they were "beneath" me; besides no one ever invited me, and I always feared no one would accept an invitation from me. But I was becoming a teenage Norwegian, and everything was different.

I invited a girl from Torild's third year English class: Solveig Nilsen. Solveig was one of the six AFS finalists I had interviewed as part

4. juledag kl. 20,00

Studentballet —61

Nr. 039   RUSSEN—62

of my responsibility as an AFSer. She was the first choice of the committee, so there was a good chance she would end up in America the year I returned. Why Solveig Nilsen and not Lillian? I had a good excuse: I didn't *have* to invite Lillian.

Although she didn't go out with anyone else, she told me it was all right for me to go out with other girls. "You must taste a little bit of everything," she had said, "to know what you like the most." But the reason I didn't invite Lillian was that I remained completely committed to my excruciating ambivalence toward her and toward my feelings about and for her. For someone as keen as I was to have a girlfriend, I did everything in my power to avoid having one.

Solveig and I went to a small *fest* at Adele's first and then to the ball. It was a "ball," not a "*fest*," so it was *hyggelig* (pleasant) not *artig* (fun). As expected, there was a band and a lot of dancing.

"You dance pretty well," Solveig mentioned at one point.

"I didn't dance much in America," I said. I didn't feel especially competent as a dancer in Norway, compared to kids (and adults, and even small children) who did it much more regularly.

"But they have all these neat rock 'n' roll dances in America," Solveig said, excited at the prospect of going to America.

"I know, but I wasn't as popular in America as I am here," I said, "and I didn't go to many dances. I'm not very good at the fast dances."

"But you manage quite well with this kind of dancing, the kind we do in Norway."

"I went to dancing school when I was in fifth grade." It was true, but it had been years since I had ever thought of that experience. All those little kids in a barn near the Post Road in Westport. All the boys wearing sports coats and ties; all the girls wearing frilly dresses and white gloves. Learning how to ask a girl to dance and knowing that the girl couldn't say "no." Learning the steps and learning how to lead, but at such an awkward age I was surprised that the memory of it remained with me.

"Do you know," Solveig asked, "that we have *danseskolen*—dancing school—in Tromsø, too? But our *danseskolen* is for teenagers. It's held every January."

"No one mentioned anything about it to me."

"It doesn't cost much," Solveig continued, "and lots of the kids from the *gymnas* go. I think you'll find it fun."

"And I certainly could use some improvement, given how often I have to dance here," I said genuinely.

The second social event of the "season" was New Year's Eve: *nyttårsaften*. (*Norsk* combines what in English are often multiple words into a single one—*nytt*/new, *års*/year's, *aften*/evening—and generally dispense with capitol letters.) *Nyttårsaften* was the culmination of *juletida* in Norway, just as it was in America.

My date was Lillian. We met at about 8:00 that evening on Storgate. Neither of us had any plans, but we knew if we walked back and forth long enough, plans would emerge. It didn't take long: Gunnar was having a *fest* at his house. We were invited and walked over to his house with him. Walking Storgate was not only a way to pick up dates, it was a way to pick up parties. Even parties were rarely planned in advance; generally they emerged spontaneously, the way dates did, as people walked Storgate and looked for something to do.

When we got there, we found ourselves in the midst of a *fest* of about twelve, mostly *russ*, but also including Gunnar's younger *søster*, Anna. Per, Odd, and Franck from Gunnar's class were there, along with Jorunn, Arnulf, Randi, Erika, and Knut from our class. I had visited Gunnar's house often and knew both Anna and his parents quite well; *fru* Brox had cooked, but otherwise she and Brox stayed out of the way.

We sat and talked for a couple of hours. It was one of those situations where my friends ganged up on me in a way only friends could. It was similar to a time at college when four of my best friends literally encircled me in a corner of the dining room and proceeded to let me have it for two hours, telling me how obnoxious I had become and how poorly I was treating everyone, including my friends. They had answers for every excuse I tried out on them; they had planned well, anticipating my every move. That conversation at Gunnar's *fest* was a little less well-planned, but it reflected a similar caring.

"So, Pete," Gunnar said, "what were you and Lillian planning to do this *nyttårsaften*?"

"I figured if we walked Storgate long enough something would turn up."

"Is there any place," Jorunn asked, "the two of you *don't* hold hands?"

"I have never seen any signs forbidding it. Did I miss them?"

"How come you never do anything special with Lillian?" Erika asked.

"Being with Pete is special for me," Lillian said.

"Being with my *russ* friends is special for me."

I Was a Teenage Norwegian

"How can Lillian know you really care about her," Randi asked, "if you don't invite her out, like to the Student Ball?"

"I don't mind," Lillian said.

"It was just a dance. It wasn't even a *fest.*"

"When are you going to invite her to the Thyholdt's?" Gunnar asked.

"When are you going to meet her parents?" Arnulf asked.

"When are *dokker* going to let us make out?"

"That sounds nice," Lillian said.

We ate at about 10:30 or 11:00. It wasn't exactly a typical *aftens.* The table looked at bit like the *julebord* at Grand; that was how full it was. And twelve hungry teenagers could only manage to eat about half of what was on it. There were cookies, cake, *kaffe*, tea, and even a little home-made ice cream. That was the first time I had eaten ice cream since coming to Tromsø. It was a cold climate, but no one had a freezer.

At about 11:30 we all grabbed our coats, put on our boots and *russelua* and walked back to the *sentrum*. By then, the fireworks were just beginning. What was great was that the traditional fireworks were mixed with a *coastal* Norwegian version: many of the ships let loose their rescue signals at the same time. The result was spectacular. The sky was hot, lighted, and lively.

Just as intriguing was Storgate itself. Tromsø had a population of between 10,000-12,000 people; Tromsdalen added, perhaps, another 3,000. By the time we got to Storgate my friends (who had been through this many times before) estimated that there were somewhere between 3,000-4,000 people out that *nyttårsaften*. And it was a typical New Year's Eve crowd: shouting, yelling, congratulating (there was a lot more congratulating than I was used to, for both *nyttårsaften* and *juletida* generally), kissing and hugging.

Some of us made it back to Gunnar's between 3:00 and 4:00 in the morning. *fru* Brox was still *våken* and put the water on for *varmepølser* (warm sausages), Norwegian hot dogs. That was the only time I had hot dogs for *frokost*. I finally made it home and to bed by 6:30, after having walked Lillian home.

"Did it bother you," Lillian asked as we walked, "what the other kids were saying at Gunnar's house?"

"I was a little uncomfortable," I said.

"Why?"

"I'm used to having serious conversations with my friends," I explained, "but I'm not used to talking with them about my...girlfriend."

"I guess I'm more used to their joking," Lillian said, "even when they're serious."

"You guys have known each other for so long."

"But they like you," Lillian insisted. "Do you understand that? That's the only reason they talk that way."

"I guess."

"And I like you to," she said as she kissed me good night.

New Year's Eve was for me, throughout my teenage years, a time for taking stock, more than a time for resolutions. Part of that stock-taking had to do with Lillian and my relationship with her. Although I was still spending time with other girls (Solveig for the Student Ball, for example), that was happening less and less frequently. In spite of all this, however, I didn't understand what was happening to me. And I continued in my need to hang on to an American girlfriend I obviously no longer had.

With the perspective of thirty years, there are, perhaps, some real questions as to whether or not I *ever* had Sue as a girlfriend. It certainly never struck me at the time that I needed an American girlfriend to insure that I wouldn't have a Norwegian one. But a Norwegian girlfriend was exactly what Lillian was becoming, whether I acknowledged it or not. We held hands all the time, I was on the verge of dating only her, and we were soon to enter our hot and heavy make-out phase. Taking stock, Lillian was certainly getting pretty close to being my Norwegian girlfriend.

My more formal stock-taking took place, as it so often did, in my letters.

den 1. januar, 1962

Dear Mom and Dad,

When I began writing this letter, a mood had just come over me. I figured it to be one of my "blue" moods, edged on by a slow, moody record on the radio. I was wrong: it is a mood of thanks, gratitude, and rich, pure happiness. It is quite a feeling to be entering the New Year with.

Probably for the first time in my life I've been really and truly thankful: thankful that I'm here in Norway, in Tromsø, hos Thyholdt, thankful for living, thankful for the good luck that has been following me ever since I was born (from the gifts of brains to the ability to use them), thankful for all the wonderful friends I have, thankful for the wonderful loving family I have, and, yes, even thankful for the WONDERFUL world I live in.

And I'm happy: happy for Tromsø and it's people who are able to, pretty much, forget the world and its problems, happy for the people here in Tromsø who are so purely happy themselves, happy for everyone, and just plain happy.

I only hope that all of you are as happy as I am. It would hurt me and break my bubble of happiness if you weren't. But then, the communications problem we have is good for something after all: by the time I've heard that you're unhappy, my bubble will have already gone. Did I ever tell you: It's fun to be happy. But I guess you've known that for quite a while now, n'est ce pas?

About 3 months ago, a last drop of pessimism came dribbling out of me. I said then that it would be impossible for me to meet new people and make new friends. During these past 3 months I have continually been seeing how wrong I was. Almost every week, it seems, I meet someone new and/or make a new friend.

I Was a Teenage Norwegian

I remember my thoughts of how impossible it would be to make new friends. I sort of call that moment "pessimism's last stand." But I have been learning a lot about people through this experience...making it worth-while as well as fun. I have also learned a lot about making friends and keeping them, though much of what I have "learned" is just a visual proof of what you have told me through my seventeen years in America. My great number of friendships also makes my job here easier because I don't have any problems in that area and my mind can concentrate on my important matters as I begin to act both more automatically and naturally. I'm having it pretty good, man, pretty good indeed!!!

Love,
Pete

-24-
Bragerevy

Although there was a *russefest* earlier in December, *juletida* literally called out for another one, and the *russ* were most susceptible to that kind of call. They "rented" a *kafé* on the outskirts of the *sentrum*, the Polarkafé on the north side of town. The Polarkafé was a little different from the other *kafés* we had used; it had a stage at one side where various local groups could hold theatricals or other events. But there was a kitchen and glass counters with food and *russ* selling *øl* to make money for their various *russ* activities.

"I think the time has come," I told Lillian after our first dance, "for us to add a little something different to our *russefester*."

"What do you mean," she said, with that knowing smile on her face. We had spent enough time together that she knew when I had some wild idea brewing.

"This is our fifth *russefest*, right?" I asked.

"*Ja*," she said cautiously, counting in her head. "The fifth."

"And what do we do at each *russefest*?"

"Dance. Drink. Discuss. Drop."

"That's what I mean. Same old stuff each time. The *russ* have their traditions to maintain, but we need something Different."

"Why do I get the feeling," Lillian said, "that you already have something in mind?"

"Drama. That's what I have in mind. I'll need your help." There were a lot of different skits on the SEVEN SEAS. I had seen one skit I thought Lillian and I might adapt to my emerging jokester personality and translate into my emerging *norsk*. I explained the broad outline of the skit to Lillian and what I needed her to do.

"*Dokker, dokker*," I shouted out at the end of one of the dances. "Listen up."

"Enough of this drinking and dancing, enough of discussions and dropping drunk. What we need is a little drama." I pulled one of the chairs from around the edge of the room into the corner near the kitchen and sat down on it.

I Was a Teenage Norwegian

"I would like to share with you," I began, "the story of the bee and the honey. Although you probably think that you see Pipe sitting before you, what you really see is a sad Queen bee in her bee hive. Why is she so sad, you might ask? She's out of honey."

As I talked, Lillian scouted up a couple of recruits for our little drama. She started with Gunnar; everyone expected the funniest from Gunnar. I could see her explaining to Gunnar what he had to do.

"So," I continued, certain that Lillian had readied everything and everyone, "I need to get one of my famous worker bees to take a trip out of the bee hive and gather some honey for his poor, starving queen." My *norsk* was barely up to the task. Lillian had taught me the new words that I needed: bee, bee hive, Queen bee, worker bee. My brother Tom loved honey, so that was one word I already knew.

"There is a Gunnar-bee. Gunnar-bee, get over here. I have a job for you." Gunnar stuck his hands under his arm-pits, flapped them slightly, made a buzzing sound, zig-zagged over to the chair, and stood obediently in front of me.

"Yes, my Queen," he said.

"Gunnar-bee, I need honey. Go out of the bee hive and get some. When you come back, touch my nose, I'll open my mouth and ask for the honey, and you can give it to me. Do you understand?"

"*Ja*, my Queen," Gunnar answered. He flapped his hands slightly, turned around two times, made a buzzing sound, zig-zagged around the room, through the attentive audience, and into the kitchen. Lillian provided him with what he needed and within fifteen seconds he was zigging and zagging back toward me. He stood obediently in front of my chair and touched my nose. I opened my mouth and said: "Give me my honey."

And he did. He spit a mouthful of water all over my face. He flapped his hands slightly, turned around two times, made a buzzing sound, and zig-zagged away. The audience exploded with laughter, I wiped my face with my hands, and I looked around the room.

"I never could trust Gunnar-bee," I said. "What I need is the most trust-worthy worker bee. That would be Jorunn-bee. Jorunn-bee!" I shouted as loud as I could. "Get over here. I have a job for you."

Jorunn stuck her hands under her arm-pits, flapped them slightly, made a buzzing sound, zig-zagged over to the chair, and stood obediently in front of me.

"Yes, my Queen," she said straight-faced.

"Jorunn-bee, I need honey. I had some problems with Gunnar-bee; he never was too reliable. You are the most trust-worthy bee in the bee hive. You are the President of the Bee Workers Union. Go out of the bee hive and get some honey for me. When you come back, touch my nose, I'll open my mouth and ask for the honey, and you can give it to me. Do you understand?"

"*Ja*, my Queen," Jorunn answered. She flapped her hands slightly, turned around two times, made a buzzing sound, zig-zagged around the room, through the attentive audience, and into the kitchen. Lillian provided her with what she needed and within fifteen seconds Jorunn was zigging and zagging back toward me. She stood obediently in front of my chair and touched my nose. I opened my mouth and said: "Give me my honey."

And she did. She spit a mouthful of water all over my face. She flapped her hands slightly, turned around two times, made a buzzing sound, and zig-zagged away. The audience exploded with laughter and I wiped my face with my hands.

"Okay, Okay," I said, looking as hurt and wounded as I could. "I think I get the idea. Now we'll see who is the smart one. Lillian-bee," I shouted. "Get over here and sit down in that chair."

Lillian had come out from the kitchen and was standing among the on-lookers. She walked over to the chair and sat down in it. She looked as serious as she could: mouth closed, no smile, eyes on me.

"Look, Lillian-bee. We need some honey, see? I'm going to go out of the bee hive and get some honey, understand?" Lillian nodded her head solemnly. "When I come back, I will touch your nose, you will open your mouth and ask for the honey, and I will give it to you." I gave a knowing, conspiratorial glance to the assembled crowd of *russ*. "Do you understand?"

Lillian nodded her head again. I stuck my hands under my arm-pits, flapped my hands slightly, turned around two times, made a buzzing sound, zig-zagged around the room, through the attentive audience, and into the kitchen. I gulped a mouthful of water and within fifteen seconds I was zigging and zagging back toward Lillian. She sat obediently on the chair in front of me, I touched her nose, and she spit her mouthful of water all over my face. The crowd roared. Slapstick—as I was finding out at the *Bragerevy* rehearsals—was the king of Norwegian comedy and Pipe was the king of kings...and Queen bees, too.

Bragerevy: The Brage Revue. Karl Arvid Román was the President of Brage and Karl Arvid had spent a little time explaining to me about the *Bragerevy*, but I hadn't really understood any of what he said. I didn't even know for sure that I was supposed to be in it. I went to Brage meetings and the *Bragefest*; I belonged to the Brage group. One of the important parts of my life in Tromsø was becoming a part of a number of different groups: *russ* specifically, the *gymnas* generally, Brage, the Norbye family, the Thyholdt family, and so forth.

Although we did have a couple of Brage meetings, and even a *Bragefest* in the fall, it wasn't until the meeting in November that the serious work on the *Bragerevy* began. We began in our November meeting to talk specifically about the *Bragerevy* and Odd Kjellman (Ragna's father) talked to us about the show, his script, and some of the skits. Karl Arvid was the master of ceremonies and Odd Kjellman was the director and the author.

I Was a Teenage Norwegian

"What would you like to do?" Karl Arvid asked me.

"Watch?" I suggested.

"*Nei*, really, what would you like to *do?*"

"It's a tradition," Franck Pettersen said, "Joanne was in last year's *Bragerevy*." Joanne was the AFS student in Tromsø the year before me.

"I'll do whatever you want me to do," I said, sounding as enthusiastic as I could.

"Can you sing? Can you dance? Do you play an instrument?" Karl Arvid asked.

"Pipe's really funny," Franck said. "He created this funny skit at our last *russefest*: The Bee and the Honey. It was really funny."

"I guess I can sing," I volunteered, with less enthusiasm than before.

"American songs?" Odd Kjellman asked.

"I know some American folk songs. I'd have to sing them in English."

"You can explain them in *norsk* first," Kjellman suggested. "Singing them in English is fine. American folk songs is good."

"And we can work you into a couple of the skits," Karl Arvid said. "We'll just see what works out and where you'll fit." And that was that; I was in the *Bragerevy*.

Practicing began in early December. We had the rehearsals at school, but not frequently. Rehearsals began in earnest as soon as school broke for the Christmas holidays. We practiced every day during the vacation, for at least a couple of hours. It was comprised of a series of dances, musical numbers, and comedy skits.

At the end December, we moved our rehearsals from the *gymnas* to the Worker's Union Hall, where the performance was to take place. We had four solid days of rehearsal, the first session from 12:00 noon to 3:00 PM; after a break for *middag*, we came back to the Hall and rehearsed from 6:00 til midnight.

Some of my *russ* friends were in the *Bragerevy*: Franck Pettersen was in the comedy sketches; Bitten Brigtsen (the Christmas virgin) was one of the dancers; Per Sparboe and Steinar Hansen were both in the band. But most of the *Bragerevy* participants were from the younger classes at school. There were many of my friends: Solveig Nilsen, Elin Fosse, Gunn Mathisen. There were also many brothers and sisters of my friends. And there were lots of new people to meet and enjoy.

During those four days of rehearsal, we spent most of our time in the audience, watching the rehearsals, waiting for our turn to rehearse, and making trouble. None of us was particularly attentive. At one point, when we were exceptionally disruptive, Odd Kjellman turned around from his chair on the stage.

"What are you doing?" he yelled at us. "We can't concentrate up here. Why don't you read a good book while you're waiting."

That was exactly what my grandfather would have said. In fact, that was exactly what my grandfather said to me all the time. In spite of that, I never carried a book with me, let alone a good book. The same was true for everyone else around me. But I did have my pocket *ordbok*; I carried that little book around with me everywhere I went. So, I took it out, opened it to a random page (page 272, as it happened), and started to "read."

I didn't exactly read. I took almost anything as an excuse to work on my *norsk*, so I took "reading a good book" as an excuse to memorize words. Page 272 happened to be the last page of the letter N and it contained many words I had never used (or seen) before; I was in heaven. I just read and memorized from the beginning of the page to the end. If nothing else, I learned a few words and kept out of Odd Kjellman's hair.

The *Bragerevy* was the major fundraiser for the *gymnas*, supporting Brage itself and the *russetur til* Kjøbenhavn, the senior class trip to Copenhagen in June. The first show was on

N nybygd	272	nåvel
vice;-bygd,*s* settlement;	dance; ende, *a*
- bygger, *s* settler.	this; present.
nydelig, *a* charming, nice.	nød,*s* want,distress;-brem-
ny|fiken, *a* curious; - født,	se, *s* emergency brake.
a newborn; - gift, *a*	nøde, *v* compel; press.
newly married; - het, *s*	nødhjelp, *s* make-shift.
novelty, news.	nødig, *av* reluctantly.
nykke, *s* whim.	nød|lidende, *a* indigent; -
nylig, *av* lately.	løgn, *s* white lie; -
nymfe, *s* nymph.	rop, *s* cry of distress;
nymotens, *a* new-fangled.	- sake, *v* force; i - sfall,
nynne, *v* hum.	in case of need; -
nyre, *s* kidney; - stykke,	tvungen, *a* forced; -
s loin; - talg, *s* suet.	tørft, *s* necessity; -
nys(e), *s* (*v*) sneeze.	ig, *a* (strictly) necessary;
nysgjerrig, *a* curious, pry-	- vendig, *a* necessary;
ing; - het, *s* curiosity.	- - gjøre, *v* necessitate;
nysilt, *a* new.	- - het, *s* necessity;
nyss, *s* hint, inkling; *av*	- - vis, *av* necessarily;
just now.	- verge, *s* self-defence.
nyte, *v* enjoy, taste; - lse,	nøkk, *s* nixie.
s enjoyment; - - ssyk,	nøkkel, *s* key, *fig* clue.
a pleasure-seeking, self-	nøktern, *a* sober.
indulgent.	nøle, *v* hesitate; - n, *s*
nytt, *s* news; - år, *s* New-	hesitation.
Year; - - saften, *s* New-	nøste, *s* ball; *v* roll.
Year's Eve.	nøtt, *s* nut.
nytt|e, *s* use, utility; *v* be	nøy|aktig, *a* exact, accu-
of use, avail;(be-)utilize;	rate; - het, *s* accu-
- ig, *a* useful.	racy; - e, *a*, *av* precise,
nær, *a* (*av*) near, at hand.	accurate; *vr* content
nære, *v* nourish; *fig* che-	oneself; - - regnende,
rish, entertain.	*a* nice, particular; -
nær|gående, *a* forward, in-	som, *a* frugal; - - het,
delicate; - gåenhet, *s*	*s* frugality.
indelicacy; - het, *s* neigh-	nøytral, *a* neutral; - itet,
bourhood, nearness.	*s* neutrality; - isere, *v*
nærig, *a* stingy, near.	neutralize.
næring, *s* food; trade, busi-	nå, *av* now; *v* reach, gain.
ness; - smiddel, *s* article	nåd|e, *s* grace, mercy;
of food; - svei, *s* trade,	- estøt, *s* death blow;
livelihood;-svett,*s* thrift.	- ig, *a* gracious, merciful.
nær|liggende, *a* neighbour-	nål, *s* needle, pin; - e-
ing; - me, *v* draw	skog, *s* pine-forest; -
(bring) near; *vr* ap-	estikk, *s* prick; - etre,
proach; - - re, *a* nearer,	*s* bot conifer.
further; - -st, *a* nearest; -	når, *cj* when; if; - som
next-door, *av* rather; -	helst, *cj* whenever; *av*
synt, *a* short-sighted; -	at any time.
tagende, *a* sensitive; -	nå til dags, *av* now-a-days;
vær, *s* presence, atten-	- vel, *av* well.

Friday, January 5th. It ran for five days and was a financial success. The 400-person Hall was sold-out every night except Friday (and there were about 300 people that night). The Friday night show wasn't the best; unfortunately, that was the show that got reviewed in the newspaper.

The show began at 8:00 PM and Kjellman had us all get there by 6:00; no time to *sove middag* that day. All told, there must have been close to 40 students participating. There was a small room off the side of the stage where we gathered, made ourselves up, and got into our "costumes." The dancers had real costumes; the rest of us had whatever we could gather or fabricate ourselves (somewhat like the *juletog* costumes, although less colorful). Most every costume had been found in an attic or been made by the kids themselves. At Staples, the boys and girls in theatricals had separate dressing rooms; not in Tromsø. In Tromsø, there was one room for everyone, and everyone dressed (and undressed) as the need arose. By December,

I Was a Teenage Norwegian

I had gotten used to a lot of differences—kids driving to a *hytta* unsupervised, kids drinking at parties (and never driving), kids walking up and down Storgate for an evening's entertainment—and the single dressing room was just one more of those differences; I went with the flow. The same situation occurred on other occasions throughout the rest of the year, on other *hyttatur* the *russ* took and on a trip to Harstad in February to watch the Norwegian Speedskating championships; but by then I was already a teenage Norwegian and I, too, thought nothing of it.

The final element of our preparation was the make-up. Everyone took care of himself or herself. Painting on new eyebrows, mustaches and beards, ruby-red cheeks, all on top of a shiny base. I couldn't tell how necessary it was or if it was just fun and part of the experience. It was a sight to see all these teenagers squatting in front of mirrors making themselves up. All except me. About all I managed was to send everyone into fits of laughter as I drew lips on my nose and eyebrows on my chin. At least there was no end of volunteers to help me out.

The show itself was a combination of dance, song, and comedy skits. The music was provided by a small band—1 saxophone, 2 trombones, 1 piano, 1 double base, and 1 set of drums—led by *russ* Steinar Hansen. I didn't particularly like the music; the dancing, on the other hand, was excellent. The comedy skits were generally funny, but too well-scripted for my taste. I would have preferred a bit of ad-libbing, but Kjellman didn't allow any of that.

I performed in two skits, and there was my famous song. The first of the two skits involved a song that was sung by Marit Wilhelmsen, one of the girls in my class. The scene was a night-club. There were five or six people sitting at tables listening to Marit sing "Blue Moon"; American songs were popular in Norway. The piano player in the band played the piano, Marit sang, and everyone else sat around and pretended to listen and drink. When the song was over, I came on stage and banged loudly on the door to the nightclub.

"*E' de' noen her som heter Da—vid—son?*" I yelled. Is there anyone here by the name of Davidson? I strung Davidson out so that it took close to 3-4 seconds for just the name. That alone got many laughs.

"*Ja,*" one of the boys (men) answered, opening the door, "my name is Da—vid—son." He mimicked my way of saying Davidson, taking perhaps 4-5 seconds just for the name. It was the first time someone had mimicked my Norwegian. That made me feel even more Norwegian.

I stormed through the door, grabbed him by his collar and proceeded to beat him up, throwing him around the night-club. I was dressed as much like a "gangster from Chicago" as I could: black shoes, my "charcoal grey" suit, dark shirt buttoned up to my neck, no tie (wouldn't Mom have been pleased to know I got a second use out of my funeral suit). The fight scene lasted perhaps 30 seconds (slapstick was big in Tromsø) and I departed, closing the door gently behind me.

252

Everyone looked at the man I had beaten up, writhing on the floor. Slowly he got up and slowly he made his way back to his chair and slowly he lowered his worn body into the chair. Then he started to giggle.

"I fooled him, but good," he said. "Actually, my name is Sparboe." It brought the house down.

Karl Arvid Román was the Master of Ceremonies of the *Bragerevy*. He had worked on much of the writing with Kjellman and had a number of short monologues throughout the show, along with parts in some of the humorous skits. He was also responsible for introducing some of the acts, and it was Karl Arvid who introduced me when the time had come for me to sing.

"We have a student at school who is from America." Karl Arvid began. "He will sing an American pop song and will himself explain what it is about."

As soon as Karl Arvid introduced me, the stagehands rolled out onto the stage three large barrels, one for me and one each for the two boys—Brynjulf and Erik—who accompanied me. All the other musical numbers were accompanied by the orchestra; I had my own personal guitar players. We were all dressed in light-colored pants, white shirts, and red bandannas tied around our necks. We jumped upon on the barrels, and when we were all seated, I began.

"The song is called The Sloop John B," I explained in *norsk*. This was by far the largest audience I had faced in *norsk*...close to 400 people. But I had rehearsed; I was ready.

"In *norsk*, the song would be called Sloopen Jon B. A sloop is a boat. It is a seaman's song. It begins with the seaman asking someone to please tell the captain that he wants to leave the boat and travel home. In the first verse, he talks about what happens on the boat in the evening. Mostly drinking. In the second verse, he talks about an officer who has drunk too much and the sheriff had to come and take him away. In the third verse, he talks about the cook who became crazy. First, he threw away lots of food and then ate up the rest."

I had actually asked Kjellman why I bothered to explain the song, since most people understood English and I doubted that anyone much cared about the words anyway, whether or not they understood them. He just wanted to make sure everyone in the audience understood I could speak *norsk*. I had never thought of that.

> We came on the Sloop John B
> My grandfather and me,
> Round Nassau town we did roam.
> Drinking all night, we got into a fight,
> Oh, I feel so break up,
> I wanna go home.

I Was a Teenage Norwegian

I went through all six verses. My song may not have been the hit of the show, but it did go well and I made it through each performance without a hitch...both the *norsk* explanation and the English song.

My final skit was typical of Norwegian humor at the time, mixing politics, poking fun at politicians, a heavy dose of dialect, and a long wait for a tame, off-color punch-line. I played an American sailor whose part required that I speak English. Two old Tromsø ladies were standing at their windows, listening to Einar Gerhardsen, the Prime Minister of Norway at the time, giving a radio address about the Common market.

Gerhardsen: There must be no doubt about where we stand on this issue. People have a reasonable desire to know. Let me, therefore, explain it in this fashion, simply and clearly: We are in favor of the Common Market and we are against it. There are advantages and drawbacks, and it will take time. We cannot underestimate what it will cost to become a member, and we can't avoid the fact that we can lose and go crazy, but we must go together into the future with the other European countries in organic fellowship and we must stand shoulder to shoulder with them.

Fru Anniksen: Well, good day, *fru* Kalvigsen.

Fru Kalvigsen: Well, good day, certainly, *fru* Anniksen. You can imagine that I just heard something terribly interesting on the radio. It was all about the Parliament and the Common Market.

Fru Anniksen: Parliament, isn't that a new sit-com?

Fru Kalvigsen: They were talking about the Common Market.

Fru Anniksen: Well, it's not all that clear what it is. In any case, those in the Parliament that are for it don't know what it is. And then there were those who were neither for or against it.

Fru Kalvigsen: That's true. There are always those who sleep while Parliament is in session.

Fru Anniksen: And if one doesn't read in the newspapers about what takes place in Parliament...

Fru Kalvigsen: ...one knows just as little about it as those that are in Parliament.

Fru Anniksen: But you, *fru* Kalvigsen, you who read the newspaper every day, can't you tell me what this Common Market is all about?

Fru Kalvigsen: You understand, the Common Market, that's where all these different countries band together so that everyone can travel anywhere they want and sell whatever goods they want anywhere, without having to pay any tariffs. In that way, the customs office becomes superfluous and customs officers eliminated. That way the governments save enormous amounts of money because there are fewer government workers.

Fru Anniksen: My, my, *fru* Kalvigsen; you certainly know how to use your mouth. But it all went a little too fast for me. I still don't understand anything about the Common Market.

Fru Kalvigsen: Look here, can't you understand that in those countries in the Common Market, people can sell their goods just as cheaply to everyone in all the countries?

Street-walker: *Åååååååååh.....*

American Sailor: Ooooooooh (The English equivalent of the Norwegian *Åååååååååh*). The boat! The boat! It leaves in an hour! Good-bye.
[I pass, in as obvious a manner as possible, a KR10 bill to the painted lady.]

American Sailor: So long, darling....

Street-walker: *Åååååååååh....*

Fru Anniksen: Well, I can see she wants to be in the Common Market. She's always selling something to someone.

At the start of my journey on the SEVEN SEAS I found that I had plenty of opportunities to express different sides of myself. Clearly the playful, joking side had more than enough opportunities; I loved to joke and fool around. But that was only a part of me and, I felt, it was often the only part of me that other people saw. I didn't often get a chance to express my other sides. I doubted that I would get much of a chance to express those parts of me in Norway, either.

The *Bragerevy* certainly allowed me to express that jokester, playful side. But Norway as a whole had, in fact, given me the opportunity to express more sides of myself than I could ever have imagined. My playful side emerged full force. My linguistic side was given free reign. My serious side was given more chances for expression than I acknowledged. My social side blossomed. And my intimate side was given every opportunity, in spite of all my efforts to the contrary.

-25-
Finally a Girlfriend

There were *russefester* and there were *russefester*. We had *russe-fester* all year but I hadn't experienced the most special *russefest* of all: the *Daabsfest*. At least that was what all my *russ* friends told me. I loved my friends; they were such a large part of what made my year in Norway. They loved surprises, and they loved breaking their own rules. There was a Norwegian saying they always quoted to me: *"Om du sier A, må du sier B."* If you say A, you must say B; Don't tell me half the story. But my *russ* friends always told me A without telling me B. They told me that the *Daabsfest* was the biggest *russefest* of the year, but they didn't tell me what was so special about it. They told me that *"daab"* meant baptism, but they didn't tell me what a *russ* baptism involved. But I was used to their surprises and I had never met a *russefest* I didn't like.

It was still winter, and it was still dark, and it was still necessary to walk to the *fest*. But it was January, and I was a teenage Norwegian, and the *Daabsfest* was at the Nyløkken Kafé, and I knew my way.

Lillian picked me up. I always walked home from *fester* with other kids; I almost always walked there on my own.

"Pete," *mor* shouted from the kitchen, "there's someone at the door for you."

"I'll get it," Tom shouted from his room, racing out into the hall toward the front door. Lillian had never been to the house, in spite of *mor* telling me I could invite her, and Tom had never seen her. He was my kid brother; he was curious.

"Hei," he said opening the door. "I'm Tom."

"Det gleder meg," Lillian said with her motherly smile. Lillian had more different kinds of smiles than anyone I had ever met: a knowing smile, a wise smile, an understanding smile, an angry smile, a motherly smile. a girlfriend smile. I felt I could always tell so much about her without her ever uttering a word. "I'm Lillian. Is Pete in?"

"You mean Pipe?" Tom said proudly, using the nickname no one in my family ever used. Jorunn and Lillian were the only two of my friends who continued to call me Pete.

"*Ja,*" she smiled the knowing smile.

"*Takk,* Tom," I said, standing in my own doorway, surveying the scene. I almost couldn't believe how wrong I had been wanting and hoping for a brother my own age. Tom was the greatest brother I could have had. He was funny and fun to be with. He was attentive to me and my needs. He looked up to me without idolizing me. He was curious about my life and friends without being overly intrusive. I got such a kick out of watching him and Lillian.

"*Ha det,*" I shouted to *mor* and *far* upstairs. "*Ha det,* Tom."

Lillian and I held hands as we walked the same shore route I had walked months before on my way to the first *russefest* at Nyløkken. I knew the road and recognized many of the houses. I felt at home, geographically and emotionally.

"Are you going to tell me," I pleaded, "what the *Daabsfest* is all about?"

"Of course," Lillian laughed. He laughter was followed by complete silence.

"Now?" I wondered out loud.

"Oh, no," she said. "Not now. You wouldn't understand anything I said now, *before* the *Daabsfest.* I'll explain it *afterwards.* Then you'll have enough experience with the *Daabsfest* to truly understand."

"*Takk,*" I said in my most sarcastic voice, a voice I tended to use less and less as the year wore on.

"*Ingenting å takke for,*" Lillian said, and I could feel her mischievous smile. Norwegians thanked for everything and had, therefore, a number of ways to say "you're welcome." Most of them were straightforward, literal translations, such as "*værsågod.*" Lillian had used the more jocular "Nothing to thank for," which, in that case, was most true.

Nyløkken was set up in a completely different way for the *Daabsfest.* The tables and chairs were pulled together, arranged as if for a banquet. There was no band. The kitchen area was full of *kafé* workers but no food was displayed in any of the counters and the *russ* weren't selling *øl.*

"*Værsågod å spise,*" Jorunn shouted out to all of us. Please eat. And we did. The *kafé* workers rushed out with their trays laden with food. This was not a *russefest*; it was a banquet, with many of my favorite foods: Øl and Solo (for Pipe) to drink, *poteter* (of course), roast pork, and *surkål,* a sweet version of sauerkraut (browner than the German version, because of the sugar, and loaded with caraway seeds). Almost all sixty of us were sitting around the tables eating and laughing, talking and joking. I could never have imagined a *russefest* without drinking and dancing, and I would never have imagined everyone would be having so much fun without their two staple *russefest* activities.

"Would you all stand and pray." I hadn't noticed Steinar Hansen until that moment. He sat at the head of the table and he was wearing a black robe and a white, circular, pleated collar.

"Who is Steinar supposed to be?" I asked Lillian.

"I said you wouldn't understand the *Daabsfest* until you experienced it," Lillian smiled. "Steinar is the *russeprest*, the *russ* priest."

"We are gathered together," Steinar began, with all the *russ* standing, holding glasses of *øl* or (in my case) Solo, "to witness the baptizing of this year's *russ*. It is a solemn occasion...."

"It must be," Gunnar Brox interrupted him. Gunnar was also wearing a black robe and a collar, although his collar was made of simpler material and hung too loosely around his neck. "It must be if no one is drunk yet."

"It is a solemn occasion," Steinar continued, undaunted, "and I'll drink to that." He led the others in downing their drinks.

"Friends," Bengt Mikkelsen rose, and he was a towering hulk when he stood up. "This is my first *Daabsfest*, but I feel great! It's great to be a *russ*; I only wish I could be one for more than one year!"

"If you don't study for your *artium*," Odd shouted, "you might be."

A number of other kids stood to speak. Bjørg gave a lengthy speech analyzing the *russ* as an example of the class struggle and the *Daabsfest* as the liberation of workers. Jorunn put the *Daabsfest* in a cross-cultural perspective. Arnulf talked about the psychology of baptism and the profound effects it had throughout adulthood. Per and Odd sang a duet in which they compared the *Daabsfest* with all the other *russefester* we had during the year. The *russ* knew how to have fun.

The tables were pushed aside after *middag* and chairs spread around. Gunnar, Steinar, and Per Sparboe, the three priests, set up their "altar:" a couple of tables under the archway separating the two rooms, in full view of the others sitting in the chairs. The table was laden with bottles of *brennevin*, wine glasses, and a large pitcher, full of an orange-colored liquid. There was a stack of large, white posterlike papers on the table and Steinar held one of them in front of his face while he read. He had added a white, cardboard cross to his outfit, to make everything official.

"Is that Solo in the pitcher?" I whispered to Lillian and Jorunn, both of whom sat next to me.

"Not exactly," Lillian smiled.

"It's *russebrus*," Jorunn said. *Russ* juice. "The *russeprest* mixed it up special for the *Daabsfest*."

"It has some Solo in it," Lillian explained, "and just about every-thing else Gunnar and Per could find."

"They may even," Jorunn continued, "have put some *tran* in it, because it is the worst-tasting *brus* you could ever imagine."

"What...."

"We'll explain later," Lillian interrupted. "They're starting."

Apparently, the three priests (along with a committee of other *russ*) had spent the previous two weeks creating *Daabsattest*, or baptismal certificates. They were elaborate documents, with hand-drawn pictures depicting something characteristic of each particular *russ*, and bordered by small photographs of each *russ*. In addition, the *Daabsfest* committee had decided on a nickname for each *russ* and had "baptized" each *russ* with his or her *russ* nickname.

One by one, each *russ* was called and Steinar went through the litany involved in baptizing/naming that person with his or her new *russ* nickname. Each candidate was required to drink a glass of *brennevin*, and all three of the priests had a glass each, too. It didn't take long for the three priests to be roaring drunk, and even more funny than they had started.

"What do I drink?" I asked Lillian, when my name was called. I never drank anything but Solo.

"That's what the *russebrus* is for," Lillian smiled, the mischievous smile again.

"But you said," I said turning to Jorunn, "it's worse-tasting than *tran*."

"You can't be baptized without drinking," Jorunn said.

"You have a choice," Lillian said. "There's always *brennevin*."

"But I can't...."

"Enjoy your *russebrus*," they both said, pushing me toward the alter and the three drunken *russeprest*.

"Oh, Pipe," Steinar slurred. "Glad you could join us."

"What will you have to drink?" Gunnar said, barely intelligible.

"What do you have?" I asked, hoping to avoid the inevitable.

"I think for you," Per knowingly poured me a glass from the pitcher, "we'll try a glass of our delicious *russebrus*." There were cheers from the onlookers. They all knew how vile it tasted from reputation only; I was the first to taste it.

"In the name of the *russ* gods," Steinar intoned, handing my *Daabsattest*, "we name you Uncle Sam."

I downed my glass of *russebrus*. It lived up to its advanced billing: it tasted worse than *tran*, and I didn't have a month to get used to it. I took my *Daabsattest* back to my chair, showing it to Jorunn, Lillian, and a number of others. There I was in the photo: King Pipe, sitting in my throne, surrounded by *småpiker*.

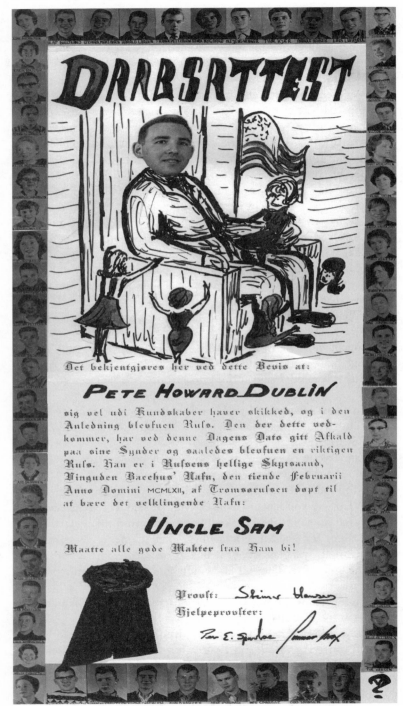

"Uncle Sam," Jorunn laughed. "It could have been worse."

"They originally wanted to call you The Ugly American," Lillian explained, "but they were afraid no one had read the book."

With the conclusion of the *Bragerevy* and *Daabsfest*, school became a major focus of my life in Tromsø. I remembered my grandfather's remark: "So, you're going to trade a year of study for a year of play."

I wouldn't say that Baba was 100% accurate, but he wasn't too far from the mark. Norwegian high schools had two kinds of exams at the end of the year, even though they were collectively referred to as the *artium*: written and oral. Each major subject had a final written exam. For English, we would have that final written exam at the end of year; same for Norwegian. Minor subjects—History, Religion, Biology—didn't warrant a written final...ever; they were "oral" subjects and there was only one oral exam each year. 24 hours before the oral exam, we would be told which subject we would have; then we would start studying for it.

I remember struggling through my World History textbook at the beginning of the school year. It had taken me hours just to read a single page. After three or four weeks I had asked Arnulf one day how much time he spent studying.

"History?" he asked incredulously. "I haven't read a single page yet."

"But what if you are called to recite?" I asked.

"I can always think of something to say," Arnulf boasted confidently. "And as long as I don't recite loudly, I won't wake up Sætter, so he won't mind much what I say."

"But what about tests?" I continued my barrage of apparently irrelevant questions.

"We don't have tests during the year in an oral subject. The only exams that count in Norway," Arnulf explained patiently, "are our final exams, those that make up the *artium*. We've had some of our written exams already last year. We've got three written exams and only one oral exam. If it turns out that History is the oral exam, then I'll study History."

And because I didn't take Biology and English, there were large parts of each day I spent with other classes. Most of those classes were in the *gymnas*, but there was one exception. The three-story *gymnas* building had an attic floor, and housed in this attic floor was the *husmorskolen*, the school for homemakers or housewives. This was one of my favorite haunts. In part, I loved it up there because no one else in the school ever went there; it was my secret garden, so to speak. It wasn't as if the *husmorskolen* was hidden or that none of the *gymnas* students knew it was up there. The students in the *husmorskolen* were considered "lesser" students than those in the *gymnas*, because none of them passed the admissions test for the *gymnas* at the end of elementary school.

The other reason for my interest in the *husmorskolen* was that its student body was populated entirely by teenage girls; I was the only boy ever there. They were not *småpiker*; a few of them were younger than me, but

I Was a Teenage Norwegian

most of these girls were my age or even a little older. Being up so high in the school just reinforced my feelings that I traveled to heaven once or twice a week. Of course, that was never the reason I gave the *husmorskolen* students.

"I want to experience," I told them in as serious a voice as I could muster, "all different kinds of experiences in Norway." I didn't fool anyone, certainly not the teacher.

But I did learn on my frequent visits to the *husmorskolen*: I learned to cook a number of Norwegian dishes. I didn't know if the students learned anything other than cooking; whenever I visited, we cooked. I learned how to cook a number of my favorite Norwegian foods, and some I didn't much care for: the porridge that was the most typical Saturday meal (which, luckily for me, only the Norbyes ever ate), Norwegian *vaffler*, which were cooked on a waffle-iron but eaten cold with cheese or jam, and a number of different chocolate cakes.

But most of my time outside of 5GE was spent with other classes in the *gymnas*. I held *foredrag*, or talks, in all the classes in the school. Each *foredrag* was essentially one class period of 45 minutes. I held at least four of those *foredrag* in each *gymnas* class, and sometimes more. I must have had 45-50 foredrag in the high school portion of the *gymnas* and the same in the *realskolen*.

But I didn't mind, because I felt that was the best way to help my Norwegian friends learn a little about America and understand it and its problems a little better. Most of the time, I told the class to ask me questions pertaining to ANYTHING about life in America.

"Do all high school students have cars?"

"Are there really gangsters in Chicago?"

"Does everyone like President Kennedy?"

"How do Whites think of the Negroes?"

"How do the Negroes think of the Whites?"

The kids were interested and we usually talked right through the *friminutter* and even after school. The class got a special exemption from inspection when I was the one who kept them inside.

I held most of the *foredrag* in *norsk*, but by January I told the English teachers that I was willing to hold some in English. One of my more linguistically fascinating *foredrag* was a two-period session in one of the 4th Year English classes on the topic of Negro History in America. Perhaps because of the much more homogeneous nature of Norwegian culture, there was always a fascination with race relations, and I was often asked questions about Negroes, the relations between the races, and Negro History.

That was one of the few school *foredrag* for which I prepared; I had spent a couple of afternoons at the USIS office reading through some college textbooks and other materials. It was a rather strange and problematic *foredrag* because it was the first time I had spoken English in two or three months. I found that I thought primarily in *norsk* and translated into English as I spoke; that was definitely a first for me. I thought I was doing a pretty good job, but occasionally the class laughed. Normally, laughing wouldn't have surprised me…but I hadn't said anything intended to be funny. It happened five or six times during my *foredrag*; other than those outbursts, I thought everything went well.

"*Takk*, Pete," *fru* Engelsen said to me in *norsk* as I finished my longest of *foredrag*.

"*Værsågod*," I said to her, thankful that I could speak in *norsk* again at last.

"That was a very interesting *foredrag*," she continued. "And your English was quite good, too."

The class broke up again, and I realized what had happened. I was thinking in *norsk*, translating into English, and giving the *foredrag* in English. Occasionally (those five or six times, I presumed) I would intersperse my otherwise "pretty good" English with *norsk* words and phrases.

School was filled with many such linguistic experiences. One of my favorite classes to visit was one of the third year English lines. I had a lot of friends in that class, including Torild Norbye, Elin Fosse whom I had known most of the year, but with whom I had become much better friends during the *Bragerevy*, and Solveig Nilsen, my date for the Student Ball.

I liked that class as well for its location; it was the only classroom not on the school grounds. The *gymnas* was a big, old brick building that looked like the Norwegian equivalent of an American junior high school built in the 1930s or 1940s. There was a lot of pressure on the school over the years to expand and take more students. High schools in Norway were much more selective than in the America. Students took exams at the end of the seven-year elementary school to get into the *realskole*, and a lot of kids there graduated with grades too low to get them into *gymnas*. Northern Norway had the fewest number of high schools, which made them the most difficult to get into in the whole country.

In the late 1950s, the school did expand, just a little. The result was a small, one-room pre-fab a couple of hundred meters down the road from the *skolegård*. That was where Torild and her class met. Torild maintained it was rather fun, being off alone together with all her friends. The room had its own identity because of its separateness, and that was one of the reasons I liked visiting there.

On one of my visits, Elin asked me about my religion. That was an obvious question for a Norwegian to ask an American, since 96% of Norwegians belonged to the state Lutheran Church and Americans could be virtually anything.

"What are you, Pipe," she asked.

"My background is Jewish," I said. Elin didn't understand how difficult a question she had asked. She didn't understand that for many Americans, Judaism could be either an ethnic group, a religion, or both. For me, it was just my ancestry that was Jewish. "My religion is Unitarian."

"What is Unitarian?" Elin asked. I was not surprised that she had never heard of that purely American religion.

I Was a Teenage Norwegian

"That's difficult to explain," I responded. And it was difficult to explain, in English, let alone in *norsk*. Since that time, I met a Unitarian minister who explained to me that Unitarians share only one belief in common.

"They don't shoot moose," he said. It was a difficult religion to explain.

"Why don't you talk to us during religion class next week about religion in America?"

I had another *foredrag* on my calendar. I was back the next week. I began talking about the variety of religions in America. We had spent a lot of time in LRY studying other religions, including visiting a variety of other churches, so I knew from some personal experience about some of that content. The difficult part was explaining that I was Jewish, but not of the Jewish religion. Even harder was explaining about how Unitarians constituted a religion with virtually no common beliefs (I hadn't heard about the moose yet).

At one point, I was talking about praying and used the word *bønne*.

"What do you mean by *bønne*," Elin asked me.

I knew that *et bønn* meant a prayer but I couldn't remember the word for *to pray*, so I simply converted the noun into a verb by adding an "e" at the end, since most regular *norsk* verbs had an "e" at the end.

"You know," I said, *å bønne*. And I put my hands together to illustrate my meaning.

"*Nei*," she smiled, since by February she didn't get that many opportunities to correct my *norsk*. "It's *et bønn*, the noun, not *å bønne*, the verb. The verb is *å be*."

"Oh, right," I said and instantly came out with: "*Be, ber, ba, bedt.*"

Everyone in the class looked at my with completely blank faces.

"*Be, ber, ba, bedt,*" I said again. They got it, and laughed. When I had heard the infinitive of the verb, I instantly conjugated it—pray, prays, prayed, has prayed—without a moment's thought. I had spent hours, especially in the fall, sitting in the back of the 5GE classroom, when I couldn't understand the teachers, memorizing verbs. And the minute I heard that one, my reflex action was to conjugate it, because that was the way I memorized it when I first learned it.

Elin played an even more important part in my life than simply providing me one of my better linguistic jokes. She enabled me to substantially change my relationship with Lillian.

January was the month of my last non-Lillian date. I didn't realize that when I made it, but I knew by the end of it. There was nothing wrong with the date but there was a change in me. The date was simple: I went out to the movies with Elin Fosse. Elin was one of my best friends, and had been since the fall. She was the one Gunn and I had made faces at while she worked in the bookstore. During the *Bragerevy* practices, we began improving our friendship. During the rehearsal time before the show started its four-day run, I invited Elin to go with me to the movies.

I met her in the *sentrum*; we walked Storgate. Then we went to the *kino*. After the movie was over, we walked Storgate a few times and had Solo and dessert in one of the *kafés*. I walked Elin home. I had been there before; I knew her mother and her older brothers. I was as much a friend of the family as Elin was my "date."

When I got home, *mor* and *far* were still *våken*. They were having their night-cap...for their circulation.

"So," *mor* asked, "who did you go out with tonight?"

"Elin Fosse," I answered.

"Ah, Elin Fosse," *mor* remarked, sitting back in her chair. "She's the daughter of Anna Fosse."

"That's right," *far* added. "The sister of Ragnhild Jacobsen."

"The daughter of Britta and Tor Jacobsen," *mor* said.

"Tor's brother," *far* added, "used to work for my father."

And on and on it went. The two of them recreated before my very ears the entire family tree going back four or five generations.

I enjoyed the date, and I even enjoyed the grilling on the part of *mor* and *far*. After the *Bragerevy* had finished its run, there was a small *Bragerevyfest* and I invited Elin to that, as well. The *fest* started off fine, Elin and I got a little friendlier, and then we made out. I told myself I wouldn't, but I did anyway.

The next day, I had a good, wonderful, warm, kind of tingly feeling in my stomach instead of the empty one I was accustomed to after making out. I felt that for the first time in my life that what I had done the night before was beautiful, which was the way in which my American father had always described to me what making love felt like. Maybe I wasn't there yet, but I was on the way. I realized that I really liked Elin a lot.

Throughout that Sunday, the feeling kept growing and growing. Elin and I met in the *sentrum* that evening and after a few trips up and down Storgate, I followed her home. Since there were so few "dates" in Tromsø, following a girl home was the most common event corresponding to an American date, although it was a lot less formal.

But everything was different; she wasn't the same as the night before. I could hear my Dad saying to me: 'So, you had a little fun Saturday, and now it's Sunday. It's as simple as that.' I had convinced myself that making out was "cheap," but it was different with Elin; I felt she was a "nice" girl. We talked a little about the situation, her feelings, and my feelings.

"Yesterday was Saturday," she said. "Today is Sunday."

"I can't forget my former boyfriend, even though my parents made me stop seeing him because he's five years older than me."

"We should remain friends."

Sue had told me that she thought it was "bad" to make out if love was not behind it all and I had come to the conclusion before I left for Norway that Sue was right. That Sunday, after talking with Elin, I sensed that it couldn't be "bad" to make out just for the fun of it. I thought of all the wonderful kids I knew in Tromsø. None of them were "cheap" and almost all of them had a "make out because it's fun to make out" philosophy. I couldn't think of that philosophy as "bad" or "morally wrong;" it was simply different.

But the feeling for Elin wasn't gone. I still wanted her to be more than just a friend. I was unwilling to let things stand; I had to ask her if she thought it might work for us, even with her "unforgettable" boyfriend. I asked her in school on Monday and she said no. No arguments: she said no, and no it was.

As I look back on that incident thirty years later, I realize how important an event it was for me. It represented the first time after such an "episode" that I was able to remain friends with the girl. We were still good friends; we remained, in fact, best of friends throughout the entire year. Elin and I still write to each other and I visit her and her family every time I am in Tromsø. And, years after I turned my failed romantic efforts with Elin into a strong and lasting friendship, I was often able to maintain friendships with other former girlfriends, too.

In addition to such long-term results, the incident with Elin enabled me to see my relationship with Lillian differently. I remained ambivalent about my relationship with Lillian; Lillian had a typical Norwegian attitude about making out and I was still mired in my own repressed notions. The situation with Elin made it possible for me to think in different terms. I knew that evening as I went to bed that Lillian was different and, in some way, special. Elin was a close friend; Solveig Nilsen was a date; Lillian was my girlfriend.

I wandered through all of my "romances" from third grade on: playing duets in 5th grade with Joanne Luptin, kissing Debbie Howell in the back seat of our car (with Dad driving) in 8th grade, Di Langford at Camp Sloane, hitch-hiking to see Jill Coughlin at Rowe Camp when I was sixteen.

I thought about my last interaction with Sue before boarding the bus in New York for Montreal.

"Sue, let's walk a little more. I've got something to give you before I go."

"Really?"

"I want you to have this necklace," I said as I gave her the necklace that Peg had given me the previous year. My younger sister was always looking out for me; she had given the necklace to me so that I would have something to give to a girl. I hoped I was not doing anything wrong. I had wanted this gift for a special girl. I hoped Sue was the right girl, and that I wasn't thinking irrationally about this just because I was going away for a year.

"That's lovely, Pete," Sue gushed, in her usual way. "It's really important to me to have something of yours while you're away. It really is."

"You mean a lot to me," I looked at her.

Joanne Luptin, Debbie Howell, Di Langford, Jill Coughlin, and even Sue Osborne were in the past. Lillian Ingebrigtsen was the present.

-26-
Danseskolen

Soldagen. The day of the sun. It was difficult to explain, and equally difficult to fully appreciate, what it is like to live a two-month-long night. The sun had gone to bed November 21st. The *mørketida* was a special, if unwelcome, time . It meant one or two hours more sleep each night, and I would *sove middag* virtually every day. It meant *tran*, the world's most foul-tasting food supplement. It meant the constant shock of coming out of the newsreels on Saturday afternoon into pure darkness. It meant watching construction workers using bright lights in "daytime." It meant more drinking and more suicides. As a teenage Norwegian, I never really got used to it and I was never convinced that even the "real" Norwegians did.

Perhaps the only saving grace of *mørketida* was that it created the need for *soldagen*. *Soldagen* was January 21st and it marked the return of the sun to Tromsø. *Soldagen* occurred on a Sunday in 1962. Sunday was a family day so I got to celebrate *soldagen* with my family.

Family life in Tromsø was different from what I had experienced with my family in Westport. The biggest difference was the apparent lack of togetherness—not a lack of love—between members of the family. I didn't find that any of my families did much together; I experienced the Norwegian family more as a group of individuals than a family unit or team.

When my family did "something together" in America, it usually took the form of a trip to the movies or the beach, a short drive "in the country," possibly a walk, a vacation trip, a trip into New York City, or "family fun" (I cannot think of charades except within the context of family fun). A trip to the movies in Tromsø was not much of a family affair because everyone went so often it wasn't much of a change to go together. Family fun didn't exist in Norway. Every now and then a play or a *revy* or a concert came to Tromsø. There was a chance the whole family might go together, although we did that only once that year.

A family walk was the most frequent family activity. Sunday was Norway's one day free of school and work and most people didn't want to "waste it" going to church; instead, they would take a walk. Many families had a *hytta*, usually within a one- to two-hour drive from Tromsø. It was common for families to take a few trips in the winter and many more in the summer; a few families spent their whole summer at their *hytta*, with the father commuting to work. We went to the Thyholdt *hytta* a couple of times during the winter and a couple of times again during the spring before I left.

On *soldagen, mor, far*, Tom, and I walked out the front door, down to the water's edge, and headed south. We walked for about forty-five minutes to the *sydspisen*, the southern tip of Tromsøy. Going to *fester* there meant that I had never done the walk during the day. Going to the *sydspisen* for *soldagen* meant that I still hadn't.

We got there around 1:00 in the "afternoon." The sun was due to appear briefly at about 1:15. By the time we got to the *badestrand*, there must have been 2,000 to 3,000 people there already.

It was awesome. It was, after all, just the sun, but on *soldagen*, the sun wasn't just the sun. It crept up over the horizon and the assembled multitude cheered. It rose slightly; it only had about ten minutes visibility. There wasn't a cloud in the sky as the sun shimmered over the ice-cold water. It was big; no, it was huge. It was magnificently bright. It was round, and yellow, and welcome…and then it was gone.

However close I felt to my Norwegian family, there was one part of my life in which I didn't involve the Thyholdts at all: my relationship with Lillian. I hardly ever talked about Lillian with *mor* or *far*; Tom was the only member of my family who had seen her. Although *mor* and *far* knew her family, I never introduced Lillian to them, even after I took *mor* up on her invitation to invite Lillian over to our house.

Because of the way our house was set up, I could have Lillian come over without anyone else in the house knowing; actually, they probably *knew*, but they never *saw* her come over. In the evening, when I brought Lillian home with me, my parents were always upstairs. I could bring Lillian into the house and straight to my downstairs bedroom without having to introduce her to them. In fact, not only did Lillian never meet my parents, I never met hers. I walked her home often, but she never invited me into her house and never introduced me to her family.

I often spent as much time with a friend's family—I visited with Gunnar Brox's and Elin Fosse's families all the time—as I spent with the friend. That was not unusual in Tromsø, although I probably was on the extreme side of being friends with my friends' families. My own Norwegian family was clearly important to me, and I sensed Lillian felt the same about hers, but there was something in our relationship that we kept apart from our families. We had great fun together when she came to my house. We made out, we had long talks, we joked and laughed, she got mad at me when I teased her, but I isolated Lillian, an integral part of my life as a teenage Norwegian, from my family, an equally integral part of that life.

If Norwegian families didn't do as much together as I might have expected, Norwegian teenagers did more together than I could have ever imagined. There were *fester*, and *hyttatur*. We *plukka poteter* and we had our *juletog*. Perhaps there were no after-school clubs, but there was Brage, with its meetings, rehearsals, and its *Bragerevy* (and its *Bragerevyfest*). There was walking Storgate, going to *kafés*, and going to the newsreels on Saturday after school. I had some time to myself, a little time with my family, and huge amounts of time doing a variety of activities with my friends. Not least of all was the *Harstadtur*, the trip to Harstad to see the Norwegian Speedskating Championships.

I had heard about, and signed up for, the trip in December, even though it wasn't scheduled until early February. By the time the buses were ready to roll, seventy kids had gathered in the *torvet*, along with a couple of sets of parents as chaperones. American kids rarely got to take trips of that sort and, when they did, there were half as many chaperones as there were kids. In Norway, the chaperones were largely symbolic. Adults accompanied the "kids," but there were never enough adults to actually supervise them. Harstad was reachable by the *hurtigruten*; taking the *hurtigruten* took less time than the bus but it was more expensive. We piled into the two buses at about 5:00 PM and were off on our eight-hour journey.

Beautiful described the sights between our window and eternity. There was a big, almost huge Norwegian moon floating in the sky. The sky itself was, for the most part, pitch black and shiningly clear as warm, melted tar. With that majestically dark background, the moon stood out as the crown itself. With its dazzling whiteness, almost blinding brightness, it shone on its nocturnal kingdom and lit it up as a lone candle on the top of a Christmas tree in a murky room. It spread its beams evenly on the snow, ice, and the sea. The snow was soft and new. The light of the moon rebounded sometimes, other times it found a home in the soft luxury of the snow…making for rolling hills, shaded here and there, but still decked in a dull lightness for the most part.

The ice was brisk and sharp, reflecting the moon's challenge with all the vigor of sun-sparkling snow. The whole effect was one of low, smooth hills and fields, clothed in whites and blacks, changing its garb with the onward rush of the bus. The sea, with its back to the wall of mountains, rippled calmly under a slightly straining wind. The moon shot its remaining life down upon it and, as with the ice, the sea would have nothing to do with it. It dispersed its latest gift, creating a sparkling splendor to match the snow's. The mountains towered in the background: tall, majestic chaperones.

With a turn of my head from the windows on the right to those on the left, whirling out from the mountains, came a long, thin streak of perforated light: *nordlys*, the Northern Lights. Seemingly coming from nowhere and leading to nowhere, that physical law-defying wonder brightened up the sky, only to suddenly shift to emptiness. From nothingness to a new design was as quickly accomplished, and once again the long curving streak made its journey out from its source hidden in the mountain.

I Was a Teenage Norwegian

Harstad was a small town of between 6,000-8,000 inhabitants, about half the size of Tromsø. It was west of Narvik, still north of the Arctic Circle. It was situated in a beautiful Norwegian coastal setting, surrounded by sea and mountains. We arrived at 1:00 in the morning and, although prior arrangements had supposedly been made, we had trouble getting sleeping space, even though "space" meant just that: floor space with, if we were lucky, mattresses. We rode to one school, but they wouldn't let us in. We waited outside for about half an hour, but they still wouldn't let us in. It was, after all, the Norwegian Speedskating Championships. There must have been 10,000-15,000 additional people in Harstad to watch them, more than doubling the size of the town. There were virtually no hotels, and certainly none of us would have stayed in them anyway. Most people coming for the championships were looking, as we were, for floor space.

We all piled back into the bus, which was fairly cold by then. The road into Harstad was perilous, and the bus had to back down one or two hairpin turns. The result was that we had broken a couple of windows in an attempt to turn one or another corner as we approached Harstad and we were now paying for the bus driver's mistakes. The bus temperature was just a shade warmer than the outside air: somewhere around 20°F. We approached another school, which was also full. Harstad just didn't have that many schools, so we went back to the first one; that was the one where we had made "prior arrangements." The second time we wouldn't let them say no. Oh, we let them say no, but then we brought our gear in anyway and made camp in the hallways. By then it was 3:00 AM. After much clowning around, we finally got to sleep around 5:00 AM.

We made our trip to Harstad during the last week of February. By that time of year in Tromsø, we had almost six hours of sunlight each day; in Harstad, we had almost seven. By 10:30 AM and the sun was just coming up. That was the earliest the sun had come up in almost five months, and it gave me a chance to check out yet another northern Norwegian town. Although Harstad did make Tromsø look "big," the two towns had much in common. They were both coastal towns; water was in view everywhere. There was a small downtown, with one tall, modern building (seven or eight stories). The rest of the town consisted mainly of small, two-story wooden houses. The bright sun reflecting off the completely clean snow made a picture-perfect view.

The snow is always clean, always completely clean, in Northern Norway. Roads rarely are plowed. Snow comes regularly and in small amounts. The total is huge; I couldn't see out of my window at home because of the two-meter snow banks outside. But it comes slowly and gradually, and there is rarely a need to plow. The temperature never rises above freezing...not once between November and April. Once the snow lands it stays, and it remains white. I didn't notice its whiteness as much during *mørketida*. But in Harstad, with seven glorious hours of sun, I became aware of its whiteness. I still had almost two more months to enjoy that whiteness before the "warm" weather came in May.

The main reason I thought we came to Harstad was to watch the Speedskating Championships. I soon found out the main reason we came to Harstad was to have fun...the seventy of us and about 10,000 to 15,000 others. Winter sports are *it* in Norway; it is what Norwegians are famous for and they produce world-class athletes. Cross-country skiing, ski-jumping, figure-skating, and speedskating are *the* Norwegian sports. Those who couldn't come to Harstad had, I was sure, their ears glued to their radios; there was no television in Tromsø.

The day's events started around noon. The throng of spectators walked to the "stadium." By late February, I was enough of a teenage Norwegian not to be shocked by what Norwegians called a stadium. It was a natural bowl, a flat plateau built into a hill about halfway down from the top of the

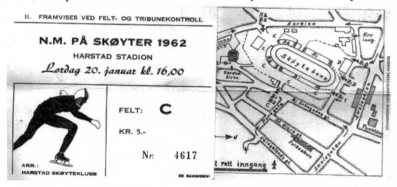

hill toward the water. There was no structure; there were no seats. On one side, built into the hill, the ground was inclined, making it possible for thousands of people to stand and still see over those in front of them. On the other side, it was flat, accommodating fewer people. In the middle was a flat area about the size of a *fotball* field. It was, in fact, where the Harstad teams played *fotball* during the warm(er) weather. The field was flooded and frozen, and it was on that surface that the championships took place.

I was warned (by my more experienced friends) to dress warmly. I wore long underwear—top and bottom—wool knickers with beautifully hand-knit woolen leggings, a woolen shirt covered with a beautifully hand-knit woolen sweater. I wore my *russelua*, a scarf *mor* had made me bring, and my beautiful hand-knit woolen mittens. On my feet I had a pair of woolen socks under my woolen leggings and my reindeer boots. It was 10°F above zero. I was freezing, and I was not alone. All 10,000 of us were constantly jumping up and down to keep warm.

"Did you bring any newspapers?" Odd Johnson, one of my *russ* friends on the trip asked.

"Newspapers?" I asked incredulously. "This is a hell of a time to want to read a newspaper."

"Nei," he laughed. "Not for reading: for insulation."

Odd had brought enough for both of us. We took off our boots, wrapped our feet in newspapers, and put the boots back on. Then we put the rest of the newspapers under our boots and stood on them, or jumped up and down on them as the situation warranted. The newspapers helped, but not much. The jumping up and down helped, but not much. This was Northern Norway in winter time; I went with the flow…even if the flow was frozen.

Some of the shorter distance races were exciting. There were only four races: 500 meters, 1,500 meters, 5,000 meters, and 10,000 meters. The 500 meters were the most exciting to watch. The 10,000 meters were too long, even for most of my friends. Some of us went *til byen* and ate, and still got back in time to see the remaining races.

Saturday evening was much more pleasant than the night before. We knew where we were staying and we could horse around in style. We were on our own; I never saw the chaperones. The boys had one classroom and the girls had another. We shared the same bathrooms and brushed our teeth together in the hall. We serenaded the girls to sleep, but otherwise we left them alone. It was quite enough fun to have thirty-five to forty boys all stuffed in their sleeping bags on mattresses on the floor pretending to go to sleep, rolling over each other and moaning in the dark. None of us slept and none of us much cared.

The trip back began at about 8:00 in the evening on Sunday. After about three hours of driving, we realized that we had left Karl Arvid Román in Harstad. I was shocked, but no one else looked either surprised or worried. Luckily, he hitched a ride and caught up with us at one of the ferry stops. Other than that excitement, some of us tried unsuccessfully to sleep while others tried unsuccessfully to make jokes; at least *they* succeeded in laughing at them. We got home at 4:00 AM and were in school by 8:30. Not bad for teenagers.

So much of what I did as a teenage Norwegian was to be a teenage Norwegian. Some of it was, in a way, easy, because there was no American counterpart; the trip to Harstad represented that kind of activity. But there were teenage Norwegian activities which had bad-memory analogies in America; *danseskolen* represented that kind of activity.

"Pete," Randi asked one day as we walked *til byen* after school, "are you going to *danseskolen?*"

"Going to it?" I asked in response. "I only heard of it once—at the Student Ball—and I assumed it was some kind of joke."

"It's not really a school," she said. "It's more of a dance class."

"Wait a minute," I said, as I got into gear. "How old do you think I am? How old do I look? In America, we go to dance class in fifth grade."

"You're not in America any more, Pete," Randi smiled. "You're a *Tromsøværing* now. In Tromsø even *russ* go to *danseskolen*. In fact, I think you'll find that almost all of us *russ* are going."

"This I have got to see," I said smugly. It wasn't that I didn't believe Randi; I had encountered stranger habits in Tromsø than *russ* going to *danseskolen.* It was just that I couldn't believe it. "Sure," I continued. "Whatever the *russ* do, I'll do, too. You know me."

"The first class is tomorrow night," Randi said. "I'll find out where it is and tell you in school tomorrow. Are you going home now or are you going to walk Storgate?"

"I'll walk a little with you," I answered, "at least to see who's here. Maybe you can explain to me why *danseskolen* is so popular among the *russ.*"

"Even I can tell you that," Arnulf surprised us from the rear. "I'm surprised you can't figure it out, Pete, smart American that you are.

"What's the difference between a smart American and a smart Norwegian, smart Arnulf?"

"I don't know."

"That's the difference; I do."

"I liked him better when he couldn't make jokes in *norsk*," Randi said to Arnulf.

"You may have noticed, my smart sometimes American, sometimes Norwegian, always *Tromsøværing* friend, that there isn't exactly a great deal to do in this town."

"How can you say such a thing?" I exclaimed. "We can walk Storgate."

"My point, exactly."

"But, Arnulf," Randi interrupted, "you're from Lyngseida. Tromsø is the big city for you."

"Will you guys let me finish?" Arnulf said with mock exasperation. "I can't even answer the simplest of questions. There is so little to do in this town, when something like *danseskolen* comes along, almost everyone jumps at the opportunity."

"Are you going?" I asked.

"Of course," he answered.

"It's getting close to *middag*," I said, noticing that it was already after 3:30 and my stomach was telling me that *middag* was expected. "I'll see you guys tomorrow," I said as I continued south and they turned again northward. "Randi, don't forget to let me know where *danseskolen* is."

On Tuesday, Randi told me *danseskolen* would take place in a small building a little north of the *kino*. After *middag*, *mor* asked me if I was going *til byen*.

"I'm going to *danseskolen*," I answered, still somewhat sheepishly. I couldn't quite get over the fact that I was seventeen years old and I was going to dance class.

"Your mother and I went to *danseskolen*," *far* said in his usual thoughtful manner. "It must be almost forty years ago. Are they still having it in that small building just north of the *kino*?"

"*Ja*," I said, before *mor* had a chance to give us the name of the building, its exact street location, the person who built it, the date it was built, and various other aspects of Tromsø's architectural history.

"Well," *mor* said anyway, "make sure you tell us who you meet there."

"I know, *mor*," I smiled

It was about a twenty to twenty-five minute walk, which gave me just enough time to get nervous.

"*Hei*, Pete," Randi and Arnulf greeted me in unison as I entered the hall.

There must have been more than 100 kids, maybe 150, milling around waiting for *danseskolen's* first lesson of the year to begin.

"You weren't kidding, Arnulf," I said to him. "I would never have believed *danseskolen* would get this kind of turnout. How long have you been coming to this?" I asked .

"Three years," he answered.

"We are ready to begin," the instructor loudly proclaimed. "Choose a partner."

The feared moment had arrived; no avoiding it now. I looked at Arnulf, but he was no help; he had already asked Randi and they had moved off into the middle of the hall. Where were my friends when I needed them? I couldn't even see any *russ* girls who weren't already paired up with *russ* boys. Everyone was always joking about how I spent so much time with the *småpiker* I figured might as well try my luck with them there.

"Do you want to dance," I asked one girl cautiously.

"*Ja*," she replied simply, grabbed my arm, and walked with me toward the center of the floor. That was it? That was easy. I could handle that.

In fact, that set the pattern for the whole evening. I asked girl after girl to dance, and I was never refused.

"Why would a girl say no?" Arnulf asked incredulously. "They came to dance."

The problem I had in Westport of always getting "no" for an answer (at dances, not dance class) was reversed, for none of the girls ever said no. And from my conversation with Arnulf and other *russ* friends, it was clear that if you were asked to dance in Tromsø, you accepted, whether at *danseskolen* or *fester*. Kids didn't attach a great deal of social meaning to the act of dancing; they just liked to dance. In Westport, girls wouldn't dance with someone they didn't like; being asked to dance was something like being asked out on a date. In Tromsø, there was no such extra layer of meaning or importance. Tromsø, where had you been all my life?

After an hour or so, I noticed Karl Arvid Román talking with a group of kids. I was particularly struck by one of the girls he was talking with. When I caught him alone a few minutes later, I asked him if he would introduce me.

"Sure," he said. "As soon as this dance is over."

As the dance ended, Karl Arvid corralled me and walked me over toward the group.

"I want to introduce Pete Dublin," he said, somewhat proudly. "This is Helga."

"*God dag*," I said formally.

"*God dag*," Helga replied.

"This is Kirstin," Karl Arvid continued.

"*God dag*," I said.

"*God dag*," Kirstin replied.

"This is Nøste," Karl Arvid said, finally introducing me to the girl who had initially caught my eye.

"Nøste?" I asked.

"Nøste," Karl Arvid repeated. "It's a nickname. It means..."

"I know what it means," I said. "Something to do with yarn."

"Nøste, this is Pete," Karl Arvid tried again to introduce us.

"Page 272," I said.

"What?" Nøste looked at me as if I was as strange as I sounded.

"Page 272," I repeated. "The word '*nøste*' is on page 272 of my *ordbok*."

"Your *ordbok*?" Nøste asked.

"His pocket *ordbok*," Karl Arvid chimed in. My pocket *ordbok* was quite famous at the *gymnas*; any one who knew me knew of my pocket *ordbok*.

"*Nøste* is on page 272 of my pocket *ordbok*," I said again. I slowly took the *ordbok*, carefully—and dramatically—opened it to page 272, and showed the now quite large crowd page 272. There, toward the bottom of the second column, was the word '*nøste*' and its definition: ball of yarn.

Needless to say, the reaction from the crowd was substantial and instantaneous. The reaction from Nøste was equally gratifying: we danced together most of the remaining hour of that first lesson at *danseskolen*.

The next day, the word had gotten around. Even as I entered the *skolegård* in the morning, I sensed that my reputation had increased noticeably. Kids came up to me all day, asking about my *ordbok*, asking about page 272, asking me what page "*fjell*" was on, and what words were on page 119.

During one of the *friminutter*, Karl Arvid came over to me. He still couldn't quite believe what I had done.

"Everyone at school is convinced you have read your entire *ordbok*, that you know all the words in the *ordbok*, and that you know which page each word is on. I just figure it's a trick, like magic. How did you do it?"

"Do you remember," I asked Karl Arvid, "the rehearsal for the *Bragerevy*? We were all sitting around, waiting our turn to rehearse our scenes. Kjellman turned around and told us to read a good book, given how much time there was to wait. Well, I didn't have to wait until the next rehearsal to bring a book; I always carried one with me. So, I started to 'read' my *ordbok*."

"You read your *ordbok*?" It was now Karl Arvid's turn to look incredulous. "What do you mean you read your *ordbok*? Just started at page one and read the whole thing?"

"*Nei*," I smiled. "I just opened to a page at random and started to memorize all the words on that page. It was one of the ways I use to learn *norsk*. It just happened to be page 272."

"You mean..." Karl Arvid began.

"That's right," I interrupted. "It just happened that the one page I memorized had '*nøste*' on it."

"And everyone in the school..."

"...thinks I know the whole *ordbok*," I finished his thought.

-27-
Å Gå På Ski

As winter drew toward its end, I broke the language barrier. I spent large amounts of time in the fall and the winter working on my *norsk*. For the first few weeks of school, I spent one class period a day concentrating on whatever the teacher said. By the end of September, I had graduated to understanding perhaps 10%. But by December, I understood most of what the teachers said and by February I didn't really think about it at all: I was just a teenage Norwegian going to school. I still didn't understand much of what Andreassen said, but I learned early on that none of the other kids in my class did either.

The symbols of breaking the language barrier were my pocket *ordbok* and my pocket mirror. For days at the start of school I was known as "the American with the sign." After the baseball game in my classroom, I was known as the "American with the sponge." Throughout my entire year in Tromsø I was known as the "American with the *ordbok*" and the "American with the mirror." I always carried both of them in my back pocket. The *ordbok* came in handy at the *Bragerevy* rehearsals and page 272 helped to enhanced my linguistic reputation.

The *ordbok* was benign; the mirror was an object of fear. Everyone knew I had it and everyone feared I would use it. I would be walking Storgate, talking with someone. I would often say a word my friend couldn't understand. He or she would ask me to repeat it; I would repeat it; the person would indicate that I had mispronounced the word; the person would pronounce it correctly; the person gasped in horror at his or her mistake. Out came the mirror. I made my friend repeat the word correctly over and over again. I would do the same, doing my best to mimic exactly his or her pronunciation. All the while, I was looking at my mouth in the mirror, up at my companion's mouth, back at my mouth in the mirror, and so on until we were both satisfied that I got it. I didn't care where I was or with whom; I was determined to speak without an accent.

Lørdagkveld. Saturday evening. Because we went to school on Saturday mornings, the weekend social life was relegated to one evening:

lørdagkveld. February 24, 1962, wasn't a particularly special *lørdagkveld*. It was, perhaps, a little busier than usual, but not that much.

The evening started with the last presentation of the *Bragerevy*: a special, shortened version we put on at the Teachers' College. Not having performed in almost seven weeks, we were just a little rusty…perhaps a lot rusty. At least it was only an hour long, with no intermission.

Afterwards, I walked back to school to join a *russefest* in progress. That was the only *russefest* all year at the *gymnas*. Called the *grisefest*, or the pig party, it was a special *fest*, related to *russ* traditions, which was why it was at the *gymnas*. All year long, we *russ* wore little red *russ* hats pinned to our coats to indicate to the world (or at least the people of Tromsø) that we were *rødruss*. There was a tradition for *russ* to wear small pig pins attached to those small *russ* hats. For some reason, it was necessary to have a special *grisefest* for the *russ* to get their pigs. I assumed that the *russ* simply looked for any handy excuse to have a *fest*, even one at school. The *fest* went from 8:00-12:00 PM, although the *russ* who were in the *Bragerevy* didn't get there until about 10:00. We got our pigs and danced a bit (there was no drinking allowed in the *gymnas*).

I was with Lillian; we were an item. That meant we spent a lot of time together at the *fest*, but we were not with each other exclusively. That was pretty much the case for all the "couples" among the *russ*—Arnulf and Randi, Gunnar and Erika, Knut and Bitten—although there weren't that many couples. I danced with Lillian more than I danced with any other girl, but I danced with other girls more than I danced with Lillian.

Lillian and I left the *fest* at midnight and headed off toward another *fest* at Harald's house. His parents had already gone to bed; they must have stuck cotton balls in their ears if they were able to sleep through the raucous noise we made. We danced to records played loud enough to push the cotton balls out of any ears. We sang songs at full tilt: traditional Norwegian folk-songs and traditional *russ* drinking songs. The drinking was as extensive as at any *kafé russefest*; I genuinely feared for the Larsen's furniture and carpets. It was so wild that one of the boys took a bath in the middle of the *fest*.

But it wasn't what Lillian and I wanted, so we headed on down the road to a third *fest*. That one was a much smaller affair: just six of us, including Gunnar and Erika and Arnulf and Randi. We talked and ate *smørbrød*.

"Can you get *geitost* in America?" Lillian asked me.

"I doubt it," I answered.

"*Du* Pipe," Gunnar looked genuinely concerned. "What are you going to do without your *geitost*?"

"And Solo," Erika began, "what will you do if you have to go back to drinking that awful Coca Cola instead of our delicious Solo?"

"Maybe you'll just have to stay with us in Tromsø," Lillian suggested.

"What about my poor parents?" I asked rhetorically.

I Was a Teenage Norwegian

"From what I understand," Lillian said, "you weren't all that pleasant a son when you left. Maybe they won't mind if you don't come back."

"I keep forgetting," Arnulf added. "I keep thinking Pipe is the Pipe he is now, not the Pete he was when he first got here. If I were your parents, I wouldn't want that Pete back, either."

"But that's not who they'll be getting back," I argued.

"But they don't know that," Randi interjected.

We slow-danced to records and made out. Pretty typical for a small *fest* from 2:00-4:00 AM.

At about 4:00 AM I walked Lillian home. From the *fest*, it took almost forty-five minutes, but walking was so normal and natural for me by then I hardly noticed how long it took.

"Do you think much about going back to America?" Lillian asked, holding my hand.

"I think about how little time I have left here," I answered.

"But do you think about what it will be like at home?"

"I'm at home here."

"No." I felt her wise smile through the darkness. "I meant, what it will be like when you're with your parents back in your American home."

"Not really. I'm too happy here and thinking about leaving makes me too sad to think about America."

"But you must be happy to be going home," Lillian insisted.

"It's too difficult to think about."

On my way home to Balsfjordgate, I dropped in on Gunnar again, unannounced. We cooked fried eggs and bacon and ate them Norwegian style: cut a slice of bakery bread, placed it on a plate, placed the bacon on top of the bread and the eggs on top of the bacon, and ate the preparation with a knife and a fork. There we were in his kitchen at 4:30 in the morning, looking out the window at the darkness, eating our *frokost* and talking like friends who had known each other all their lives. It would have been a more special moment if Gunnar hadn't been his usual dead drunk self. He passed out by 5:00, I washed the dishes, and left. It was only a little more than a half hour's walk to my house from Gunnar's, so I was home by 6:00 AM...well before anyone was even up!

By March, I was counting my remaining months in Tromsø. Not because I wanted my year to end; quite the contrary. I wanted to savor every minute. But I knew the year was slowly coming to an end, and I found myself thinking constantly about how close that end was coming. In March, it was still months away, and I thought in terms of months. But months would not last long as the currency of time. Less than four months to go. With less than four months to go, I was reminded of the letter I wrote to my parents at the end of my voyage on the SEVEN SEAS. Its mixture of accurate and inaccurate projections was particularly relevant as I felt my year coming to its end.

June 17, 1961

Dear Mom and Dad,

We are now approaching the end of the beginning...and we shall arrive in Rotterdam tomorrow morning a little ahead of schedule. I guess I might as well go out on a limb a little and try to explain to you, my parents, what I will try to do and what I will hope for this coming year. I will be candid and not hold back one thought, not even where sex is concerned. We all know each other fairly well so that we can talk about such subjects, don't we, Mom?

Naturally, my first obligation is to represent myself in a manner that I will be proud of. Most people would rather have me say in a manner that God would be proud of, but I still do not feel that I belong in a group with the theists. And this time, I will make a sincere effort to show all parts of me. I feel it would be as disastrous to show these people merely the serious side of my character as it has been to show this group of AFSers the lighter side, and I will try to steer away from either extreme.

I had begun a simple "Hello. Good morning. How are you?" campaign at Staples this year and I think it will be pretty easy to continue that in Norway.

I will try to live my life at my new home in a way that is much like my life in Westport; in other words, I will try to be helpful in making my bed and doing the dishes (naturally, only if things like these are actually done by the Norwegian kids themselves). And possibly an experience such as this will make me all the more helpful to Mom when I get back.

I am realizing more and more the effect that Sue has on me, for I have done absolutely nothing sexually this trip (you both must realize that sex for me is necking and making out, nothing more). Maybe I have never told you that Sue is very dogmatic in these matters and she will NEVER make out with or kiss a boy unless she feels very strongly about him. And she has begun to infiltrate me with her ideas, and I think I am glad she has. Therefore, I feel that I will be able to act in this same manner in Norway, at least I am hoping that I can (that is a pretty trite statement by now) and that I will have no trouble in controlling whatever impulses may invade me.

As I mentioned once before, I am becoming a little less of a pessimist and truly thinking more positively, sometimes even to such a degree that I think I fulfill the responsibilities that I myself have undertaken. But no more of this; now you know a little more about me, your own son.

Give my love to everyone and keep what remains for yourselves. I am well and not too moody and I think of you when I can imagine what you are doing and how you are feeling. I am looking forward to this year that is still unknown.

As much love as I have,
Pete

Less than four months to go in my year in Norway and not one mention of the one sport most closely associated with that country: skiing. Although there was snow in Tromsø since October, by the time there was enough snow on the ground for skiing (late November), *mørketida* had arrived. Skiing wasn't much fun in the dark, and it was even less fun to *learn* how to ski in the dark. But by late February, there was plenty of snow and some daylight, and by March, I was almost as skillful as a normal Norwegian three year old.

The first step in the process was the purchase of skis and boots. In America, I would have gone with my parents; in Tromsø, I went with my friends. One day after school, toward the end of February, Jorunn made it clear to me what was next on my teenage Norwegian agenda.

"I think," she announced, "it's time for Pete to get a pair of skis."

"Definitely," Arnulf agreed.

"I don't even have any money," I said.

"Where is your account?" Jorunn asked.

"At the Post Office," I said.

"No problem," Arnulf chimed. "We'll get you fitted and we can walk to the Post Office while they put the bindings on."

As we walked down the hill toward Storgate, I remembered the one time I had skied in America. My grandmother had a small house in North Conway, New Hampshire, and she had invited our family to visit for a week during the winter school vacation when I was fifteen. None of us kids had skied before, and we all took lessons on the "bunny hill." We weren't alone; lots of other kids my age were taking lessons. By the end of the first day I was able to take the rope-tow up the bunny hill myself and ski down without hurting myself (but not without falling). Within another day, I had graduated to the next hardest hill, and by the middle of the week I was taking the T-bar up the "regular" mountain and making it down the easiest trails all by myself. I wasn't great, but I more than managed. I didn't love it, but I did enjoy it.

I felt I knew what to expect when Jorunn, Arnulf, and I walked into the sports store on Storgate. But I didn't see what I expected. I expected wide skis, and all the skis I saw were narrow. I expected huge, elaborate bindings, and all I saw were bindings with a small elastic wire and a locking mechanism. And I expected monstrous boots in which it was impossible to walk, and all I saw were small boots (not much bigger than regular shoes) with a narrow indentation at the back of the heel for the elastic wire.

"You look surprised," Arnulf said as he pulled out skis for me to look at. "Haven't you been skiing before?"

"*Ja*," I answered. "I went skiing for a week two years ago. But none of this looks familiar."

Arnulf looked puzzled; I had been skiing but the skis didn't look familiar. Jorunn, who had been in America, understood at once.

"You went downhill skiing?" she asked.

"Of course," I said, in an inexcusable, yet understandable, fit of cultural parochialism.

"We don't do downhill skiing in Tromsø," Jorunn explained. "We do cross-country skiing."

"But skiing is skiing," I continued naively. It was like telling an Eskimo that there was only one kind of snow.

"Not at all," Jorunn explained patiently. "We have slalom, downhill, cross-country, and even ski-jumping. All we do in Tromsø is ski-jumping and cross-country, and I don't think you're ready for the jumping!"

Two weeks later I did, in fact, get an opportunity to see a ski-jumping competition and Jorunn was right; I wasn't ready for that. A group of us from school went on a Saturday afternoon in mid-March while there was still a modicum of light. There was a rather steep hill and a rather large ski jump built off the hill. The competitors climbed up the hill holding skis even wider than I was used to in America. They came racing down the jump and flew through the air for what felt like an endless amount of time. They landed, knees bent, on the skis as if what they did was nothing at all out of the ordinary.

Eventually, Jorunn, Arnulf, and the salesperson picked out what I needed: a pair of blue, wooden, cross-country skis, two bamboo poles, a strange-looking elastic metal binding, and a pair of ankle-height boots. It all came to KR100, an entire month's spending money from AFS. We walked over to the Post Office where I had my bank account. I loved my red *postsparebank* (Post Office Savings Bank) book, with its little colored stamps representing my deposits.

I took out KR100, walked back to the sporting goods store, handed the money over to the salesperson, hoisted the skis onto my shoulders, and walked home...feeling very Norwegian.

I Was a Teenage Norwegian

The next day, Tom gave me my first lesson in our driveway. It was as if I had never been skiing before. I could barely stand up. The skis were so narrow; being made of wood, they appeared too inflexible. Standing beside Tom (who looked as if he had been born on skis), my feet felt as if they were constantly coming out of my skis, which they were. The front of each boot was locked into the binding, but the rear of my boot was attached only by the weird-looking elastic metal loop, which meant the heel of my foot kept coming off the ski.

"My foot keeps coming off my ski," I complained to Tom.

Tom looked carefully at my boots and bindings, checking to make sure everything was attached correctly.

"*Nei*, it's not," he said after careful examination. "Everything's fine."

There was no reason to argue with a fourteen year old real Norwegian. Both of us, unfortunately, were right. My foot kept coming off, but not more than it was supposed to.

For about an hour, Tom did everything he could to help me. By the end of the hour, I had made it out of the driveway onto to Balsfjordgate. To the right of our house, Balsfjordgate dropped steeply going down toward the water; to the left, Balsfjordgate went straight and flat for a while, and gradually downhill. On that Sunday, left was my only realistic option.

Tromsø had its advantages and disadvantages as a place for a teenage Norwegian to learn to ski. The main benefit was that I could walk into the garage, put on my boots and skis, grab my poles, and head out the door onto the "slopes." I could ski from our house, along Balsfjordgate, all the way to the *sykhus* and back again...as often as I wished. What few cars appeared on the street were well aware of the kids skiing there and drove slowly and observantly. There was no need to get in a car, drive five hours, pay lots of money for lift tickets, and wait forever in lines. Tromsø provided instant skiing.

There was one major disadvantage to learning to ski in Tromsø: I was the only person in town over the age of two who didn't already know how to ski. On Sundays, I would see parents walking one year old babies with skis on. The child was between the parents, each parent holding a hand, and the three of them walked and skied down the street together. I would literally be out on Balsfjordgate practicing with three- and four-year olds who were so much better than I was, that they thought my inability to ski was about the funniest sight they had ever seen in their still short lives. The falls and spills I could take; they were part of the learning experience. What was harder to endure was the laughter of kids who couldn't read or write but could ski circles around me.

By the end of March, I practiced *bak om meieri*, behind the dairy. The town's only dairy was only a two or three minute walk/ski from our house. When I had mastered Balsfjordgate, I began to ski over *bak om meieri* and practice with the "big kids," those kids in our neighborhood who were between the ages of eight and twelve. The little kids on Balsfjordgate thought I was the funniest event they had seen since the circus; the big kids thought I was beneath contempt. They weren't exactly mean; they were disdainful. They let me practice with them, but their attitude was somewhere between showing off their skills and pretending I didn't exist. I didn't let it bother me. I had spoken *norsk* when about all I could do was mutilate the language. I had gone to *danseskolen* not knowing (or remembering) a step. My exchange student shield protected me from just about any form of embarrassment, and it certainly protected me from the disdain of eight to twelve year olds. But I did marvel at what they could do on their skis. They would build a two or three meter snow mound and jump off it. I could see how some of them, at least, would be up on the real ski jumping hill within a few years. My agenda was to learn and to polish my few skiing skills...which I did, alone in the midst of a group.

As had happened one day in the fall, when the principal had given the entire school a half-day off to go climb a mountain, in the winter he gave us a half-day off to go skiing. I went home, put on my skis, grabbed my poles and mittens, and made it all the way back to the *gymnas* all by myself. Within ten or fifteen minutes, almost all of the *russ* had assembled and we started skiing on the roads, up the hills toward the top of Tromsøy. Even though I had lived higher up on the island when I had lived with the Norbyes, I had never spent much time there, and never near Prestvannet, the large lake on top of the center of the island. In 1962, Tromsø was still a small town on a bigger island, and much of the island was empty of houses and wooded. That was where we *russ* headed.

"Pete," Gunnar said to me as we began walking/hiking/skiing across Prestvannet, "you've gotten pretty good at this." He had heard that I had never used cross-country skis before coming to Tromsø.

"*Takk*," I said, huffing and puffing and doing my best to keep up with him and the others.

"But I think," Franck said, "Pete will have to go with the girls."

Now, ordinarily, that was music to my ears. Even though they were *russ* girls, and not *småpiker*, I rarely gave up an opportunity to spend my time with the girls. But Franck, friend that he was, hadn't suggested this for my benefit; he was suggesting that I wasn't strong *nok* to keep up with the boys. He was not only right about that; I had trouble keeping up with the girls.

It wasn't simply a matter of strength; it had more to do with skill, experience, and stamina on skis. I did the best I could, but I couldn't keep up with the girls, who were, luckily, more patient and willing to slow down to let me catch up.

"How are you doing?" Lillian asked, as she lagged behind the others.

"I...." It was difficult talking in between all the huffs and puffs. At least I had come so far as to be able to huff and puff in *norsk*.

"You look like you know what you're doing," Lillian continued.

"*Æ e' ikkje så dum som æ se' ut*," was about all I could manage. At least I could still joke.

"Take a break," Lillian suggested, stopping herself.

"What about the others?" I asked.

"The girls will wait for us," Lillian said. "We're better company than the boys, anyway."

Part of the problem was that I fell most of the time, particularly on even the smallest of downward inclines. It was fun swooshing down, but I had no control whatsoever. Since I followed in the skisteps of the girls, I had it easier on flat ground; my skis always went in the paths that they had made for me. Coming downhill, however, I could never get my skis out of those ruts, which made it difficult to stop. Luckily, there was always my butt, which was what I generally used for stopping.

That *skitur* was a breakthrough experience . In some ways it was analogous to the hour-long conversation I had with Jorunn at the Román house the day before school started. I had been working on my *norsk* for two months. I listened a lot and spoke a lot, but always in small, narrowly defined ways. Then Jorunn and I talked for an hour, in real sentences...a real conversation. That was a linguistic breakthrough for me. For the month prior to that first *skitur*, I had worked on my skiing. I watched others do it and did a lot myself, but always in small, narrowly defined ways, in our driveway, on Balsfjordgate, *bak om meieri.* Then that first *skitur:* two hours, on the move always (except when I was on my butt)...real skiing. That was a skiing breakthrough.

Throughout March and April, I went skiing all the time: after school, on weekends, with my friends, with my family. At Easter, our entire family went to our *hytta* on Kvaløya. We drove to the western part of Tromsøy, took the ferry to Kvaløya, and then drove a bit more. We spent almost the whole week at the *hytta*, as did many of my friends and their families at theirs. By then, the sun was out twelve hours a day, and skiing in bright sunlight was a special treat.

All of that, it turned out, was just preparation for my marathon. On the last weekend of our Easter vacation, we returned home early so that I could go on a serious *skitur* with a number of *russ* friends. We were driven across Tromsøbrua then north along the coast. Our task: to ski back home. I had no sense of distance, but I was with friends and we just did it. Coming downhill was more fun by this time: I hardly ever fell and I enjoyed the brief exhilaration that the speed brought. The cost, however, was steep...as steep as the hills we had to climb from the bottom of our downhill sprints. Up and down, through the woods we trudged and hiked. I was so pleased with myself, being able, more or less, to keep up with everyone, girls and boys. I was a part of the group, a teenage Norwegian, just another *russ* out for a spectacular *skitur* along the northern Norwegian coast to end another Easter vacation.

After five hours of that heavy-duty exercise, we skied across Tromsøbrua, up (but not down) Storgate, and I eventually made my way home to the comfortable living room on the second floor of Balsfjordgate 43.

"How was it?" *mor* asked as I fell dramatically into her chair in the living room.

"Great," I said, still huffing and puffing. "It was great. I kept up with everybody; nobody had to wait (often) for me."

"We'll be having *middag* in about half an hour," *mor* said.

The *skitur* was fabulous, but it felt good in that chair, too. I hadn't realized how tired I was as long as I was still on the skis; now that I was off my feet, I realized how sore I was. I hadn't ever exerted myself so fully and for so long in my entire life. I certainly deserved a half-hour's rest.

"*Værsågod å spise,*" *mor* said, inviting me to eat.

"*Takk,*" I said, starting to get up. And that was as far as I got: starting to get up. I never finished getting up; I never even got close. My legs were like rubber and they remained that way for close to five hours. I *sove middag* during and after *middag*, right in that chair. I drank *kaffe* and ate after-dinner cakes in that chair. I ate *aftens* in that chair. It was the only time in the seven months I lived at Balsfjordgate 43 that I ever sat in *mor's* chair, and I sat in it all evening. I finally got enough strength in my legs to get up, walk over to the stairs, down the stairs, into my room, and into my bed. It wasn't until I awoke the next morning that I could walk and move in a way approximating normal. Five hours on skis and five hours recovering in *mor's* chair.

Less than four months to go.

-28-
Narviktur

I loved Tromsø. I loved my life there; I loved all those parts of me that I had rarely expressed before I got to Tromsø; I loved being there. Although I knew I would be returning to Westport, my family, and America, there was a part of me that never wanted to leave Tromsø.

At the same time, I wondered frequently how typical Tromsø was and how "Norwegian" my time in Tromsø was. Although my life in Tromsø was dramatically different from my life in Westport, there was a part of me that felt the difference was as much the difference in the sizes of the two towns as it was the difference in the two cultures.

I yearned to visit other places in Norway, to get a better perspective on Tromsø. Unfortunately, independent trips were out-of-bounds to AFSers. I could travel with my family, which I had done occasionally: with the Románs to northern Finland to a track-and-field competition and with the Thyholdts to their *hytta* on Kvaløya. I was allowed on one long trip, to Harstad to see the Norwegian Speedskating Championships, because there were adult chaperones, thus satisfying an AFS rule. I was even allowed to spend weekends with other *russ* at their *hytter*, but I was never allowed a trip by myself...until March, when I was allowed to travel to Narvik.

Narvik was the nearest town to Tromsø. It was south of Tromsø; there wasn't much north of us. It was about 250 kilometers away. On the autobahns of Germany, most cars could have covered that distance in two hours...or less. But there were no super highways in Northern Norway; there were no highways in Northern Norway; there were no paved roads in Northern Norway; on some parts of the trip, there were no roads at all. There was a bus from Tromsø to Narvik and the ride took a little over six hours.

"Do you have everything?" *mor* asked me, as I finished packing the second of two small bags.

"*Mor*," I sighed, "I'm just going away for a week." Which meant, to me, that I hardly needed to take anything at all. Narvik was on the coast, like Tromsø, which meant it was relatively warm (relative, that is, to its latitude), but the temperature still wouldn't get above freezing and there was no need for two sets of clothes, one warmer than the other. The Norwegian rules I had acquired for changing clothes were quite different from those I was used to in Westport:

shirt	once a week
socks	once a week
underpants	once a week
sweater	once every 3 weeks
pants	once every two weeks
shower	once a week

The way I figured it, I didn't need to bring anything except my toothbrush, my comb, and my electric razor. But *mor* was *mor*, and I took as much as I could so she would feel better.

By the time I finished my extensive packing and walked out into the hall, *far* had come down to join *mor* to wish me well on my journey.

"You've got everything?" he asked.

"More than everything," I responded.

"You have all the addresses and phone numbers?" *mor* asked, as only a mother could. I figured I was allowed to go on that trip in large part because I had the names and addresses of somewhere close to half the population of Narvik. *Mor* was from Narvik and still had relatives living there, including her *søster* and my four Narvik cousins. There was Les Rhea, the closest the American AFSer to Tromsø. And there were Román relatives, and Norbye relatives, and the list was endless. One of my bags was for clothes; the other bag had all the addresses and telephone numbers.

"*Ja, mor*," I said tolerantly, as only a teenager could say to his mother.

"I hope you enjoy yourself," *far* said, silently slipping something into my hand. I snuck a glance: a KR10 bill. I was completely floored.

It wasn't the money itself that took me by surprise. My AFS allowance was KR100 a month, so even KR10 wasn't that much money. It wasn't the money that was so significant; it was the symbolism of the action.

The Thyholdts were my family. I had felt a part of the family almost immediately. *Mor* was a mother to me; Tom was my brother. *Far* was *far*, but he never showed any emotion. He talked with me, listened to me, argued with me, laughed *with* and *at* me...but he never showed any emotion. Until he slipped that KR10 into my hand.

From that moment on, I was his son. He loved me as a son, and I knew it. No words ever passed between him and me that day, and no words expressing feelings or emotion ever passed between us. But he had shown me he loved me as a son, and I knew it; I felt it. Because he was never overt, never explicit, I never knew if he knew I knew; I never felt that he felt I felt. But none of that mattered because I knew what I knew and I felt what I felt. Everything was different for me from that moment on, and everything remained different throughout the rest of my year with the Thyholdts. Everything was different for me from that moment on and every feeling I had for my *far* remained with me until I said good-bye to him on his deathbed over twenty-five years later. Everything was different for me from that moment on and every feeling I had for *far* I still have today: I was his son and I loved *far*.

Of course, I didn't mind getting the KR10.

It was late Friday afternoon and the bus left from the *sentrum*. *Far* had offered to drive, but I preferred to walk. With one bag in each arm, I walked out the front door, down the driveway, and along Balsfjordgate toward the *sentrum*. I arrived at the bus with ten minutes to spare. There really wasn't a bus station, as such. The buses simply waited at the *torvet*, the town square. The *torvet* was right on the water, and fishing boats docked there to sell their daily catch. In summer, people sold fresh vegetables. In early March it was still too cold; there were only buses. I threw my two bags in the baggage area underneath the back of the bus, found a window seat, and we were off.

"So, Pete," the woman across the aisle said to me as we approached Tromsøbrua, "who are you visiting in Narvik?"

"Family," I answered.

"Román or Thyholdt?" she asked.

I didn't even know the woman, and she knew who I was. She knew who I was, she knew where I was going, she knew more about my family (my families, actually) in Narvik than I did.

"Tante Maria," I said.

"Of course," the woman smiled. "Per must be about your age. Have you ever met him?"

"*Nei*," I responded. "I don't think so." Don't think so? I didn't even know who she was talking about.

"You'll like him. He's an interesting boy. Well, you must remember me to Tante Maria. Just tell her you talked to *fru* Henrickson on the bus to Balsfjord; that's where I get off. She'll remember me."

Most of the first hour of the trip was along the coast...along Balsfjord, actually. I had gotten a sense of Norwegian *fjords* on the *hurtigruten* ride up from Bodø in the summer: steep, sheer mountains coming directly down into the sea. From the water, the *fjords* were spectacular. From the bus, even in the darkness, they were equally magnificent. In most places, there was perhaps a 100-200 meter buffer of reasonably flat ground, on which people could farm. But the farther away from the coast we got, the steeper the mountains and the buffer zone of flat ground virtually disappeared. There were no paved roads in Northern Norway and the more into the interior we drove and the more steep the mountainsides, the more exciting the roads became.

"Lyngen," the bus driver announced, stopping the bus in front of a *kafé* alongside the road. I couldn't see any other element of the town. "Half an hour." I had been on the bus for about an hour and a half and I was ready to stretch my legs and fill my stomach.

Everyone piled out of the bus into the *kafé*, which looked similar to those in Tromsø: a glass-enclosed counter with all the *smørbrød* and cakes on display and tables and chairs scattered throughout a single, large room. Women were behind the counter ready to serve.

"*Værsågod*," one of the women said to me, smiling.

"*Geitost og Solo*," I replied.

"*Solo?*" she asked, pointing to the orangish yellow soda bottle on the shelf behind her.

"*Jada*," I answered. "*Bare Solo er Solo.*" Only Solo is Solo, I repeated the advertisement for my favorite orange soda I had seen in the magazines and heard on the radio. I felt proud of my ability to make jokes in *norsk*, even bad jokes.

I went outside after I finished my snack and stood around with a number of the other passengers. *Fru* Henrickson had already left the bus back in Balsfjord...the town, not the *fjord*.

"Are you enjoying your trip?" one of the men asked me.

"*Ja*," I answered. "It's beautiful, even in the darkness. Especially Balsfjord."

"Have you been into the interior before?" he asked me again.

"Last summer. A couple of times."

"But not in the winter?"

"*Nei*. Not in the winter."

"Well, then," the man continued, "what do you think the temperature is outside now?"

To be honest, I hadn't thought about the temperature. I hadn't noticed much difference between the temperature there and what I was used to in Tromsø. I didn't get what that man was driving at, but I paused and *felt* the temperature as best as I could. I still didn't feel any difference from what I had become used to.

"It feels about normal to me," I said. "I guess it's about 5 cold degrees."

Temperature was measured in Celsius in Tromsø and all over Norway. Freezing was 0°C. Anything colder wasn't referred to as "minus" degrees, the way we were used to in America. Norwegians called "minus" degrees "cold" degrees. Five cold degrees was -5°C, or about 25°F. That was the temperature Tromsø settled into, day and night...or night and night as I thought of it during the *mørketida* of winter.

"5 cold degrees, you say?" The man looked at me with a broad smile on his face. He walked me over to the side of the *kafé* and showed me a small wall thermometer attached at eye level near the corner of the building.

"Looks a little closer to forty cold degrees to me," he said, pointing at the thermometer.

I couldn't believe that, but I looked at the thermometer and that's what it showed: 40°C. I had never experienced -40°C but I knew a great deal about it, because it was the only temperature where Celsius and Fahrenheit were the same. Which meant that I was standing outside, in a one-*kafé* town, 150 kilometers north of the Arctic Circle in -40°F temperature.

I Was a Teenage Norwegian

"But it doesn't feel any colder than in Tromsø," I remarked to the man. "In fact, when I walk home and the wind is blowing, I feel much colder than I do now."

"Tromsø is a *wet* cold," the main explained patiently and pleasantly. "When the wind blows off the sound, the cold is even wetter. Here, in the interior, it's dry and the cold is a dry cold. The temperature is much lower, but it doesn't feel colder. I thought you might be interested."

I certainly was. Every day I learned something new, either about Tromsø, Norway, or myself. Who would have thought I would learn something about the weather on a bus trip to Narvik? And my learning on that trip was far from over.

"Before you get back on the bus," the man said, "take a look over there, toward the mountain. *Nordlys.*"

Nordlys? The newspaper, I thought to myself as I turned my head. A faint light low in the northwest drew my attention. It was just above the mountains and was like a green phosphorescent band. It just sat there, or moved very slowly. It died out, but that was not the end of *nordlys*—the Northern Lights—it was just the beginning. I had seen *nordlys* once before, briefly, on the Harstadtur. That was a prelude; this was an extravaganza.

A new band appeared. It moved from the northwest, where I first saw it, higher up in the sky. It curled, and the curl floated along the band from west to east like a wave. A new band was lit up in the northwest and moved upward, And another band. Waves and curls were moving along the bands. Was there a red color there, too? The light was getting stronger and I could see only the brightest stars through the bands and arches of the northern lights.

Then, within a few minutes, the sky exploded. Rays of light shot down rapidly, forming bands like drapes that spread all over the sky, reminding me of curtains flickering in the wind. The curtains were still green, but now they were decorated with a violet and red trim at the lower and upper ends. The bands were moving and undulating all over the sky, disappearing and forming again as new rays shot down from space. Above my head I could see rays going out in all directions. The mountains in the background were illuminated by the light and energy from space.

The bands spread out, getting weaker; they finally dissolved into a diffused light all over the sky. I couldn't see any more bands or arches, but I discovered that the sky background looked grayish green and I couldn't see many stars. The lighting reaching us from all directions was so strong that I could easily see details around me: the bus, the *kafé*, the people watching that display of *nordlys*. I looked carefully and it appeared that the clouds were being switched on and off, as though by an electric light switch, every five or ten seconds. And then it was over.

About half an hour from the *kafé* snack stop we came upon our first ferry. When we approached a ferry, the bus stopped and all of the passengers got off. The bus drove onto the ferry, with as many other cars as were there; there were never too many cars. Most of the ferries had a small space inside where people could sit on benches; one ferry was big enough to have a small *kafé* with *kaffe*, Solo, and cakes. But for me, it was standing outside that was the most enjoyable place.

Northern Norway must have been one of the world's most expensive places to build roads. Just coming from Tromsø to Narvik, we had driven alongside the ocean, climbed up and down mountains, and encountered *fjords*...which had to be crossed or driven around. Building bridges was not viable: the distances were much too long and the traffic much too sparse. Just think how long it had taken to build a bridge from the mainland to Tromsø, and there the distance was only a kilometer and the people crossing it numbered in the thousands per day.

"What about building the road around the *fjord?*" I asked the man standing next to me on the ferry.

"Take this ferry," he explained. "Do you know how far a road would have to go to avoid that ferry crossing?"

"It's too dark to see anything," I answered, "let alone the length of the *fjord.*"

"I don't know exactly, of course," he said, "but I would guess between 10-12 kilometers. And building a road alongside a *fjord* is no easy matter: cutting into the mountainside, removing the rocks, getting it straight and level under pretty difficult circumstances."

"But wouldn't it be worth it to shorten the trip?"

"That's a great deal of money to save an hour," he said.

"Personally," a woman behind us chimed in, "I wouldn't spend any money on roads to replace the ferries. I love the ferries, no matter how much more time they take."

And I had to admit, I loved the ferries, too. In fact, they were far and away my favorite part of the trip to Narvik...and the trip back from Narvik...and the trip to Harstad...and the trip back from Harstad. Riding the ferries was one of my most pleasurable and memorable experiences in Norway (of course, I never missed the last ferry of the day).

Most of the ferries were small: enough room for the bus and five or six cars. The biggest ferry still couldn't hold more than a dozen cars. I could walk around the cars, walk from one end of the ferry to the other, hug the side rails, or even stand at either the front or the back, always looking out over the water. Each time I took a ferry the feeling was a little different, depending on the time of day more than the weather or the temperature. When I took the ferries in the spring, it was during daylight and I could see everything around me clearly: the water, the roads, the mountains, the houses. But I still preferred riding ferries in the dark.

Most of the ferry rides on my Narviktur were in real darkness: stars but no moon. It was eerie hearing the water lap against the ferry, mixed in with the engine noises and the the sounds of the seagulls following us, ever hopeful that someone on board would throw them a scrap of anything. I couldn't *see* anything, but I felt I could *feel* everything: the history of the place, the seafaring mentality of the people, the overwhelmingness of nature. On the trip back to Tromsø, the moon was out during most of the ferry rides, and that was even better. There was enough light to see almost everything: the shoreline, the mountains silhouetted against the almost black sky, the white-caps the ferry made plowing through the semi-rough sea.

I felt as much at peace on these rides as I ever did at that point in my life. There was virtually no human sound; I felt completely alone. I was an almost Norwegian in the midst of a most Norwegian situation. I was an introspective seventeen year old, in both English and *norsk*, and those fer-ryboats and ferry rides were a kind of hallowed ground. Looking out over the water, feeling the hum and vibration of the boat, deep in my thoughts and myself, wallowing in my almost Norwegian-ness: for an atheist, it was damn near spiritual.

Our bus finally pulled into *Narviksentrum* late that evening and Les Rhea was there to meet me.

"How did the bus ride go?" she asked as I got my two bags out from under the bus.

"On the one hand, long," I answered, "and on the other hand, fantastic."

"Fantastic?" Les asked.

"*Nordlys*. The ferries."

"I couldn't stand the ferries," Les explain as we walked through *Narviksentrum*. "They made the trip so much longer when I came up to Tromsø with my family in October."

I smiled as we walked together, two American teenagers walking along in a small Norwegian coastal town more than 150 kilometers north of the Arctic Circle, talking to each other in passable *norsk*.

Les and I had so much in common, both coming to a faraway strange place that we hadn't chosen and whose language neither of us had spoken prior to our arrival. We were the same age, the same color, from more or less the same economic background. Yet we obviously saw some things in a quite different way. I felt I was coming off an almost-religious experience on the ferries, and Les just saw them as adding time to an already long trip.

"I've arranged for you to stay with another AFSer in Narvik," Les explained as we walked.

"I thought you were the only one," I joked.

"A *former* AFSer," she laughed when she realized I could joke in *norsk*. "Her name is Unni. Unni Larssen."

Les and I talked as we walked. Her *norsk* was good, but I thought mine was a little better. I spoke a little more quickly than she, but not as distinctly. It was a little difficult for me to be certain because I had never really heard myself talk in *norsk*.

"Pete," Les began as I took off my boots just inside the Larssen's front door, "this is Unni."

"*God dag*," I said, shaking her hand and nodding my head, in typical Norwegian fashion.

"I'll leave you now," Les said, "and meet you at school tomorrow morning. *Ha det* you two. *God natt.*"

"*God natt*," Unni said closing the door behind Les. "*Stig på*, Pete, and meet my family. This is my brother, Karl Erik, and this is my father."

"Thank you for having me," I said.

"It's our pleasure," Larssen said. "Would you like to *drikke kaffe*?"

"*Ja*," I answered.

"Can I have some, too?" Karl Erik begged. He was a little younger than Tom, just about as tall, with untypically dark hair...like his sister's.

"*Nei*, Karl Erik," Unni said pleasantly but decisively. "It's too late."

"Please," Karl Erik begged again.

"Off to bed. You'll get to see Pete again tomorrow."

I had assumed he just wanted to eat. Although I thought of myself as the unpopular Pete of Westport, most people I met in Norway saw me as the intriguingly strange Pete of America, and a Norwegian-speaking American at that. It always took me a little by surprise when I realized I was something of a celebrity; even by the end of the year, that reality never quite fit my self-image.

Unni went off to the kitchen and fixed the *kaffe* and *smørbrød*. She was about my height with almost jet-black, curly long hair. I found her exceedingly pretty, but in an un-Norwegian kind of way.

"How was your trip?" Larssen asked.

"Fantastic," I answered. "I saw *nordlys* for the second time, but this time was so explosive. I've never seen anything quite like it. And the ferries; I loved the ferries."

"A lot of people want the government to get rid of the ferries," Larssen commented. "They say it adds too much time to the trip. But I like them. I like their relaxing nature. Everyone now is in a hurry; I like to take my time."

"*Værsågod*," Unni said, setting the *kaffe* and *smørbrød* down on the table.

"Where were you in America?" I asked her, as she poured the *kaffe*.

"Oklahoma," she said, pronouncing the word with a slight midwestern accent.

"What was your year like?"

"It was great. I had a wonderful family. My sister was terrific. My parents were wonderful to me. I felt so at home. My school was great, too. I had so many friends and they were all so nice to me. My sister still talks to me about coming to visit me here in Narvik. It was such a wonderful year. I only hope your year in Tromsø will be as good for you as my year in Oklahoma was for me."

Larssen had already endeared himself to me with his comments on the ferries. He was a small, quiet man, basking now in the radiance of his daughter. The affection he had for her was spread all over his face.

The next morning, Unni put out the cheese, jams, and bread for *frokost*. Only Larssen prepared his *matpakke* for lunch since the three of us had only a half day of school on Saturday.

I Was a Teenage Norwegian

"Here's your *tran*," Unni pushed the bottle across the table to me. She was just like *mor*. As far as *tran* was concerned, Narvik was just like Tromsø.

I spent the morning at the *gymnas* in Unni's class. The school building was newer and one of our classes was in this seemingly huge (with hindsight, it was only large) European-style lecture room, the kind I had seen in the movies: a blackboard in the front, a lectern in front of it, and rows of seats on increasingly high levels. But other than those two differences, I found school in Narvik to be quite similar to the *gymnas* in Tromsø. We stayed in the same room (except for the science class in the lecture room) and the teachers came to us. There were ten-minute breaks between classes when everyone had to go outside, except the *russ*. Everyone stood up when the teacher entered the room. The students respected some teachers, and not others. Students were called upon to recite, and reciting in Narvik meant spitting back the book verbatim just as it did in Tromsø. I came to Narvik for perspective, and I got it.

After school, a group of us walked *til byen*. We didn't go to see the newsreels, but we did walk Storgate. But the "one-side-of-the-street" policy that was so strictly enforced in Tromsø wasn't the hard-and-fast law in Narvik.

"Do you want to see the iron ore?" one of the kids asked me.

"What do you mean, iron ore?" I asked.

"Come on. You cannot visit Narvik and miss the ore."

They took me to a part of town that had railroad tracks and cars. Although I knew the Norwegian railroad didn't go any farther north than

Fauske, the railroad cars in Narvik came from Sweden, not Norway. Narvik was the nearest port to large iron mines in northern Sweden, so the Swedes had built a railroad from Sweden to Narvik just to ship the ore. It was that industry, to a great extent, that made Narvik a richer and more expensive town. I noticed, for example, that hot dogs cost KR1,25 in Narvik while they only cost KR1 in Tromsø.

Unni cooked *middag* for the four of us, and I *sove middag* there just the way I did at home in Tromsø. I was certainly relieved that to *sove middag* was not merely a Tromsø custom.

Unni stayed home with her father and Karl Erik while Les and some of her friends picked me up. We started the evening at an *Unge Høyre* meeting, the "Young Rights." Norway has many political parties; *Høyre* was one of the non-socialist, conservative parties. Each of the parties had an *ung* section for youth who were not able to vote but wanted to participate in politics in some fashion. Karl Arvid Román had worked at the *Unge Høyre* office the previous summer. The meeting was boring, but I did get a chance to meet some other kids. Afterwards, we all went back *til byen*, walked their Storgate, and stopped in the *kafés* for *øl* (for them) and *brus* (for me).

"Did Unni tell you about her time in America?" Les asked me as she walked me back to the Larssen's.

"She sure did. What a great time she had."

"She didn't tell you what happened?"

"She just talked about how much she liked her family. And how everyone treated her so well."

"She didn't tell you she got sick?"

"*Nei.*"

"After about four months in Oklahoma," Les explained, "Unni got sick. I don't know what it was, but it was serious. She had to go into a hospital."

"She didn't mention anything like that. She just said how much she enjoyed everything."

"She ended up staying in the hospital for the rest of her year in America."

I was floored. Unni hadn't said a word to me. She hadn't mentioned anything about that. And she wasn't putting on an act; she was too sincere. There was no remorse for what she *hadn't* gotten in America, only joy for what she *had*.

"What about her mother?" I asked, having been too embarrassed to say anything to Unni directly. "Where is she? Unni does everything for her father and brother."

"No one told you?" Les asked with surprise.

"Told me what?" I asked.

"Her mother died just after Unni returned from Oklahoma. She died of cancer. Unni has had to take care of the household and finish *gymnas* all at the same time."

I Was a Teenage Norwegian

I went to Narvik for perspective. I wanted to get some sense of how I was doing with my *norsk* by comparing myself to Les. I wanted to get some sense of how typically Norwegian my school experience in Tromsø was by attending another school. I wanted to see if my Storgate experience in Tromsø was the same as Narvik's Storgate. I wanted to get a sense of how typically Norwegian my family life in Tromsø was. The trip was, in that sense, a success.

But I got much more than I bargained for. I saw love in *far* when he handed me the KR10. I saw the colorfully explosive *nordlys* light up the night sky. I saw more hairpin turns that I ever wanted to see again. I felt the ferries touch me in a most unexpected way. And I met Unni Larssen.

I met someone who, quite unlike me, could always (and, perhaps, only) see the best in others and the best in any situation. She spent almost eight months in a hospital in Oklahoma and all she could talk about were the four months she lived with her family and how wonderfully everyone treated her. If Les hadn't told me that her experience included illness, I never would have known. And I never would have known because Unni clearly didn't think of that part of her year in Oklahoma. She wasn't hiding anything from me; that part of her year was not what she treasured. And she came back to a dying mother and a life where she had to be *søster*, daughter, mother, and housekeeper all together. And never an angry word about her fate. She had a way of viewing situations positively. I had never met anyone like her.

For the two years between the time I returned to Westport, and when I made my first trip back to Norway in the summer of 1964, I continued to write to Unni once or twice a year, and she would always write back to me. We told each other about our lives at college (for me) and university (for her), our friends and family, that kind of thing. As my return trip to Norway approached, I wrote Unni that I was coming back and that I wanted to see her. I told her, as best I could in a *norsk* that was not used to expressing feelings, how impressed I was about the way she talked and felt about her AFS experience, how impressed I was at the way she took upon herself so many obligations, how special a person she was, how much I wanted to see her again, how much I wanted to be with her again. Unni was one of the most memorable people I had met in Norway seeing her again was one of the reasons I wanted to return. I didn't hear back from her.

Instead, I received a letter from Karl Erik, just a few days before I left for Norway. Unni had died. She had been sick with cancer off and on for the entire two-year period. She never mentioned anything to me, probably because she didn't think about her sickness...just the enjoyable experiences (which couldn't have been many) she had at university. Karl Erik told me that she had received my letter and reading it was one of the last things she did. I cried. I've never forgotten Unni Larssen.

Less than three months to go.

-29-
Søttendemai

As the end of the year approached, I became more and more aware of what had happened to me over the year. Sometimes the clearest place to see these changes was in my letters home. A mid-year letter and an end-year letter; a somber, introspective, self-reflective letter and a chatty, upbeat, almost playful letter.

December 15, 1961

Dear Mom and Dad,

I could not describe my present state in one word, but instead, it would be necessary to use two; for I am both happy and sad. So many times I realize the responsibilities resting upon my shoulders, and I realize my inadequacy to meet all of them successfully. And I do so many wrong things and there are so many things that I do not even know if I consider them kosher or not, that I cannot help but feeling a little blue and melancholy at times.

And I do miss home and all my friends...a very great deal. I'm not sure about my love (if any) for Sue, but I am positive as to my love for my family. And my inadequacy in the language here is such a disheartening thing at times that I am almost ready to give up and call it quits...for it just seems beyond my capabilities and abilities to master the language quickly enough and to my own satisfaction.

How lucky, in a way, I was not to know a great deal about this "other side" of AFS before I came; I might not have accepted. And, I certainly have spoken enough about all the good points: my ready acceptance, the happiness of the others here leading to my own happiness, a slow but steady change for the better in several respects. And with the coming of a fluency in norsk (if it is coming) an understanding and a real love for these people for what they are is sure to come...the possibilities are enormous. And, to be sure, the good solidly outweighs the bad (for I am happier than I am sadder).

But no matter; I know for certain that everything will turn out for the best and everyone concerned will be happy. Liz visited last week and she said she noticed a change in me from unknowing, undecided, and indefinite to just the opposite. And I, when looking at this paragraph and some of the first ones I wrote (say, from Montreal), can notice it, too. This

I Was a Teenage Norwegian

clean, healthy Norwegian atmosphere might indeed be rubbing off on me...it certainly might.

I won't even make a prophesy as to what will happen to me or what I'll do during the rest of the year. I've done some thinking, but it will definitely have to be changed anyway, and I'll just keep my ideas in my own head. I'm dissatisfied with what I'm saying, and when I am, I shut up. And so it is....

> Much, much love,
> Pete

den 15. mai, 1962

Dear Mom and Dad,

On Sunday, May 13th, Karen Mentzoni (daughter to mor's brother) was confirmed (she is 15), along with 170 others. In the evening (half 5) we went over to their house to eat the confirmation dinner. In one manner or another, we found things to do until midnight. We ate dinner from half 6 until half 7 and then talked until about half ten, when we ate aftens *of coffee and cake. We talked a little more and then played a game. The object of the game was guess how many people had sent greetings to Karen (either a card or a telegram). I won the small prize when I guessed 133; there were 143 in reality! By about half 12 I was ready to leave. I hadn't gotten much sleep the previous night (I had slept* hos *Gunnar) and I was dead tired.*

I had completely forgotten about my birthday but the others hadn't. When the clock struck 12, I was made to play Happy Birthday to You with my one-fingered technique on the piano and to go around shaking everyone's hand as I said takk, takk to their Gratulerer med Dagen *(Congratulations for the day, a phrase people here use for almost any occasion).*

I slept until half 12 the next day and I woke up feeling 18!! We had delicious fish cakes for dinner (my second choice, because there was no fresh halibut). I received a song played on the piano by Tom, a Tromsø pillowcover from Olemann, and a pair of sandals from mor og far. *We had a* russemøte *in the evening to plan the* russetog til søttendemai. *I came home to fresh-baked chocolate cake in the evening and whipped Tom in casino 14-0. That was the real high point of this day!!!!*

We had a couple of inches of snow-fall Saturday evening, but otherwise we expect Spring in a couple of weeks...or so.

> Much snow-white love,
> Pete

Søttendemai. May 17th. The Norwegian National Holiday. The July 4th of Norway. It was a truly momentous day, for three reasons. First, and most important, it is the year's most important day for Norwegian *russ.* Second, May 17th meant there were only six more weeks before I left Tromsø. Third, it was an anniversary for me, as well as for Norway: on May 17th, 1961, I heard I was going to Norway to spend a year in Tromsø.

Søttendemai formally began at 12:01 AM, and that was just about when it actually began for us *russ*. We were not about to miss even one minute of that day.

We gathered at the *gymnas* to prepare for the *søttendemaitog*, the May 17th parade. The preparations were similar, yet more elaborate than at Christmastime. As I walked into the art room at midnight, most of the *russ* were already there, working away. Gunnar was standing on a chair with a piece of wood under his feet and a saw in his hands, furiously cutting the stick to the proper length. Per Sparboe was next to him, having arranged his stick of wood across a table to make the sawing easier. Bengt Mikkelsen was bent over—not an easy feat, given his size—with paint in one hand and a paint brush in the other, working attentively on a colorful drawing of some sort or other on a big sheet of brown wrapping paper. Hans and Knut were helping someone adjust a face mask made out of burlap with two small metal plates for eyes.

"It's going to be a gas mask," Hans explained to me, sensing my ignorance.

I was a *russ* and I participated in everything the *russ* did: *juletog, søttendemaitog, russefest*, and whatever else was part of the *russ* tradition and experience in Tromsø. My lack of history as a teenage Norwegian meant that, although I did everything, I didn't necessarily know in advance what was involved in doing anything.

The *russ* planning the *søttendemaitog*, had decided upon certain humorous political statements the *russ* would make that year. Even in the *Bragerevy*, I was in a skit that had to do with the European Common Market. Although at midnight I still didn't know what the theme, or its various points, would be, I could see that a gas mask was to play an integral part in at least one of those points. And I thought I noticed a rocket in the making, too.

"Pipe," Elna Seim called to me. She was wearing a smock to protect her clothes as she painted a sign on one of the benches. "Are you here to help or just watch us work?"

"Can you use a hammer?" Ole Jens asked.

"*Ja*," I answered. "What do you think? I'm an American?" We had a running joke by that time of year as to whether I was an American or a Norwegian. They figured Norwegians could do everything and Americans nothing...thus my response.

For the next hour, I hammered into sign frames all of the sticks that Per, Gunnar, and others had sawed to (more or less) accurate lengths. I hammered together four pieces into a square perhaps a meter and a half wide by a meter deep. And then I attached a 2-3 meter stick down the middle, both for additional support and as a handle. I assembled eight or ten of these sign frames while others provided me the pieces and still others painted the actual signs which were then attached to the frames.

I Was a Teenage Norwegian

At the other end of the art room there were still other *russ* who were putting together costumes, although costumes weren't quite as important for that *tog* as they were for the *juletog*. I had already been told that most of the *russ* would wear their *søttendemai russ* outfit, but clearly some would be in costume. And, a final group was assembling some large structure. It looked like a rocket or a missile: long, cylindrical, with a pointed front end. I didn't even bother to ask; I knew the rest of the *russ* liked to surprise me as much as I enjoyed surprising them.

We finally finished at about 2:00 AM. After all that hard work, we needed a bit of food to sustain us through the rest of our "day." But first, came our *russ* uniforms. I walked home from the *gymnas* where *mor* had already laid out my outfit: She had sewn long, thin red stripes down the outer edge of the two legs of my gray slacks. It was like a garish tux; nothing subtle about *russ* red. She had also sewn a red Eiffel Tower on the upper right hand side of the back of my green sports coat. Tromsø had adopted for itself the nickname *nordensparis*, the Paris of the North. I could never figure it out, and no one ever explained it to me (or, perhaps, there was no real explanation, save for community pride or tourism). Next came my white shirt and a pretty *russ* red bow tie. I had never worn a bow tie before (nor have I ever worn one since), but all the *russ* boys wore one. Next came a red vest. A number of *russ* girls had sewn red vests for all of the *russ* boys; I buttoned up the vest and put on my green sports coat with my red Eiffel Tower on the back. Finally, came the red *russehua*, the official *russ* hat. The *russehua* was not to be confused with the *russelua* that the *russ* girls had knit for the *russ* boys during the winter.

The *russehua* was not an informal arrangement, as was the *russelua*; the latter were something we *russ* had decided to have, but the *russehua* were "official" *russ* attire. They were similar in size and shape to the more formal, black hats *russ* would wear at their graduation, except these were bright red. They were the same shape as the small *russ-hat* pins we had gotten at the *grisefest* and had adorned with our little pigs. They had a small, black, plastic brim and a long tassel coming out of the top. With my *russehua* on my head, I was definitely ready for *søttendemai*.

"You look very Norwegian," *mor* commented on the final product she saw before her. She had worked too hard on too much of that outfit not to stay up to see me put it all on for the first time. She had experienced *søttendemai* three times before; she knew the routine.

"Can you take a picture of me?" I asked *far*.

I walked out onto the garage roof, now clear of winter snow. I stood as upright as I could manage at 2:30 in the morning, in all my *russ* attire and holding a small Norwegian flag in my hands. We were still four or five days short of the *midnattsol*, but by 2:30 the sun was already visible again, providing all the light *far* needed to capture me in all my Norwegian glory.

Then I walked over to Gunnar's house. Even at that hour of the night/day, neighbors were hanging clean clothes out to dry in preparation for the day's festivities.

Brox, *fru* Brox, and Anna had arranged a "little something:" *smørbrød* of all sorts, *vaffler* with jam, *kaffe*, Solo (for me), and even chocolate cake. Since even 3:00 AM wasn't one of Norway's many official mealtimes, the Brox family could combine elements from both *frokost*, *kaffe*, and *aftens* as they saw fit. Most of my *russ* friends were there and already eating.

"You look very Norwegian," Anna Brox said as she handed me an open-faced *geitost smørbrød*.

"*Takk*," I said, both for the *smørbrød* and the compliment.

"Where's your *russehua*," Lillian asked me.

"Right here," I said, taking it off the table and placing it on my head.

"Do you know what the tassel is for?" she asked.

"*Nei*."

"We use it to mark how many nights we stay up," she explained, "between *søttendemai* and graduation. Every night you stay up the whole night you can tie a single knot in the tassel. Stay up two nights in a row, you can tie a double know in the tassel."

"We have about three weeks," Gunnar said, "and I expect many knots from you, Pipe."

"Are you guys all set," Franck bellowed. "We have work to do before the sun rises." A little Northern Norwegian humor.

Although I had understood our work at the *gymnas* was all for the *søttendemaitog*, apparently some of the posters were destined for buildings on Storgate. By the time we got to Storgate, some of the *russ* had been home and back again with ladders. Most of us watched while the more daring climbed the ladders and posted the signs on many of the buildings. On *søttendemai* there were many more, smaller signs than the single huge one we hung at Christmas. The first sign went up over Wilhelmsen's Book Store: *Ha det, gymnas. Ha det, bøker.* Bye, bye high school. Bye, bye books. Down the street we met the *grønnruss*, the Green Seniors from the *realskole.* They had hung up their own sign over Kaffistova, one of the more popular *kafés*: Next year it's our turn.

We saved our best and most elaborate sign for the *kino* where we spent all of our Saturday afternoons and many of our evenings. It was in the form of a movie announcement, which we pasted up over the real posters announcing real movies. Our film was entitled: *Høvdingen på Nordens Par(a)(d)isøya.* The translation was a bit awkward: The Chieftain from the North's Par(ad)is(e) Island. It starred Hansen, our assistant principal, playing himself in the main role and our beloved principal was the director. Pictures of those two and other teachers playing supporting roles were plastered throughout the poster. It may not have been Bergman, but it was pretty impressive.

"All right, boys and girls," Odd Johnson shouted as we put up our last poster. "The fun is over; it's time to get to work."

I followed along as we all walked down Storgate and up the hill back to the *gymnas.* There, as if by magic, appeared out of nowhere three, large *russ* red trucks.

"Climb aboard," Jorunn nudged me.

"No chance you might tell me what we're doing?"

"None at all," Jorunn just smiled.

"You'll find out soon enough," Lillian reminded me.

All sixty of us jammed ourselves standing up in the back of the three trucks. As we climbed up, we were given old-fashioned metal horns, which everyone started blowing before the trucks had even started on their way.

"Isn't this a little noisy?" I asked no one in particular. "Won't we wake people up?"

"That's the point."

"*Han e' ikkje så dum som han se' ut.*" A slight change: He's not as stupid as he looks.

"With brains like that, he must be Norwegian."

What we were doing was driving around the island waking up all of our teachers. As we made our way up toward the highest point on the island, I was amazed at how much snow was still on the ground. Storgate and Balsfjordgate were at sea level, and they were completely clear of snow. Even the *gymnas*, up thirty or forty meters, had no snow. The topmost point on the island couldn't have been much more than 100 meters above sea level, but there was still half a meter's worth of snow on the ground, although the roads were clear. First snow: October. First snow permanently on the ground: November. Still snow on the ground: May.

So there we were, sixty red-capped *russ* driving around the roads of Tromsø at 4:30 in the morning blowing our horns as loud as we could. If there was a detailed plan, I never could figure it out. As far as I could tell, we drove around, stopping at the first teacher's house we could find. It happened to be Sætter's house, a two-family house. I felt sorry for the other family, but perhaps they were used to it. The informal rule was that only the students who had that teacher that year could wake the teacher up; that meant us from 5GE. We climbed out of the truck and some of us huddled around the front door while others found a way to climb up on the balcony on the second floor (*russ* intelligence had discovered that Sætter's bedroom was on the second floor). We all stood blowing our horns frantically, as if we had another twenty teachers still to wake up. Sætter was hardly *våken* during History class; I didn't expect much of him that morning. He stuck his head out between the bedroom curtains and pretended to be *våken*.

"That's considered '*våken*' for Sætter," Arnulf shouted down from the balcony.

"Anything more would be out of character," Knut echoed.

We all climbed back up into the trucks and off we went to our next victim: Andreassen. His house sat alone up on a small hill, with a big picture window facing east, toward the mainland and the mountain. Both the English and the Math Lines had Andreassen in Norwegian; that made close to forty of us. We circled the house (as we had our Christmas tree) and danced around it, blowing our horns and encouraging Andreassen to join us. He didn't. He didn't join us and he didn't even acknowledge our presence.

"Sætter is asleep when he's *våken*," Arnulf said, "and Andreassen is in some other world. It's not surprising he's in another world when he's sleeping, as well."

"We heard," Jorunn explained, "that sometimes he simply goes to his *hytta* on *søttendemai* to avoid the *russ*."

"Whatever the case," Gunnar gathered us back into the trucks, "he gets no more of our valuable time."

The Engelsens had a smallish house with a balcony-like porch on the first floor. A number of us climbed up onto the porch and serenaded both Engelsen and *fru* Engelsen. Suddenly, Engelsen himself walked out the door onto the porch, resplendent in a silk bathrobe.

"*God morn*," he said in his typically cheery voice.

"*Morn. Morn. Morn.*" We all responded, sluggishly but equally cheerfully.

"And *velkommen*," Engelsen continued in good spirit. I was struck by how typical the response of each of the teachers was. Engelsen had always been my favorite and he came through with flying colors that morning.

The prize, however, went to Senum, a physics teacher that both the Natural Science and Math Lines had that year. I knew nothing about him and had no idea what to expect. He lived in one of the island's large apartment buildings. We certainly couldn't climb up on his balcony, let alone encircle his building with noisy dancers. We settled for staying in the trucks underneath his balcony and blowing our horns as furiously and loudly as we could. Suddenly, Senum appeared on his balcony, the one on the fourth floor with five small Norwegian flags decorating it. He was dressed in his Sunday best: suit, white shirt, and tie; and he returned our serenade, playing a lively tune on his trombone.

"*Frokost*," Gunnar shouted as we finally made it to the last of the teachers' houses by 6:00 AM. "We're already late."

The trucks returned us to the *skolegård* at the *gymnas*, we all piled out of the trucks and headed back down the hill (for the third or fourth time that "night") toward the restaurant, one of the few in the town. With sixty of us (and at 6:00 AM), we had the restaurant to ourselves. We were a little weary, but still in pretty lively spirits. We hadn't slept at all during the "night," and we had a full day ahead of us; we definitely needed a little sustenance. We ate a typical *frokost*: *kaffe*, milk, and *smør-brød*. No *tran*; winter was over.

After *frokost* we walked Storgate. In part, we wanted to check out our handiwork from the night before. All the posters we had put up during the "night" were still there. Anyone wanting to go to a movie would have our *russ* selection as one alternative: The Chieftain from the North's Par(ad)is(e) Island. And almost all of the shop windows were decorated. The main decoration was the inclusion of Norwegian flags into the display. But many of the windows also paid homage to us, the *rødruss*: some windows included a *russehua*, others had congratulatory words for the graduating *russ*, still others had doctored pictures to include red-hatted students. It was an even more festive atmosphere than I had experienced at *jul*.

By 10:00 AM all the *russ* had assembled (again) at the *gymnas*; almost twelve hours had elapsed since we started working on our posters and costumes the previous "night." But everyone was still together; we hadn't lost anyone to sleep or boredom. The *skolegård* had (during our absence) been prepared for *søttendemai*: a large, three-meter Norwegian flag hung from the balcony outside the principal's office, the same balcony from which he had announced our fall (mountain-climbing) and winter (cross-country skiing) half-days off. And sitting in the *skolegård*, directly in front of the flowing flag was the last item for preparation: the *russebil*.

Ole Jens owned a car, of sorts. It was a 1930s Volvo. The headlights were not built into the body, but attached to its outside. It did, however, have an electric starter; Ole Jens didn't have to crank it.

"All right, you guys," Ole Jens challenged us, carrying buckets of paint. "Let's make this *bil* a genuine *russebil*."

And paint it we did. There was no roof to paint, but we painted the body blue and the trim red, especially the somewhat shaky running boards. The fenders got a coat or two of red, as well, as did the radiator at the front and the radiator-like slits on the sides of the hood.

"Just in case people don't understand," Gunnar explained, red paint brush in hand, "I think we had better label the parts."

Gunnar proceeded to paint "*Inngang*" (entry) on each door and "*Motor*" on the hood. There was no radio antenna to replace, but Franck attached small Norwegian flags (on the ends of meter-long sticks) on each side of the windshield. A couple of red Eiffel Towers and a red *russehua* completed the decorations.

"Where's Jorunn?" I asked as we headed back into the art room to put the final touches on our posters.

"Don't worry about Jorunn," Lillian said, working hard to suppress a smile.

We spent the next hour or so putting the posters together. Those who were wearing costumes put them on. Steinar Hansen was wearing his priest outfit from the *Daabsfest*. Most of us, however, were just wearing our *russ* outfits, with our red-striped pants, Eiffel Towers on our backs, and a *russehua* on our head. As the time approached for our leaving the *gymnas*, I looked around at our red-splotched group. We looked somewhere between impressive and funny-looking.

"Where do you think you're going dressed like that?" Gunnar asked me.

"Aren't we ready to go?" I asked.

"You're not," Odd said.

"Sure I am," I said again

"*Nei*, you're not," Per Sparboe echoed the others.

I had obviously missed something. Per and Odd were still wearing their white shirts, their red bow ties, and their red *russ* vests. But neither of them had his *russehua* on his head; instead, each wore a large, red duncecap. I hadn't even seen anyone making them, let alone trying them on. Each had a drum strapped over his shoulders and each was wearing a red skirt instead of pants. And Per was holding another skirt in his hands, while Odd was holding another duncecap and Gunnar was holding a third drum.

"*Værsågod*," Per said to me, handing me what I quickly guessed was my skirt.

"*Værsågod*," Odd said, handing me my cap.

"*Værsågod*," Gunnar said, handing me my drum.

As I took off my pants and put on my costume, the rest of the *russ* crowded around me to make sure I did everything correctly.

"Now you're ready to go," Lillian smiled, kissing me affectionately on the check. "And now we're all ready to go."

And off we went, out the *skolegård*, following the *russebil*. We assembled with all the other participants in the *søttendemaitog* at Tom's elementary school near the *gymnas*. We were the last group to march in the *søttendemaitog*, which gave me a chance to see all the other groups. The graduating 7th-graders from the elementary school marched, as did their school band, Tom included. The graduating students were all dressed up in their finest sport coats and slacks, and each one carried a small Norwegian flag on a short stick. The band looked great, with its leader in the front, along with three drummers with tall fur hats, sort of like the guards at Buckingham Palace. There must have been close to forty or fifty members, all in their white jackets, white caps, black slacks or skirts, and red ties and belts. I was so proud of my little brother.

The *grønnruss* marched, with their green *russehua*, but there were lots of other students, as well. There were nursing students from the *sykhus*, teachers from the Teachers College not to far from Balsfjordgate, and, my favorite, the *husmorskolen* students, the girls I visited frequently in the fourth floor attic at the *gymnas*. Although a few of them wore their traditional *bunads*, folk costumes representing the county from which they came, most of them wore blue blouses and white aprons and had white kerchiefs tied around their hair. Although most groups marching led with Norwegian flags, the two students leading the group of nursing students carried large Red Cross flags.

But no group was as grand (and amusing) as the *russ*. Tor Kjær led our group, carrying the *gymnas* flag. He was followed by the *russ* dressed up only in their *russ* outfits. Then came the posters. There was a baby still in diapers taking off on a rocket ship, to commemorate the flight of John Glenn. There was a poster of Charles DeGaulle (with a nose even bigger than in real life) struggling with the Algerians. There was a poster announcing the Association of Tromsø Principals, with three of the *russ* huddled together in a wagon made of thin tree trunks resembling a prisoner's wagon from the Middle Ages. The soldiers in gas masks preceded the *russebil*, which had mounted on it the large missile "Wilhjelm," named after our honored principal. And the *russ* drummers—Per, Odd, and Pipe—followed the car, in our cute red vests, duncecaps, and skirts, pounding away on our drums, not exactly in unison or to any particular rhythm. We were quite a sight.

The parade was surprisingly long, probably close to a kilometer. And, we walked along the shore road that I took home after walking Storgate. We walked up alongside the *sykhus* past the end of Balsfjordgate, where I could wave (and drum) at *mor* and *far*. We walked along many of the streets I was used to walking on: past the *gymnas*, down into the *sentrum*, and, finally, the length of Storgate from the Grand Hotel to the *torvet*.

I was too busy to notice that Jorunn, our *russeformann*, our class President, had never joined the parade. As we approached the *torvet*, I noticed that there was a large platform erected in the center, with a small set of stands behind it. No one was on the platform and no one was even on the stands behind it.

"There she is," Per yelled to me.

"Who? Where?"

"Over Tromsøbrua," Odd pointed and shouted simultaneously.

Sweeping in over our famous Tromsøbrua was a helicopter. I hadn't seen a helicopter since coming to Tromsø. In fact, I hadn't seen anything in the air at all, since Tromsø didn't have an airport. Taking a plane from Tromsø meant taking a six-hour bus ride to Bardefoss, the nearest military airport, which had a few civilian flights as well. But I could see a helicopter, and it was definitely a *russ* helicopter, draped with a Norwegian flag and with a red Eiffel Tower and *russehua* painted on the cockpit.

The helicopter landed on one of the docks adjoining the *torvet*, and out stepped our *russeformann*, Jorunn Pettersen. She climbed onto a throne, which was attached to two long 2 x 4s and hoisted onto the shoulders of Bengt Mikkelsen and seven of the strongest *russ* boys. They marched her over to the platform; the rest of us had already climbed up onto the stands behind it. Steinar Hansen began with a mock prayer and Jorunn gave a rousing speech, a mixture of half-hearted patriotism and full-fledged *russ* humor. With her red *russehua* and her flowing red cape, she looked like a queen, which is more than I can say for the bunch of us behind her, hooting it up (with our mouths and our horns). And the crowd watching those antics was huge: it overflowed the *torvet* into Storgate and even up the hill toward the police station.

I assumed the speech was the end of our day, but I was wrong. We did get a bit of a break. After the parade and the speech, we were allowed to return to our homes and have *middag* with our families.

"But make sure you don't go to sleep," Lillian warned me.

"But I always *sove middag*," I protested.

"Not today," she reiterated. She gave me back my pants and *russehua*, which she carried for me during the parade. She knotted the string holding the tassel before she gave it back to me and I put it on my head.

"That's one night without sleep," Lillian explained. "That's for staying up last night. If you *sove middag* today, you won't get credit for tonight and you won't earn your second knot."

"And for two nights in a row without sleep," Jorunn explained, as she removed her red cape, "you get a double knot: the sign of a real *russ*."

The day went downhill from the excitement and exhilaration of the *søttendemaitog* and Jorunn's speech. I went home for *middag* with my family and I made sure I didn't *sove middag*. And I went out later that evening to our *søttendemai russefest*, at the house of one of the *russ* instead of one of the *kafés*.

"I wasn't certain," Gunnar had explained to me when we met on Storgate that evening, "we would have enough energy to dance."

He had a point. We did have our *russefest* and we all (at least those 20-30 who made it to the *russefest*) stayed up all night to earn our double knot...but barely. We sat up talking about the days events. For the others, the high point was definitely the helicopter.

"Tromsø had never seen anything like it," Jorunn explained to me. "Every year, the *russeformann* makes a speech, but never has a *russeformann* entered in such a dramatic fashion. This was definitely a first for Tromsø."

We all sat around talking, still in our *russ* outfits. As the night wore on, we undid our red bow ties and the jackets started coming off. By the "morning," most of us had undone the buttons on our vests, as well. By then, we were a sorry sight: barely in our clothes, drooping and slouching in our chairs, hardly able to talk (let alone laugh). The Solo was gone, and we were gulping *kaffe* just to keep *våken*: Erika, Bengt, Jorunn, Randi, Arnulf, Gunnar, Odd, Per, Bitten, Bjørg, Lillian...even Pipe.

"It's six o-clock," Jorunn announced. "We made it!"

"And now we can go home," Arnulf shouted.

"What do you think of *søttendemai* now, Pete," Lillian asked me as I walked her home, holding hands.

"This one," I smiled, "was a little different from my last one."

"Perhaps," Lillian suggested, "that one was more exciting but this one was more fun?"

"This one was certainly longer," I said.

"I have looked forward to this day for years," Lillian said to me. "But I never would have imagined sharing it with you, Pete."

"I never even imagined this day," I responded, "but I'm glad I could share it with you."

I walked Lillian home (and got more than just another kiss on my cheek for my efforts) and then walked myself home. I stumbled through the door and into my room by 7:00 AM. *Mor* (bless her heart, and her experience with three former *russ* children) had made my bed, making it that much easier for me to fall into it, ending my first *søttendemai* as a teenage Norwegian. And I knew that I would keep the memory of this *søttendemai* well into my future.

Less than two months to go.

-30-
Home Alone

Alone. That was what I felt, ironic as it was. It was the first week of June and I had been in Tromsø almost a year. I had lived with three families. I had gone to school for almost ten months and had made tons of friends. But now that my *russ* friends had all left for two weeks, now I felt alone. The *russ* had saved all year for their big trip: the *russetur til Kjøbenhavn*. Every senior class in every Norwegian *gymnas* took a *russetur*, and almost all of them went to Kjøbenhavn. Even though the Tromsø *russ* had chaperones for their trip, none of the other *gymnas* with AFS students had chaperones, and AFS decided it would be unfair for only one AFSer to participate on the *russetur*. So I, too, stayed home alone.

den 3. juni, 1962

Dear Mom and Dad,

I began writing my last Kjære Venn *letter about May 17th, but I couldn't finish it. The russ are now in Kjøbenhavn; they went last Monday morning. After they had gone, I almost felt like throwing up, which is quite paradoxical since my stomach was nothing more than an empty pit. I do not believe I have ever felt so completely alone as I did then and as I still do now. I think only of them and I how I love them so; I count the days until they are back with me here in Tromsø.*

But this is but a part; I have just four more weeks and then this whole fairy tale of a dream will be destroyed by the awakening of reality. Four more short weeks and then it's all over. I could even count the days now, but it's too sickening a thought.

This year has been too great. What was it Willa Cather said in A Wagner Matinee: *"Don't love it so well, Clark, or it may be taken from you." How true; how true. I guess old Willa wasn't that bad after all. I feared all along getting involved with a girl because I would just have to say good-bye, but I forgot about my love for Tromsø and all that this year has meant for me. And now it's too late.*

I should have hated my stay here; then it would have been easy to leave. They ask me if I'm looking forward to leaving, and I can't really say I am. If they only know how much I'm not. I can't wait to get home; if I could only accomplish that without leaving!!!!

I Was a Teenage Norwegian

I still haven't heard from Sue (it's been two months now; not even a birth-day card) and that may be just adding to my "downness." But I'll be fine next Tuesday when the russ *are back, and then I'll begin doing some of the stuff I should be doing. Please try to pick out a couple of nice presents for my two Norwegian families; you know how much they mean to me. But I'm sure you'll do your usual good job; you always do.*

Much "down" love,

Pete

School was over for the *russ*, and that meant school was over for me. I could sleep late every day, which I did. That was of particular importance because I rarely went to bed before 3:00 or 4:00 in the morning in June. There were three major reasons why an eighteen year old boy whose class-mates had all left for two weeks stayed up until the wee hours of the morn-ing. The first was the *midnattsol.* It was light all day and all night, which made staying up late easy. The second and third reasons had to do with what I spent much of my time doing while my friends were away: work-ing at Figenschau and walking the mountain.

On Storgate, across from the Tromsø Cathedral was one of Tromsø's most famous landmarks: a life-size polar bear. It stood on the sidewalk, on all fours, in front of one of the oldest and largest tourist shops in town: Figenschau. Figenschau was a combination tourist store and fur store. The polar bear was its most distinguishing feature, although its windows, full as they were with wooden trolls, ivory carvings, and colorful lapp outfits, were among the most attractive in town. Kids rode on the bear's back and tourists took their pictures with it. There were even Tromsø postcards with the Figenschau polar bear as the central image.

Two days after my *russ* friends had boarded the bus for Narvik—to catch the Swedish train to Stockholm and Kjøbenhavn—I wandered down Storgate and into Figenschau.

"*Værsågod,*" the woman behind the countered greeted me.

"*God dag,*" I responded. "I'd like to talk with someone about a job."

"Just a minute. I'll have to get *fru* Holm."

The brief intermission gave me a chance to look around the store. I had passed the store over 1,000 times, walking Storgate as often as I did. And yet, I had never once been inside. I wasn't a tourist, and I wanted to make sure I NEVER did anything a tourist might do. I figured working there was all right, as long as I didn't shop in the store.

"*Ja,*" an older woman said to me. "How can I help you."

"I was wondering if I could work here, a job," I said. I felt I was stum-bling with my *norsk*, since I was entering what were for me uncharted waters. That conversation was the closest I had ever been to talking like an adult instead of a teenager. Apparently, *fru* Holm didn't notice.

"Why aren't you in school?" she asked.

"I'm a *russ.*"

"Why aren't you on your way to Kjøbenhavn?" She asked again.

"I didn't get permission."

"From your parents?" She continued her questions.

"*Nei*, from AFS."

"You're American?"

"Yes," I answered, proud not because of my country of origin but because I had fooled another Norwegian into thinking I was born and raised in Tromsø. To me, I was a teenage Norwegian. To *fru* Holm I was just a Norwegian teenager...and a Norwegian teenager skipping school.

"You're Pete?" she asked. I hoped it would be her last question.

"*Ja, æ e'* Pete," I answered in my most exaggerated *Tromsøværing* dialect.

"So...you want a job, Pete? Why didn't you say so? I could use some extra help when the ships are in."

"You mean the *hurtigruten?*" I asked.

"*Ja*, but not just the *hurtigruten*. We get the two *hurtigruter* every day now that it's summer, but we also get larger tourist ships a couple of times a week, especially in June."

"Isn't it a little cold for tourists?" I wondered aloud.

"No one comes to Tromsø for warm weather," *fru* Holm laughed. "They come for the *midnattsol*, and June's the best month for *midnattsol.*"

"Well, that sounds fine to me," I said. "I didn't want a full-time job, just something to do while the *russ* are away and a different Tromsø experience."

"I think you'll find this quite different," *fru* Holm smiled.

"There is one problem, though."

"*Ja.*"

"I can't make any money. I'm not allowed to get paid for work as an exchange student."

"That may be a problem for you," *fru* Holm laughed, "but it's not a problem for me not to pay you. But how about this: I won't pay you money, but you can earn store credits."

"I don't understand."

"I'll pay you a regular hourly wage, but I won't give you the money. I'll pay you KR4 an hour. You work for ten hours and I'll pay you KR40. But I won't give you money. I'll give you store credit, which you can use to buy whatever you want from the store."

"That might be okay," I said.

"And as a Figenschau employee, you'll get a standard 30% discount."

"That's great. I can buy all my coming home gifts that way. It's a deal. When do you want me to start?"

"Come back this evening around 11:30. The boat docks at midnight and the tourists are wandering through Tromsø for about two hours."

"Great. *Takk.* I'll see you then."

I Was a Teenage Norwegian

For the next month, I worked at Figenschau from four to seven hours a day, depending on whether or not one of the large tourist ships stopped in Tromsø that day. The store wasn't tiny, but it wasn't especially large, either; perhaps the size of a couple of our classrooms at the *gymnas*. About a third of the store was devoted to the furs. That was *fru* Holm's department, both for the women from Tromsø and the tourists. *Fru* Holm spent a large part of each day in the office or selling fur coats to the women of Tromsø. But she was on the floor and behind the counters with the rest of us when the ships came in.

"This is how Figenschau got started," *fru* Holm had told me one day when things weren't especially busy. "In fact, this is one of the oldest stores in Tromsø. We will celebrate our 100th birthday in 1964. Paul Hansen Figenschau started the company as a grocery store, but within a few years he was buying and selling skins, to both Norwegians and tourists."

The rest of the store was stocked with everything imaginable that a tourist might like to buy. There were two or three racks of Norwegian sweaters, both hand-knit (the more expensive ones) and machine-knit. Those were among the most popular items, and among the most expensive. There were also lots of hand-knit mittens and caps. The most common items were the hand-carved wooden items: *trolls*, fishermen, lapp boys and girls, and the like. The window had a couple of mannequins dressed in lapp clothing, which was also for sale. There were lots of little items made of sealskin: wallets, eyeglass cases, small seal dolls, etc. My favorites were the carvings made of seal tusks: letter openers, knife handles, elaborate decorations depicting eskimo fishing and hunting situations. And there were plenty of hand-painted *rosemaleri*, the typically Norwegian painted bowls, plates, and even large chests.

That first night I was quite nervous. I never worked in a store before. I babysat and mowed lawns, even did odd jobs for people. But I never had anything approximating a real job, and never waited on customers. When the first wave hit, I stayed back and watched how the women handled everything. After fifteen or twenty minutes, I felt I could handle it and moved closer to the counter.

"You got any trolls?" an American tourist in idiotic Bermuda shorts literally shouted across the counter at me.

"Yes, we do," I answered calmly in English, showing him the most mundane of the wood carvings.

"You think we'll see any of these from the boat?" Mr. Obnoxious asked what I assumed was his charming wife. I guess he thought he was funny.

I knew I had to speak English to the tourists but I had decided to speak English with a Norwegian accent.

"Gooood evening," I said.

"Do you have any trolls?" one of them might ask.

"Yes, we dooo," I answered. "We have a very fine seeelection. If you will folllllooow me, I will shew them toooooo yoooooo."

"This is very nice."

"Yes, that is especially nice. It was made by a local craftsman here in the north of Norway. You can see how carefully he has carved the face toooooo conform to the Norwegian traditions," I continued, raising and lowering the tone of my voice to make it sound as singsong as possible.

"You speak very good English," they would invariably say. "How long have you been studying it?" And everyone working with me, including *fru* Holm, would burst out in laughter...even though I did this at least once every day.

Working at Figenschau was great for me during my time alone, but it wasn't enough to keep me busy. One of the other ways I filled my time was giving *foredrag*. I had done this in school, but toward the end of the year I wanted to expand my audience.

I put a small advertisement in both town newspapers: *Tromsø* and *Nordlys*. "Speeches About America (the miniscule headline went). I will be

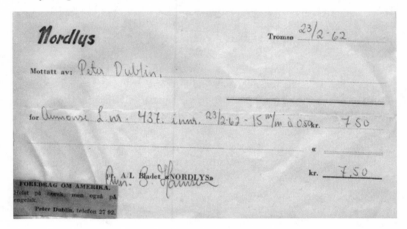

glad to talk to your organization about any topic. Send request to Box 123. Pete Dublin." The result was that during May and June, I gave eight or ten such speeches to different organizations around Tromsø. Often, during the day, I would walk over to the USIS office and get Appelbaum to help me with my research. The most intriguing invitation and speech was when I was asked by a group similar to Alcoholics Anonymous. I decided to give a speech entitled "Prohibition in America"; it was quite well received.

In June I felt more alone than at any time since Trollvasshytta, although at Trollvasshytta I was also a little homesick. In June, in Tromsø, I was at home; I just felt alone at home. In addition, I was reaching the end of my year in Tromsø; it was time to take stock. I had begun that process in some of my letters home. And in June I found a way to reflect upon my year in Norway while I was still in Norway, a way to wind down from the excitement of the year, a way to quietly, peacefully say good-bye.

I Was a Teenage Norwegian

My way was to walk to, up, and around the 2,000 foot mountain on the mainland directly across from Tromsø. This mountain had a special significance for me because it was so visible. I could see it from Storgate, or at least glimpses of it down the side streets leading to the water. I could see it from the third floor windows of Gunnar's and Franck's Math Line classroom at the *gymnas*. I could see it every day from the picture window in the living room at home. In June the sight was especially spectacular at night, with the *midnattsol* reflecting all its glory off the mountain. That was the mountain we had walked up and on the previous fall when the principal gave the entire *gymnas* the afternoon off and told us to "take a hike up the mountain."

Three or four times a week, I headed for the mountain. If I worked at Figenschau that night, I would sometimes go before work, leaving at 7:00 or 8:00 PM and returning to the store by midnight, when the *hurtigruten* docked. Other nights, I started at around 10:00 and returned at 2:00 or 3:00 in the morning. And many times, I began my evening's journey after I had finished work at Figenschau at 3:00 AM; then I didn't get back home until *frokost*, having earned (all by myself, no less) another knot in my *russehua* tassel.

I particularly enjoyed going later. At that time of "night," even Storgate was deserted. It was a little eerie to walk up an empty Storgate, but it was an intriguingly different kind of experience and it felt appropriate as a way to start my four or five hour evening's journey. With no people on the sidewalk to talk to, I focussed on the stores and store windows in a way I rarely did at other times. And I always walked on the "correct" side of the street, even when there was no one else in town to notice. I was a *Tromsøværing*; there was only one side of Storgate one walked on...day or day, in company with others or completely alone.

Tromsøbrua was a toll bridge. It cost only KR1 to walk over *Tromsøbrua*, and Tromsø had instituted one-way tolls well before any of the bridges and tunnels in America had done so.

"And the tolls," *far* had told me when I asked about them, "will only last

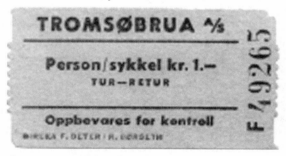

as long as it takes to pay off the construction costs." *Tromsøbrua* was about a kilometer long, about a ten-minute walk. I rarely made it in that amount of time on my way *to* the mountain. I loved walking across *Tromsøbrua*. I loved walking up its steep incline. I would sometimes stand for half an hour at its topmost point and look down at the boats under me...and there were always boats, no matter what time of day or day. And if I was walking over *Tromsøbrua* around midnight, I was confronted with *midnattsolen*. I could see it while I stood on the southern edge of *Tromsøbrua* and looked toward the south. I could see it, sometimes just inches above the mountainous islands to the south of Tromsøy, shimmering off the water. I would have watched it for hours if it weren't for the fact that seeing the *midnattsol* from *Tromsøbrua* was only my second favorite place to view that treasure of nature; my favorite place was always from the mountain.

The foot of the mountain was a ten-minute walk from the bridge. Arriving there, I was confronted with one of life's little choices: walk or ride up. Tromsø had a *fjellheis*: a gondola car. If I took it I was up on the mountain in five minutes. And it wasn't especially expensive: KR15 for a ten-ride ticket. I did buy a ticket and I did use it, although I didn't use up the ticket completely. Not because the ride wasn't pleasurable and easy, and not because the view from the *fjellheis* wasn't spectacular.

I generally walked both up and down the mountain because the walk was even more special than the *fjellheis*. I started on my walk up the mountain from the bottom terminal of the *fjellheis*. The *fjellheis* was already up about fifty meters above sea level and, perhaps, 100-200 meters away from the coast. Within five minutes, I was walking in an isolated woods. Within another five minutes, I was out of the woods; the tree line ended pretty close to sea level.

I had a series of special stopping places as I walked up the mountain. One was just at the edge of the trees. One was in the midst of tall grasses and small bushes. One was on an outcropping of rocks, seemingly in the middle of nowhere. What they all had in common was a spectacular view of Tromsø. The walk itself took only about forty-five minutes, but I hardly ever just walked. It was as if the walk up was as much an excuse to visit my special stopping places as it was a reason for good, healthy exercise.

The mountain was too steep to walk straight up, and I wound around a bit to the north. The final five minutes had me climbing up a steep set of rocks, so that I always felt a bit of a surprise as I actually made it up to the plateau and the restaurant adjacent to the top terminal of the *fjellheis*, both of which I could see so clearly from my living room picture window. I usually ended my mountain trips at the restaurant, sipping my hot fruit toddy at the large expanse of windows providing me with another special place and view of Tromsø. I often started my top-of-the mountain hike by walking out on the the roof of the restaurant—a fenced-in deck or platform—with its own view of Tromsø.

I Was a Teenage Norwegian

In an objective sense, every view of Tromsø was the same, but every view was different for me. Each view from one of my special stopping places had significance because of the nature and physical surroundings of the stopping place; somehow the view was different through tall grass and bushes than from on top of an outcropping of rocks. The view from inside the restaurant was influenced by the warmth and the taste of the hot toddy. And the view from the roof deck was affected by my close proximity to the tourists.

The primary purpose of those mountain walks was to provide me with an opportunity to reflect on my year in Tromsø and on myself. Even though I had grown during the year to a point where I could look at myself in terms of myself, I still had a strong tendency to define myself in contrast to others. I got a secret thrill standing on the roof-deck at the railing, looking out over Tromsø and Tromsøy in the midst of (primarily) American tourists, feeling even more my teenage Norwegian-ness. I wasn't one of them. I wasn't speaking English. I wasn't even an American. I hadn't taken the easy way up the mountain. I wasn't making foolish, ignorant, and silly comments about being 300 kilometers North of the Arctic Circle. I was a teenage Norwegian, taking an evening's stroll up my local, neighborhood mountain.

I spent most of my time up on the mountain itself. I walked away from the restaurant and across the plateau. I walked up to the small summit. I walked past the rock formation I remembered stopping at with my *russ* friends the previous fall. I walked, sometimes for hours, out as far as I could along the edge of the mountain that faced Tromsø, because looking at the island was such a central part of the experience for me.

But it was not simply looking at Tromsø that made those mountain walks so important to me; looking at the *midnattsol* was important, too.

Describing *midnattsol* as sun at night doesn't capture its magnificence, its power, its spirituality. Describing it as sun at night doesn't at all explain why I could sit and watch it for hours on end, and never tire of it. Describing it as sun at night doesn't explain how it pulled me almost every night for a month back to the mountain to bask in its radiance.

Because that was what I did for almost all of June, even after my *russ* friends return from Kjøbenhavn. I watched the sun reflect off the water as I crossed the Tromsøbrua. I peeked at the *midnattsol* from my special stopping places on my hike up the mountain. But most of all, I watched the *midnattsol* from atop my mountain. Depending on the hour and my position, I could see it off to the south of Tromsøy or I could see it directly behind the *sentrum* and the island. If there were clouds in the sky, there would be colors as well; not the brilliant and vivid colors of a sunset, but the sparkling and powerful colors of the *midnattsol*. I could see Tromsø in shadows as the sunlight reflected off the water surrounding the island.

The *midnattsol* was a powerful physical presence, but that wasn't its most compelling factor. It was an even more powerful emotional presence. The warmth it radiated was as much emotional as physical. I loved to look *at* it, but I appreciated even more looking *into* it. I was in there, and so were all my families and friends. My whole year, my whole existence as a teenage Norwegian, was in the *midnattsol*. I saw myself and my life every time I saw it from my mountain. I wasn't religious in any way; I was, in fact, proud of my atheism. But my lack of religion didn't translate into a lack of spirituality, and the *midnattsol* tapped into that spirituality like no other phenomenon before or since.

Most of the time, I went up on the mountain and walked around by myself, but once I brought Liz with me. Liz provided me with a unique perspective on myself. She wasn't family and she wasn't a peer, but she had known me almost the entire time I was in Norway. She was my *norsk* teacher at Trollvasshytta. She was the one who knew about my holding hands with Lillian for the first time almost before I held Lillian's hand. She had been an AFSer herself.

"You've changed, Pete," Liz said to me as she stood next to and I leaned up against a huge cairn near the edge of the mountain.

"*Kem æ?*"

"*Ja, du.*" Liz smiled, appreciating the *Tromsøværing* joke more than *mor* did.

"I feel as if I have," I said to her.

"You were angry when I first met you," she said.

"Angry?" I was puzzled.

"You didn't yell or shout or anything like that. But you were angry inside. Everything was so serious for you. You wanted everything to mean something. You wanted to have conversations like this one six hours a day."

"I see what you mean," I said.

I Was a Teenage Norwegian

"You're much more playful now," Liz continued. "You don't demand that others have to be with you in any certain way. You meet other people more on their own terms. You're happier...less angry."

At one level, Liz was just telling me things I already knew. But having her tell me them, hearing them from someone else's mouth instead of hearing them in my own thoughts, made that knowledge different and more accessible to me.

Walking down the mountain was different from walking up and walking home was different from walking to the mountain. I walked down much more quickly and I rarely stopped at any of my special stopping places. It was as if I needed those few minutes to clear my mind of all my reflections and so I concentrated on the physical aspect of coming down. I would stand at the top of the small hill overlooking Storgate from the north and I could see the twenty-foot-long shadow created by the ever-present *midnattsol*. The streets were empty of people, but they were still *my* streets and Tromsø was still *my* town and it was still full of memories and import even without any people and even at 3:00 in the morning.

Even during *mørketida*, I enjoyed the walking. It was good exercise and, probably, one of the reasons I kept my weight down to where it had dropped during my stay at Trollvasshytta; the healthy *fisk og poteter* diet didn't hurt in that regard, either. But walking provided more than mere physical exercise; it also provided a kind of mental exercise. I talked to myself, throughout my walk, out loud and silently, sometimes sung songs—either to myself or even out loud, there being no one within earshot to embarrass me—always thinking and reflecting on my life and life itself. Walking was the perfect escape for me.

The first few months I was in Tromsø, I carried on conversations in my head with myself in English about Westport, my family there, and my LRY friends. By the time school had begun at the end of August, and certainly soon thereafter, the content of those walking conversations had switched to Tromsø: what was happening in school, with my family, with my new-found friends, the *fester*. The language was still English, but the content had made the transition from America to Norway.

By the time I moved into the Thyholdt household, I began to talk to myself in *norsk* about my Norwegian life. I wasn't really thinking in *norsk* yet; I was talking *norsk* almost exclusively, but I still did a lot of mental translating from English to *norsk* as I talked. I felt like one of the United Nations interpreters who had to translate what was heard, speak it immediately thereafter, and simultaneously listen to the next sentence while speaking the translated version of the last...or something like that. But even though I wasn't thinking in *norsk*, I had decided to talk to myself in *norsk*. There I was, walking by myself with no one around, talking to myself and deciding to talk to myself in *norsk*. I was so Norwegian-aggressive that I talked to myself in *norsk* in bed, as I was going to sleep. By mid winter, I thought in *norsk* and talked to myself in *norsk* while I walked.

Walking also provided a means for discovery. There were some things I learned as a result of walking. The first of these discoveries came in the spring, however brief and fleeting that season was in Tromsø. I had moved in with the Thyholdts in November. There were one or two meters of snow already on the ground and days were replaced by nights. For the next five months, I walked to school along the same path: down Balsfjordgate, in back of the *sykhus*, and so forth.

By April, the snow began to melt and the days were days again; it was even light in the morning as I walked to school. On one of those days, I discovered a fence. The reason I had never seen it before was that it was covered with two meters of snow; I had walked over that fence every day for five months without knowing I was walking over anything. For the next month, I continued to discover objects all over Tromsø as I walked to school, *til byen*, and to friends' houses, objects that were new discoveries for me since I had only walked over them during the winter.

The second discovery was quite different. It involved a man I saw many times, at least once or twice a week from the time I moved in with the Thyholdts until I left Tromsø. Although I saw the man many times, I never met him, never talked to him, never even knew him. In fact, I never even saw his face. The only time I ever saw the man was when I walked home from the *sentrum* to Balsfjordgate. The Grand Hotel was at the southern end of the up-and-down Storgate walk. When I started home, I walked past the Grand, past the store where Jorunn's mother worked, and past the brewery and its *ølhall*.

From that point on, I walked along the coast, or at least the coastal edge of the island. In winter, it was a bitter cold walk, with the wind often fiercely whipping off the water.

I Was a Teenage Norwegian

It was during that stretch of walk that I often saw a man, presumably also walking home. He wore a blue smocklike outfit, like that worn by many shop-workers in town. It had a tie belt, buttons down the front, and was a bit longer than a suit jacket. I doubt that was all he wore in winter, but that was the only image of his clothing that I retained. The other memorable feature was that he always walked with his hands clasped together behind his back. I had never seen anyone walk like that before coming to Tromsø and, although I occasionally saw other people in Tromsø walk in that fashion, I never saw anyone walk only in that fashion. Perhaps that is why I can still remember so vividly that man I saw so often and never met and never knew.

As I walked behind that man two or three days a week on my way home, I imagined what he would be thinking and saying to himself, just as I was thinking and talking to myself. I didn't have the faintest idea, of course, but I thought about him as a person, a person with feelings and experiences, with feelings and experiences as important to him as mine were to me. We walked the same route day after day, not knowing about each other and not knowing each other. I wondered what he was like, what his life was like, knowing that his life was as meaningful to him as mine was to me, even if I never knew anything about him. In an odd way, that stranger, that person I always saw and never knew, helped me see the world and the people within it in a new way, a more sensitive way, at least in part.

And in a way I have never forgotten. I will see someone on a subway and wonder what her life is like, what she is thinking about, knowing I will never know her and never know anything about her. I get out of the subway, and the person is gone from my life, after a brief moment of almost interaction. And I think of my Unknown Norwegian, hands behind his back, walking home in his smock. I never knew him and, apparently, I can never forget him.

I felt alone during the two weeks in June that my *russ* friends were away on the trip in Kjøbenhavn. They were to return during the end of the third week of June.

"Why don't you go to Narvik," *mor* suggested to me, "and meet them?"

"What do you mean?" I asked her. We were sitting in the living room the evening before they were due back and I was telling her how much I had missed them and how happy I would be to see them all again.

"Take the bus to Narvik," she said, "and surprise them." She was my *mor*, she knew I loved surprises.

"I don't get it."

"How are the *russ* getting home?" she asked patiently.

"Train to Narvik."

"And from Narvik?"

"Bus."

"And how is the bus getting to Narvik?"

"From Tromsø."

"And is the bus going to be empty on its trip to Narvik?"

"*Ja.*"

"And is the bus driver going to be lonely on the long trip to Narvik?"

"*Ja.*"

"And are you going to be on that bus keeping him company?"

"*Ja.*"

It was the end of my year in Tromsø, I had already traveled to Narvik on my own, I didn't even bother to ask Liz for permission.

I went to the school the next day and took advantage of the skills I had acquired on *søttendemai*. I built myself another wooden poster frame, with another long handle. Then I drew a large pipe on a large sheet of brown wrapping paper. Inside the pipe I printed in my best handwriting: *Velkommen hjem Tromsørussen*, Welcome Home Tromsø Seniors. I put the sign together, feeling pretty good about my accomplishment.

The bus ride was different, but just as memorable, as my previous rides to Narvik and Harstad. The main difference was that I could now see in the clear daylight of Northern Norwegian summer night, the tundra and mountains that had only been shadows before. The best part of that trip was still the ferries.

We arrived at about 6:00 AM, just in time for me to race out of the bus with my sign as the train pulled into the Narvik train station. The *russ* stumbled out of the train, most with their eyes still closed from a last night of carousing and lack of sleep. They were genuinely surprised and pleased to see their old Pipe waiting for them, with his sign and his *russehua*.

"*Du* Pipe, *du* Pipe," Gunnar threw his arm around my shoulder. "What in the world are you doing here?"

"*Kem æ?*"

"How did you get here," Lillian asked.

"*Æ e' ikkje så dum som æ s' ut.*"

On the trip back, I sat holding hands with Lillian the whole time, listening to everyone's stories about their escapades in Kjøbenhavn, in the midst of 10,000 other *russ*. I was back with my friends, no longer alone. Maybe I had only two more weeks in Tromsø, maybe I had only two more weeks as a teenage Norwegian, but at least I no longer felt alone.

I spent most of my final two weeks in Tromsø with Lillian. We met almost every day, held hands wherever we went, did things together even when we were with groups of other kids. She also came over to Balsfjordgate a lot, and we spent all of our time together in my room. This was one of the main advantages of having the bedrooms on the first floor. I could come home with Lillian, and we could go into my room with no one even knowing. Of course "no one knew" in the same way that kids in school think teachers don't know they're passing notes; the teachers see everything but the kids think they're invisible. I'm sure *mor* and *far* knew everything, but I could at least feel that Lillian and I were "invisible."

We laughed and joked and talked, but mostly we made out. It was the best making out I had ever experienced. It was full-body making out. We never took off our clothes, but our bodies ground together. Ejaculation without penetration. Ever since that first time in Gunnar's *hytta*, sex had never been the same. I am sure now that *Lillian* would have been more than happy to move beyond even full-body making out, but *I* clearly was not ready.

And I clearly was not ready for any kind of commitment. Something was going on for me in those final days. I spent more time with Lillian than ever before. We did all kinds of things together and I enjoyed being with her all the time. I got as close to her then as I had ever gotten to any girlfriend. But I imposed limits on myself. I still pretended Sue was my girlfriend. I felt guilty after sex. I never fully opened myself up, to either Lillian or myself. I may have been a teenage Norwegian, but there were still pieces of the old Peter Dublin I just couldn't shake.

Less than one month to go.

-31-
The Journey Ends

den 17. juni, 1962

Dear Mom and Dad,

I guess this is really the last letter, really good letter, I'll be writing you from Tromsø. I'm not exactly sure when I'll be leaving, but it shouldn't be much later than July 1.

My jobb *is going pretty well. I work from about 4 or 5 until 7 or 8 in the evening. I work together with some jovial females (all married) and I have a lot of fun!!*

My artium *results were quite disappointing: T (C) in English and* måtelig *(F) in Norwegian (the second lowest of six grades: S, M, T, Ng, Måt, Ikke). I must be worse than I imagined in Norwegian and I must have forgotten more than I imagined in English. My* norsk *is pretty good, but it's better suited to speaking than writing: lots of familiar expressions and words that can't be used in such a serious paper!*

In the winter I was always tired...no matter how much I slept. Now, in the summer, I'm never tired...no matter how little I sleep. I usually sleep from 6:00 in the morning til 2:00 or 3:00 in the afternoon. I'm just never tired before 5:00 or 6:00 in the morning. NEVER!

I've a calender in my room; it hangs on one of the walls. I've just paid it a visit—as I do each evening—and crossed off June 17. There are now but 13 numbers—each representing one day—remaining uncrossed. The seventeen other numbers—each also representing one day—have a couple of No. 90WB Washable Blue Wearever Pen ink lines through them, something which means these are days which will never be lived again, never in the same spirit as they have now been lived, at least. Perhaps in the spirit of memory, but that's not enough.

It's just about over now; I've not much time left before another year of my life will have been. I should be happy that I've had these thirteen days, not depressed on account of this past year. But I'm happy I've had this past year and depressed on account of these thirteen days. Each evening, as another day bites the dust, I can't help but feeling a little blue and lonely. I've had a most wonderful year, but it's over now.

I Was a Teenage Norwegian

You, Mom and Dad, have lived most of my life with me. You've experienced my happiness and sorrows and have seen me grow from seventeen to eighteen. But you can't help me now. I am alone, but I wish to be so. I've been helped throughout this year: by you, fru Román, fru Norbye, fru Thyholdt, Román, Norbye, Thyholdt, Adele Berg, Jorunn Pettersen, Harald Larsen, Gunnar Brox, Lillian Ingebrigtsen, Liz Arnet, Unni Larssen, Ragna Kjellman, Engelsen, Tom Thyholdt, Arnulf Berg, and even many more. Now it is that the results of this help should begin to appear and I wish to be alone.

In another five weeks I'll be home in Westport, then they'll be only memories. Now I've still got thirteen days. I'll try to use them, but I'll always be thinking of this past year. It's meant a lot to me and it's opened my eyes to the goodness of the World. That's why I'll continue to live these thirteen days as I begin to unravel the past. I'm pretty happy, I guess; I'm alone, but I'm not really lonely.

Much, much love,
Pete

Pain. Loss. Tears. None of them could be avoided. It was my last day in Tromsø. It was the day my return journey began.

I wandered around throughout the day, both physically and emotionally. I had packed the night before so that I felt free to wander on my last day. I wandered past the *gymnas*, empty of students, all of whom, like me, were on vacation. I walked past Torild Norbye's and Elin Fosse's separate classroom building and past my *"be, ber, ba, bedt" foredrag*. I walked past the *skolegård*, and past where I had gotten my *småpiker* to knit sweaters for me. I walked past the classrooms and past the memory of squeezing the baseball sponge on Gunnar's surprised face. I walked past the cemetery and past my grey flannel suit. I walked past Prestvannet and past the *skitur* where I could barely keep up with the girls. I walked past the Holt farm and past the *poteter* we *plukka*.

And there were even more places too far to walk past. I couldn't walk past the *sydspisen* and the *soldagen* it represented. I couldn't walk past the Nyløkken Kafé and the *russefester* it represented. I couldn't walk past Lillian's house and the parents I never met. I couldn't walk past the Kjellman's house and the *Bragerevy* it represented. I couldn't walk past the Fosse's house and the friends that house represented. I couldn't walk past the *danseskolen* building and the page of my *ordbok* that it represented.

At 2:00 AM that evening, *far* turned to me. "It's time to go," he said simply. A man of few words and much feeling.

"I know," I said. "You drive; I'll walk." That was my wish. *Far* had sent four large boxes of my clothes, books, sweaters, and my Figenschau "wages" to Rotterdam already. They would be waiting for me on board when I walked up the GROOTE BEER gangplank. But that still left two large suitcases in the car. I would have to carry them often enough in the next eight or nine days; *far* offered to drive to the dock with them. For myself, I wanted to walk *til byen* one last time.

At least I didn't have to say good-bye to anyone as I walked out the front door; *mor*, Tom, and Olemann had accompanied *far* and the two suitcases. It was easier leaving an empty house than one full of *mor's* laughter. I started my exit from the kitchen, remembering the weeks it took to get used to *tran*. I walked from the kitchen into the dining room, remembering our fresh salmon last supper. I walked through the living room, looking out the picture window at the sun bouncing off the mountain on the mainland. That was it for the upstairs and I walked down the stairs. I never walked down those stairs without looking at the clock and remembering the half-hour night's sleep during *mørketida*. I spent the most time in my bedroom, making sure that everything in it—the sink in the corner, Paal's pictures on the wall, the couch-bed, the desk—stayed indelibly etched into my memory.

I opened and shut the front door for the last time and walked out the driveway into Balsfjordgate. Past the playground, now empty at 2:15 at night, but still bright from the *midnattsol*. Past the grocery store where *mor* shopped and the *sykhus*, down to the water's edge. No wind; no cold winter air. Just the *midnattsol* at the back of my head and the water and the mountain off to my right. Past Mack's brewery and *ølhall*. And onto Storgate, for one last up-and-down stroll...starting at the Grand Hotel. Past Figenschau's, where the tourists were still busy gobbling up souvenirs, even without the help of the salesperson who spoke surprisingly good English. Past Pedersen's *bakeri*, closed for the evening; I had eaten my last *halvmåner* and *skillingskaker* earlier that day as part of my leave-taking. Up to the *kino* on the other side of the street, on which I still couldn't walk...always the proper *Tromsøværing*. Back past Anne Marcussen's mother's knitting shop where I bought the *garn* for my many sweaters and Peder Norbye, where *far* Norbye always had a little something for me. Past the cathedral and Sagatun, my favorite *kafé*, and the Post Office, where they knew more about me and my families than I knew myself. To the dock, where the majestic-looking, weather-beaten *hurtigruten* was awaiting me.

But it was not just the boat that awaited me. Both families were there, the Thyholdts and the Norbyes. And many of my friends: Jorunn, Arnulf, Randi, Gunnar, and Lillian. Pain. Loss. Tears. None of them could be avoided. It was my last day in Tromsø. It was the day my return journey began. And the people closest to me were there, making it even harder for me.

There were almost no words, but no words were needed. I could see in each face, and feel in each hug, the love we shared. One after the other said good-bye in silence. Pain. Loss. Tears. None of them could be avoided.

The time had come. I took a suitcase in each hand, put the sleeping bag Tom had given me under my arm, and walked up the gangplank. The time was 2:55 AM. The sun was bright, Tromsø was magnificent, and the boat was ready. And when it started to move, the tears started to flow. I thought my stomach would drop to the deck, the feeling of loss was so great. It was the end of my year; I could never recapture it. It was over, gone…at least that was the way it felt to me at that moment. I wanted to jump off the *hurtigruten* and return to Tromsø. I knew I couldn't, but I wanted to because I didn't want to lose that year. I didn't want to lose my family and my friends. What I couldn't understand was that I never would.

I had the strangest feeling as the *hurtigruten* pulled away from the dock and away from the shore and away from Tromsø. Just as we pulled *away* from the dock, I remembered that moment the previous year as the *hurtigruten* pulled *into* the dock, as I approached Tromsø for the first time. I didn't know whether I was coming or going. But I was going. I was on the *hurtigruten* and I was on my way home. I stood on the deck, at the railing, looking at Tromsø as it became smaller and smaller as we moved farther and farther away. The *hurtigruten* rounded a corner, and Tromsø was gone.

The *hurtigruten* was the same, but it felt completely different. I hadn't ridden the *hurtigruten* since the year before, but it looked familiar, as if I had ridden the *hurtigruten* my whole life. I felt I knew my way around the boat the moment I stepped onto it. I talked with the crew as if I was one of them, not with the tourists, as if I was one of them.

The year before, I felt as if *I* was the curiosity; now I felt that the *tourists* were the curiosity. I got such a kick out of listening to them and to their questions:

"What time does the sun go down?"
"Is it always this cold in the summer?"
"Does the water freeze in the winter?"
"How can people live so far north?"
"How can people live in so isolated a place?"
"How can people stay up so late?"
"Why are there so many people on the streets in the middle of the night?"
"How can they live without television?"
"How can they live without steak?"
"Do you really believe they only boil their potatoes?"

I heard myself as a teenage American in those questions, and laughed at them as a teenage Norwegian.

The *hurtigruten* trip was the same as it had been. We traveled the same route down the coast, stopping at the same towns. We took the same little tourist detour into the same picturesque *fjord*, for no other purpose than to allow the tourists an opportunity to photograph the steep mountains as they dove directly into the sea. I still crowded to the railing to look at the *midnattsol*. I still slept on the deck in a sleeping bag.

The *hurtigruten* trip was the same but it felt different. I saw the isolated houses and fishing villages, but they appeared warmer and cozier. The mountains and islands were familiar, not at all strange. When I walked through the small towns at each stop, I was walking through little Tromsøs. Before I was a stranger in a strange land; now I was a teenage Norwegian wandering through towns not unlike my own. Looking at the *midnattsol* was layered with meaning. Even sleeping on deck felt less of a challenge; I managed six hours of sleep, no sweat. I just locked my arms in position and locked the sun out of my already closed eyes.

The *hurtigruten* landed in Bodø at 3:00 AM, twenty-four hours after we departed Tromsø. There was no one to meet me, but I didn't need anyone to help. In the intervening year, the Norwegian railroad was extended from Fauske to Bodø so I could get on the train in Bodø and avoid the bus ride. The train didn't leave until 7:00 in the morning, but I had no trouble wandering around the town by myself until the bakeries opened and I could sample the Bodø versions of my favorite Norwegian pastries.

The train was the same train I had taken the previous year but the ride was different. I had traveled the year before in almost complete silence, listening to the people around me talking a language I couldn't understand. On the return trip, within a half an hour of leaving Bodø, I encountered fifteen *grønnruss*. I would not travel the return trip in anything even approximating almost complete silence.

"Where are *dokker* going," I asked in my best, thickest *Tromsøværing*.

"Oslo," a couple of them answered cheerfully, in unison.

"*Russetur?*" I asked. I had never heard of *grønnruss* taking a senior trip; they certainly didn't in Tromsø.

"*Ja,*" answered one of the prettiest Norwegian girls I had seen all year.
"Are you on a *russetur*, too?" asked one of the other girls.
"*Nei.*"
"But you have your *russehua* on," the girl said.
"Why aren't you on a *russetur*?" the pretty girl asked.
"I didn't get permission," I answered. I knew what was coming and I was milking the situation for everything I could.
"What do you mean permission?" asked one of the boys. "Where are you from?"
"Tromsø," I answered.
"Didn't the *Tromsøruss* go to Kjøbenhavn?"
"*Ja.*"
"Aren't you a *Tromsøruss*?"
"*Ja.*" I was almost there.
"I don't understand the thing about permission," the pretty girl asked.
"I'm an AFS exchange student," I said, "and I didn't get permission to travel on the *russetur.*"
"What do you mean, an exchange student," one of the boys asked. "I thought you said you are a *Tromsøruss.*"
"I am, but I'm also an exchange student."
"From America?"
"*Ja.*"
"Norwegian-American?" Always the same questions, always the same routine.
"*Nei.* No Norwegian heritage."
"But you sound like you're from *Tromsø!*"
"*Takk for kompliment,*" I said. Thanks for the compliment.
The group of fifteen *grønnruss* were from a small town— Straumsjøen—on a small island in Vesterålen, a group of islands just south of the more famous Lofoton Islands. In Straumsjøen, for most kids being a *grønnruss* was the most schooling they could hope for and, therefore, a bigger deal and a *russetur.*
The pretty girl turned out to be Sylvi Olsen. I found out that my interest in *småpiker* had not waned since I left Tromsø twenty-four hours earlier. I also found out that the attraction I had for *småpiker* was not limited to Tromsø *småpiker.* Sylvi and I sat next to each other, talked, and flirted all the way from Bodø to Oslo. The trip was more like a non-stop *fest* than a train-ride.
We got off the train only once on the trip, in Trondheim where we had to change trains. I weighed myself on a penny-scale: 78 *kilos,* 172 pounds. I had lost fifteen pounds since I had left America the year before. I probably lost most of it at the beginning in Trollvasshytta, but I had not put anything on, in spite of what I perceived to be the vast quantities of food I consumed in Tromsø: four or five meals a day, *kaffe* and cake sometimes three or four times a week, my side-trips to

Pedersen's *bakeri*, and on and on and on. It must have been the staple diet of *fisk og poteter*...and walking ten or twelve kilometers a day.

I said good-bye to my new *grønnruss* friends as the train pulled into the Oslo station at around 7:00 the next morning. Bente Dahl, one of our teachers on the SEVEN SEAS and at Trollvasshytta, was there to greet me.

"I see you found some friends for the trip," she smiled as she shook my hand.

"*Grønnruss* on their *grønnrussetur*," I said. "They're from Vesterålen. The school is a lot smaller than the *gymnas* in Tromsø. For most of them, this is their last year of school, so a *russetur* for them is really important. In Tromsø, on the other hand...."

"I see you are a bit more talkative than a year ago," Bente smiled. "And I notice that you have developed a fondness for *småpiker*."

"Are we going back to Trollvasshytta?" I asked as we headed out the station toward the street.

"*Nei*," Bente answered. "There so many fewer of us now. We're going to stay at a *hytta* in Larvik. We'll have to take a train."

"But we're leaving the train station," I said.

"We need to take the train from the other station," Bente smiled. "We'll take the *trikk*."

"I remember taking the *trikk* last summer," I said. "It was so different from the subway in New York City, which was what I was familiar with. I felt so Norwegian taking it, listening to everyone talk, even though I couldn't understand anything. I remember when Tom Holbrook and I went down by ourselves and had to make our way around the city by ourselves. I remember how scared I was and...."

"This is where we get off," Bente interrupted my nonstop monologue.

"...I remember," I continued, not missing a beat, "going to the store to buy a map and feeling so great that we could manage to buy anything in *norsk*...."

"Pete!" Bente screamed at me, stopping me dead in my tracks. "You're in Oslo, now, not Tromsø. We have traffic lights."

I was astonished. I had almost walked through a red light into an oncoming car. I hadn't seen a traffic light in Tromsø; I had hardly seen any traffic. I never even had to look before I crossed Storgate, where there actually were a few cars each day. I had not only become a teenage Norwegian, I had become a teenage *Tromsøværing*. It was a good thing I had Bente with me. The previous year, I had trouble navigating Oslo because I had never been in Norway before. A year later I had trouble navigating Oslo because I had spent too much time in small town Tromsø.

We took the train to Larvik, a small coastal town south of Oslo. The other eight year-long AFSers were already there. Everyone talked fluent *norsk*. A couple of the kids had even passed their Norwegian written *artium* exam. I didn't even come close. I was genuinely impressed. On the other hand, no one *spoke norsk* better than I did. And no one, no one at all, spoke it with as strong a local dialect as I did. I enjoyed having something about which I could feel proud. It wasn't as much an issue of being better than they were; it was my need to be different. I still needed to define myself in opposition to others.

Everyone liked having been in Norway, but no one struck me as having had as profound an experience as I had. The sense I got was that for everyone else, the differences between where they were in Norway and where they lived in America were not that great. They had all come from urban or suburban America, and they had stayed in urban or suburban Norway. There was a much greater difference for me between what I had come *from* and what I had come *to*, and that difference was an important ingredient in shaping my Norwegian experience.

Few talked about unique or special experiences. Tom Holbrook had taken his guitar onto Karl Johan (Oslo's Storgate) and played folk songs to earn money for the *russetur*, even though he couldn't take it. That was cool and different, but there weren't many other stories like his. There were no sponge baseball stories, no *Narvikturs* to surprise the homecoming *russ*, no memorizing pocket *ordbok* pages. I had come desperately wanting to be someone else, to find other, unexpressed parts of my personality. I left Norway not only as a teenage Norwegian, but as a different Peter Dublin.

After our three days together in Larvik, the nine of us AFSers and Øystein (the same Øystein from Trollvasshytta) boarded the train for Kjøbenhavn. Pulling out of Oslo, I couldn't shake the feeling that I had been there before. I could remember vividly the impressions I had arriving in Oslo by train the year before. I could remember all the Norway-bound AFSers crowding the windows as we entered Norway from Sweden, so early that frosty morning. I was leaving the same way I had entered, but a different person.

As we had done the previous year, we stopped in Kjøbenhavn to change trains and to eat. Before it was Danish pastries at a restaurant near Tivoli, the famous park in Kjøbenhavn. A year later it was a full meal, but only in the railroad station restaurant. All ten of us sat down at the largest table we could find, the waiter brought us menus, and we talked away, as we had since the moment we all met in Larvik. We talked for almost an hour before we noticed that the waiter had never returned to take our orders.

"I think I know what the problem is," Øystein said, getting up and walking over to where the waiters were standing.

"The problem is," Øystein explained when he returned, "we're speaking Norwegian. The waiter thought we were Swedes. Although *norsk* and Swedish may sound similar to Norwegians, they are often indistinguishable to a Dane."

There was a lot of tension between the Danes and the Swedes. Some of it was historical. The two countries had fought over Norway for hundreds of years, taking turns owning and governing it. Some of it was more recent. The Swedes were "neutral" during World War II, and profited financially during the war while Denmark was occupied by the Germans. It was difficult for many Danes to forget.

"I told him," Øystein continued, "that we are Norwegians."

Within a minute, the waiter had returned to our table and had taken our orders, which were clearly rushed through the kitchen, given how quickly the food arrived. I wondered if we would have been served so quickly if Øystein had told him we were Americans.

We were off again, on the final leg of our train ride to Rotterdam. We were leaving by boat from the same port we had arrived at the previous year, but without the other hundreds of AFSers on their way to Norway, Sweden, and Denmark. There were just the nine of us (and Øystein) and the ride was much quieter and more reflective. Gone was the anxiety and anticipation, replaced by just anticipation.

We boarded the GROOTE BEER in Rotterdam, a ship a little smaller and a little faster than the older SEVEN SEAS we had used the year before. Here, too, there were just the nine of us; everyone else was a tourist, or an immigrant, or a European student traveling to America. It was a long trip—nine days—but not an unpleasant one. Although we were all looking forward to getting to our American homes, all of us wanted to retain our teenage Norwegian-ness as long as possible. We all continued to talk to each other in *norsk*, and spent little time talking to anyone else. That was the closest we got to a *russetur*.

I was impressed with the comparisons and contrasts between my trip *to* and my trip *from* Norway. I took the same *hurtigruten* between Bodø and Tromsø. I slept outside on the same deck. I looked at the same scenery. Going *to* Tromsø I was an American teenager: I was frightened, I was on my own, I could talk to no one, I knew not what to expect. Coming *from* Tromsø I was a teenage Norwegian: I poked fun at the tourists, I talked to crew members incessantly, I felt completely at home.

I took the same train (with the exception of the Fauske bus) between Bodø and Oslo. It took the same twenty-four hours. I looked at the same scenery. Going *to* Tromsø I slept most of the trip, I spoke to no one, I was awestruck by the scenery. Coming *from* Tromsø I hardly slept at all, I talked to fifteen other Norwegian teenagers for almost twenty-four hours non-stop, I took the scenery in stride as if I had seen it all my life.

I spent time in Oslo with the other AFSers. I was with many of the same kids. I was with the same two adults. Going *to* Tromsø I was so depressed I was almost sent home, hated to study Norwegian, anxious to get out of there. Coming *from* Tromsø I was as happy as I had ever been in my life, loved to speak my newly acquired *norsk*, and wished I could stay in Norway forever while anxious to get out of there.

I took the same train between Oslo and Rotterdam. I was with many of the same kids. I was with the same two adults. Going *to* Tromsø

I Was a Teenage Norwegian

I stayed up all night partying with the other Americans, ate Danish pastries, was a little frightened about my future. Coming *from* Tromsø I slept peacefully, had the singular experience of being mistaken for a Swede, and partially wished the train was moving in the other direction.

I took the same kind of boat between Europe and America. I took about the same amount of time to travel between the two continents. Going *to* Tromsø I partied with eight hundred other Americans, hated to study Norwegian, wondered why AFS had selected me. Coming *from* Tromsø I reflected on my life with eight other Americans, spoke *norsk* in a last gasp effort to maintain my teenage Norwegian-ness, and worried about whether or not I would fit in when I got to my new/old home.

I woke up on the final morning looking out the port hole in much the same way I did the year before. In 1961 I saw Rotterdam, the first land in ten days; in 1962 I saw Hoboken, the first land in nine days. I stumbled up to the deck, meeting and greeting the other eight AFSers, all of whom were already there. We all knew that the end had come, that our fantasy lives had ended, and that we would have to continue with our real lives. I looked out into the awaiting crowd with a mixture of sadness and joy.

I saw my family the moment I started walking down the gangplank from the boat to the dock: Mom, Dad, Tom, and Peg. We got my bags, piled them into the back of the station wagon, and headed off on the two-hour trip to Westport.

"You've lost weight," Mom remarked.

"You look good," Dad said. "How was the boat trip?"

"It was fine," I said. "It wasn't as exciting as the SEVEN SEAS, *men* it was a good ending for the year. There were nine of us AFSers and we spoke *norsk* to each other pretty much all the time."

"I hope," Tom said, "you're not going to wear those sandals when we get to Westport. Bruce Lawder wore his sandals all the time when he came back from France; I hope you're not going to be like him."

"I guess," I continued, "now that I am back here, I'll have to be *mer* like an American, won't I? But it will be difficult, *fordi* I feel like I still want to eat *geitost* for breakfast and I doubt I'll get that in Westport."

"What's *yate*...whatever you said?" Peg asked.

"It's my favorite cheese," I answered. "I like *nøkkleost* and *jarlsbergost* and even *primulaost*, but *geitost* is my favorite. There were days when I would eat *geitost* three or four times a day. I would eat it on fresh-baked bread, or *knekkebrød*, or even on *flatbrød*. And *fisk*, I'd eat that all the time, too. I never liked it here, but now I love it. They just boiled it, and they served it with boiled potatoes. And on special occasions, we had melted butter with the boiled potatoes. We had a treat for desert once a week, too. Sometimes it was peanuts, although sometimes it was *fruktsuppe*."

"It's good to have you back, Pete," Mom said with a smile as we finally pulled into our driveway on Red Coat Road, "but you'll have to work on your English."

Which I did, for the rest of the day. It was a whirlwind day, visiting people and places I hadn't seen for a year: Staples, Compo Beach, the Unitarian church, even downtown Westport. I even enjoyed seeing people I had never liked, and even more the few people I had liked. By the time it was time for bed, I crawled into it and fell asleep almost immediately.

I dreamt that night. I was at the dock in Tromsø, where the *hurtigruten* was awaiting me. But it was not just the boat that awaited me. Both families were there, the Thyholdts and the Norbyes. And many of my friends: Jorunn, Arnulf, Randi, Gunnar, and Lillian. Pain. Loss. Tears. None of them could be avoided. It was my last day in Tromsø. It was the day my return journey began. And the people closest to me were there, making it even harder for me.

There were almost no words, but no words were needed. I could see in each face, and feel in each hug, the love we shared. One after the other said good-bye to me in silence. Pain. Loss. Tears. None of them could be avoided.

The time had come. I took a suitcase in each hand, put the sleeping bag Tom had given me under my arm, and walked up the gangplank. The time was 2:55 AM. The sun was bright, Tromsø was magnificent, and the boat was ready. And when it started to move, the tears started to flow. I thought my stomach would drop to the deck, the feeling of loss was so great. That was the end of my year; I could never recapture it. It was over, gone…at least that was the way it felt to me at that moment. I wanted to jump off the *hurtigruten* and return to Tromsø. I knew I couldn't, but I wanted to because I didn't want to lose that year. I didn't want to lose my family and my friends. What I couldn't understand, even in that dream, was that I never would.

-32-
Reunion

"I had another Norwegian dream," I told Jana as our eyes opened simultaneously that morning. "It's been twenty-five years and I still dream in Norwegian four or five times a year."

"What was it about this time," Jana yawned.

"All I remember," I was completely wide awake, "is the part where I'm hitch-hiking in Norway. I hitched from Oslo to Tromsø and back again when I went back to Norway in 1964, the summer after my sophomore year at Oberlin. But I never hitched while I was an AFSer.

"But all of my Norwegian dreams are almost more about Norwegian than they are about Norway. They're always set in Norway. People talk to me in perfect Norwegian, which means I can at least hear and imagine perfect Norwegian...and speak it, in my dreams. I talk to them in broken Norwegian, with a heavy English accent, fumbling for some of the Norwegian words. I'm aware of how bad my Norwegian is and it's almost as if that's what the dream is about."

"I don't think that's what the dream is about," Jana said, half asleep and half professionally. Jana was a child therapist and although she didn't work with adolescents (which is what I was when I thought in Norwegian), she brought that perspective into many of our conversations.

"I know."

"Have you thought about going back?" she asked.

"I always *think* about going back," I answered. "But it's difficult going back because I feel so selfish doing it."

"But it's important to you. I understand that. I don't like you being away, but it's important for you to go back."

"It's been...when was the last trip? I feel like I have to count on my fingers: 1964, 1968, 1971, 1981. That's it: 1981. I can't believe it was six years ago, but that was the family reunion."

I spent the summer after my sophomore year at Oberlin in Norway, the entire summer. I hitch-hiked from Oslo to Tromsø, attended my brother Paal's wedding, and even spent a week in Straumsjøen with Sylvi Olsen, whom I had met on the train to Oslo on my way home in

1962. I went back for a couple of weeks in the summer of 1968, just before I started teaching in New York City. In 1971, I went back as part of a textbook-writing project.

Then in 1981, I went back for a Thyholdt *familietreff:* family reunion. I received a letter from my brother Tom that spring, telling me about the reunion. I knew I had to go; Jana knew I had to go. But I was into surprises, still. I wrote Tom, telling him how excited I was about the reunion but that I wouldn't be able to attend…and then I made my travel plans to go.

The only thing I knew about the reunion was that it was to be held in Trondheim, Norway's third largest city with over 100,000 inhabitants. I arrived in Oslo, spent a day or two with Jorunn and her family.

The next morning I had to figure out where the reunion was being held. It was a Friday morning and I called *Brødrene* Thyholdt, the company *far* and *onkel* Edvard had founded and Tom and Olemann ran.

"*Brødrene* Thyholdt *værsågod,*" the receptionist answered.

"*God morn,*" I said, in my thickest *Tromsøværing* dialect. "I would like to send some flowers to the Thyholdt *familietreff* in Trondheim, but I don't know where it is."

"It's being held at the Esso Hotel," she said pleasantly.

"*Tusen takk,*" and I quickly hung up.

I took something of a risk coming all that way without knowing where I was going, but I always knew I would figure out a way to find out, and I did.

I took a trolley out to the hotel. And I waited. About 7:30 in the evening, I saw them pull up to the main entrance. I walked out to greet them.

"*Takk for sist,* thanks for the last time," *far* said and he shook my hand, as if it had just been a few weeks since we had seen each other.

"So, it was you," Tom hugged me and laughed, "who called about the flowers. The receptionist told me some *Tromsøværing* called, but she didn't recognize the voice."

That was the last time I had been back: 1981.

As I rummaged through my closet to find a shirt (I gave up my Norwegian habit of wearing the same shirt every day), I noticed my *russevest,* my red *russ* vest.

It was the oldest piece of clothing I owned. It was a simple red vest and I hadn't worn it since May 17th, 1962. I knew it was still in the closet, all the way over on the right side of the hanging things. It wasn't my style to wear vests, with or without a sports coat; perhaps that's why I never wore it. Or perhaps, it was better kept as a memory, as a reminder of when I was a teenage Norwegian.

"*Det har blitt lenge sia sist,*" I said to the vest: It's been a long time since the last time. Although I hadn't even noticed the vest in ten or fifteen years, it felt natural to talk to it (and myself) in Norwegian. My Norwegian was the main vehicle for keeping alive my thoughts and memories of that year. The minute I reverted to Norwegian, I slipped back in time and place to Tromsø, even if only for a brief moment or two, as I did in the closet.

Clearly, as Jana would say, the dream and the vest were signs. When I came home two days later, I read the letter from Jorunn with the invitation to the Tromsø *Gymnas* Class of 1962 Twenty-fifth Year High School Reunion.

"You have to go," Jana said emphatically to me after I translated the letter and the invitation. "You know you have to go."

"I know, but I still feel selfish going alone," I said. "Why don't we all go together?"

"If that's what you really want."

"I don't know," I said. "I talk about Norway so often and I would like you, Maja, and Max to experience this important piece of myself."

"I would love to go, and I'm sure Maja and Max would, too."

"But going with you will completely change the experience. That's what makes the decision difficult."

"It's your decision," Jana said sympathetically. "You have to go; it's too important an event to miss. We'd love to join you and share some of what is so important to you. But, I can understand why you might want to go alone, and if that's what you decide, I'll support you in that decision."

Jana knew well the tension with which I struggled, for we talked about it often. The year in Norway was a powerful experience for me, and I had committed myself (for whatever reasons) to never let go of it. That's why I continued to dream in Norwegian; that's why I refused to let my language go, even as I forgot more and more of it. And my language was, in many ways, the key to the process of retention.

I had some opportunities to speak Norwegian in America, but I rarely did. Norwegian wasn't part of my adulthood; it was part of my youth. Norwegian was my transport back in time to that year I lived in Norway. My Norwegian had ossified; it hadn't changed over the twenty-five years. When I spoke Norwegian, I became the person I was when I learned Norwegian, because the Norwegian remained the same. I couldn't talk about anything that had happened to me in the twenty-five years since I left Tromsø in 1962; I couldn't talk about my work, about my parenting, about current events in the world. I could talk only about family and friends, parties and food, going to the movies or walking Storgate. When I started talking Norwegian, I become seventeen years old. I felt my body and my personality change. I was more outgoing, I was more upbeat…I was Pipe!

In many ways, my year in Norway was a fantasy. Everything was perfect, at least in my memory. I had a loving family, a fun-to-be-with brother with no sibling rivalry, great friends, and great times. I was known throughout the school and the town; I was a personality. I was popular; all the *småpiker* wanted me. Speaking Norwegian enabled me to relive that fantasy anytime and forever. Whenever I returned to Norway, I went back in time and back in personality, and I relived my fantasy. I could do it over and over again forever, just by returning to Norway and speaking and thinking in Norwegian. Norwegian was the key that unlocked that fantasy world.

That was the tension. Going back with Jana, Maja, and Max would change the experience, because going with them would change the language. My trip would be in Norwegian and English. I feared the magic spell, the fantasy, would be broken. Peter Dublin would travel to Norway, not Pete, not Pipe. Jana understood that as well as I did.

Maja was 14 and Max was 10, both still at an age where they enjoyed traveling and spending time with us. They were genuinely excited at the prospect of visiting Norway. Maja was so excited she asked me to teach her Norwegian. We spent almost two months before the trip working together on her Norwegian. It was a great experience for me…a special father/daughter time. Maja picked up the language quickly, and spoke with little American accent. By the time we got to Norway, she refused to speak a word of it.

I wanted to replicate some of my first time experiences in Norway on this return journey; I wanted my family to experience some of what I had experienced, even though they wouldn't be able to feel what I felt. I planned the first week of our two weeks in Norway to follow the same path I had originally followed, with stops along the way to visit Norwegian friends.

Our first stop was Oslo, where we stayed with Jorunn and her new family. Jorunn married her high-school sweetheart, Tore. Because Jorunn was a Norwegian AFSer, she had to take her senior year of *gymnas*. She was a *russ* with us, but she spent the rest of her school years with the class ahead of us and I had never met Tore while I was a teenage Norwegian. I had, however, met him often on my return trips to Norway. He was bright and intensely funny…and I had a real effect on him.

"You know Pete," he said to me, "I have lived in Oslo longer than I lived in Tromsø."

"I know," I said. "I can hear it in your accent."

"I speak now like an *Osloværing*," he said. "But after two days with you, I think I'm speaking like a *Tromsøværing* again. Your Tromsø accent is starting to rub off on me."

Jorunn and Tore lived in a bright, sunny, wood-paneled house on the Oslofjord. The most striking part of their house was the large wall in their living room. The wall was covered with thirty or forty paintings created by Tore's sister, Marit Bockelie. They were all of Tromsø and its surroundings: Storgate, Claudiusbakke (the hill we walked down from school to the *sentrum*), my mountain across the sound on the mainland, *soldagen*, winter snow on the trees, and on and on. Looking at that wall for me was like going back to Tromsø.

I Was a Teenage Norwegian

Jorunn and Tore didn't have a *hytta*; instead, they had a 40-foot sail-boat. Around 10:00 in the evening, we decided to go into Oslo and Tore suggested we take the boat. There wasn't enough wind to sail so we used the motor, but it was still an exciting adventure. Tore let Max take the tiller; the guy was in little kid's heaven. I feared Max would chew off his tongue, as he concentrated so intently on avoiding the other boats in the *fjord*. Tore brought us up to one of the docks and we walked around a set of old buildings which had recently been converted into a shopping mall. I was in Norway (the signs were in *norsk*) but it felt more like America. But Oslo never was Norway for me; only Tromsø was Norway to this teenage Norwegian.

All four of us took the same train North that I took over twenty-five years before. We travelled over the mountains to Trondheim, where we stayed in the only hotel of our two weeks' stay. Just staying in Trondheim had already broken the original pattern; it was even more broken when we had *middag* with Karl Erik Larssen, Unni Larssen's "kid" brother. Larssen, their father, was visiting Karl Erik (although I doubt his visit was coincidental), which made the evening in Trondheim even more emotional than I assumed it would be. I had never shared my feelings about Unni, feelings which had grown and solidified over the years.

What astounded me was that Jana understood and followed our conversation. Maja and Max were outside all evening (it was light until just past 11:00 PM) playing with Karl Erik's kids and other kids from the neighborhood; Max taught everyone how to play baseball. The five adults were inside, four of us having this emotionally dripping reminiscence in *norsk*. I can't explain how she did it, but Jana understood more of what we said than I would have ever imagined possible. I was struck on a number of occasions when I switched into English to explain something to her and Jana said that she already understood. Perhaps Jana wasn't surprised that emotions can transcend the language barrier, but it surprised me.

The next day we continued our train journey northward. At Bodø; we were met again by a former AFSer: this time by Svein Lundestad and his family.

While I was in college, my family had a Norwegian AFSer "staying" with them. It was an unusual situation. My family was Svein's family, but Svein went to a private boarding school, and was with my family only during vacations. None of us saw much of him, but what we saw we liked. Svein was tall, blond, and funny. We kept in touch with him over the years and he even came back to the US with his family for a visit. I still remember taking them all to the NBC tour at Radio City in New York. We got to a stop on the tour where there were clocks representing the time from cities throughout the world.

"Does anyone come from another country?" the guide asked our group.

Svein raised his hand. "I come from Norway."

A man next to us turned to Svein and asked, "Do you know Einar Haugen? He lives in Bergen."

Without missing a beat, Svein answered. "No, I don't know Einar," Svein said pleasantly. "I wonder if you know Robert Smith? He lives in Kansas City."

It's a shame the man asking the question didn't get it. On the other hand, if he had gotten the joke, he wouldn't have asked the question.

We spent one night in Bodø with Svein, and the next night we boarded the *hurtigruten*, right at midnight, just as I had over twenty-five years before. The *hurtigruten* trip from Bodø to Tromsø still took twenty-four hours, it still started and ended at midnight, and it still took place entirely in daylight. I could share with my family the *midnattsol* that I came to love so dearly from my teenage Norwegian years.

The *hurtigruten* was still a big, old coastal steamer. There was no swimming pool and no entertainment, except for the magnificent scenery. The food was ordinary. The most significant difference for me was that we had cabins. For once, I didn't need a sleeping bag and I didn't have to sleep on a wooden bench outside on an uncovered deck. The cabins were cramped and uncomfortable, but they represented a degree of luxury and a symbol of adulthood I couldn't have envisioned as a teenage Norwegian.

Maja and Max had gotten used to the late nights ever since we arrived in Oslo. But on the *hurtigruten*, they experienced the real thing: *midnattsolen* and no night. The voyage started in clouds, but within an hour the clouds disappeared, revealing the *midnattsol*. I felt its power even as Jana and I watched it reflect off the icy Norwegian coastal waters. For Jana, the moment was special: her first *midnattsol*. For me, however, it was even more special, because seeing *midnattsolen* again, especially within the context of this re-enactment, brought to the surface all of the associated memories of my teenage Norwegian year.

For Maja and Max, the trip was simply a trip. They raced around the boat, playing tag. They had never been on as large a boat. There were other Americans they talked to, and members of the crew often tested their English on them. They found some German tourists with whom to play cards. *Midnattsolen* was cool primarily because it enabled them to stay up until 2:00 in the morning. They loved sleeping on the bunk beds in the cramped cabins, which weren't cramped at all to them. The breakfast *smørgåsbord* was a fantasy-land for them; they didn't mind trying everything, because they knew that if they didn't like something, they could eat something else. They even enjoyed it when the boat made its little "tourist detour," wandering into the picturesque *fjord* to allow people to take pictures. And they loved stopping every few hours and walking around the little coastal towns, watching the fishermen get their boats ready, and tasting whatever bakery treats they badgered their parents into purchasing for them.

And then there was Tromsø. I had approached Tromsø a number of times before and in a number of different ways. Twenty-six years ago, I had approached by boat. I saw the island for the first time; it was striking, but unfathomable. On previous trips, I had approached by air, arriving at the new airport on the island. Seeing Tromsø magically appear out of the sky all of a sudden was a special way of seeing this place I loved. But approaching it on the boat that time was, perhaps, the most striking and the most special of all. Seeing the *sydspisen* as we rounded a corner of the coast, recognizing the *badestrand* on which I spent *soldagen*, passing familiar sights on the way to the dock, watching the dock grow bigger and bigger as we approached, seeing the *sentrum* and glimpses of Storgate...all that and being able to share it with my family, that was my most special approach to Tromsø.

And, as was the case twenty-six years before, my family was still on the dock, waving to me/us. It was just a Thyholdt family that time, no Norbyes. And it was a new generation of Thyholdt family. It wasn't *mor*, *far*, Olemann, and Tom; that time it was Tom, Berit, Arne, Sverre, and Morton. Tom built a smaller, more compact house for *mor* and *far* on the west coast of the island, facing Kvaløya. Tom, Berit, and their three boys moved into the Balsfjordgate house. Same family, different family; different family, same family.

We all piled into a van they borrowed and drove away from the docks. I was struck by the similarities and the differences. The Sagatun Kafé and post office were still in their old, familiar places. Most of the stores looked similar. But all the roads were paved. The Mack brewery was at least three times as big as it was in my youth. And the old *sykhus* building was dwarfed by the two or three new additions to it. As we drove down Balsfjordgate I was saddened to see that the old playground where I watched the neighborhood kids play was a small apartment building. Otherwise, the houses were mostly the same, and even the same colors, and the grocery store *mor* shopped at every day was still on the corner.

And Balsfjordgate 43 itself looked exactly the same. The same grey color. The same living room picture window overlooking the water and the mountain. The same garage roof-deck outside my bedroom window. The same doorway and even the same door. The same bedrooms on the first floor, although they had all been remodeled, looking nouveau Scandinavian. The upstairs, too, was similar in layout, but different in appearance.

"We've remodeled since you lived here, Pete," Tom explained to me in *norsk*.

"*Værsågod*," Berit beckoned us all to the living room coffee table, already laden with my favorite foods: *geitost smørbrød, vafler, sjoko-ladekake*, and Solo.

"Do you like it here in Norway," Berit asked Jana in *norsk*, which I translated into English.

"Yes, I do," Jana answered, "very much."

"Can we go up there," Max pointed to the mountain through the picture window.

"Is that really snow?" Maja asked. "In summer?"

"Yes, it is," Tom answered in halting English.

"Can we go up there?" Max asked again.

"I think tomorrow, perhaps," Tom suggested, still in English.

We ate and talked, in a mixture of English and *norsk*. Before we knew it 2:00 o'clock had come and gone, and all of us were completely wide awake. I had experienced this phenomenon before, but it was new and exciting for Jana and the kids...perhaps more exciting for Maja and Max than for Jana.

"Off to bed," I said.

"But it's still early," Max said.

"Check the clock," I suggested. It was a different clock but in the same place as the clock I checked after my memorable half-hour sleep night so many years before.

"It can't be right," Max complained, genuinely feeling that it must be earlier.

Jana took the kids down to their rooms and went to bed herself; Berit went, too.

"I really like Jana," Berit said as she hugged me good night.

The next day, while the kids played outside and Tom went off to work, Berit and I took Jana on a walking tour of Tromsø. Luckily, whatever the changes, they were not momentous. We walked the back roads to the *gymnas*, the same path I took all those days all those years ago. The building looked the same; the *skolegård* looked the same. We walked down the same hill to the *sentrum* and Storgate.

Storgate had changed. It was now a pedestrian mall for almost half its length. Where it wasn't a pedestrian mall, the automobile traffic was overwhelming. Where it was a pedestrian mall, the pedestrian traffic was overwhelming. There were now two, four-story department stores, with escalators. Many of the same stores were still there, and they probably outnumbered the new ones, but the look and feel of Storgate had changed. Tromsø was still a small town, but it didn't *feel* like a small town any more. Tromsø may still have been 300 kilometers north of the Arctic Circle, but it didn't *feel* isolated any more; I saw long hair, beards, and jeans.

"And drugs," Berit added, "lots of drugs. And nightclubs. Tromsø has more nightclubs per capita than any other city in Europe."

"I would like to look at some Norwegian yarn," Jana told Berit, even though I need to translate for her.

"I know a good store," Berit struggled in English. The she turned to me and asked in *norsk*, "Do you know about *rester*, leftovers?"

"*Nei*," I said.

"They're an easy way to make a sweater," she said. "I'll show you when we get to the store."

The store was on Storgate; I was sad to see that Anne Marcussen's mother's store was no more.

"Sometimes," Berit explained to me and I explained to Jana, "factories find small mistakes in their machine-knit sweaters. They make them in pieces and if they find a mistake, they don't put the pieces together. Instead, they sell the pieces to stores and the stores sell them. The mistakes are almost always small and they are usually marked. If you find something you like, you make the sweater by sewing the pieces together. It's very easy."

It was easy, but it is also sacrilegious. Jana loved knitting and she bought enough yarn for two sweaters. But she liked the idea of *rester* and asked me if they had a cardigan.

I was her guide to Norway and I decided to take charge myself; no need to work through Berit.

"I'm looking for a *kofert*," I said in my best *Tromsøværing* to the woman attending us.

She looked dumbstruck. She clearly didn't understand a word I said. She and Berit talked in *norsk*, so it wasn't that.

"*Kofert*," I said again. It's an easy word to pronounce. There can be no misunderstanding it.

She looked dumbstruck. She didn't understand a word I said.

"*Kofert*," I said again in my best *Tromsøværing*. "You know, the kind of sweater with buttons down the front not the kind you pull over your head."

"Oh," she said smiling, her face exuding understanding. "*Kofta.*"

I was so cool. I was going to take charge. I was going to handle the business transaction in *norsk,* and demonstrate to Jana my complete linguistic competency. I asked the poor woman for a suitcase instead of a cardigan.

In the evening, the four of us borrowed Tom and Berit's car and drove across the Tromsøbrua to the *fjellheis.* There was no toll; the Norwegians toll the truth. I wanted to replicate as much as possible my former experiences on this trip, and share as many of those experiences as I could with my family. I suggested hiking up the mountain; they opted for the *fjellheis* and a walk on top of the mountain. We took the *fjellheis* to the top, finding an empty, burned-out shell of the former restaurant. It had burned years before and was not worth restoring.

Other than that, my mountain hadn't changed. We could still walk out on the roof-deck and admire Tromsø through the backdrop of the *midnattsol.* We could still walk along the edge of the mountain, enjoying its magnificent views of Tromsø, Tromsøy, Tromsøbrua, the outer islands, the water, and the *midnattsol's* reflections off the water. We could even find the large cairn that I leaned against as Liz and I had our final talk.

What was new was snow. The highest part of the mountain was almost completely snow-covered.

"Let's go there," Max squealed. "It looks cool."

And cool it was. After we trudged up through the snow to the highest spot we could easily reach, we stripped off our coats, made sleds of them, and slid down the snowy incline on them. Here it was, 12:30 at night. The sun was so bright we wore sun-glasses. The weather was so cold we wore jackets. And we slid down an incredible snow-covered incline 300 kilometers north of the Arctic Circle. I was no longer a teenage Norwegian, but we were having one hell of a good time.

I had two stops to make before the reunion began. The first stop I needed to make alone; it was my visit to the Románs. I wanted Jana to experience everything, but I wasn't sure about this visit. They lived in the same house and it, like the Balsfjordgate house, looked the same.

"Pete, you don't have to take off your shoes," *fru* Román said as I took off my shoes. I might be a guest but I was damned if I was going to act like one.

"We heard you were in town," Román shook my hand. Why was I not surprised they had heard?

"As you can see," *fru* Román continued, "it's just Román and me here, now. All of our children are grown."

"Even Bergljot?" I asked plaintively, not wanting her to be anything other than the seven year-old I remembered.

"Even Bergljot. We're all older, aren't we? And what about you, Pete?"

"Well, I have a family now. Jana, my wife, is with me, and our two children. Maja is fourteen and she learned Norwegian for this trip and won't speak a word of it now that she's here. Max is ten and he has already had a chance to be captain of Jorunn and Tore's boat in the Oslofjord. I have a small company in America and we develop educational materials for school children, books and computer software."

"I think, Pete," *fru* Román said with a grandmotherly smile, "that we might have gotten along better, if you had answered all our questions then as you answered my question now."

She hadn't changed, but perhaps I had and perhaps she was in part correct. I still felt that they could have done much more to have made my stay with them more comfortable. But the teenage Norwegian that was talking to them as an adult, was a far different person than the teenage American that lived with them that summer. I didn't leave their house that day feeling that everything had been my fault, but I left their house that day feeling a little less angry at them.

If nothing else, I was indebted to them for enabling me to visit my next family, for I never would have been able to visit the Norbye's that afternoon if the Románs and I had handled our own relationship better.

The Norbye house on Holtveien was the same as I had left it twenty-five years before, even though Torild and Helen had each built houses on their parent's property. As Jana and I walked into the living room and saw that same coffee table with that same *sjokoladekake* on it—the best *sjokoladekake* in the world—I felt as if the past twenty-five years had never happened.

"So, Pete," *far* said as we sat down, "we're all here together to *drikke kaffe*."

"And we are so happy to meet you, Jana," *mor* said in her best English.

"Pete," Torild spoke excellent, almost unaccented English. "I was sure you would marry one of the *småpiker*, but Jana is really nice. Maybe she's too good for you? What do you think, Helen."

"I don't know if I will even speak to Pete," Helen answered. "I'm still mad that he never asked his older sister's permission to marry Jana."

"For years I have heard how *mor's sjokoladekake* is the best in the world," Jana said to *mor*. "Peter is right. This is the best."

Mor beamed. It wasn't just the compliment. She liked Jana. She was happy for me that I had found someone like Jana. She was happy that our little family was together again, even if slightly enlarged. She was still *mor*.

The reunion itself began the next evening, at *middag*. Unlike some American school reunions, only the *russ* were allowed to come, so Jana and the kids stayed at home. Like American reunions, I received the same "reunion shock." The first night's *middag* was held in a small, older building five minute's walk beyond the old *kino* at the northern end of Storgate. There were a couple of meeting rooms, and as I walked into the building I passed a room with a lot of older people in it. I continued on to the next room, looking for the *russ* and their *middag*. The other room was empty. We were the "older" people.

Between forty and fifty of the sixty *russ* made it, and almost all of my friends: Gunnar, Jorunn, Arnulf, Randi, Erika, Franck, Odd, Per.

Some had changed a great deal: Bengt Mikkelsen (the giant) was just as tall but almost gaunt, half of the boys/men had put on substantial amounts of weight, and many had lost substantial amounts of hair. But everyone was easily recognizable.

"Where's Lillian?" I asked Jorunn, who had flown up after we left her in Oslo. "Isn't she coming?" Jorunn was one of the planners of the reunion.

"She said she was coming," Jorunn answered. "Maybe tomorrow."

Jorunn and the others planning the reunion sent out questionnaires to all of us and most of us returned them. Jorunn and the others put them into a little booklet and sent the booklet out in advance. Lillian wrote a little something about herself: she was a secretary at the local *gymnas* (unheard of for a *gymnas* graduate with an *artium* degree), she had two daughters, and she was a little "thicker" than she was at school.

There were raucous songs, a lot of eating and drinking, reminiscing, good and bad old jokes. No one expected me to return, which made it even more special that I was there. Everyone was impressed at how well I spoke *norsk*. No one suggested it was better after twenty-five years, but a number of people remarked that I had more of a *Tromsøværing* accent. The *middag* went on for four or five hours and ended with a group picture outside...using, of course, available light. I walked home, as I always used to do.

Saturday morning I walked to school. It was just like the first time I was in Tromsø, that is, walking to school on Saturday morning. All the *russ* were waiting just outside the *skolegård*, just as they did twenty-five years ago. That morning, however, the *skolegård* itself was empty. We were the only "students" coming to school on that Saturday morning. There were many new faces, who missed the previous night's *middag* and *fest*, but still no Lillian.

Jorunn herded us into the teachers room, a large room in the basement I had never entered before. A number of our former teachers were there: Engelsen, *fru* Engelsen, Aschim, Hansen. Some of them nodded to me in recognition.

"I want to welcome you all," Jorunn began, "to the twenty-fifth reunion of *Russ*, 1962. We have a great deal planned for the next two days and I want to get started right away. I want to especially thank all of the teachers who have joined us now. I hope most of you will still be willing to join us for *middag* and our *russefest* this evening, after you hear what Franck Pettersen has to say. Franck."

Franck had always wanted to be an actor, and he was teaching drama at the newest *gymnas* in Tromsø, in Tromsdalen.

"*God dag*," he said to us, almost formally. There was still a lot of the actor in him. "As some of you may know, throughout my *gymnas* years, I kept a notebook. In this notebook, I wrote down amusing incidents which happened in my classes. I still have this notebook, and I thought it might be interesting to use it to help us remember our-

I Was a Teenage Norwegian

selves—and our teachers—and how quiet and well-behaved we were in those days of our youth.

"The following conversation took place during a lesson on the Second World War. I wonder if even Aschim himself remembers it?"

Aschim: How did the winter battle go between Finland and the Soviet Union?

Wiggo: Finland lost.

Bengt: 2-0.

"Then there was the time that Magnus went up to the board and was given the task of inflecting the verb 'to tax'."

Harald: What does "tax" mean?

Steinar: It's *nynorsk* for taxi.

"I will never forget *fru* Engelsen and her valiant attempts to get us to pronounce English the way she wanted. I wonder if she would like to take the time now—we're most of us all here now—to try again."

Engelsen: What is the plural for "*støvler*" in English?

Gunnar: Boats.

Engelsen: Boots, Gunnar.

Gunnar: Bow—t—s.

Engelsen: Boo I said. Booo. Boooo. Booooo.

Franck: You can't scare us!

"I remember this incident right before one of our exams. Riksheim came into our class."

Rektor: Everyone in the class will meet in the drawing room during first period on Monday morning.

Harald: What for?

Bengt: Last rites.

"Aschim wasn't the most demanding of teachers. But every-now-and-then, he decided it was his job to pretend to be a teacher."

Aschim: Knut, didn't you read the homework last night?

Knut: Of course, but I don't remember anything. But that's an exception. I was just unlucky.

Odd: He sure was unlucky...to get called on.

"And Aschim, even when he decided to be demanding, wasn't always the most clear of teachers. You could almost tell when he was about to depart this world: his head would tip up a little, his eyes become distant...you must remember."

Aschim: Bjørn, where's your paper?

Bjørn: It's not finished. I can't hand it in.

Aschim: I'm going to handle this in exactly the same fashion that another history teacher did when a student came to her the day before a paper was due and said he couldn't hand it in because it wasn't ready. "You must hand it in," she said. Well, the assignment was handed in, and it was an excellent paper.

These words were followed by a long and complete silence.

Bjørn: So? What's the point of that little story?

"*Fru* Engelsen was at the other extreme. She was brutal in the way she handed out discipline, especially to us unruly boys."

Engelsen: Steinar Hansen, be quiet during the exam! If you have something to say, you can say it to me.

Steinar: Well, I just threw a snowball at Arnulf. I just wanted to ask his forgiveness.

Franck: Steinar, I think you better ask *fru* Engelsen's forgiveness.

"Hansen was just as severe, in his own way. He never was frightened at handing down even the most strict of punishments."

Hansen: Odd, how long has it been since you had a haircut?

Gunnar: He can't count that high.

Hansen: Odd, if you don't get a haircut, you're never going to get your Physics tests back.

Odd: I'll never get another haircut!

"Gunnar Brox was by far the most serious of students. Even today, looking at him now, the man is all business."

Engelsen: What's so funny, Gunnar?

Gunnar: This question you gave us.

Engelsen: How so?

Gunnar: You asked "Why did it take Henry so long to throw up?" when I think you meant "Why did it take Henry so long to grow up?"

Class: Roars with laughter.

Engelsen: I hope you'll find the test as funny.

Gunnar: We will, if you give us the same question.

"Over the years, as you all can see, Bengt has slimmed down; he's still as tall as ever, but not quite as broad. So, you'll all have to close your eyes and remember Bengt as he was in our youth—huge—to fully appreciate this episode. Hansen was in the middle of a physics lesson and ready to select the next victim for recitation."

Hansen: So…next is Bjørn. Where are you, Bjørn? (There was no answer. The room was silent.) Is Bjørn absent today?

Bengt: He's sitting behind me.

Hansen: Coward.

"Then there was a time when Harald finally had to admit that Hansen was right, for once."

Hansen: So, Harald, I'm not so stupid after all.

Harald: Hansen, I never said you were stupid.

Odd: *Nei*, you never *said* that.

"What continues to amaze me as I read through these notes, is how well we students understood our teachers. This incident took place as Vidar Brox was explaining a mathematics problem at the board."

Brox: Why did I place the minus sign there?

Odd: Is there anyone besides me and Brox who doesn't know why?

I Was a Teenage Norwegian

"I can see that Hansen is enjoying this. But does he remember the Norwegian Speedskating championships and the havoc they wreaked in his math class?"

Hansen: Steinar Hansen, what is it you're doing up at the board. I've never seen you destroy an equation the way you're doing now.

Steinar: It's the National Speedskating Championships, Hansen.

Hansen: What about them?

Steinar: They're in Harstad.

Hansen: I know they're in Harstad, Steinar. I think we all know they're in Harstad, Steinar. What's the point?

Steinar: I have a bad case of travel fever, that's the point.

Odd: What's her name?

"And Aschim, does he remember the havoc Bengt wreaked?"

Aschim: Bengt, put away your Physics book.

Bengt: It's not my Physics book; it's Geography. I fooled you!

"And Odd, sitting smugly in the corner there, pretending now to be an adult. Does he remember the havoc he wreaked?"

Brox: Odd, even if you aren't interested in learning anything, you must let Sverre listen.

Odd: Sverre's not interested either.

Franck went on like this for close to forty minutes. Joke after joke, funny situation after funny situation. He had all of us, teachers and students alike, rolling on the floor with laughter. These were my friends, and many of the teachers were my teachers, and I knew them and I saw them in these stories. This was a homecoming to bring back the fondest, and funniest, of memories. When Franck finally sat down and I pulled myself up off the floor and into my seat again, I looked around the room. There was Lillian: a little "thicker" and laughing, laughing, laughing.

We looked at each other. It had been twenty-five years since we had seen each other. It had been twenty-five years since we had communicated with each other. I had a number of unresolved issues with her but I had no idea how she felt about me. I didn't know what to do. As usual, Lillian did. She got up, walked over to me, smiled, said "*din tosk*, you fool," and gave me a huge hug. I did likewise.

For the rest of the morning and into the early afternoon, Lillian and I were just part of the gang. We stayed in the school for a few more hours, talking to our former teachers and listening to stories, of both past and present. We walked to the *sentrum* and up and down Storgate, as we did so often in the past. About a third of the class still lived in Tromsø; almost all of the others returned to Tromsø with some frequency, at least to visit family still here. Some of us stopped for *kaffe* and cakes, Solo and *geitost smørbrød* at Sagatun, one of the few remaining *kafés* of our youth. Our next scheduled event was the *russefest* that evening: *middag*, speeches, and dancing.

348

I walked home from the *sentrum* along my old route, wondering if I would see my "Unknown Norwegian," in his blue shirt-coat, his hands clasped behind his back, his face still hidden from me. The *ølhall* was still there, the *sykhus* was still there, the *kiosk* where I sometimes bought secret treats was still there, but my walking friend had moved on.

I walked into the house and up the stairs expecting Berit to be putting the final touches on *middag*. Instead, Tom was in the kitchen boiling the *fisk og poteter*...my reunion request meal. Berit and Jana were out on the small deck, sunning themselves, knitting together, and talking away...in their own way. In many ways, that scene described perfectly the changes in our family over the years.

When I was a teenage Norwegian, *mor's* place was in the kitchen. She raised the kids and took care of the house. Unlike my Mom, who (I felt) was always frustrated by her place in the family structure, *mor* was completely satisfied and fulfilled with her role. Both Tom and I had made dramatic, but easy, breaks with the past. We both spent just about as much time in the kitchen as our partners, and we are both comfortable there. To have seen *far* in the kitchen would have been a real shock; to see Tom there, was not. That commonality reinforced in our adult lives the bonds we forged as teenage Norwegians.

Jana and Berit's relationship turned out to be equally strong. By the time we got to Tromsø, Jana had spent time with three other Norwegian families: Jorunn Pettersen (Bockelie), Karl Erik Larssen, and Svein Lundestad. Jana related well to the women in each of these families, all of whom spoke excellent English. All of the women were professional women, and Jana could talk to them about her own professional life and theirs. Given my hopes that this reunion trip would have meaning for me yet still be enjoyable for Jana, I was pleased at the way in which Jana related to the women as we wended our way together north through Norway.

Berit was different. She grew up in a small, rural town in Northern Norway, even smaller and more isolated than Tromsø. She had been a *grønnruss*; that was the end of her schooling. She spoke little English. She was more quiet and less assertive than the other women Jana had met. And yet, the attraction between Jana and Berit was virtually instantaneous and it was clearly strong; the two were inseparable. They talked for hours, even though they could hardly understand each other's language; they simply created their own way of communicating. They were like sisters.

In the evening I walked back *til byen* and our *russefest*. Getting together brought back all the memories, most of them good when colored with time. Getting together enabled me to see what happened to all those people from my youth. Getting together provided an opportunity to reflect upon my life by comparing myself to others, a foolish but obvious part of any reunion.

I Was a Teenage Norwegian

But this reunion was different. Other reunions took me into the past for a brief glimpse of that past. This reunion took me back into the past of a still active fantasy life.

Fifty-two of the sixty *russ* were in attendance. Two had died; two were "too far away" to make it; four were anti-social. It was a treat to see so many; it was most fun for me to see Gunnar Brox again, or at least the party Gunnar. He had divorced two or three times and he was still on the look-out, even at the reunion (even though Erika hadn't come). He hardly looked a day older; his hair was full and still bright red. He drank as much as ever and he got drunk just as quickly. The speeches were funny, the *middag* Norwegian, the time pleasant.

The evening was primarily a personal reunion for Lillian and me. We sat next to each other and held hands, just like old times. Although we danced with others (the rules of a *russefest* hadn't altered), we danced mostly with each other. And when we danced slowly, we held each other tight, feeling our past, feeling our relationship. But mostly we talked.

"I have thought a lot about how I was then," I started, talking in an awkward *norsk*. I rarely shared my feelings in *norsk*, but I was committed to *norsk*, whatever damage I did to the language.

"You can talk in English if you want," Lillian said sympathetically.

"*Nei*, I can't" I answered, astounded that she even asked. But she didn't know the "adult" Pete and his teenage Norwegian fantasy. There was no way I could come to Norway and speak English. It was difficult enough to have to share my Norwegian fantasy in English with Jana, Maja, and Max; there was no way I could burst my fantasy bubble at the reunion. I could express myself better in English, especially about my unresolved issues with Lillian, and she would have no difficulty in understanding anything I said; her English was better than my *norsk*. But that wasn't the issue. I needed to live out the fantasy in *norsk*, otherwise it didn't exist. Lillian didn't understand that because we hadn't communicated in twenty-five years. I somehow expected her to know that.

"I don't think I ever treated you well," I continued. "I was unsure of myself. I kept thinking that I had a girlfriend at home even though I didn't. I mean, I don't think she was my girlfriend from her point of view and I probably knew that although I didn't know if I knew that I knew it. I realize now that it was difficult for me to commit myself to anyone at that time in my life. In fact, I wasn't able to love anyone for many years. I don't understand why, but I feel bad...."

I stumbled on like this for what felt like hours. I had all these feelings to share and not the language with which to do it. Lillian held me tightly as we danced, and listened patiently to everything I said. She maintained her wise smile, the same smile she had as a teenager.

"*Du var umoden*," is all she said. You were immature. Here I had spent, perhaps, three or four minutes giving my typically (both as a teenager and as an adult) rambling, convoluted, intellectual analysis, and Lillian cut through the bullshit with three words.

"But what was it like for you?" I asked. "How did you put up with all of that from me? If you knew I was that way, why did you stay with me? I mean, you knew I couldn't commit to you and you knew I was going to leave and you knew...."

"*Men æ elska dæ,*" Lillian said simply again. Because I loved you.

One of the things I liked best about my college reunions was that they reinforced my sense that I had good judgment in people. I saw these impressive adults and I said to myself: you picked good people as friends in your youth. This was the case with Lillian...in spades. She may have become a little "thicker," but what a remarkable woman she had become. She was still full of life; her smile was still full of love and understanding; she had become even wiser.

And she was centered. She received an *artium* diploma, a rare commodity in those days, and she became a *gymnas* secretary, a job well-below what most *gymnas* graduates would expect. She took it because that was what she wanted to do. She wanted to work, she wanted to work with kids, she didn't want to go to school any more, she wanted to have time and energy for her own children and her partner. She knew what she wanted, and she cared not at all what other people might think of her.

And she kept the memories of our relationship alive and well in her mind. She continued to feel the love for me she had as a teenager, without that love interfering with the newer and more mature love she felt for her partner. In so doing, she made it possible for me to do the same. My time with Lillian, twenty-five years after the fact, had a profound effect upon me. On the one hand, it helped me think back upon that year in somewhat of a new way, adding Lillian's perspective to that of my own. Spending time with her at the reunion enabled me to reflect on who I was at that earlier time. How unable I was at that time to commit to anyone. Why I had continued to feel I had a girlfriend in Sue, making it easier not to commit to Lillian.

On the other hand, my time with Lillian helped me think about my life as an adult. I couldn't spend the time I did with Lillian and experience my feelings for her if Jana didn't, in her own quiet way, give me permission. I knew I could be with Lillian and feel whatever I felt, because Jana knew it was important to me to experience those feelings. She knew that experiencing those feelings for Lillian in no way affected my feelings for her, except perhaps to enable those feelings to grow. Life is not a zero-sum game. As I experience my love for Lillian, my love for Jana grows.

I have led a lucky adult life. I have no regrets. I wouldn't change a thing. My work has been satisfying. My family has been satisfying. Jana has been more than anyone has a right to expect. And I understand that "you can't change one thing." To alter even the most insignificant event in one's past, undoes everything. I understand that. And I have no regrets.

I Was a Teenage Norwegian

My year in Tromsø was a special and formative year. I learned more about families than I could have ever expected. I learned more about myself than I knew there was to learn. I came out of my shell. I discovered parts of myself that I had refused to acknowledge. I made life-long friends. I was ready to experience Oberlin to the fullest, in a way not possible if I had spent my senior year at Staples. And all I have to do is return to Tromsø and start speaking *norsk* to become seventeen again. And I understand that "you can't change one thing." To alter even the most insignificant event in that year, undoes everything. I understand that. And I have no regrets.

But I do regret that I was not able to love Lillian, that I was not able to experience her love for me. I could feel it at the reunion. She had lived her life and loved her family, as I had lived mine and loved mine. But there was still a little part of me that wished I had been open to her feelings (and mine) in 1962. Those were special feelings that I never knew, that I never allowed myself to know. And I understand that "you can't change one thing." To alter even the most insignificant event in that year, undoes everything. I understand that. And I have no regrets. But....

Mor and *far* had moved to a smaller house on the edge of Tromsøy, facing Kvaløya. *Mor* was fine. When we went to her house to *drikke kaffe* she still put out quite a spread and she still laughed as she always had. Every time she laughed I could feel myself drifting back in time.

Far was not doing well. Tom informed us the first night we arrived that *far* was in the hospital. "*Du*, Pete," Tom had said to me in *norsk*. "We need to see *far* tomorrow, in the *sykhus*."

I had known *far* had been sick for a number of months. Tom had warned me as we planned this trip. But I hadn't known how sick he was until I saw him in the *sykhus* that next day. He was pale and frail. He had always been thin, but now he was a wisp of a man. So different from when I saw him last, six years before at the family reunion. Then he was up til 3:00 in the morning, dancing with everyone in sight: *mor*, his *søster*, his daughter, and even his grand-daughters. Now he was dying.

"Is that you, Pete," *far* asked weakly.

"*Ja, far*," I answered, taking his hand. He had always loved me as a father, although it took me a while to understand the ways in which he showed it. But I knew it as I held his hand, and I could see it as I held his hand, and I could feel it as I held his hand.

"I'm glad you could come," was all he managed. We held hands silently for a few moments and then Tom took me back to the house, leaving *far* with *mor*, my *søster*, Astrid from Oslo, and Olemann.

The next day, our other brother, Paal, came up from Oslo. He went to the *sykhus* immediately. *Far* was in bed, lying on his left side, facing into the room.

"Is that you, Paal," *far* asked.

"*Ja, far*," Paal said. "I'm here now."

"Is that everyone?" *far* asked. "Is everyone here?"

"*Ja, far,*" Paal answered. "Everyone's here."

Far took one last look, turned over onto his right side, faced the wall, and was silent. He had waited almost ten days for everyone in his family to come to Tromsø. He literally kept himself alive until he could say good-bye to everyone. Then he turned to face the wall so he could die in private. I'll never know if *far* included me in "everyone;" I think and I hope he did. But, I included myself in everyone.

Twenty-five years before I had waved good-bye to *far* from the *hurtigruten* as I left Tromsø. I felt I was leaving a big part of me behind. This was worse, for this time a part of me died when *far* died. He was a part of me, had been a part of me for twenty-five years, and when he died, that part of me died with him. But it was only a part of me that died with *far*. The rest of me, and both my families, was alive and well and feeling more on that reunion trip than I could have ever hoped for.

I returned to Balsfjordgate late that "night" after I had said my goodbyes to Lillian, and everyone was still up. We got the kids to bed just before 3:00 AM and the four of us stayed up even later, just talking. I was so pleased that the four of us had, in our own way, forged a new family, a new generation of family. Tom and I were brothers in adulthood as we were in our teenage years. And, we had more in common as adults than we had then: we both shared domestic chores, we both ran our own businesses, we both talked about our emotions, we both took our parenting seriously, and we both allowed our role as parent to play a major part in our self-definition. And Jana and Berit were sisters in adulthood. They managed to form an incredible bond between themselves, in spite of their linguistic incompatibilities.

I was even more pleased at how this trip had helped me better understand my relationship with Jana. After we went to bed, I shared everything that happened between Lillian and me. She listened and was genuinely pleased for me. Without ever saying so, Jana had given me permission to be with Lillian in a way that might have been threatening for other partners. She enabled me to re-establish a relationship with Lillian, and to discover the love I had for Lillian, even though I never acknowledged that love as a teenage Norwegian. The fact that I could talk about this with Jana, and that Jana had allowed me to experience these feelings made my love for Jana even stronger than it had already become...and that I had already acknowledged.

We left Tromsø the next day, taking the plane after *middag*. Just before we headed to the airport, the four of us, in our new family configuration, sat in the living room, looking at the mountain through the picture window, talking. For the first time, I noticed that Tom and Berit had a Marit Bockelie print on their living room wall: *Soldagen*, a color print of the sun showing its face for the first time in two months. I had a color photograph that Tom took on that day in 1962, and it had always been one of my favorites from that year.

"I love that picture," I said to Tom in *norsk*. "I had never seen any of her work until we stayed with Jorunn and Tore. They have a wall in their house with thirty or forty of Marit's pictures. I love her style."

"Take it with you," Tom said, walking over to the wall and taking the picture down.

"*Nei*, I couldn't," I said.

"*Værsågod*," Tom said. "We have *soldagen* every year in Tromsø. I can walk down to the *sydspisen* every year on January 21st and experience *soldagen*. You can't do that in America."

"*Takk*," is all I could say.

"Now," Tom continued, "you will always have something to remind you of Tromsø. Now, you will never forget us."

And I never have.

Teenage Norwegian-English Glossary

Norwegian has twenty-nine letters in its alphabet, the twenty-six letters of the English alphabet and three additional letters: *æ*, *ø*, and *å*. These three additional letters come at the end of the Norwegian alphabet. When you see words beginning with *æ*, *ø*, or *å*, look for them at the end of this glossary.

aften: evening
aftens: evening meal
artig: fun
artium: high school diploma
badestrand: beach
bak om: behind
bare: only, just
be: to pray
bestemor: grandmother
betyr: to mean
bil: car
bok(bøker): book(s)
bokmål: one of the two official Norwegian languages
bra: good, well
Brage: the closest equivalent in Tromsø to a high school club
Bragerevy: Brage Review, the closest equivalent in Tromsø to a high school play
Bragefest: a party involving those kids in the *Bragerevy*
Bragemøte: a meeting involving those kids in the *Bragerevy*
brenne: to burn
brennevin: hard liquor, aquavit
brus: soda
brødrene: the brothers
byen: town
da: then
dag(en): (the) day
deilig: delicious
denne/dette: this
desverre: unfortunately
det: it, that
Det gleder meg å treffe deg: Pleased to meet you
Det går bra: (everything's) fine, literally "it goes well"
din(e): your
dokker: you (plural) in *Tromsøværing*; you guys
drikke: drink

drikke en kopp kaffe: drink a cup of coffee
drikke kaffe: eat the coffee meal (coffee and cakes or sweets)
du(deg): you (singular)
dum: stupid
dyne: (down) comforter
eftermiddag: after dinner time
eller: or
en/et/ei: one; a; an
engelsk: English
er: is, are
Fanden: damn
familie: family
familietreff: family reunion
fant: found
far: father
femte: fifth
fest(en): (the) party
fester: parties
fisk: fish
fjellheis: mountain lift, gondola car
fjord: a narrow inlet of the sea between cliffs or steep slopes
flatbrød: Norwegian flat bread
fordi: because
formiddag: literally "before dinner;" closest equivalent is afternoon
forsikringsselskapet: life insurance company
forstå(r): to understand (understands)
fotball: soccer
friminutter: recess
frokost: breakfast
fru: Mrs.
frukt: fruit
fruktsuppe: fruit soup
første: first
førstejuledag: First Day of Christmas, that is, December 25th
få(r) lov: (to) get permission
får vi være med: can we come along?
gammeldags: old-fashioned

garn: yarn
geitost: goat cheese
god aften: good evening
god dag: good day; hello
god mor(ge)n: good day; hello
god natt: good night
god jul: Merry Christmas
grei: straight-forward
gris: pig
grønn: green
grønnruss: junior high school seniors
gummistøvler: rubber boots
gymnas: senior high school
gå: to go; to walk
gå en tur: go for a walk
gå på ski: ski, go skiing
gå til byen: go (walk) to town
ha(r): have
Ha det (godt): good-bye; literally: have it (good)
halvmåner: a kind of Norwegian pastry, literally "half moons"
han: he
han e' ikkje så dum som han se' ut: he's not as stupid as he looks
hei: hello, hi
heia: an informal *norsk* greeting, somewhere between "hi" and "hello"
helveta: hell
her: here
heter: is called, is named
hilsen: greeting, used to conclude a letter
hjem: home
hos: with, at the house of
hua: hat
hun: she
hurtigruten: Coastal Express
hus: house
hvem: who (*bokmål*)
hvilke(n)(t): which
Hvor mye koster det: How much does it cost?
Hvordan står det til: How are you?
hybel: apartment or room (for students)
hyggelig: pleasant
hytta: cabin, cottage
hytter: cabins, cottages
hyttatur: trip to the cabin, cottage
høyre: right
igjen: again

ikke: not; turns any affirmative into a negative
ikkje: not; turns any affirmative into a negative (*Tromsøværing*)
i morgen: tomorrow
inne: in
inspektør: assistant principal
ja: yes
jada: emphatic yes
jarlsbergost: Jarlsberg cheese
jeg: I or me
jente: girl
jul: Christmas
juleaften: Christmas Eve
julebord: Christmas buffet
julefest: Christmas party
juletida: the Christmas season
ka: "what" in *Tromsøværing*
kafé: café
kaféfester: parties held in cafés
kaffe: coffee
kake: cake
kan: can (to be able)
Kan jeg få: Can I get
kart over: map of
kem: who (*Tromsøværing*)
kino: movie theater
Kjære Venn: Dear Friend
kjøpe: buy
klasseforstanden: main teacher at the *gymnas*
kofert: suitcase
kofta: cardigan sweater
komme: to come
kompliment: compliment
kopp: cup
Kor det gar: How are you? in *Tromsøværing*
kort: card
koster: cost
knekkebrød: crisp bread (Rye Crisp)
krone: crown; dollar
kroner: dollars
kval: whale (*Tromsøværing*)
Kvaløy: Whale Island
kveld(en): (the) evening
leke: to play
like: to like
lua: hat
lykke til: good luck
lørdag: Saturday
Mackøl: Mack beer, the local Tromsø brew
mai: May

mange: many
matpakke(r): lunch pack(s)
meieri: dairy
melkesjokolade: milk chocolate
men: but
middag(s): literally "midday;" refers
to dinner
min(mitt): my, mine
mor: mother
morn: hi, short for *god morn* or *god
morgen*
mørk: dark
mørketida: darkness (two months
during winter without daylight)
møte: meeting
må: must
natt: night
nei: no
neste: next
nordlys: Northern Lights
noen: someone
nok: enough
norsk: Norwegian (language)
nu(nå): now
ny(tt): new
nynorsk: one of the two official
Norwegian languages
nå: now
ofte: often
og: and
også: also
om: if
onkel: uncle
ordbok: literally "word book," dictionary
ost: cheese
pen: pretty
plass: place
plukka: pick
postkort: postcard
postsparebank: Post Office savings
bank
potet(er): potato(es)
prest: priest
prøve: to try
pølse(r): sausage(s)
realskole: junior high school
reise: travel
rektor: principal
rester: leftovers
rosemaleri: a typical Norwegian
form of decorating bowls and
plates
russ: seniors

russebil: (the official) *russ* car
russefest: senior party
russefestformann: the social chairman of the *russ*
russeformann: *russ* president
russetog: senior parade
russetur: senior class trip (traditionally to Kjøbenhavn)
russevest: red *russ* vest
rød: red
rødruss: high school seniors
sentrum: town center
si(er): say, says
sjokolade: chocolate
sjokoladekake(r): chocolate cake(s)
skolegård: school-yard
skillingskaker: a kind of Norwegian
pastry
skynd deg: hurry up
slår: hits, strikes
smørbrød: sandwich(es)
smørgåsbord: buffet
småpike(r): literally "little girl(s);"
refers to younger girl(s), particularly those in the junior high
school
snakke(r): to speak (speaks)
snakk langsomt: speak slowly
sol: sun
soldagen: the day in January when
the sun rises for the first time in
two months
sov(e) middag(s): literally "sleep dinner;" refers to an after-dinner nap
spise: to eat
stig på: come in
storefriminutter: literally "large
recess;" lunch break at school
Storgate: Main Street
strøm: electricity
stykke: piece
støvler: boots
surkål: sauerkraut
syd: south
sydspisen: Southern tip (of Tromsøy)
syk: sick, ill
sykhus: hospital
søster: sister
søt: sweet
søtten(ende): seventeen(th)
takk: thanks
takk for livet: thanks for life
takk for matt: thanks for the food
takk for nå: thanks for now

I Was a Teenage Norwegian

takk for sist: thanks for the last time (we were together)

til: to

tog: train (alone), parade (at the end of a word)

torsk: cod

torvet: town square

tosk: fool

tran: cod liver oil (the world's most disgusting taste)

tre(r): tree(s)

trikk: trolley

Tromsøbrua: Tromsø Bridge

Tromsøværing: a person from Tromsø; the Norwegian dialect spoken in Tromsø

Tromsøy: Tromsø Island

tur: trip

umoden: immature

ung(e): young

unnskyld: excuse me

vaffler: waffles

varm: warm

varmepølser: hot dogs

velkommen: welcome

venn(er): friend(s)

vi: we

Vi sees imorgen: see you in the morning (tomorrow)

vil: will

vin: wine

vinerbrød: pastries

vitaminer: vitamins

værsågod: here you are (when someone gives something to someone else); may I help you (in a store); your welcome (in response to thanks)

våken: awake

æ: I or me in *Tromsøværing*

æ e' ikkje så dum som æ se' ut: I'm not as stupid as I look

øl: beer

ølhall: Beer Hall (the the brewery)

øre: ear; penny

ører: pennies

øy(a): (the) island

øye: eye

øyeblikk: literally "blink of an eye;" a minute

år: year